Burgundy

Burgundy

Art · Architecture · Landscape

Editor-in-chief Rolf Toman
Text by Ulrike Laule
Photographs by Achim Bednorz

h.f.ullmann

FRONTISPIECE:
Saint-Seine-l'Abbaye, Côte-d'Or
View of the town and surrounding countryside

© 2007 Tandem Verlag GmbH
h.f.ullmann is an imprint of Tandem Verlag GmbH

Project realization: Rolf Toman, Espéraza; Birgit Beyer, Cologne;
Nikolaus Hoffmann, Bergisch Gladbach
Editing: Ulrike Weber-Karge, Dresden
Picture research: Astrid Schünemann, Cologne; Simone Firtion, Espéraza

Cover design:
Peter Feierabend, Erill Vinzenz Fritz

Front cover illustration:
Bazoches
Village and surrounding landscape
Photo: Achim Bednorz
© Tandem Verlag GmbH

Back cover illustration:
Vézelay
Ste-Madeleine, main portal
Photo: Achim Bednorz
© Tandem Verlag GmbH

Original title: *Burgund. Kunst, Landschaft, Architektur*
ISBN 978-3-8331-1418-2

© 2007 for this English edition
Tandem Verlag GmbH
h.f.ullmann is an imprint of Tandem Verlag GmbH

Translation from German: Marion Schneider and Uta Hoffmann in association with APE Int'l.
Editing: Eric Martinson in association with APE Int'l.
Typesetting: APE Int'l., Richmond, VA
Project management: Tammi Reichel for APE Int'l.
Project coordination: Nadja Bremse-Koob

Printed in China

ISBN 978-3-8331-2012-1

10 9 8 7 6 5 4 3 2 1
X IX VIII VII VI V IV III II I

CONTENTS

OPPOSITE:
Saint-Saulge, Saint-Martin, 16th-century stained glass window.

Burgundy – A Brief Overview

Pinot-noir grapes
The famous red wine of Burgundy is pressed almost exclusively from these grapes.

"A year ago, I returned to the land of my childhood. In Vézelay, not far from Clamecy, I settled down to enjoy the peacefulness of the spacious, pleasing countryside of my home: the softly undulating contours of the blue hills, the clear rivers winding through meadows and lined by rows of poplars, and the architectural treasures which the province owes to the centuries during which noble Rome and ancient France reigned here." These are the words with which Romain Rolland described his native province of Burgundy in 1939. He is one of the last in a long line of scholars, authors, and poets born in Burgundy who remained deeply committed to this land, honoring it in their works. During the 18th century Abbot Claude Courtépée, Dom Plancher, Dom Merle, and Peincédé all described Burgundy in works of many volumes and in such minute detail that they might have been doing an inventory. In the 19th and 20th centuries, the romantics, realists, and naturalists followed suit: the writings of Alphonse de Lamartine, Sidonie-Gabrielle Colette, Marie Noël, Gaston Roupnel, Achille Millien, Claude Tillier, Maurice Genevoix, and Franc Nohain are loving memorials to the people of Burgundy and its quiet countryside.

Traveling around Burgundy it is easy to understand why it is so highly esteemed. Burgundy is a quiet country, peaceable and gentle, bearing the imprint of nature and history. It is thinly settled, and extensive areas of the Yonne and Nièvre departments are almost devoid of humans, an extremely rare phenomenon in central Europe. Its other two

departments, Saône-et-Loire and Côte-d'Or, where mining of the Le Creusot coal deposits began in the 18th century, are more densely inhabited. In the 19th and especially the second half of the 20th century, Dijon and its surroundings as well as the Saône valley became middle-class industrial centers. Greater numbers of towns and villages are also found in the hills west of the Saône, in the famous wine-producing regions of the Côte and the Haute-Côte. The population density in Burgundy is only half of the national average, whereby Dijon itself has a population of just 150,000. Mâcon, Auxerre, and Nevers, the three other department capitals, have between 35,000 and 45,000 inhabitants, and almost all the other towns are markedly smaller.

So in Burgundy you come across two phenomena that have become rare in today's world: the small city and the small village. Cities like Semur-en-Auxois, Tournus and Tonnerre have just over 6,000 inhabitants, Saulieu has a bit over 3,000, and Noyers only 837. Nevertheless they are cities, pure cities that essentially have not increased in size since the beginning of modern times and have kept so many of their old buildings that they are truly "historical." As for the villages, many have barely 100 inhabitants, yet boast a château or a *maison forte* in which the estate owner occasionally still resides today. Dreamy and old-fashioned in a thoroughly endearing manner, these rural farming villages nestle between hills whose peaks provide views over the next hill and the ones behind it onto the plains, and even beyond to the high plateaus.

PREVIOUS TWO PAGES:
Blanot / Saône-et-Loire,
view of the town.

Pastures near Issy-l'Evêque /
Saône-et-Loire with
Charollais cattle.

Between the woods and the extensive meadows, cattle and sheep graze.

To witness the stillness and the darkness of night in such villages is an experience in itself. We who live in cities and densely populated areas, who never really experience complete dark or silence, are strangely moved by the dark night of these villages in which the barking of a dog carries for miles. The countryside has surely always been like this, and if you are lucky, the quiet, the light, and the season combine to create an atmosphere in which you can feel the breath of an era long past.

The TGV offers a harsh contrast. The French high-speed train zooms through Burgundy, connecting the cities Dijon, Nevers, Beaune, and Mâcon with such centers as Paris, Lyon, and even Marseille. It has a way of appearing unexpectedly and disappearing just as suddenly, but its path is recognizable at any time by the wires of its overhead contact line.

The products grown and cultivated here—cattle from Charollais, poultry from the Bresse, wine from the Côte-d'Or or from Chablis—are among the best and most sought-after, both in French cuisine and internationally. There is an historical dimension to these goods too, as they are mentioned in accounts of the banquets of Burgundy's dukes. Modern tourists travel to Burgundy not only because of the great art treasures, but also because of its famous cuisine and excellent wines. This explains why hotel rooms have to be booked long in advance for the time of the grape harvest.

This is the season in which the country takes on new colors. The green of the meadows and woods and the delicate hues of the roses give way to the crimson of the grape vine and the yellows and browns of the forests. Fall mornings are often misty and damp, and the hidden sun blurs contours. Fallen leaves drift like islands on the innumerable streams and canals. Still later in the year, hoarfrost covers the grasses and glitters in the first rays of light, disappearing in puffs of steam in the midday sun. This may well be the lovliest time to travel to Burgundy.

Burgundian art had two great periods of creative output: the Romanesque and the late Middle Ages. While Burgundy had to compete with other artistic centers such as the Provence, Normandy, and Alsace in the 11th century, it was almost without rival during the era of the dukes. Just as 200 years later the elaborate court ceremony of the court of Louis XIV at Versaille came to embody the ideal of an age—definitive not only for the nobility of France, but for the aristocracy of all Europe, even for the czars of Russia—so the court of the dukes of Valois was the measure of the feudal world for a period of 100 years. Even the emperor himself was judged by

the standard set by the Valois dukes. Compared with Philip the Good or Charles the Bold, he was embarrassingly poor.

The Romanesque period, which lasted until about 1200 in Burgundy, left behind an abundance of splendid buildings, the largest and most important of which, unfortunately, were lost: the Romanesque abbey church of Saint-Bénigne in Dijon and the third church of Cluny. The latter, however, still

Beaune/Côte-d'Or, Hôtel-Dieu, from 1434, south wing.

The Canal de Bourgogne near Tanlay/Yonne.

lives on through its many "daughters" in Paray-le-Monial, Autun and Saulieu, in Semur-en-Brionnais and Beaune. Sainte-Madeleine in Vézelay is also still standing; like Saint-Lazare in Avallon and Anzy-le-Duc, it belongs to the tradition of groin-vaulted buildings. In addition to these highlights, the Romanesque period in Burgundy left behind a truly astounding number of beautiful village churches.

Burgundian sculpture of this period is also magnificent. The sculptures at Autun are the earliest that can be associated with a name: Master Gislebertus. Beginning in about 1120, figures were freed from their background. Their anatomically formed bodies became separated and life-like, conveying the Christian message to viewers in a wealth of scenes. Unfortunately, the paint has completely worn away. Only a few traces attest to the original coloration, the effect of which can hardly be overestimated.

Gothic art succeeded the Romanesque period in about 1200. Magnificent cathedrals were constructed in France, which to some extent overshadowed the significance and popularity of Burgundian Gothic. But it is important to remember that many Gothic building projects had to be discontinued during the Hundred Years' War, and that when construction was later resumed, these buildings were completed in the Flamboyant style.

Not only in Burgundy is the Hundred Years' War associated with the names of the dukes of the House of Valois. They were skillful tacticians, allying themselves at times with France, at other times with England, placing Burgundy and the Netherlands among the great powers of Europe. It was during this period that the name Burgundy took on the enchanting connotation that it still has today. This atmosphere allowed the art of the van Eycks, Rogier van der Weyden, and Claus Sluter to develop and their schools to thrive. Architects of the new style were Raymond du Temple and the Dammartin brothers. Philip the Bold built, renovated, and restored in many places simultaneously with an almost frenzied energy. His son John the Fearless (Jean sans Peur) lacked the time, and his grandson Philip the Good preferred to focus on administration of the court, expensive banquets, and splendid outfits and processions. In addition, he spent far more time in the Netherlands. In Burgundy, meanwhile, the nobility was busily renovating its family estates according to the ideal of the duke's buildings. In the forefront of this activity was the chancellor Nicolas Rolin who, like Philip the Bold, was an almost fanatical builder. But many other nobles were involved as well, from those in the duke's innermost circle right down to the lesser noblemen. A large portion of these estates have been preserved, and they add to Burgundy's charm and atmosphere just as much as the churches, monasteries, and small cities. In these lovely buildings, which are located primarily in the countryside, Burgundy's great era comes alive again.

OPPOSITE:
Map of Burgundy with the departments Côte-d'Or, Saône-et-Loire, Yonne, and Nièvre.

30,000 Years of Culture – A Glance at the History of Burgundy

It has often been observed that Burgundy, the region between Champagne and Auvergne, Franche-Comté and Centre, has no natural borders, and therefore has always served as a passageway. Its history is correspondingly complex and eventful.

In about 30,000 BC hunter-gatherers settled in the river valleys. The most famous archaeological site is the rock of Solutré near Mâcon (illus. left), a place which was used for hunting and butchering by large groups of people over many years. Due to its famous cave paintings, the site is considered one of the key locations in Franco-Cantabrian cave art. In the Upper Paleolithic era a farming civilization settled a broad, continuous strip of land extending from southern Spain to northern Burgundy and Lake Geneva, and across the Côte d'Azur down into Italy. Many of the exhibits in city museums house archaeological finds from this era that testify to a high level of artistry, including weapons and tools made of stone and bones, skeletons, and objects placed in graves to accompany the dead.

At the same time the western Mediterranean was colonized by the Greeks, who founded Massalia (Marseille) in about 600 BC, a social transformation began to take place in Burgundy. On the strategically advantageous rock plateaus, various tribes began building hill forts, city-like settlements, under the leadership of a tribal prince. The precious burial objects found in the grave of the princess of Vix—a heavy, finely wrought diadem of gold and the so-called Krater of Vix, the largest bronze vessel of the ancient world ever excavated (illus. below and pp. 108/109)—prove that the tribes of the Seine and Saône not only traded actively with the Greeks, but also that they lived in a differentiated and strictly organized society. This, too, might have been due to contacts with the colonizers. Trade routes were the rivers Rhône, Saône, and Seine, on which barges carrying goods were probably drawn upriver by teams of oxen.

In 121 BC, the Romans founded a province in southern Gaul that was later renamed Provincia Narbonensis after its capital, Narbonne. With this province, the Romans finally replaced the Greeks as the most important power in the western Mediterranean. At first, nothing essentially changed for the Celtic tribes of the north, but when the Aedui found themselves in dispute with the Helvetii and asked

LEFT:
The cliff of Solutré near Mâcon/Saône-et-Loire.

ABOVE:
Relief on the neck of the Krater of Vix, ca. 530 BC. The frieze is 5½ inches (14 cm) high and repeats itself eight times. Châtillon-sur-Seine/Côte-d'Or, Archeological Museum in the Maison Philandrier.

Alise-Sainte-Reine/Côte-d'Or,
sculpture of Vercingétorix, 1861/
1865, copper, height 23 feet (7 m).

Rome for help, Caesar saw his chance. The Aedui, who inhabited the region that later became Burgundy, were the most important tribe in Gaul aside from the Arverni. In 58 BC Caesar began his campaign for the conquest of those parts of Gaul that had not yet been colonized. Vercingétorix, the young prince of the Arverni, united the Gallic tribes and led them in their struggle for liberation from the might of Rome. He became a tragic hero when he and his troops were defeated in 52 BC. The Romans laid siege to Alesia in two concentric rings, took Vercingétorix captive, and led him through Rome in a triumphal procession. After seven years of imprisonment he was finally murdered.

Nevertheless, on a cultural level, the Roman conquest made hardly any changes. The Celtic peoples had already used coins as a means of payment, they had given their settlements names, they had cultivated the arts and crafts, and had even begun to cultivate vineyards on their sunny slopes. The Romans adopted the Gallic oppidum, and excavations reveal that Romans and the natives of Gaul lived and worked together in various sectors.

In 43 BC the Provincia Lugdunensis was established with its capital at Lugdunum (Lyon). Autun was built at the foot of Mont Beuvray, soon to become the main city of northeastern Gaul. Autun was called the "City of Augustus," replacing the oppidum Bibracte at the top of the mountain.

In the second century, missionaries began to arrive from Rome, preaching Christianity and converting the Gauls to the faith. The next two centuries are considered the era of the French saints. In the name of Christ they founded churches, established the first dioceses, suffered martyrdom, and fortified the Christian faith in Gaul. When Clovis, king of the Franks, was baptized in the late 5th century, the Catholic church had finally established itself in Gaul.

In 443 the Romans resettled the remaining Burgundians—on the principle of dividing the land—into the Saône-Rhône area. This was an event of great historical import, as it associated the name of Burgundy for the first time with the region that later attained tremendous political significance in Europe. The earliest records of the Burgundian people date from the first century. They emigrated from the island Bornholm (Burgundarholm) in the Baltic Sea, moving into the lower valley of the Vistula River. In the 3rd century, a larger group appears to have occupied the region formerly belonging to the Alemanni on the Main River and allied themselves there with the Roman conquerors. In 406/407 they crossed the Rhine, where the first kingdom of Burgundy in the Rhine area, under its "phylarchos" (leader), Gundahar, is historically documented. It is likely that the history of this people forms the basis of the Niebelungenlied poem. War against Aetius, Roman governor of the area of present-day Belgium, and perhaps also against invading Hungarians, so weakened the Burgundians in 435/436 that contemporary sources speak of their complete extinction. This catastrophe marked the end of the Burgundian realm on the Rhine.

Autun/Saône-et-Loire,
Roman theater, 1st century AD.

Berzé-le-Châtel / Saône-et-Loire, double tower gatehouse, ca. 1430/1440.

The survivors of this battle can be found again in 443 in the Provincia Lugdunensis. They were given land in Sapaudia (now Savoie), an area settled by the Romans south of Lake Geneva. One third of every Roman farm had to be handed over to an immigrant family. With this ruling, the Romanizing of the East Germanic Burgundians became inevitable. However, it seems that they quickly recovered their self-esteem and continued to pursue their own interests. Within one or two generations, the Burgundians established an extensive state on both shores of the Rhône and Saône Rivers, between the increasingly powerful Franks to the north and the Western Roman Empire to the south. In about 500, this kingdom reached the height of its power under King Gundobad (480–516). His royal residences were located in Geneva and Lyon; his greatest achievement was the formulation of a code of Burgundian law, the Lex Gundobada, and another a few years later for his Gallo-Roman subjects, the Lex Romana Burgundionum. This code is a mixture of late classical vulgar law with elements of Germanic law, and it remained the most important basis for the government of the Burgundians, who

had by then come to dominate the Roman population in Sapaudia.

Despite their marked opportunism and a strong instinct for intelligent diplomacy, the Burgundians were not able to survive between the two power blocks for long. In 534, almost exactly 100 years after the catastrophe at the Rhine, the Burgundians were again defeated, this time by the Franks in the Battle of Autun. Even the marriage of Clotilda, the daughter of the Burgundian king Chilperic II and niece of Gundobad, to Clovis, King of the Franks, did not work to the advantage of the Burgundians. King Godomar III was defeated in 534 by two of Clovis' sons, Chlotar and Childebert, shortly after Clotilda had ordered the murder of Godomar's brother Sigismund, her cousin.

According to the terms of the victors, subjugated Burgundy was absorbed into the Frankish Empire. Nevertheless, the Burgundians clearly managed to preserve their region as a state, allowing them to maintain something of their ethnic identity. At first, Burgundia was divided among the living heirs of Clovis, that is, among his two sons Childebert and Chlotar and his grandson Theudebert. The Frankish

Semur-en-Brionnais/Saône-et-Loire, 13th-century donjon.

kingdom had previously been divided into three parts for them. By the year 558, all the male heirs of Clovis were dead except for Chlotar, so at the end of his life Chlotar again partitioned the entire realm anew among his four sons. With the death of Charibert I (567), this four-way division again became tripartite: Sigebert I received the eastern kingdom with Metz and Reims, which Gregory of Tours had already named Austrasia; Chilperic controlled the west kingdom, called Neustria or Francia with the cities Soissons and Paris; and Guntram ruled the enlarged Burgundia with the new residences Orléans and Chalon-sur-Saône. Due to its large number of influential, Roman-trained civil servants, Burgundia soon became the most powerful of the three.

When King Guntram died in 592, leaving no heir, the country fell to his nephew and adopted son, Childebert II of Metz, whose lineage likewise ended in 613. Then the united realms of Austrasia and Burgundia fell to Chilperic's son, Chlotar II of Neustria, though it is perhaps overly optimistic to speak of a united realm. The former division into Austrasia-Neustria-Burgundia had established itself. The noblemen of Austrasia had consolidated their position and power by holding important political offices, and they were able to effectively keep royal power in check. Austrasia and Neustria were united only insofar as both sought to circumvent the politi-

cal prominence of Burgundia. Finally, the Pippins, the Austrasian mayors of the palace, won this play for power, and the Carolingians entered the political stage. Carolingian rule was legitimized when Pippin the Younger was crowned in 751. The kingdom was thoroughly reorganized, orienting itself towards the Germanic east (to the states along the lower and middle Rhine), and Burgundia was relegated to the sidelines.

When the Carolingian Empire was divided in the Treaty of Verdun in 843, the inheritance of Charlemagne, that is, of his son Louis the Pious, was

Marmagne/Côte-d'Or, former Cistercian abbey of Fontenay, cloister.

again divided among his three sons, taking little note of the old regional affiliations of Burgundy. The north-south division into East Frankish, Lotharingian and West Frankish kingdoms also split Burgundy into eastern and western halves. The east—present-day Switzerland, Alsace, and the Franche-Comté—as well as regions on both shores of the Rhône went to Emperor Lothar I. Northern Burgundia, including Chalon-sur-Saône, Autun, and Auxerre, belonged to the West Frankish kingdom of Charles II the Bald. Charles the Bald became emperor in 875 as his brother's heir. In or before 880, he made West Frankish Burgundy into a duchy, giving it to his brother-in-law Richard the Just. This was the duchy of Burgundy that would play such a critical role in the affairs of France for 600 years.

Through further divisions due to the treaties of Mersen in 870 and of Ribémont in 880, Boso and Rudolf, the two brothers-in-law of Emperor Charles III the Fat, succeeded in acquiring for themselves the two kingdoms of Upper Burgundy and Lower Burgundy from Lotharingian Burgundia. At the end of the 9th century, three neighboring realms existed in the area once known as the second Burgundian realm, all of which retained the name Burgundy. Upper and Lower Burgundy remained dependents of the German emperors for centuries, while the West Frankish Burgundia, the duchy of Burgundy, became a vassalage of France through the consoli-

dation of the western state. In 1031, the French king Henry I placed it in the hands of his youngest brother, Robert, giving him the right to bequeath the duchy to his heirs.

At this time, the monastery of Cluny, the center of an enormous network of monasteries throughout all of Europe, was already 120 years old and had almost reached the zenith of its power. Emperors and kings, archbishops and cardinals, even the pope himself, came to Cluny and presented *Cluniacensis ecclesia* with gifts and privileges. In the 1080s, Abbot Hugh began the construction of the third church, Cluny III, which was to become a proud and gigantic work, even larger than the old church of St. Peter in Rome. But the history of the monastery ended essentially with the completion of this church. In 1075, the monk Robert of Tonnere had founded a reform monastery in Molesme which was re-founded in Cîteaux in 1098. Under its third abbot, the Englishman Stephen Harding, the monastery was austerely organized. Just as the monks of Cluny had once espoused an ascetic life, so now the Cistercians demanded that monks give up their property and all comforts; even pictorial illustrations of the Bible and any adornment of their buildings were forbidden. These reforms were directed against Cluny. In fact, the Cistercians managed to supercede Cluny, even though they never attained their adversary's secular power. The development of both these orders is taken up in detail at a later point (see pp. 120 ff. and pp. 268 ff.).

Fate favored the Capetian dukes in Burgundy, and their dynastic succession was ensured for more than 300 years. At the death of each duke, his heir stood ready, and so the subsidiary Capetian line could consolidate and expand their power in the duchy longer than their relatives on the throne of the French kingdom. However, when Philip of Rouvres died at the age of 17 in 1361, the duchy fell back to the crown, which at the time had come under great pressure due to English ambitions to expand their territory. Burgundy had suffered greatly when the English troops used it as a passageway to Paris—it had been plundered and deeply impoverished. John II the Good gave the duchy to his youngest son Philip (later the Bold), who was able to make his fortune with it and secure it for his successors. The extremely exciting and unusual story of the dukes of the House of Valois follows at a later point (see pp. 23 ff.).

The Valois dynasty seemed near its end in 1477 with the dreadful death of Charles the Bold on the battlefield of Nancy. But his only daughter, Mary, married Maximilian I of Habsburg. Even though Mary fell off her horse and died at the age of 23, she left behind two children, Margaret and Philip. The latter's son Charles was to became Charles V,

Tournus / Saône-et-Loire, former monastery church of Saint-Philibert, Romanesque Madonna.

TOP LEFT:
Berzé-la-Ville, Saône-et-Loire, Romanesque chapel in Château des Moines, detail of apse painting.

Countryside in Nivernais.

the French king whose empire came to dwarf the political dreams and ambitions of his great grandfather. Charles, however, never had control over the duchy itself. After 1477, the duchy fell to France and Louis XI never bestowed it to anyone, probably with good reason. He turned it into the province of Burgundy with Dijon as the seat of administration. The resulting surge of building activity there, which culminated in the construction of the splendid Palais des Etats in the late 17th and early 18th century, marked a final zenith for the city.

At that time, the province of Burgundy consisted essentially of those areas that became the departments of Côte-d'Or, Saône-et-Loire, and Yonne after the French Revolution, with only minimal border changes, as the partitioning took old county borders into consideration in many places. The county of Nivernais, which together with the Bourbonnais adjoining it to the south now forms the department of Nièvre, was a border jumper. In the 9th century, Richard the Just, in competition with his step-brother Boso of southern Burgundy, had brought the *pagi*—that is, the administrative entities (later counties) of Nivernais, Auxerrois, and Mâconnais—under his sway. Nevertheless, in 880, when the duchy was constituted out of West Frankish Burgundy, the rights to these lands were again withdrawn from the feudal contract. Only under the dukes of Valois did these areas return to Burgundy—first the large and important Nivernais

in 1384, and later the small counties of Auxerrois and Mâconnais in 1435. In that year Philip the Bold married Margaret of Flanders, the heiress of Louis van Maele and granddaughter of Margaret of France. In addition to other extensive territories, she also brought the Nivernais into the marriage.

In 1477, during the time in which control of the duchy returned to the crown, the Nivernais was again removed from the union. In 1491 it came under the control of the House of Kleve. In 1539 Nivernais became a duchy itself, and later came into the possession of the Gonzagas of Mantua, of Cardinal Mazarin, and the Mancini family. In 1789 this land became a part of the newly created French Republic as the department of Nièvre, but was not considered to be part of Burgundy. Almost 200 years would pass before Nivernais returned to the fold. Finally, in 1960, the economic region of Bourgogne (Burgundy) was created, which included the departments Cote-d'Or, Saône-et-Loire, Yonne, and Nièvre. In 1972, France was divided into 22 regions without further changes to this partitioning.

Thus the name Burgundy once again refers to those territories which Richard the Just had brought together at the close of the 9th century. Burgundy has enjoyed a certain continuity over the course of the centuries, left somewhat at the sidelines and unhindered by great political dramas, a position that has allowed it to develop its own culture and its own special magic.

Uant le prince de
galles dist que com
batre le conuenoit et
que le cardinal de
pierrefort sans riens exploittier
sen raloit. Il dist a ses gens en
les encourageant Beaulx seig.
se nous sommes vngz pou cotre
la puissance de noz ennemis si
ne nous esbahissons mie pour ce
Car la victoure ne gist mie ou
grant nombre de peuple mais
ou dieu la veult enuoyer. S il
aduient que la iournee soit po
nous nous serons les plus hon
nourez gens du monde se nous

sommes mors. Tay encores mon
mon pere et de beaulx freres et
aussi vous auez de bons amis q
nous contreuengeront. Si vous
prie que vous vueilles huy ente
dre a bien combatre. car sil plaist
a dieu et a mons samt george
vous me verrez huy tresbon chle
De ces paroles et de pluss. aultres
belles raisons que le prince de
galles remonstra ce iour a ses
gens et fist par ses mareschaulx
remonstrer ilz furent tous re
confortez. Deles le prince pour
le garder et conseillier estoit
messire Jehan chandos ne oncqs

Burgundy and the Dukes of the House of Valois

Philip the Bold –
The Brilliant Founding of a New Duchy

The Hundred Years' War reached a dramatic climax on September 19, 1356. The French army was defeated by the English in the Battle of Poitiers, and the French king, John II, who bore the epithet "the Good," would spend the next four years an English prisoner. His four sons had also taken part in the battle. While the dauphin, the future Charles V, had fled from the enemy, the youngest prince, 14-year-old Philip, had fought at his father's side with particular courage. It was in honor of this bravery that the king gave the duchy of Burgundy to his youngest and favorite son as an appanage seven years later. Although Burgundy had been impoverished, plundered, and devastated by the English, the land nevertheless had a long and fantastic history.

Philip, who later received the epithet "the Bold" (le Hardi), was born on January 17, 1342 and was just 21 years old when he became the duke of Burgundy. He was tall and strong, with a bulky frame, a broad, protruding chin, and a somewhat hooked nose, "a man of dark complexion and ugly," wrote Christine de Pisan, a contemporary who chronicled conditions at the French court in the early 15th century. But she also emphasized that he was of "exceptional understanding and council." He was not only unusually brave on the battlefield, but also possessed exceptional political skills, an admirable mind, and an unusually engaging personality—and he knew how to use the opportunities offered to him.

Supported by his brother Charles, Philip was successful in wooing Margaret of Flanders, the heiress of Louis of Maele. Margaret had already been betrothed to Philip of Rouvres and to Edmund of Langley, a son of Edward III of England. As granddaughter of Margaret of France, she brought the rich and fertile lands of Flanders, Artois, Nevers, and Rethel as well as the Franche-Comté ("free county") as royal feudal territories into the marriage. By eliminating the rival Englishman and winning over Margaret as a vassal of France, Charles V gained an important victory over England.

On the other hand, in this constellation, the seed for future conflicts had already been sown. At that time Flanders enjoyed the most highly developed trade of any European country, and was dependent on the raw material wool, which it bought from England. Nevertheless, Philip remained completely loyal to France. In fact, he saw himself above all as a French prince. This was noted by another contemporary, Jean Froissart, when he wrote of Philip that he was "wise, cool-headed and inventive, and very far-sighted in his affairs, and [he] wanted no difficulties for the kingdom of France but tried to keep peace among all the parties as well as he could, and [he] did not want to trouble these lords, neither King Charles (V) his brother, nor King Charles (VI) his nephew."

Incidentally, like the young Christine de Pisan who was some decades his junior, Froissart numbers among the most important exponents of French court historiography. Froissart was the author of a chronicle many volumes in length that records the events at the court of Charles V, a work which he rewrote numerous times before his death in 1404. In 1370 Philip called himself "son of the king of France, Duke of Burgundy, Count of Flanders, Artois, the county of Burgundy, Lord of Salins, Count of Rethel, Lord of Mecheln." Both his inherent power and the pride he took in his titles were evident in the duke's court. Philip employed not only the most talented painters, architects, and sculptors of his time, but also supported an entire cadre of musicians, goldsmiths, illuminators, tapestry weavers, poets, and historiographers who recorded his life and political deeds for contemporaries and for posterity. His exuberant patronage is legendary, and he competed therein eagerly with his brothers, King Charles V and the dukes of Berry and Anjou, John and Louis. The brothers exchanged lavish gifts, and artists and craftsmen traveled from one court to another, building and adorning the residences of these men so passionately involved with the arts and so competitive with one another.

Philip's special passion seems to have been architecture. With truly hectic zeal, he adorned, beautified, and modified the castles and palaces of his countrysides and the houses (hôtels) of his cities. Reports of their beauty and splendor fill the pages of the chronicles and—above all—the duke's account books. The buildings on which he lavished his attention incorporated such features as modern baths, covered galleries, and colorful windows embellished with historical figures.

Furthermore, Philip and his brothers took part in every military engagement that had drawn the English army into France since the breaking of the treaty of Brétigny in 1369. Philip made great contributions to the negotiations that brought about the truce of 1375.

In 1380, King Charles V died and left two sons, Charles VI and Louis of Orléans, both of whom were still under age. Just as the Battle of Poitiers

Duke Philip the Bold,
French school, last quarter of the 16th century, oil on panel, Versailles, Châteaux de Versailles et de Trianon.

OPPOSITE:
The Battle of Poitiers,
1356, miniature, Paris, Bibliothèque Nationale.

24 years earlier had been an opportunity for this, the favorite son of the king, to prove his loyalty, the early death of Philip's brother offered him another chance. Philip took over the government of France, at first together with his brothers, John of Berry and Louis of Anjou, and later alone. He was clever, circumspect, and loyal while never losing sight of his own interests.

On November 3, 1388, Charles VI, under the influence of his younger brother Louis of Orléans, dismissed his uncle and declared that in the future he would rule alone. This reign lasted four years. Then on August 5, 1392, while he was hunting in the forest of Le Mans, the king's insanity became manifest for the first time. Louis of Orléans had to accept that his uncle Philip would again become the regent, taking over the affairs of government, while John of Berry became governor of Languedoc.

In the meantime, unrest had come to Flanders. Under the leadership of Philip van Artevelde, the league of the *Chaperons blancs* ("white caps") organized uprisings in the cities of the Netherlands. They had promulgated revolutionary ideas beginning in 1375 that were causing unrest throughout Europe at this time. In the face of these urban uprisings, Louis of Maele turned to his son-in-law Philip the Bold for help, who in turn asked his nephew, Charles VI, for support. In the Battle of Roosebeke, the joint forces of a French-Burgundian army under the famous red and gold *oriflamme* (golden flame) banner brutally defeated the Flemish uprising on November 29, 1382.

In 1385, in order to strengthen his influence in the north against the interests of the Luxembourgers, Philip married his son John, the future duke of Burgundy, to Margaret of Bavaria, the daughter of Duke Albrecht of Bavaria, Count of Hennegau, Holland, and Seeland. He also wed his own daughter Margaret with Wilhelm of Bavaria, the son of Duke Albrecht. As a result of these marriages, a dangerous dualism arose between feudal allegiances owed to the empire and those due to France, a conflict of interests that would become ever more significant for the later dukes. A year later, in 1386, Philip was involved in another undertaking in the service of the French crown: a military campaign to England. Ships were brought together from all over and men were speedily armed, but in the end, the duke preferred to come to terms with the English in a peaceable manner.

Philip dedicated the final years of his life to maintaining a tenuous peace with England, which he felt best served the interests of both France and Burgundy. On April 27, 1404, Philip the Bold died in Hal and was buried in the Carthusian monastery of Champmol. Today his tomb is located in the Musée des Beaux-Arts in Dijon.

Duke John the Fearless, painting by an unknown master, oil on panel, Antwerp, Koninklijk Museum voor Schone Kunsten.

John the Fearless – Corriger la Fortune
John the Fearless (Jean sans Peur), Philip's eldest son, succeeded him on the throne of the duchy. He was born on May 28, 1371 and spent his childhood in Flanders. Unlike his father, he spoke the Flemish language. He was described as brave, daring, crafty, and infinitely ambitious. Reports indicate that he was a small, dark man with blue eyes, a full face, an unwavering gaze, and a hard chin; his skull was massive and irregular, his behavior without delicacy or grace. He found speaking difficult, he seemed not to know how to appear in public, and he neglected his clothing. In 1470 Olivier de La Marche, the secretary and ambassador of Charles the Bold, described that past time: "This Duke John had a very brave and courageous heart. And he was an earnest, circumspect, and careful man who trusted no one and therefore always carried weapons under his clothes and had his sword at his side. And he made himself feared by everyone; they, in turn, did not trust him either." Plainly he lacked his father's diplomatic talents. But he did follow through with the marriages planned by his father: his daughter Margaret became the wife of Charles VII, the dauphin; his son Philip married Michelle of Valois (Michelle of France), the dauphin's sister; his daughter Anne became Duchess of Bedford and so on. Even then, the charming phrase was already being coined: *Bella gerant alii. Tu, felix Burgundia,*

OPPOSITE:
Genealogical chart of the dukes of Burgundy.

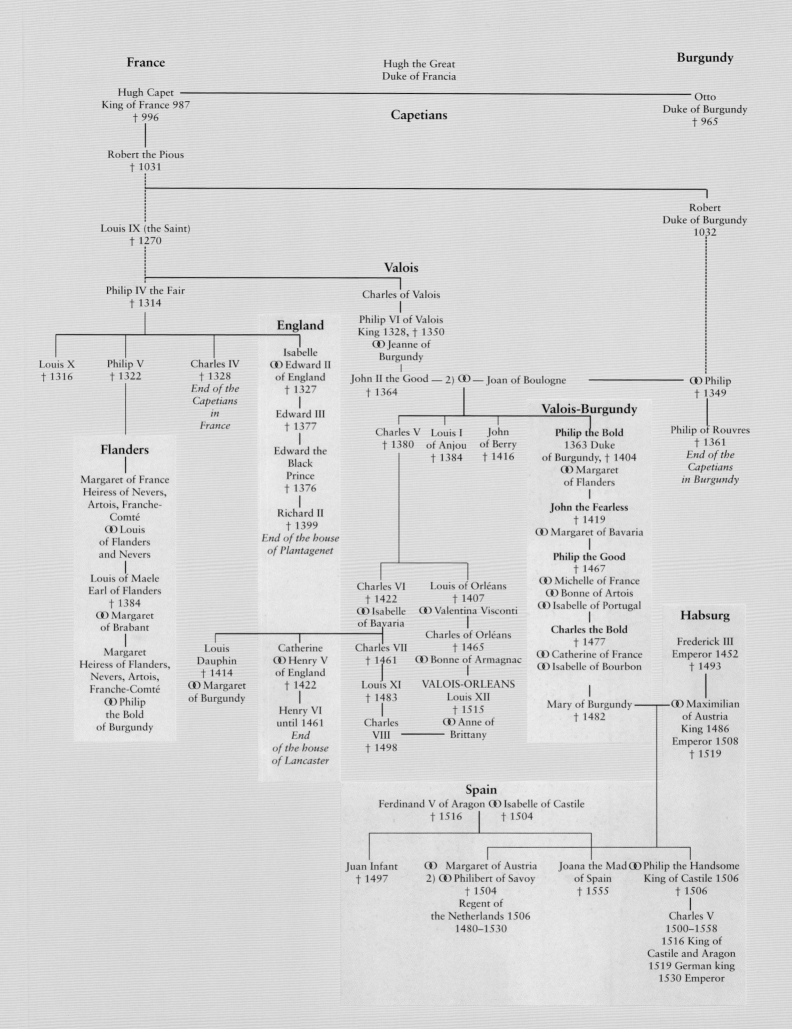

France

Hugh the Great
Duke of Francia

Burgundy

Hugh Capet
King of France 987
† 996

Capetians

Otto
Duke of Burgundy
† 965

Robert the Pious
† 1031

Robert
Duke of Burgundy
1032

Louis IX (the Saint)
† 1270

Valois

Philip IV the Fair
† 1314

Charles of Valois

England

Philip VI of Valois
King 1328, † 1350
⚭ Jeanne of
Burgundy

Louis X
† 1316

Philip V
† 1322

Charles IV
† 1328
*End of the
Capetians
in
France*

Isabelle
⚭ Edward II
of England
† 1327

John II the Good — 2) ⚭ — Joan of Boulogne
† 1364

⚭ Philip
† 1349

Edward III
† 1377

Valois-Burgundy

Philip of Rouvres
† 1361
*End of the
Capetians
in Burgundy*

Flanders

Margaret of France
Heiress of Nevers,
Artois, Franche-
Comté
⚭ Louis
of Flanders
and Nevers

Edward the
Black
Prince
† 1376

Charles V
† 1380

Louis I
of Anjou
† 1384

John
of Berry
† 1416

Philip the Bold
1363 Duke
of Burgundy, † 1404
⚭ Margaret
of Flanders

Louis of Maele
Earl of Flanders
† 1384
⚭ Margaret
of Brabant

Richard II
† 1399
*End of the house
of Plantagenet*

John the Fearless
† 1419
⚭ Margaret of Bavaria

Philip the Good
† 1467
⚭ Michelle of France
⚭ Bonne of Artois
⚭ Isabelle of Portugal

Margaret
Heiress of Flanders,
Nevers, Artois,
Franche-Comté
⚭ Philip
the Bold
of Burgundy

Charles VI
† 1422
⚭ Isabelle
of Bavaria

Louis of Orléans
† 1407
⚭ Valentina Visconti

Charles the Bold
† 1477
⚭ Catherine of France
⚭ Isabelle of Bourbon

Habsburg

Frederick III
Emperor 1452
† 1493

Louis
Dauphin
† 1414
⚭ Margaret
of Burgundy

Catherine
⚭ Henry V
of England
† 1422

Charles VII
† 1461

Charles of Orléans
† 1465
⚭ Bonne of Armagnac

Louis XI
† 1483

VALOIS-ORLEANS
Louis XII
† 1515
⚭ Anne of

Mary of Burgundy
† 1482

⚭ Maximilian
of Austria
King 1486
Emperor 1508
† 1519

Henry VI
until 1461
*End
of the house
of Lancaster*

Charles
VIII
† 1498

Brittany

Spain

Ferdinand V of Aragon ⚭ Isabelle of Castile
† 1516   † 1504

Juan Infant
† 1497

⚭ Margaret of Austria
2) ⚭ Philibert of Savoy
† 1504
Regent of
the Netherlands 1506
1480–1530

Joana the Mad ⚭ Philip the Handsome
of Spain   King of Castile 1506
† 1555   † 1506

Charles V
1500–1558
1516 King of
Castile and Aragon
1519 German king
1530 Emperor

Pierre Salmon (14th–15th century),
called "Le Fruictier", secretary of
Charles VI, "Les demandes faites par
le roi Charles VI", 1411–1413.
Geneva, Bibliothèque de Genève,
Ms. fr. 165, fol. 4

nube! ("Let others wage wars. You, fortunate Burgundy, marry!"). The House of Habsburg would later adopt this motto as its own, along with the rest of the inheritance.

John was Flemish, but he was also a passionate supporter of the king's party. His motto was *IC HOUD* (I will hold/ I will not give way). It became increasingly impossible to keep the smoldering conflict between the House of Burgundy and Louis of Orléans from breaking out under the circumstances. For a long time Louis of Orléans had been trying to draw the English into another war and

oppressing his subjects with heavy taxes to finance his extravagant court, whereas John, as his father before him, attempted to ensure the peace with England under any circumstances. John vehemently opposed his cousin's attempts to demand such outrageous sums of money, a stance which naturally won him the sympathy of the common people as well as the approval of the middle class and intellectuals, who hoped that he would introduce long-awaited reforms.

Everything was pointing towards civil war. But at that moment, the duke of Burgundy believed he could solve the problem by eliminating his cousin. On November 23, 1407 he had Louis of Orléans murdered. The notorious deed resulted in a scandal. John the Fearless left Paris and traveled immediately to Flanders. In Paris, the theologian Jean Petit held a speech before the dauphin and the royal councilors that was to become famous, justifying the murder of a tyrant and accusing Louis of Orléans of treason against the king and against France. The populace supported the duke of Burgundy, but the nobility was shocked and angry. Valentina Visconti, the widow of the duke of Orléans, lamented publicly and filed suit before the king and parliament, though finally without effect. John was able to risk returning to Paris and was given a tumultuous greeting by the people.

On March 9, 1409 the two parties made peace in the Cathedral of Chartres, a purely fictional peace. John now returned to Paris and consolidated his power—through troops and through generous gifts to those who served his interests. Isabelle, the wife of Charles VI, succumbed to his influence.

Then something unexpected occurred: Charles, the indecisive eldest son of Louis of Orléans, was married for the second time, to Bonne of Armagnac. Her father, Bernard, immediately made himself the spokesman of the Orléans party, which now called itself the party of the Armagnacs. Bernard of Armagnac not only had many followers at his disposal and considerable sums of money, he also gave his party the standing and respect it needed, for now the grandfather of the young duchess of Orléans was none other than John of Berry. Orléans, Armagnac, Berry, Clermont, and Alençon formed an alliance against Burgundy and together they began rounding up troops.

On July 18, 1411 the young duke of Orléans sent an insolent challenge to John the Fearless, who answered with equal sharpness. Civil war began.

The prize to be won was nothing less than the crown of France. The Armagnacs began the fighting with terrible plundering and devastation. John the Fearless, on the other hand, presented himself as the friend of peace. He was the great hope of the people and the intellectuals, and he sought to keep their favor through gifts and flattery. But his intentions were imperialistic, and he was later called a betrayer of the people, someone who cleverly and unscrupulously pursued his own power politics. Nevertheless, who was causing the most damage to France at this time? Was it the extravagant, plundering party of the Armagnacs, the indecisive king whose allegiance leaned first one way and then another, or the Burgundian party led by the decisive, unscrupulous John the Fearless, who continued to govern his own regions well in spite of the turmoil?

Like any war, this one followed its own laws and was soon out of control. John the Fearless, who had incited the people of Paris to revolution, could no longer restrain the populace. His followers, who belonged to widely varying stations of society, could no longer agree on a course of action. John departed from the capital, thereby leaving it to Bernard of Armagnac.

In 1415, after both parties had successively appealed to England for support, Henry V intervened, landing with his troops in Normandy. John the Fearless' situation was now precarious: as a French prince with royal blood and ambitions for the French throne, England was his arch enemy. But he also controlled extensive regions outside of his French seigniory. In the interest of those lands, amicable relations with England was a top priority.

With skillful diplomacy, he saw to it that the Armagnacs refused to sign the proposal for a mutual alliance against the English which Burgundy had offered. The Armagnacs fell into the trap and found themselves in the position of dealing with the English alone. On October 25, 1415 almost all the French nobility able to bear arms fell at the disastrous Battle of Agincourt, including the two younger brothers of John the Fearless, Philip of Nevers and Anton of Brabant.

Henry V demanded his Capetian inheritance—the French throne—and officially the duke of Burgundy negotiated with him for a truce. But behind the scenes, John the Fearless wished to bring about an English-Burgundian alliance. Burgundy, the French fief bound to support the French king, became a neutral power. In May 1417, in a secret and mysterious letter that he wrote with his own hand, John the Fearless recognized Henry and his successors as rightful heirs to the French throne, whom he would support "by any secret ways and means." This was his second act of treason!

In Paris, Bernard of Armagnac continued to rule through force and terror, but he was sorely harried by the attacks of the two secret allies. France found itself in a deep crisis. Three sons of Charles VI, successive dauphins of France, died between 1401 and 1419, that critical year in which John was

Jan van Eyck, detail from the painting *The Madonna of the Chancellor Rolin*, ca. 1435, oil on panel, Paris, Musée du Louvre.

The bridge in van Eyck's painting has been interpreted as the Bridge of Montereau, on which John the Fearless was murdered in 1419.

The murder of John the Fearless on the bridge of Montereau, 1419, Paris, Bibliothèque Nationale.

murdered. That left Charles, a 15-year-old boy, as dauphin, and under the influence of the Armagnacs he felt called upon to govern the affairs of state. His mother, Isabelle of Bavaria, allied herself with Burgundy and announced from Troyes that she had "…taken over the rule and government of the kingdom out of concern for the king." John the Fearless had his soldiers march into Paris—again through betrayal—and the dauphin withdrew to Bourges, where he resided for several years. The duke himself waited in Troyes until the tumult and the atrocities that accompanied the change of power came to an end. On July 14, 1418 he ceremoniously entered Paris, accompanied by the queen. The English continued to be a threat, however: Henry V and his troops were still in Normandy.

John the Fearless was faced with a decision. Should he make public to the world his still completely secret alliance with England, or should he try to ally himself with the dauphin? Since July there had been attempts to reconcile the two cousins; they had sworn friendship and expressed the desire to drive the king of England out of France together. Yet what was the meaning of this display of amicability that was celebrated in Paris with a Te Deum? Could the duke actually afford to be in conflict with the English king, considering his interests in the Netherlands? What tactics would he pursue next? These issues were suddenly pushed aside by an act of violence. On September 10, 1419 John the Fearless was killed on the bridge of Montereau by the stroke of an ax. He was just returning from a meeting with the dauphin. Although the exact circumstances of the deed have never been fully explained, it is clear that he was assassinated by order of the dauphin.

Philip the Good – Grandseigneur and Diplomat

Tension was in the air and emotions ran high when the third duke of Valois took over the affairs of state in 1419. He had been given the name of his grandfather, Philip, and earned the epithet "the Good" (le Bon). Born in Dijon on July 31, 1396, he was only 23 years old when he began to govern. Together with his wife, Michelle of Valois, he lived in Gent "where he enjoyed himself, went hunting and danced, according to the manner of princes and befitting his age." The young duke's appearance was considered elegant and dignified; he was tall and had pleasing features with thick eyebrows "whose hairs stood up when he was angry like the horns of a snail." His character was described as knightly and bold, but he also seems to have been quite sensitive. Georges Chastellain, who held the office of official court historiographer during the lives of both Philip the Good and Charles the Bold and accompanied both dukes wherever they went

until their deaths, emphasized Philip's "infinitely vulnerable pride and violent bursts of anger," though "a single reasonable word calmed him down again." He loved splendid processions, festivities and banquets—the descriptions of them in the chronicles still astound us today. Like his grandfather before him, Philip took great interest in architecture and furthered building projects. In Dijon, for example, the Tour Philippe le Bon (see illus. left) was built and the adjoining large logis, which remained unfinished, was begun. He ordered still larger building projects in the Netherlands. The chronicles also emphasize his noble character and his piety, which was nevertheless accompanied by an unusually liberal private life. He was known to have had 30 mistresses, and 17 illegitimate children were officially recognized and given high offices.

Philip's reign began with a violent act which demanded retribution—and the son repaid the dauphin and the Armagnacs for the murder of his father by making his secret alliance with England an official one. Revenge does not, however, seem to have been the only motive that induced the sensitive and proud duke to take this step. Rather, he seems to have followed the council of the cities as well as the advice of his family in this matter. Apparently, all were of the opinion that an alliance with Henry V of England was in the best interests of Burgundy and of the divided kingdom of France. Moreover, Parisians were angry and shocked by the murder at Montereau, and public opinion leaned towards the Burgundian party as it had in the best of times.

Aware of this shifting of opinion, the king declared from Troyes that no one should obey the injunctions of the dauphin. Even the French people looked to Henry V to save their country from the confusion caused by their country's split. Charles VI and Isabelle signed an agreement with Henry which deposed the dauphin, whom they blamed for the murder and whom they accused of "dreadful and heinous crimes." Henry was to marry Catherine of Valois, the sister of the dauphin, and be regent in France until Catherine's son could take over the French throne. This treaty, known as the "Betrayal of Troyes," has been called the most ignominious treaty in French history by French historiographers. Contemporaries, the populace, and governmental bodies, however, greeted it with great joy and applause. And in the end, whether the treaty was patriotic or not, the French royal house had nothing more to offer than a king who was mentally ill and an underaged dauphin. Two parties had been fighting for years for control of the regency, and the populace had suffered enormously.

Philip the Good, of course, placed himself firmly on the side of the king and of England, which was also the side of the victor. Over the course of his life

Dijon, Palais des Ducs, outer façade of the Salle des Gardes and Tour Philippe le Bon, from 1450 on.

In the summer of 1422, the death of the duchess of Burgundy, Michelle of France, was followed by the death of the English king Henry V shortly thereafter. In October of the same year, France's King Charles VI died. The son of Catherine and Henry V was crowned in England as King Henry VI, and the duke of Bedford was appointed to act as his regent.

In Mehun-sur-Yèvre, the dauphin, the son of Charles VI, proclaimed himself king and gathered patriots about him. The division of France was now complete: there were two kings, the king of Paris and the king of Bourges. The duke of Burgundy, who had not attended the funeral of Charles VI because he did not find it fitting to walk behind a regent in the funeral procession, turned bit by bit towards the dauphin, although he had recognized Henry VI. Philip the Good's dissatisfaction with the French regency of the duke of Bedford and his lack of desire to deal with French affairs of state combined to lead him, more than either of his two predecessors, to make efforts towards creating an independent Burgundy. Well prepared by his father and grandfather, he was able to gain Namur, Holland, Seeland, Friesland, and Hennegau. Through inheritance he also acquired the duchy of Brabant in 1430. In the process, he almost doubled the size of his original territorial inheritance. He no longer fought for supremacy in France, but profited from the stalemate between the two kings, which had evolved almost entirely to the favor of Henry VI by the year 1429.

Time and again throughout history, completely unforeseen events occur that are later hard to explain, events that completely transform a situation and change the course of history. Such a phenomenon was the appearance of Joan of Arc (Jeanne d'Arc) in the hour of France's greatest need. The visions of this young girl from the country, without education or understanding of the political situation, struck the soul of the French people like a thunderbolt; it seemed that in Joan, God himself had sent a messenger who would turn the fate of France. All at once, patriotism, strength, and the courage to fight were aroused in the French people. The story of Joan of Arc is familiar to most: under her leadership, French troops were able to free Orléans from the siege laid by the English. She then led Charles VII to his coronation and consecration in Reims, and finally fell into the hands of her enemies, the English, in Paris. She was handed over to them; her trial and execution followed in Rouen. From today's perspective, the course of this interlude was typical. It had to end with Joan's death. In this way she became a martyr who had transformed the destiny of France and strengthened nationalistic sentiments.

it becomes clear that he always placed himself on the winning side. In this case he justified his decision on the basis of his desire to revenge his father's murder. In addition, the cities of Flanders, which he had consulted for advice and confirmation after the death of his father, were inclined to favor England in any case because of their trade relations with that country.

King Charles VII of France, painting by Jean Fouquet, oil on panel, Paris, Musée du Louvre.

Philip the Good did nothing to come to the aid of Joan of Arc. It was typical of him to wait in the sidelines to see which party would emerge victorious and then decide accordingly whom he would support. As Henry VI and his regent, the duke of Bedford, grew less and less powerful, the duke of Burgundy turned his allegiance to Charles VII. His historiographers proclaimed his feelings, the feelings of a prince of royal blood who, like all the others, was filled with patriotism.

In August 1435 a large peace conference was held in Arras which was attended by all three parties. At first, England and France could not agree, and the duke of Burgundy came to terms with the king of England in a separate peace. On September 2 the English departed. The treaty signed by Burgundy and France on September 20 dissolved the secret pact of 1417 between Burgundy and the English, as well as the Treaty of Troyes. As recompense for the murder of his father, Charles VII gave Philip control of Auxerre, the Auxerrois, Bar-sur-Seine, Luxeuil, the strategically important Somme cities, the Ponthieu, and Boulogne-sur-Mer. Perhaps even more important than these territories was the concession that for the duration of his life, he was released from the obligatory oath of allegiance to the French king. This meant that he was sovereign in his French fief—and now he attempted to achieve the same status for his estate.

On February 2, 1440, Frederick of Styria was elected King Frederick III of Germany (he later became emperor of the Holy Roman Empire). His election was extremely advantageous for the duke's purposes. Philip began his diplomatic and military operations in Luxembourg, as he had hereditary rights to this duchy that conflicted with those of William of Saxony, the brother of margrave Frederick II of Saxony. Philip marched his troops into Luxembourg in August 1443 with the approval of the German king. By the beginning of the following year, he had already come to an agreement with Saxony, and the duchy of Luxembourg was granted to Burgundy for a ransom of 120,000 Hungarian gulden.

Philip's influence in France's political affairs had become negligible. His relations with Charles VII continued to be cool, and when the Hundred Years' War was revived once again in 1450 after French troops conquered Normandy and Guyenne, Burgundy remained neutral. In the meantime, the dauphin Louis, who would later become Louis XI, resided in Brabant from 1456 onwards. He had left the French court because of disputes with his father. Together with his wife, he remained the guest of the duke until his father's death. This stay did not, however, prevent Louis from becoming Burgundy's most bitter enemy later on.

Charles VII finally died in 1461, and the heir to the throne could return from exile. With him came Philip, whose generosity the royal couple had availed themselves of for so long. Incidentally, Philip had not been to Paris since he had left the capital to the Armagnacs. The young king's entry into Paris became a moment of triumph for the duke of Burgundy, who rode at the head of the procession, clothed entirely in black velvet, on a white horse with a golden harness. He was accompanied by his son Charles attired in crimson velvet, a great number of pages in black damask, and Burgundian noblemen in splendid velvet robes. Although the duke of Burgundy once again had to swear the feudal oath of fealty to the son of Charles VII, he considered himself a kind of guardian of the young king. He left no one in doubt as to his ambitions—but he had no time for political power play any more. His health was deteriorating; the last years of Philip's life were marked by mental and physical decline. On June 15, 1467 Philip the Good died in Bruges.

In conclusion, it must be mentioned that more than his father and his grandfather, Philip loved splendour, magnificent processions, and knightly tournaments. There is not enough room here to quote Olivier de La Marche's detailed description of the *voeu du faisan*, the famous pheasant feast of February 17, 1454, which the duke held in Lille to swear in the knights of the Order of the Golden Fleece before their departure on the crusade to

Jean Wauquelin presents his translation of the Hennegauer Chronicle to Philip the Good, miniature (detail) by Rogier van der Weyden, ca. 1448, Brussels, Bilbiothèque Royale Albert I.

Constantinople. The duke had founded this distinguished order to compete with the English Order of the Garter, which had steadily refused to admit him. As in all the duke's public appearances, groups in attendance were dressed alike, the archers in gray and black cloth, the squires in silk, the knights in damask. On three tables were arrayed, among other things, a completely rigged and manned ship; a fountain in a landscape of glass with rocks made of sapphires and other rare stones; a pastry in which 20 musicians sat surrounded by additional landscapes, architecture, and people; and entire scenes depicting daily life and mythological motifs.

Philip himself never participated in the crusade. In Gent, the last of the cities in the Netherlands to rebel against him, the wealthy and influential citizens rose up against Philip. He was finally able to defeat them in 1453, but by that time Constantinople was already in the hands of the Turks.

Charles the Bold – Under the Spell of Power

Philip's heir was his son Charles. After two childless marriages his third wife, Isabelle of Portugal, bore him a single son. The chroniclers called him *le téméraire*, "the bold," or *le Grand Duc du Ponant*, "the Great Duke of the West," even during his lifetime. He was born in Dijon on November 11, 1433. Olivier de La Marche, who grew up with the duke and had known him since childhood, wrote of Charles: "He was hot-headed, lively, and stubborn and almost always wanted to have his way as a child. Nevertheless, he was also reasonable and so high-minded that he could resist his inclinations, so that when he was young, you could have found no person more gentle nor more polite than he." The chronicler emphasized Charles' piety, his intelligence, his keen memory, his diligence and his reserve, his love of the sea and ships, and his love of hunting and literature. Georges Chastellain noted Charles' skill in rhetoric and his fondness for "speaking beautifully and admonishing his followers to remember the virtues, like an orator." However, Chastellain also addressed the duke's lack of restraint: "He kept no rule or measure (upon the death of his father) and behaved in such a way that all were astonished at his excessive pain." Philippe de Commynes judged the young duke similarly when he described him as impulsive, stubborn in his wishes and sharp in his words, ambitious, proud, headstrong, and incapable of being moderate. His own father affirmed the suspicious nature of the son, explaining this was something he had inherited from his mother, who was the most suspicious woman that he had ever known. In this regard, it should perhaps be recalled that a suspicious nature had also been one of the most prominent characteristics of Charles' grandfather,

Duke Charles the Bold, painting by Rogier van der Weyden or his workshop, oil on panel, Berlin, Staatliche Museen Preußischer Kulturbesitz, Gemäldegalerie.

John the Fearless, along with his admirable skill in diplomacy.

Charles' appearance seems to have been similar to that of his father. He was quite tall, a bit stooped, and had broad shoulders. He had long arms, black hair, a rather dark complexion, clear blue eyes, a wide mouth, and the projecting chin that ran in the family. Rogier van der Weyden painted two portraits of father and son that display a degree of family similarity that is almost astounding. Like his father, Charles was pious, but his piety was not paired with affability, goodness, a love of life or pleasure-seeking. Instead it was accompanied by abstinence, earnestness, and harshness.

Due to his father's long illness and decline, Charles had already become acquainted with and used to running affairs of state while his father was still living. In 1465 he had been appointed "Lieutenant General," and his influence increased. It never even occured to him to strive to obtain Louis XI's crown; his dream was rather to establish a Kingdom of Burgundy on the ruins of France.

At first Louis XI seemed to be his unwitting helper. After returning from a deeply distressing period of limbo in exile, Louis showed himself to be vengeful and ill-advised at the beginning of his rule, angering many around him. The future duke of Burgundy, at that time still count of Charollais, used this weakness of his opponent to his own advantage. With the support of large segments of the French nobility and public organizations, Charles allied himself with François de Bretagne and Charles of France, Louis' youngest brother, in the *Ligue du Bien Public* ("League for the Public Well-Being") and attacked the king. The battle ended with a stalemate and concessions of the French crown to the allies. But Louis XI had learned his lesson. He attempted to reconcile himself with his opponents, and began to play the allied partners off against each other. In addition, Charles' method of isolating his opponents and encircling them with a net of alliances is the very method that France would make use of years later against Burgundy.

At the outset, however, fortune was with Charles the Bold. On July 3, 1468, in his third marriage, he wed Margaret of York, sister of King Edward IV, and thereby once again drew closer to England. Unable to foil the marriage, Louix XI now tried betrayal. He secretly sent agents into the powerful city of Lüttich in order to incite the people there to rebel against their duke. At the same time, Louis visited the duke of Burgundy in Péronne to win him over, to deceive him, and to thwart his alliance with England. But just when the king had been received with all possible honors in Péronne, the news of the rebellion—and its instigator—arrived from Lüttich. Charles reacted with raging fits of anger and imprisoned the king immediately. Philippe de Commynes, the duke's chronicler and chamberlain, recorded the events in great detail. Finally Charles was ready for negotiations, even for a personal talk with the king, who in turn capitulated without stipulations, as he was in a precarious situation. Unfortunately, Charles knew no limits. In addition to demanding that Louis cede extensive incomes and rights, in the Treaty of Péronne he forced the king to submit to an ingenious and terrible punishment. The king had to accompany Charles to Lüttich and witness as Lüttich was burned and its people massacred en masse.

These events bred hatred in Louis, while in Charles they fomented pride and excess. He lost all sense of what was possible, because at first, nothing seemed impossible. Philip the Good had earlier set his sights on Alsace, and now his son saw his opportunity. In 1469, Sigmund of Austria-Tyrol, who was deeply involved in a conflict with the Swiss, offered Burgundy an alliance and pawned the territories of Alsace, the Sundgau, and the county of Pfirt to the duke of Burgundy. It seemed impossible that the Habsburgs, who had been impoverished for many generations, would ever be in a position to buy back their land. Immediately after the completion of this treaty, negotiations began concerning the marriage of Charles' only daughter, Mary of Burgundy, with Maximilian of Austria, son of the Habsburg emperor Frederick III. The Holy Roman Empire and England both allied with Burgundy! It is little wonder that France regarded Burgundy as a terrible threat.

A short time later the duke also considered an alliance between his heiress-daughter and Charles of France, hoping to further weaken the position of the king. He formed a new tripartite alliance with John II of Aragon, whom Louis XI had alienated, and with Edward IV. These three were further supported by several discontented feudal lords who made various promises of support. In addition, the two kingdoms of Aragon and Castile were united through marriage in 1469.

Louis XI now tried to intervene in the War of Roses, the bloody contest between the Houses of York and Lancaster over control of the English throne. Louis' motive was to break up the English-Burgundian alliance. His success was only of short duration. In 1471, Charles the Bold and Edward, who had returned to the throne of England, renewed their alliance, and took Naples as their third partner.

Without a doubt, the last duke of Burgundy does not bear the epithet "the Bold" in vain. He was audacious not only on the battlefield, but perhaps even more so in his diplomacy. Wherever he saw an opportunity to expand his powers and further his interests, he grasped it with lightning speed and left in his wake amazement and respect that compelled caution. And fortune smiled on him. Was it not serendipitous that Louis XI fell into his hands in the very moment his treachery was revealed? Was it not luck that Louis had fallen out with John of Aragon, or that his brother-in-law Edward returned to the throne? Today one might say that Charles was buoyed up on a wave of success. He was, after all, one of the richest and most powerful princes of Europe. This surely contributed to his loss of touch with reality, and explains why one of his character traits became ever stronger, to the extent that it would later be called pathological: his lack of moderation. The excessive behavior that he had demonstrated since early childhood now became boundless, because in the end, he had never encountered any genuine obstacles that could not be overcome. His ambition was unbridled, as was his opinion of himself; his demands and his expectations, his punishments and his anger, all were equally excessive. "Half of Europe would not have been sufficient for him," Commynes wrote about the duke.

Charles' ambitious plans—his attempt to seize the king's crown and even the crown of the empire—were not, however, completely due to excessive personal ambition. Philip the Good had handed down to his son a complex group of

Tapestry of 1000 Flowers from the so-called Burgundy Loot, Brussels, ca. 1466, Bern, Bernisches Historisches Museum.

King Louis XI, portrait sketch from *Le Recueil de Portraits d'Arras*, Arras, Bibliothèque Municipale.

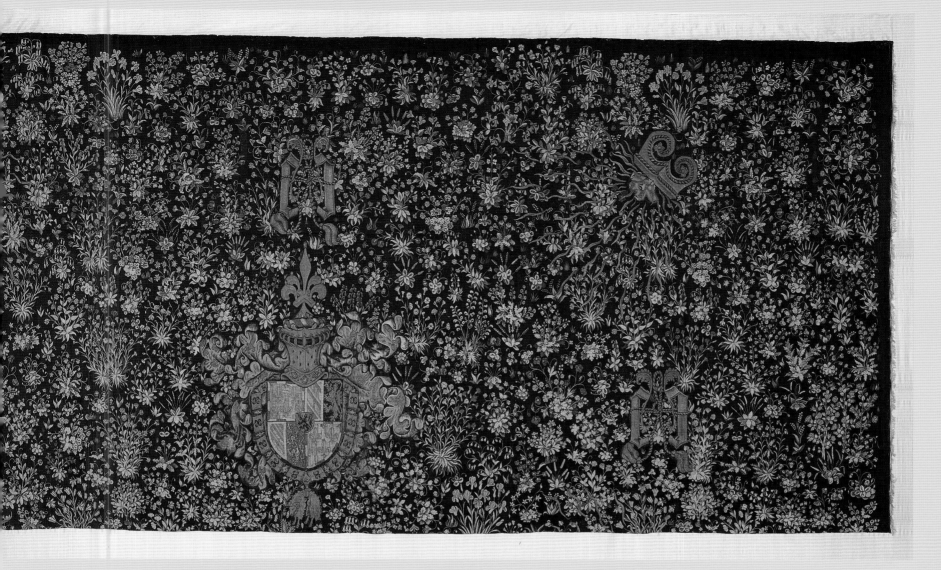

territories with varying degrees of dependence. Its existence as an entity could finally only be ensured through imperial law. Only in this way could Burgundy become sovereign in relation to France. The negotiations of the duke of Burgundy with Emperor Frederick, as impetuous and exaggerated as they might seem, were, from his point of view, absolutely logical and correct.

In 1473, the wheel of fortune began to turn, at first imperceptibly. Charles' temerity outdid itself and he lost all sense of limitations. When Charles of France, the betrothed of his daughter Mary, died in 1472, Charles the Bold believed rumors circulating that suggested the young man had been murdered, and immediately began to gather troops in Arras to seek revenge. England was not ready to renew the Hundred Years' War, so the duke impatiently led the campaign in Vermandois without their aid. He was defeated outside Beauvais and had to accept a cease-fire in 1473.

As Mary was now marriageable once again, another suitor presented himself: Maximilian. In a sincere effort to maintain good relations with Burgundy, Emperor Frederick III offered the duke—as

his father had before him—a king's crown in exchange for one of the royal fiefs. But to Charles, in light of his lofty ambitions, the offer seemed ridiculous. He wanted everything. He wanted Burgundy to become a kingdom which united the old Lotharingia with the ancient Burgundian kingdom of the 5th and 6th centuries. After negotiations broke down in Trier, he announced publicly in Dijon that the lords of France had annexed the former kingdom of Burgundy illegally, something that all its subjects regretted.

But at first the emperor and the duke met in Trier. Officially, the meeting was about the engagement of Mary to Maximilian, about a crusade against the Turks, and about reinstating peace between France and Burgundy. Unofficially, the two men discussed raising the status of the duchy to that of a kingdom, and what is more, Charles was to receive from Frederick the title of Roman king and a rightful claim to the throne of the empire. Exactly what the two men discussed remains a mystery. Did the emperor perhaps take offense at the splendor displayed by the Burgundian, which made him appear impoverished by comparison? Or was it that

Reliquary of St. George that belonged to Charles the Bold, 1471, by Gérard Loyet, height 21 inches (53 cm), appeasement gift of the duke to the city of Lüttich after the devastation in the year 1468, Lüttich, Treasury of the Cathedral.

the emperor was already secretly negotiating with Louis XI? Or did the demands of the Burgundian seem too extravagant, leading the emperor to fear the consequences of what they proposed? How else can it be explained that after two months of negotiations, the emperor secretly left Trier in the night of the 24th to the 25th of November, 1473 without so much as paying his bills?

Charles, who had already prepared the throne and the coronation robes, was disappointed, but not completely disheartened. In July, Duke Nicholas of Lotharingia had suddenly died and Charles was interested in acquiring the duchy. In addition, on July 25, 1474, he and Edward IV of England signed the Treaty of London, which incorporated the terms of the secret pact of 1417 and those of the Treaty of Troyes. Edward was planning an invasion of France and Charles assured him of his support with more than 10,000 soldiers, and that he would support Edward in his claim for the French throne. In return, Charles would be freed of all the duties of a vassal, and extensive territories would increase his possessions in France.

The invasion was planned for June or July of 1475, presumably giving Charles enough time to attend to his interests in the east. In these circumstances, it is difficult to understand why the duke of Burgundy became involved in internal German disputes over the archbishopric of Cologne, but with his characteristic obstinacy he kept his troops stationed near Neuss for months and weakened his strength just at the moment when he could have struck the decisive blow, together with England, against Louis XI. His difficulties were compounded as Louis was finally able to make clever use of alliances, which had been used so effectively against him, to defeat Charles.

In Alsace, the ducal overseer Peter von Hagenbach instituted a harsh and cruel regime. By ignoring the complaints of the people and siding with his bailiff, Charles drove the Alsatians directly into the arms of their former enemy, the House of Austria, which, like France, had begun to fear the duke more and more. Now the alliance which was to bring about the first real loss for Burgundy began to form: the House of Habsburg bought back Alsace with French money, as it had only been pawned to Charles, rather than sold outright. In 1474, a rebellion broke out in the Alsatian cities against Peter von Hagenbach, who was taken prisoner and brought to Breisach. Upon Duke Sigmund of Tyrol's arrival there on April 30, 1474, Hagenbach was quickly tried, condemned, and executed.

The Swiss, who were mercenaries of the French, supported the Alsatian cities and together they attacked Charles' troops and defeated them on November 13, 1474 near Héricourt (Belfort). From that point on, the fate of Burgundy worsened like a gathering of dark storm clouds. While Charles was still laying siege to Neuss he received the news that the English, as per their agreement, would land in France in a few months time and fully expected his military support; and that under the influence of Louis XI, René II of Lotharingia had rebelled against Burgundy.

At this point Charles finally abandoned his siege of Neuss and hurried to Calais to meet Edward IV in July 1475. Charles now waged war on two fronts, in the east and in the west. The French army was not as weak as the opponents of Louis XI had anticipated, and now that its neighbors in the west were trembling in fear at the thought of being invaded by Burgundy, it was much easier for Louis XI to win them over as partners in his alliance. Edward IV was also open to negotiations which would finally put to an end the Hundred Years' War. For this reason, Charles cancelled the Treaty of London angrily in 1475; the English-Burgundian alliance was broken. On August 29 treaties were signed in Picquigny, confirming the peace between the royal houses of England and France.

Burgundy nevertheless remained a powerful nation. The alliances with Aragon and Naples were still in effect, and since the beginning of 1475, Burgundy was also allied with Milan and Savoy. Louis XI busily wove the threads of his web. He agreed to a cease-fire with Burgundy for a nine-year period and agreed to the cancellation of the alliances with Aragon on one side and Lotharingia on the other without, however, thinking of giving up the secret support of René II.

Charles was not able to learn from his defeat. Obstinate and vengeful, he conquered Lotharingia and wanted to teach the Swiss a lesson, for they had attacked the governor of Franche-Comté, angering the duke to no end. What followed, the panic and frantic activity with which Charles sought to force a victory, can only be explained by the steady stream of success in his younger years. Only these can explain the rashness of a campaign that began in January 1476 and ended on January 5, 1477 in a complete catastrophe for the Burgundians. Charles the Bold fell in an utterly chaotic battle near Nancy. His body was found after two days, naked and contorted in the mud of the pond of Saint-Jean. Only with the help of a scar and his teeth, which had been badly damaged, could he be identified. Booty as splendid as any described in a fairy tale fell into the hands of the Swiss, for the duke had taken with him on the campaign works of art, tapestries, silverware, robes, and money in unimaginable quantities.

Charles' heiress was his only daughter, Mary. She was, understandably, a highly sought-after partner

Court Festivities, copy by an anonymous artist of an original now lost, from the circle of van Eyck, Dijon, Musée des Beaux-Arts.

throughout Europe, in spite of the fact that parts of her lands had been repossessed by France and the empire. During the negotiations that her father had held with Frederick III, she had been promised to Frederick's son, Maximilian I. Mary abided by this agreement, and this marriage essentially formed the basis of the power and wealth, as well as the court ceremony, of the House of Habsburg. In spite of the fact that Mary died very young—at the age of 23 as the result of a fall from her horse—she left two children, Margaret of Austria and Philip (later the Handsome). Philip would become the father of Emperor Charles V. The same Charles inherited many of the features and character of his Burgundian ancestor, and like him, always dressed in black. He would be known as the last Burgundian.

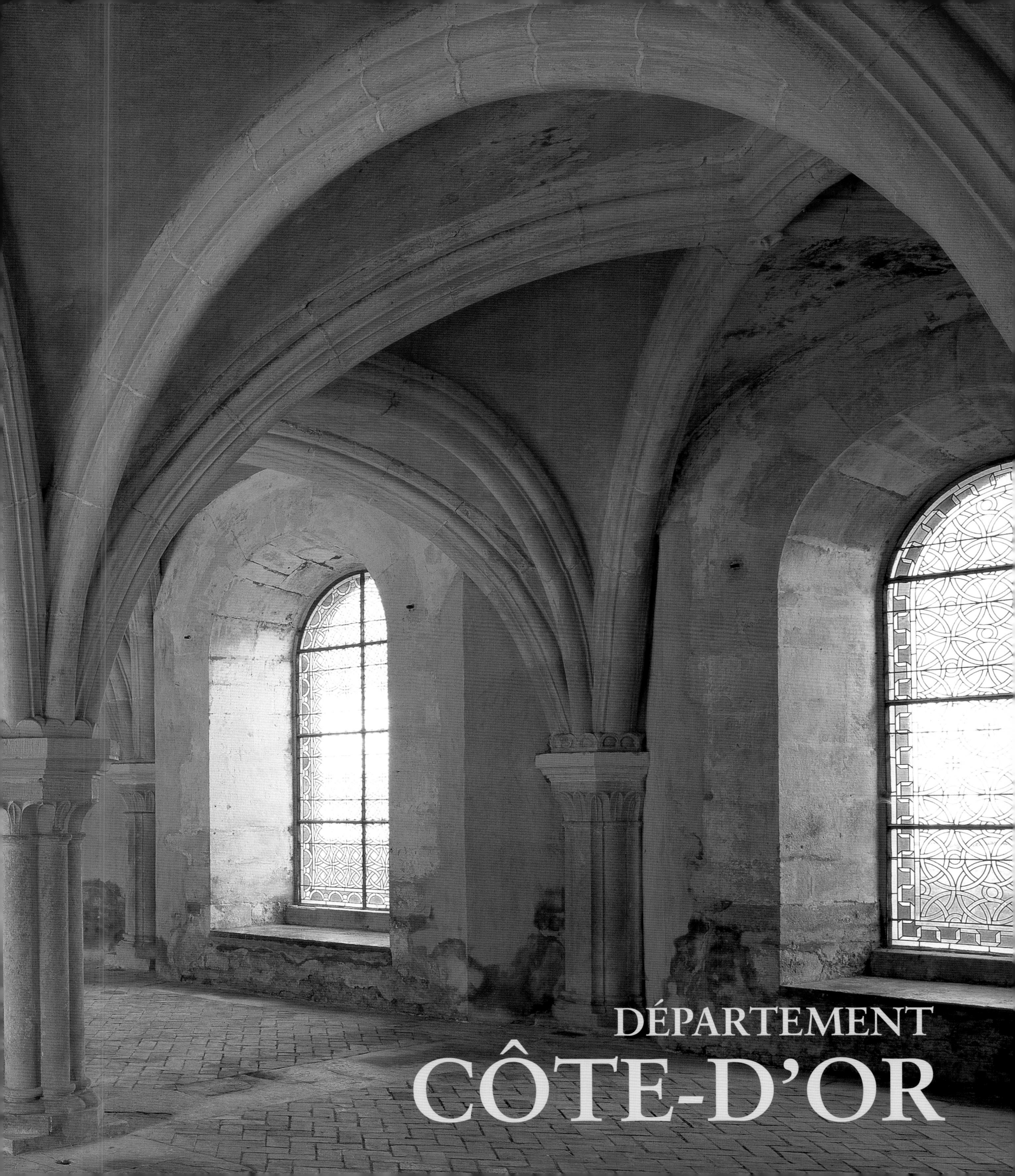
DÉPARTEMENT
CÔTE-D'OR

Together with the department of Saône-et-Loire, the department of Côte-d'Or forms the eastern half of Burgundy. The Côte-d'Or stretches to the north and south, bordered in the east by the former Franche-Comté, which was a dependency of the German Empire. Today this area has become the departments Jura and Haute-Saône. Farther north lies Haute Marne, which belongs to Champagne. To the west and south, Côte-d'Or is completely enclosed by the other departments of Burgundy. To the north and west, its contours are determined by the plateaus of Lower Burgundy, which extend primarily in a north-south direction and determine the course of the Ource, Seine, and Ozerain Rivers. The Côte-d'Or and Haute Côte further south extend almost at right angles to the plateaus, forming the southern and south-eastern slopes on which the world-famous wines are cultivated. This is a hilly countryside, in some places almost sleepy. The Canal de Bourgogne slowly meanders through it, accompanied by various rivers and wonderful avenues, in endless winding curves. If Saône-et-Loire is cast as the department of Romanesque churches and monasteries, then Côte-d'Or is the department of châteaus and *maisons fortes* standing dreamily in quiet, picturesque villages, drawing visitors into the irresistible spell of their history.

PREVIOUS TWO PAGES:
Marmagne, former Cistercian abbey of Fontenay, chapter hall, end of 12th century.

RIGHT:
Canal de Bourgogne at Châteauneuf-en-Auxois.

Dijon – The Capital of Burgundy

Dijon, view over the roofs of the city from the Tour Philippe le Bon.

Dijon today has about 150,000 inhabitants, making it the largest city in Burgundy. First mentioned in 768 AD as the capital of a *pagus* (county), from the 11th century on it was the capital first of the duchy and then of the province of Burgundy. Pre-historic and early historical finds prove that there was an early settlement here where the north-to-south trade route, running along the mountain ridge, crossed the east-west route. It was Gregory of Tours who made the first written mention of this city in the 6th century. He had seen the city himself as his uncle was Bishop of Langres. Gregory wrote of a city wall about 3/4 mile (1,200 m) long and 30 feet (9 m) high, 5 feet (1.5 m) thick, with four main entrances and 33 towers much higher than the surrounding walls. A ditch and a second wall enclosed the inner ring. This description suggests a Roman *castrum*; and in fact vestiges of it can be seen in the burial monuments and in the great stone blocks that were discovered in excavations under the dismantled church of Saint-Etienne. Gregory also had a name for the settlement: Divio.

During the second half of the 3rd century, Benignus is said to have been in Burgundy as a missionary and thereby suffered the death of a martyr. After his death he was revered with special devotion in Dijon. Nevertheless, Christianity seems to have first gained wider acceptance during the 5th and 6th centuries, and Gregory mentions a church with baptistery, a bishop's palace, and a house for the clergy in his account of his visit.

When, after 1031, Dijon's status was elevated to that of the capital of the duchy, the city was infused with a fresh economic impetus that soon made the Roman walls all too confining. Various breaks in the wall were already made in the mid-11th century in order to enlarge the church of Saint-Etienne. A circle of houses was built abutting the exterior of the walls and developed into *faubourgs*, or suburbs, with their own centers and markets. Due to the growing practice of revering saints, the small cemetery chapels evolved into parish churches and monasteries. In 1137 a major fire destroyed the city, which was rebuilt with a wall more than one and a half miles (2.5 km) in circumference, incorporating the old entrance gates to the city. The wall survived in this form until the 19th century.

Dijon got a new look starting in the 1370s as Philip the Bold began renovating and expanding the ducal palace. The conventions of the court necessitated the presence of numerous nobles, whose palaces changed the immediate surroundings of the ducal palace in particular. But over time the entire city was caught up in the economic and artistic blossoming that ensued.

After the abrupt fall of the House of Valois, Burgundy fell to the crown, and from the mid-15th century Louis XI and his successors ordered the

Dijon, view of the city from the Tour Philippe le Bon. In the foreground is Notre-Dame.

reinforcement of the city wall. From then on, a governor resided in Dijon, someone who belonged to the king's family and of course required a suitable residence. The ducal palace was renovated and enlarged by a wing; in the west, the wings of the Palais des Etats were added on. Today, the city panorama is still essentially characterized by the architecture of the 17th and 18th centuries. Due to the economic, social, and artistic flourishing of this period, Dijon became the seat of a newly appointed bishopric, a university, and of numerous associations and corporations.

Today, Dijon remains by far the largest and most important city in Burgundy. The administration of the department Côte-d'Or has replaced that of the province of Bourgogne, and modern means of transportation ensure Dijon its pivotal position as a trade center. The city offers easy access to the highways to Paris and Marseille, to the TGV (*train de grande vitesse*, or high-speed railway), and there is an airport nearby in Longvic. The Canal de Bourgogne, begun in about 1830, lost its importance as a means of transportation long ago and is now a place of recreation. The food industry, indigenous to Dijon for centuries, has now been supplemented by the electronic and chemical industries and by mechanical engineering.

Industries and housing settlements have sprung up around the city, displacing the vineyards of Côte de Dijon, which had cultivated a famous wine since the late Middle Ages. Only Marsannay-la-Côte, in the far south of the region, has remained. Almost as famous as Burgundy wines, which the first duke loved and enjoyed presenting to others as a "promotional gift" to further their good reputation, is Dijon's mustard. The Maille company is one of the oldest houses involved. That venerable firm is proud to point out that, since its founding in the year 1720, it has survived three monarchies, two empires, five republics, five European wars, and five monetary reforms.

In the city center of Dijon, its industry is hardly noticeable. Here, historic houses from five centuries (the 20th is hardly represented!) stand in close proximity, one atop the other, bearing impressive testimony to the continuing prosperity of the city. The endless stores and businesses offer an assortment of goods fortunately not aimed exclusively at tourists; instead, it reveals something of the way and style of life espoused behind the façades of the city houses, and in the idyllic villages and country estates nearby.

Bustling life fills the city of Dijon: in the city center or immediately adjoining it are administrative buildings, the court of justice, as well as the city archive, many schools, and the university quarter (Cité Universitaire).

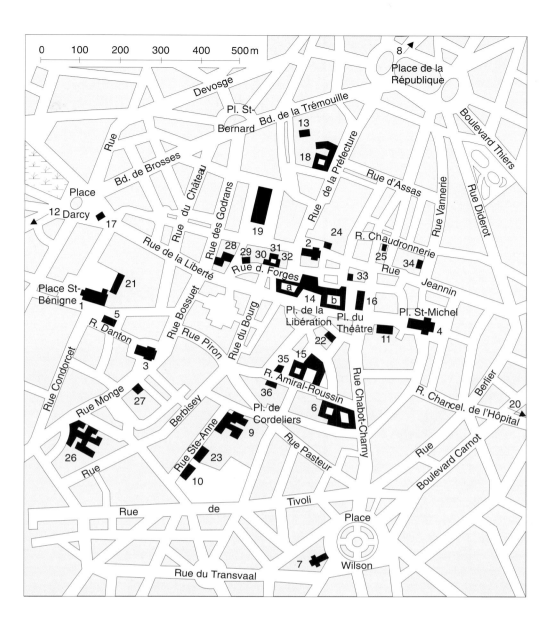

Dijon, map of the city

1 Cathedral of Saint-Bénigne	17 Porte Guillaume
2 Church of Notre-Dame	18 Prefecture
3 Church of Saint-Jean	19 Market halls
4 Church of Saint-Michel	20 University
5 Former church of Saint-Philibert	21 Musée archéologique
6 Former Jesuit church and	22 Musée Magnin
theological college; city library	23 Musée d'Art Sacré
7 Church of Saint-Pierre	24 Hôtel de Voguë
8 Church of Sacré-Cœur	25 Maison des Caryatides
9 Former Carmelite convent	26 Former Hôtel de l'Académie
10 Former convent of Saint-Bernhard	27 Hôtel Bouchu
11 Former church of Saint-Etienne;	28 Hôtel des Godrans
Musée Rude; chamber of commerce	29 Hôtel Morel-Sauvegrain
12 Former Carthusian monastery of	30 Hôtel Aubriot
Champmol	31 Hôtel Chambellan
13 Clairvaux cellar	32 Maison Milsand
14 Former castle	33 Hôtel Berbis
a City hall, former Palais des Etats	34 Hôtel Chartraire de Montigny and
b Musée des Beaux-Arts, former	former Hôtel du Commandant
Logis du Roi	Militaire
15 Palais de Justice (courthouse)	35 Hôtel Legoux de Gerland (Liégeard)
16 Theater	36 Hôtel Fyot de Mimeure

Saint-Bénigne

The former monastic church of Saint-Bénigne, now destroyed except for a few remnants, once figured among the largest and most exceptional churches of the western world. Its loss is just as lamentable as that of the monastic church of Flavigny and the three successive churches of Cluny.

A first large basilica above the grave of the saint was consecrated in 535 and became the monastic church of the monastery that was founded here later. In 989, William of Volpiano (962–1031) of Cluny was appointed abbot here. Caught up in the indefatigable reform and building activities and with an eye to the newly completed church of the mother house (Cluny II), William made Saint-Bénigne the center of its own reform group of about 60 monasteries and began building a new church in the year 1001. He did not take Cluny II as his model, as might be expected, but instead chose the architectural type of the large, five-aisle transept basilica, almost 330 feet (100 m) in length, with a west transept, a semicircular west apse, and a deep east transept with Benedictine choirs on either side of a semicircular choir set off by columns. Behind this screen of columns lay the entrance to a wide, three-aisle rotunda, three stories high, which was connected in the east to the original, almost square burial chamber through a rectangular chapel dedicated to the Virgin Mary. Eight columns surrounded the center space of the rotunda, at the apex of which is an oculus. Sixteen columns separated the first ambulatory from the second, matched by 24 engaged semi-columns on the exterior wall. The uppermost story had only one broad ambulatory,

Dijon, cathedral and former abbey church of Saint-Bénigne; view to the east into the rotunda.

spanned by groin vaults. The capitals, some of which have now been replaced, are among the oldest known sculptures in Burgundy. A round stair tower adjoined the rotunda at both the north and south sides. A crypt with exactly the same dimensions as the building above it reached well under the central nave and was accessible via a stairway under a triple arch. Under the main apse was the grave of Benignus. The eastern part of the nave was presumably reserved for the monks. Because of the crypt, it was elevated well above the side aisles and was not accessible from the west. The elevation of the nave might have been three stories: arcades over square piers, galleries, and finally a clerestory. Given these dimensions, vaulting was surely never intended. This is quite surprising, as from about 1000 onwards, every large sacred building in

Burgundy endeavored to display stone vaulting. The exterior apparently boasted a pair of towers in the west; a second pair is presumed to have been located on the west sides of the main transept arms. This building was completed in 1018.

Saint-Bénigne is not a key building in the historical development of architecture. Its rotunda was never imitated and this type of building, the unvaulted basilica, was not a common or popular one in Burgundy. The models for the crypt and the nave are probably to be found in the buildings of upper Italy, William's homeland, as well as in the double choir of Ottonian monastic churches and diocese churches of Germany, especially in Augsburg, where William's godmother, the empress Adelheid, made generous donations and endowments. The rotunda, however, remains unique. Other rotundas accessible from a crypt ambulatory by way of a three-aisled passageway had been built before, for example in the 9th century in Saint-Germain in Auxerre and in Flavigny-sur-Ozerain—the latter even had an arcaded ambulatory—but architectonically, the rotunda in Dijon took the place of the central apse of a Benedictine choir. Moreover, its dimensions bear no comparison to those of Auxerre and Flavigny. For a long time, an effort was made to establish the Burial Church of Jerusalem as the prototype, but this idea has been rejected. Although the very concept of similarity was understood differently in medieval times, there is not enough resemblance between the two structures. There is another theory today, namely that the rotunda is the product of very disparate traditions, a structure arising from the cult of the tombs of saints, the patron saints, and the liturgy of the monastery. It is probably the Pantheon in Rome that is the most important model, mainly because of such common elements as the rotunda and oculus, and because of a common liturgical program. The Pantheon was reconsecrated in 609 as the church of Santa Maria ad martyres.

The large structure in Dijon suffered serious damage in 1137. It was repaired and expanded with a narthex, and a consecration in 1147 is documented, probably only with regard to the (at that time vaulted?) eastern sections. The renovation of the nave (perhaps also rib-vaulted) with its magnificent portal took until about 1160/1170.

In 1271 the crossing tower collapsed, and the decision was made to build a completely new structure. The three-apse choir with a preceeding antebay and parts of the transept were finished by 1287. The nave, whose elevation of arcades on round pillars, triforium, and clerestory with walkway were typical for Burgundy, was not completed until 1325. It seems a bit static and eclectic, and its coating of gray paint gives it a lifeless and dull impression (illus. p. 44).

Dijon, cathedral and former abbey church of Saint-Bénigne, rotunda capital, about 1010.

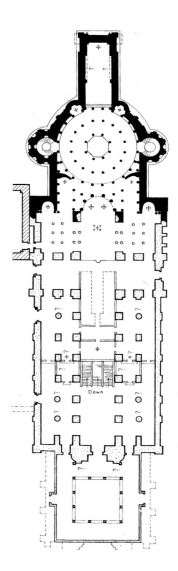

Dijon, cathedral and former abbey church of Saint-Bénigne, floor plan.

The French Revolution brought a temporary end to the monastery: it was disbanded and plundered. The upper stories of the rotunda were taken down and the crypt filled in with debris. The recessed portal of the 12th century, which is indebted to the Gothic, was torn down except for the outer frame and the base of the jambs. The original design is known today through an illustration. Christ sat enthroned in the tympanum with the symbols of the Evangelists, cherubim, ecclesia, and synagogue. The Virgin and scenes from Jesus' childhood adorned the lintel. In the archivolts were angels, childhood scenes, and the Elders of the Apocalypse. Below in the jambs were figures from the Old Testament as well as Peter and Paul. The trumeau was reserved for the statue of St. Benignus, the head of which can be seen in the museum.

Saint-Bénigne was restored to its original function as a church in 1795, and in 1805 it became a diocese church. For this occasion, the tympanum from the destroyed church of Saint-Etienne was brought here. It is a work from the atelier of Jean-Baptiste Bouchardon (1667–1742), and depicts the stoning of St. Stephen. After 1794 the interior furnishings were also brought to Saint-Bénigne from other churches. Of special interest are the marble sarcophagi of Jean-Baptiste Legoux de La Berchère and his wife from the 1630s, on which the donors kneel in eternal worship (illus. below), the tombs and epitaphs on the walls of the lateral aisles, the 18th-century choir pews from the abbey of La Charité-lès-Vesoul, and numerous very lovely figures of saints from the Sainte-Chapelle of the dukes, dismantled in 1802. When the buried crypt

ABOVE:
Dijon, cathedral and former abbey church of Saint-Bénigne, interior view facing east.

RIGHT:
Dijon, cathedral and former abbey church of Saint-Bénigne, donor figures from the two cenotaphs of Jean-Baptiste Legoux de La Berchère and his wife, 1730/1740.

OPPOSITE:
Dijon, cathedral and former abbey church of Saint-Bénigne, former dormitorium, second half of the 13th century, today in the Musée archéologique.

LEFT:
Dijon, cathedral and former abbey church of Saint-Bénigne, chapter hall in cellar; after being filled in during the 16th century, today the Musée archéologique.

OPPOSITE:
Dijon, tympana from Saint-Bénigne with Maiestas Domini and the Last Supper, ca. 1160/1170, Musée archéologique.

BELOW:
Dijon, bronze statuette of the goddess Sequana, ex-voto from the source of the Seine near Saint-Germain-Source-Seine, Musée archéologique.

was rediscovered in the 19th century, the rotunda was reconstructed according to the conceptions of that time (illus. pp. 42/43).

Of the extensive monastic complex, only the east wing of the cloister—with its chapter hall vaulted over heavy pillars of quarry stones—and the rib-vaulted dormitory have survived. The dormitory is a light and unusually lovely three-aisled columned hall dating from the second half of the 13th century (illus. p. 45). The Musée archéologique is now quartered here. Its most famous pieces are numerous votive gifts from the Sequana Grotto at the source of the Seine (illus. right), Claus Sluter's bust of Christ from Champmol (illus. p. 60), and the remains of the magnificent portal of old Saint-Bénigne (illus. opposite).

Besides the ex votos from the source of the Seine, Gallo-Roman sculptures depicting both gods and everyday people are on exhibit in the dark vaults of the basement, which dates from the 11th century. In the bright, elegant dormitory on the ground floor are medieval sculptures from Dijon, pieces of the building that previously stood on the site of the church of Saint-Bénigne, and the tympana and the busts of Christ by Sluter already mentioned. In the upper story, pieces dating from the centuries between the Palaeolithic era and the Merovingian period are on display.

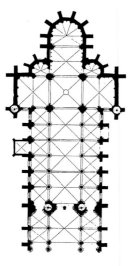

Dijon, Notre-Dame, floor plan.

Notre-Dame

In the northern part of the old city center, a new church—Notre-Dame—was built on the site of an older church by order of the magistrate. It was begun in about 1220. The choir and the eastern transept walls were probably finished by 1230, shortly thereafter the transept and the eastern nave bays. As early as 1240 there was mention of affixing the gargoyles that populate the façade in droves.

Notre-Dame is a three-aisle basilica with a transept, a square crossing, and a recessed, seven-sided polygonal apse behind a square bay (illus. below). This square grid is continued in the wings of the transept and in the nave, where pairs of bays form six-part vaulted squares. Two small, rounded apses adjacent to the choir open into the transept.

From the crossing, you look up into the tower where the triforium and clerestory are repeated. The nave and transept are three stories high: circular pillars with beautiful crocket capitals carry the ribbed pointed arches, above which are the broad triforium and the clerestory with walkway. Extremely slender vaulting shafts—three under each of the transverse arches, but only one under the central rib of the six-part vault—articulate the triforium. The elevation of the choir reveals four zones. Here, between the triforium and clerestory, is a blind arcade. This is an element of the early Gothic, as are the six-part vault and the circular pillars. Because of the slender proportioning of all the columns and vaulting shafts, the effect of the interior is that of extreme delicacy and seeming

weightlessness. Indeed, Notre-Dame is imbued with a freedom and delicacy throughout that is also evident in the narthex, the upper story of which has a gallery.

A double-tower façade was planned in the west, but this was abandoned in favor of the present façade, which is unique, revealing on the exterior the principles of design applied to the church within (illus. opposite). Located above the three-part, strongly recessed entry portal of the almost solid west wall is a two-story screen of closely set blind

Dijon, Notre-Dame, west façade.

OPPOSITE LEFT:
Dijon, Notre-Dame, view through the nave towards the east.

OPPOSITE RIGHT:
Dijon, Notre-Dame, wooden Madonna, Notre-Dame de Bon Espoir, ca. 1100.

arcades on overly slender columns. The capitals of these columns are richly decorated; they carry relief friezes embellished with vines and gargoyles (which were restored after 1881) and their number matches that of the blind arcades. Although completely medieval in its motifs, the impression of the façade is almost classical. The portal sculpture and the four figures that once adorned the spandrels of the ground floor have been lost. The design, however, is known: the jamb figures were prophets, patriarchs, and kings of the Old Testament. The tympanum of the main portal displayed the crowning of the Virgin; below in the lintel were her death and burial. On the left portal was the Adoration of the Kings as well as the Annunciation or the Visitation of the Virgin and the Announcement to the shepherds. At the right portal, the Passion and the Crucifixion were depicted. The interior furnishings were lost during the French Revolution. Only the wooden Madonna from about 1100 (illus. opposite) and the remains of old murals in the transept and the side aisles still remain.

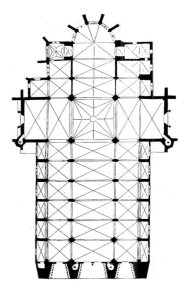

Dijon, view from the Tour Philippe le Bon over the Tour de Bar, museum, theater, and mint in the direction of Saint-Michel.

OPPOSITE:
Dijon, Saint-Michel, west façade.

Dijon, Saint-Michel, floor plan.

Saint-Michel

The parish church of Saint-Michel lies at the eastern edge of the old city. Originally, the cemetery of the canons of Saint-Etienne was situated here; a first parish church is mentioned in 889. Shortly before the turn of the 16th century, a new structure was decided upon, but it was only completed a century and a half later. A consecration in the year 1529 perhaps marked the completion of the interior. The façade was finished in 1559, while the cupolas of the towers were not built until 1667.

The floor plan and elevation were still entirely late Gothic in conception. The simple three-aisle nave is followed by a five-part transept with stellar vaulting above the square crossing, and a recessed choir with surrounding chapels. Due to the absence of a clerestory, the interior is naturally quite dark. It also contains almost no sculptures, decoration, or other furnishings.

The west façade is quite different (illus. opposite). Its ground floor, with three deeply recessed portals, consists of traditional Gothic forms, but the shape of the baldachins and the tondi on the exterior already reveal Renaissance influences. A superposition accentuates the two west towers, whose decoration recalls famous castles. The two-story central part and the two octagonal towers with cupolas are Baroque. The small monopteros, a circular, pillared temple on the terrace above the broad central portal, is a real curiosity.

Chartreuse de Champmol, Carthusian Monastery

The Chartreuse de Champmol, which once lay outside the gates of the city, was founded by the first Valois duke, Philip the Bold. He began planning his own tomb in the 1370s, when he was barely 30 years old. As he entrusted the Carthusian order with matters concerning his salvation, he founded a monastery for 24 monks near his Burgundy capital. On August 20, 1383, the duchess, Margaret of Bavaria, laid the foundation stone *par sa main mesme* ("with her own hand"), and her 12-year-old son, who later became John the Fearless, placed the second stone. The choice of architect remained a matter of disagreement until February 10, 1384, when Drouet de Dammartin, a colleague of the royal architect Raymond du Temple, came from Paris. He was entrusted with the monastery, and the duchess also commissioned him to plan and build her country estate at Germolles. Shortly thereafter, Raymond du Temple himself came from Paris to Dijon—perhaps to approve the plans and view the building site. Then construction of the church that would house the ducal tombs in its choir began; it still stands today. Of the three chapels adjoining the choir, one was two stories high and contained the private oratories of the duke and duchess. In the south was the so-called small cloister, which was connected to the great cloister by a corridor. The 24 cells for the monks and the parlatorium were grouped around this large courtyard. The small cloister provided access to the chapter hall, the refectory, and the library. This ensemble was festively consecrated on May 28, 1388.

The composition of figures for the church portal (illus. p. 58) was decided upon right at the beginning. The Virgin Mary with Child was to adorn the trumeau (illus. left), while the jambs were reserved for the duke and duchess as donors together with John the Evangelist and St. Catherine as intercessors. The two sons of the French king John the Good, both famous patrons of the arts, were the first to have portrait sculptures made of themselves and their families and arranged in dynastic composition. In 1386, Jean de Marville, the duke's court sculptor, had begun work on the portal according to the plans of Drouet de Dammartin. The molded frames, the archivolts, the tympanum with trefoils, and the consoles and baldachins for the figures were soon completed.

But in 1389 Jean de Marville died unexpectedly, making room for a true genius who almost unconditionally left the achievements of medieval sculpture far behind, creating astoundingly life-like and fantastically expressive figures: Claus Sluter from Haarlem. In 1385 he had already worked on the sepulcher and its reclining figure of the deceased. Dissatisfied with the work of his predecessor, Sluter

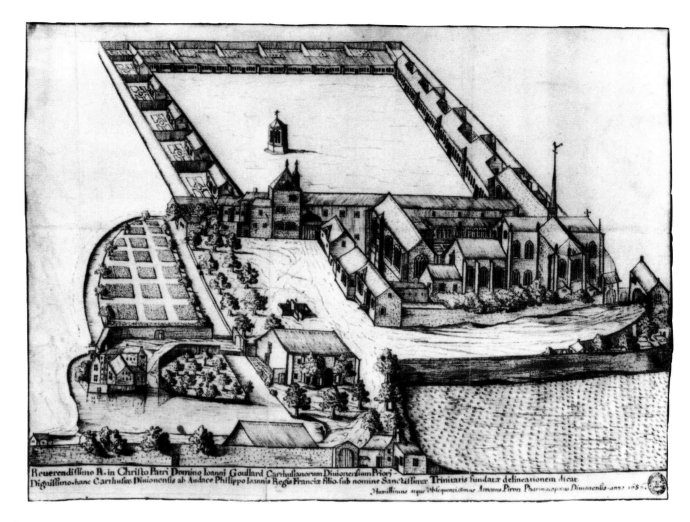

Dijon, Chartreuse de Champmol, floor plan of the church as it currently stands.

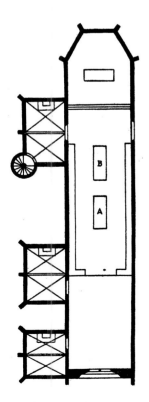

had all of de Marville's work removed, in some cases at his own expense. He could not alter the west wall, however, and for this reason, his superimposed figures fit badly into their niches. No works done by Sluter's contemporaries can measure up to his.

In 1401 the portal was completed. Sluter was also responsible for the interior decoration and furnishings. Records mention three large figures for the upper oratory of the duke, depicting the Madonna and the duke's favorite saints, John the Evangelist and St. Anthony, but unfortunately these sculptures have not survived.

In addition to the architectural sculptures, the sources also mention bells, columns of bronze for the main altar, a lectern and chandeliers, pews for the choir, wooden paneling, portals and furniture for the library, polychrome frames, murals and gilding of the duke's private oratory, a painted triptych on which the Annunciation, the Visitation, and the crowning of the Virgin were depicted, 24 panel paintings for the cells of the monks, gilded wooden reliefs, and finally, magnificent stained-glass windows. The burial chapel in Champmol seems to have surpassed all of the duke's other building projects and is a clear indication of Philip's dynastic ambitions. Only first-rate artists were engaged to work on his projects.

Still more famous than the interior of the church and the tombs today is the so-called Well of Moses (illus. pp. 60/61), although only the torso of Christ has survived. In former times, it stood in the middle of the great cloister, whose inner square was the cemetery of the monks. This fountain was Sluter's masterpiece. Statues of the six prophets who foretold the passion of Christ surround the central column of the fountain's basin. Above them, angels seem to float, carrying Mount Calvary on their outspread wings. The cross, accompanied by the Virgin, Mary Magdalene, and John, was destroyed during the Revolution.

While Sluter's surviving statues in themselves justify a journey to Burgundy, they are nevertheless only a pale shimmer of the magnificence that once surrounded the burial place of the dukes. Lively polychromy and shimmering gold, paired with the austerity and simplicity of monastic life—and do not forget the music—all gave the monastery a festively solemn atmosphere which, in the conceptions of that era, must have seemed a fair approximation of heaven. Three dukes and their wives found their final resting place here beneath the monks' choir. Even Emperor Charles V, the grandson of Charles the Bold and therefore at heart a man of Burgundy, wanted to be buried in Champmol "next to his ancestors from Burgundy."

Claus Sluter – His Art and Influence

Born around 1355/1360 in Haarlem, Claus Sluter's name is encountered for the first time in the records of the ducal court in May of 1385, when Sluter was between 25 and 30 years of age. He had come to Dijon as the second journeyman of Jean de Marville and worked on the sepulchre of Philip the Bold. Who was this man who was able to elevate late medieval sculpture to such artistic heights within two decades? Nothing is known about Sluter's childhood, his youth or his apprenticeship, but he clearly was not a beginner when the duke entrusted his sepulchre to him. Sluter continued to work on it until his unexpected death sometime between September 1405 and January 1406.

At that time, this monument completely overshadowed any sculpture that had previously been done. Although it is based on the traditional form of the stone sarcophagus with figures, in this case everything came alive. Between the base and the covering slab of polished black marble, an architectural landscape of alabaster is revealed, a rhythmic row of arcades consisting of five double arches on each side (illus. pp. 56/57). These double arches, framed by delicate pier buttresses with triangular gables, lend the impression of small interiors, for between each of them and set slightly back are two diagonally placed arches whose peaks point forward, creating the illusion of real, monumental architecture. The arches are filled with tracery and are topped by ogival arches embellished with gilded crabs and finials. In addition, gold-plated pinnacles crown the lateral pier buttresses. The upper end is formed by a triforium which follows the curve of the arches exactly, further emphasizing the illusion of a mysterious space behind them. This interior space is filled by a funeral procession of 42 pleurants, mourning and praying monks. No two figures are alike, and each is so detailed and realistic that it seems to be alive. On the covering slab rests the supine figure of the duke, his final portrait. He is accompanied by a lion at his feet and two angels at his head. Over the course of the centuries, the polychromy has been restored numerous times and today a thick coating of enamel-like paint covers the stone. Especially the flesh tones of the reclined figure and the angels, as well as the head of the lion, seem strangely lifeless, almost grotesque.

The sepulchre was dismantled early on. In 1650 the first statuettes were missing; in 1791 it was taken apart. In 1818 it was restored and reassembled according to pictorial sources. Neither the angels known from descriptions, which probably stood on the small consoles of the pier buttresses, nor the group of choirboys at the head of each funeral procession, have been recovered. Today the sepulchre is preserved in the Musée des Beaux-Arts in the Palais des Etats. It is hard to imagine how much more life-like and mystical it must have seemed in the choir of the chapel of Champmol, where Sluter had orchestrated the room and the sculpture to a continuous requiem in the midst of colorful light, refracting on the gilding of paintings and sculptures.

This sepulchre not only proves Sluter's genius as a sculptor; he was also a talented director, staging in stone the duke's imposing presence and his proud ambitions. Sluter masterfully united a high degree of realism with the demands of beauty, harmonizing the actual, physical appearance with an idealized conception of the personage. In this respect he must have been an ideal match for Philip, who desired to see himself glorified, for Sluter proceeded in the same manner in his work on the portal of Champmol and on the Grande Vis in Germolles.

Dijon, detail of the sepulchre of Philip the Bold, Musée des Beaux-Arts.

OPPOSITE:
Dijon, former Salle des Gardes with the tombs of the dukes (on the walls are altars and tapestries, in part from Champmol), Musée des Beaux-Arts.

FOLLOWING TWO PAGES:
Dijon, funeral procession of the monks sculpted on the sides of the sepulchre of Philip the Bold, Musée des Beaux-Arts.

After the death of Jean de Marville, Sluter took charge of the workshop in Champmol in 1389. Except for the archivolts, he had the work of his predecessor completely removed from the portal— probably at his own expense, at least in part. This act attests to his self-confidence and pride as an artist, which was not yet typical in his time. Sluter then created five life-size figures: for the trumeau a Madonna with Child, and for the door posts the duke and duchess in the pose of eternal worship with their two patron saints, Catherine and John the Evangelist (illus. below and opposite top). The statues are monumental and dynamic, almost Baroque; the portraits are astoundingly forceful and full of life. Here again, one is confronted with the staging of a ritual: the duke and duchess, in a humble but proud posture, are being recommended to the Virgin by two intercessors. The Mother of God, herself a queen, keeps her face turned towards her child. The difference does not lie in the fact that the figures of the duke and duchess are portraits; that had already been done on the famous Grande Vis in the Louvre two decades earlier, and the two donor figures at the portal of the Eglise des Célestins in

Dijon, Chartreuse de Champmol, church portal with the Mother of God on the trumeau and the donors with intercessors, 1389–1405/1406.

Dijon, Chartreuse de Champmol, detail of portal: Philip the Bold and St. John the Baptist.

Dijon, Chartreuse de Champmol, detail of portal: Margaret of Flanders and St. Catherine.

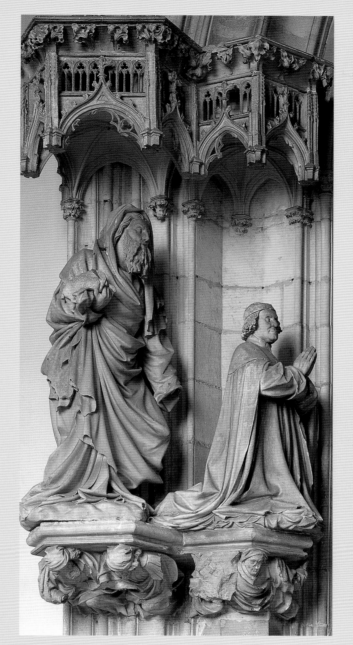

Amiens, cathedral of Notre-Dame, south transept portal, Virgin on the trumeau, called the *Vierge Dorée*, or "Golden Virgin," ca. 1240/1245.

The Madonna statue on the central column of the portal is a depiction typical of the early 13th century. This type first emerged in the High Gothic cathedrals of the Île-de-France. The *Vierge Dorée* of the cathedral of Amiens is one of the most famous examples of this type.

Paris also depict the royal couple in a realistic manner. Nevertheless, what a difference between the two pairs of figures! The sculptures of Charles V and Joanna of Bourbon are still completely Gothic. As jamb figures, they stood at the portal and gazed on the viewers, not at the Madonna who presumably stood on the trumeau. Philip the Bold and Margaret of Flanders, on the other hand, accompanied by two saints, kneel before the Madonna. They do not gaze at the viewers, but are turned away from them, their attention wholly focused on the Virgin and Child. Their faces are unsparing portraits; nothing has been idealized. They are solemn, as the divine presence demands, and the carefully draped folds of their majestic robes follow the movements of their bodies. The royal couple, on the other hand, smiles down from the jambs. Despite some personalized features, their faces are undefined, and their silhouette closed. They stand stiff and immobile, in almost unnoticeable contrapposto.

shepherd couple with a herd in the shadow of an elm tree. Again, the people were no longer depicted in isolation, but were active participants in a scene of a very private nature, one that portrayed the natural world and the favorite pastimes of the duchess. Sluter's other works for Germolles were a Madonna over the portal, who may have born similarities to the Madonna of Champmol, and probably numerous fireplaces, one of which is preserved in the Salle des Gardes.

Sluter's masterpiece was the Well of Moses in the great cloister of Champmol (illus. below and opposite). Doubtlessly the sequence of images was composed by a clergyman. Sluter worked to complete the piece between 1395 and 1405/1406, to a great extent by himself. The drilling and masonry work for the basin, the central column, and the platform alone took three years. Sluter began with the crucifixion—Christ's torso may now be viewed in the Musée archéologique in Dijon (illus. left)—and the accompanying figures of the Virgin, Mary Magdalene, and John. They were set in place in 1399. Then followed the angels, who seemed to be carrying Mount Calvary on their outspread wings, and finally the six prophets who had foretold the passion of Christ. In their hands they carry scrolls on which the relevant Biblical texts can be read. The painter Jean Malouel and two assistants then painted the well entirely in colors and gold. The prophet Jeremiah wears glasses, and Mary Magdalene a diadem. Only the lower part of the ensemble is still in situ; Mount Calvary had already disappeared before the Revolution.

As is true of all of Sluter's works still in existence, the color is now missing. Still more regretable is the loss of the gilding, as the shimmer of gold imbued the sculpture with a very special ambience.

In 1381, the duchess bought a *maison forte* in Germolles, which she then had transformed into a magnificent country estate. She, too, commissioned Claus Sluter for the masonry work. The main entrance to the splendid two-story chapel and the adjoining apartments formed the so-called Grande Vis, an external spiral stairway that probably was modeled on the steps of the Louvre. However, while life-size figures of the Valois dynasty officially received every visitor there, at Germolles, a relief plate by Sluter bearing pastoral scenes made it clear that this estate was a private residence. This relief has been lost for a long time and no sources exist that give an intimation of its appearance. The pointed arches of the portals to the chapel and the Salle des Gardes, which still exist, suggest there was a similar portal at the Grande Vis, and it seems certain that the pastoral was a flat relief in the tympanum. Here Philip and Margaret of Flanders were depicted as a

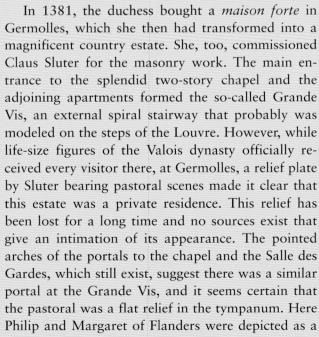

Dijon, torso of the crucified Christ from the Well of Moses in the former cloister of Champmol, 1395–1405/1406, Musée archéologique.

Dijon, Chartreuse de Champmol, Well of Moses, the prophets Daniel and Isaiah.

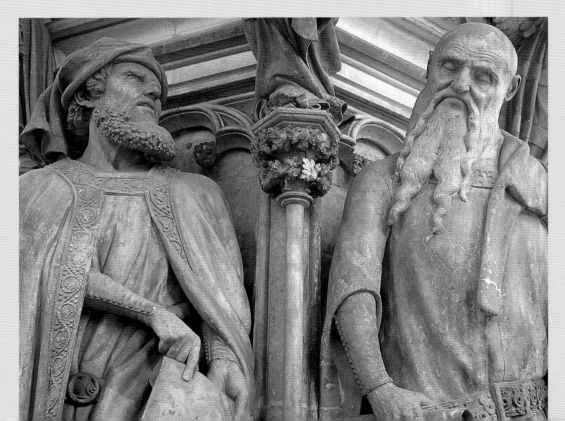

Even without color, however, the figures are masterpieces; each prophet is a type in whose face sadness and despair can be read, albeit in that spiritualized form which distinguishes them from ordinary people. Moreover, the prophets do not stand isolated; they are active and form groups. David and Jeremiah turn towards each other, seemingly engaged in conversation; Jeremiah is talking, David, listening. Daniel and Isaiah are also discussing or consulting (illus. opposite).

Monumentality and a completely new sense of space, realism, and a genius for drama are the components of Sluter's style. His works strongly influenced not only French sculpture, but also that of western and central Europe for more than half a century. His successor was his nephew, Claus de Werve. Born about 1380 in Haarlem, he is listed in the records at the end of the year 1396 as an apprentice. At first he worked on the Well of Moses, following the designs of his uncle.

After Sluter's death, he completed work on the sepulchre of Philip the Bold, again according to Sluter's sketches and with the help of another journeyman named Hennequin de Prindale. It was finished by the year 1410. Immediately afterwards, John the Fearless commissioned him to create his own sepulchre. Claus de Werve appears to have inherited all too little of his uncle's genius. His own works, of which only a few are in existence, appear mediocre, and sources report of his continual financial difficulties. He died in about 1436, with the sepulchre of John the Fearless (illus. below) not even begun. Now it was Jean de la Huerta who took over the workshop, and he received the commission for the sepulchre in 1443. The design, whether his own or that of Claus de Werve, relied heavily on Sluter's model. At the death of Jean de la Huerta in 1455, the arcades and some of the pleurants, as well as the two supine figures of John the Fearless and Margaret of Bavaria, the angels, and perhaps the

lion were finished. The reclining figures broke, however, and had to be sculpted anew, this time by Antoine le Moiturier between 1460 and 1470.

Unlike Claus de Werve, Jean de la Huerta had a large atelier. Many works originating from this workshop or from its environs can still be seen in Burgundy, for example, the beautiful Madonna with Grapes in Notre-Dame in Auxonne (illus. p. 86), the Madonna with the two Johns in Saint-Jean-Baptiste in Rouvres-en-Plaine (illus. p. 84), and the pietà in the castle chapel of Epoisses. There are also a number of related sculptures in the Musée des Beaux-Arts in Dijon, especially numerous Madonnas similar to the Virgin in Champmol. All these works share the realism of expression and life-like drapery that is characteristic of this style. In Burgundy, which continued to be a center of cultural activity long after the fall of the House of Valois, Sluter's influence continued to make itself felt even into the early 16th century.

Dijon, the double sepulchre of Duke John the Fearless (died 1419) and his wife, Margaret of Bavaria. It was begun in 1443 by Jean de la Huerta and his workshop, modeled on Sluter's sepulchre for Philip the Bold, Musée des Beaux-Arts.

Gent, St. Bavo, Gent Altarpiece, Jan and Hubert van Eyck, completed 1432, oil on panel.

The wings are closed and their exterior shows the "everyday" side. On the bottom level are the donor couple, Jodocus Vijdt and his second wife, Isabella Borluut, with their intercessors John the Baptist and John the Evangelist. In the middle zone is the Annunciation; in the lunettes are the prophets Zechariah and Micah as well as the Erythaean and Cumaean sibyls. The care and artistry with which different materials and textures—cloth, fur, metal, stone, and skin—are replicated is extremely impressive. Indeed, it would not be among the court art of Burgundy if all the figures were not dressed in rich, expensive robes.

Sluter's work had tremendous influence on other areas, most notably in Flemish painting. Under the patronage of Philip the Bold, as well as his brothers and heirs, Flemish painting reached new creative heights. Or was there a common root, a common goal, which manifested itself in related areas of art? In any case, the same realism can be found, the same painstaking care taken over the smallest details, the same jamb figures, and the same rich interrelation between the figures in the paintings of Jan van Eyck and those of his successors. Because these paintings have come down to us complete and undamaged, they can give us some idea of the enchantment that colors, patterns, and textures of clothing, jewelry, skin, and architectural elements, as well as the original lighting conditions and the intended setting, must have given to the sculpture of the Late Middle Ages.

Dijon, Palais des Ducs/Palais des Etats, view into the *cour d'honneur*, which was finally completed in the late 18th century after being under construction for more than 100 years, interspersed with numerous bouts of re-planning and delays.

Palais des Ducs/Palais des Etats

During the rule of the Capetians in Burgundy, Dijon became a bourgeois city, paying taxes and tribute to the duke in return for certain privileges. When the young and ambitious Philip took over the crown of the duchy of Burgundy in 1363, he made Dijon into a Valois capital. The Capetian dukes had also had a residence in Dijon, of course, and so Philip set about modernizing it and furnishing it anew. Philip, in fact, took over the refurbishment of many older buildings, and by doing so, he continued the tradition and rule of the Capetian dukes, thereby legitimizing his own reign as their heir and successor. At the same time, Philip was demonstrating his right to rule as a prince of royal blood, proving himself, in competition with his brothers, a worthy Valois. On the site where the Roman wall had long since been torn down, he had the Capetian ducal residence renovated beginning in 1356/1357. Here a donjon and, by all appearances, a logis were erected. To the east lay the Sainte-Chapelle, a three-aisled basilica with west towers, a transept, and a long choir with two semicircular chapels on each side. In 1802, this church was torn down. It is most unfortunate that no architectural works dating from the time of Philip the Bold have been preserved.

The residence in Dijon was the earliest of the countless renovations and new buildings undertaken by Philip. Typical for the structures of the first Valois duke was the square donjon in combination with a hall construction, the Grande Salle. Plainly, this sequence of rooms must have been ideally suited to his court ceremony. The donjon had tracery windows on the ground floor and external stair towers at the corners. Of the entire extensive complex, only the donjon remains standing, but it seems probable that the Grande Salle also had tracery windows with stained glass as well as painted and gilded wooden barrel vaulting. The subject matter of the paintings surely pertained to the history of the dynasty.

From 1433 on, Philip's grandson, Philip the Good (Philippe le Bon), began the renovation of the residence in Dijon with the addition of a utility wing. First, a spacious, square kitchen building was erected. Three of the sides contained two large fireplaces each, and a domical vault, open at the top, was erected on free-standing supports. On the north side there was a well. The *pâtisserie* (pastry kitchen) and the *paneterie* (bread bakery) followed shortly afterwards; they were built as extensions of the kitchen building. The façade consisted of large, square-hewn stone blocks and had profiled windows and portals. While the adjoining buildings were torn down in 1852/1853, the kitchen has remained intact.

About 1450, Philip the Good began to have the old logis replaced by a new one with the assistance of the architect Jean Poncelet of Lyon. Only a little more than half of the project was completed. On

OPPOSITE:
Dijon, Palais des Ducs/Palais des Etats, Tour de Bar, 13th century, and stairway to the Galerie Bellegarde, early 16th century.
The Tour de Bar is the oldest part of the complex. On the ground floor, the openings of the old tracery windows are still visible. On the side wall one can see traces of the gable of an adjoining building that served as living quarters or as a reception hall for state functions.

the northwest corner, a seven-story donjon rises up from a square base: the Tour Philippe le Bon (illus. p. 65 and opposite). Cornices separating the stories articulate the structure and high, narrow mullion windows with ogival arches let in light. A small square stair tower on a corbel gives access to the stories of the tower, and a balustrade with tracery above the eaves crowns the structure. The logis reveals the same repertoire of forms. It has three stories and contains a Grande Salle in the interior, in which the sepulchres from Champmol, among other things, can be viewed today. The chimneys on the narrow walls date from the 16th century, as the original ones were destroyed by a fire. A staircase preserved in the wall provides evidence that there was originally a rostrum that took up the entire narrow west side. Philip's great uncle, John of Berry, had had just such a rostrum in the Palais de Justice in Poitiers, and Philip, like his great-uncle, apparently used his rostrum to make festive appearances.

The street side of the logis has been preserved, though it has undergone many restorations. It is evenly articulated. Above the small ground floor windows rise the large, six-part mullion windows that light the Grande Salle (illus. opposite). The splendid dormers boast similar windows topped with delicate pier buttresses, pinnacles, and finials. These date from the 19th century, but are based on old illustrations. Interestingly, to the west, on the far side of the Grande Salle, the city façade is three stories high and no longer completely symmetrical. The court façade was segmented in the same way. Although the five-story square stair tower was probably meant to divide the façade in the middle, the windows were apparently positioned according to the needs of the room and not with an eye to exterior symmetry. Only the dormers above the balustrade with tracery were placed evenly. They, together with the stair tower, give an idea as to how long the logis was once intended to be.

After the fall of Great Burgundy, the duchy returned to the crown and Dijon became the residence of the royal governor. The ducal residence increasingly fell into disrepair, as into the early 17th century the only structures being repaired were the city fortifications. Finally, in 1614, a long period of planning and building began. First, the Galerie de Bellegarde was built, a classical gallery structure between the Tour de Bar (illus p. 65) and the still uncompleted logis. Towards 1740, the so-called Aile de Rocrois was built at right angles to the logis. It was a palace for the governor Louis II of Bourbon, who became famous under the name of le Grand Condé. In addition, sources report countless larger and smaller buildings that covered the entire court. In 1681, Louis XIV gave the Estates in the province permission to build *bâtiments dont ils auraient*

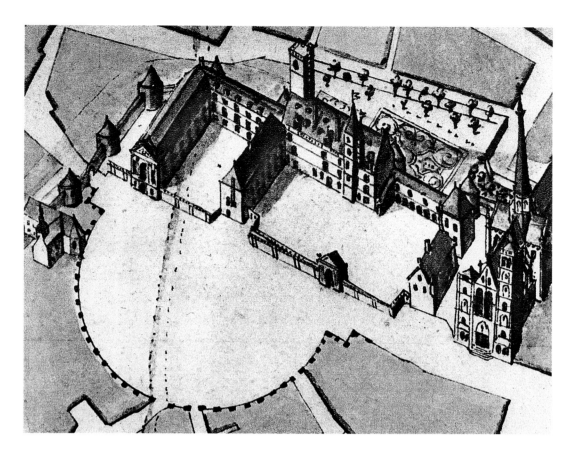

Dijon, Palais des Ducs/Palais des Etats, bird's eye view from the late 17th century.

besoin pour la tenue des Etats ("buildings they would require for the administration of the Burgundian Estates"). Immediately afterwards, the architect Daniel Gittard was commissioned, and under the site management of Martin de Noinville, the west wing of the *cour d'honneur* (ceremonial courtyard) with the large Salle des Etats and the mint were erected. The building was not yet complete when Gittard died in 1686. His successor was Jules Hardouin-Mansart. Two sketches dating from the year 1688 (illus. p. 68) show that Hardouin-Mansart respected the ducal palace, the Aile de Rocrois, and the recently finished portal, even carrying over its structure onto the front side of the west wing, though he altered the proportions somewhat. A plan dated the same year envisioned a three-wing building adjoined by two further courtyards on the east and west sides. Another horseshoe-shaped court with an equestrian statue of Louis XIV opened out to the south.

This plan was now to be realized. In 1686 construction began on the pillared arcade of the courtyard; in 1689 the exterior of the west wing was completed. The Salle des Etats, however, fitted with the exquisite wood paneling of Etienne Masson, was first used in 1695. In 1700, the Aile de Rocrois finally collapsed and work commenced on the main façade. Eight years later, in 1708, Jules Hardouin-Mansart died and Robert de Cotte succeeded him as architect in Dijon. By 1720 the rooms in the main building were also finished. Only the fireplaces with large reliefs by Jean Dubois have

OPPOSITE:
Dijon, Palais des Ducs/Palais des Etats, former logis of the Duke and the Tour Philippe le Bon, from ca.1450.
The tall, narrow mullion windows belong to the Salle des Gardes, the large festive hall of the dukes, in which their sepulchres now stand.

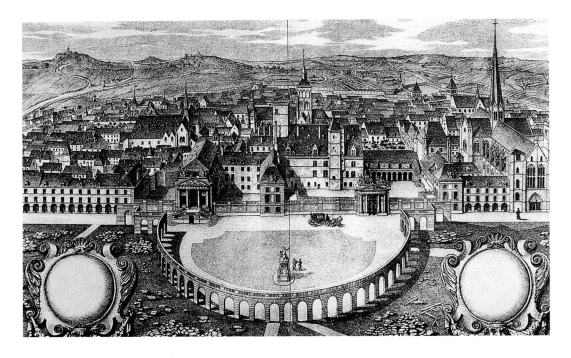

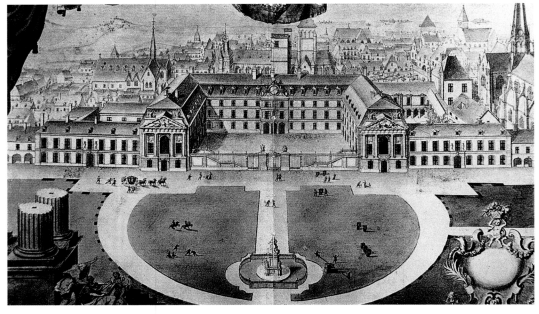

Dijon, Palais des Ducs/Palais des Etats, two models proposed by Jules Hardouin-Mansart for the redesigning of the ducal palace complex, 1688.

OPPOSITE:
Dijon, Palais des Ducs/Palais des Etats, front side of the west wing by Jules Hardouin-Mansart, 1689.

been preserved from this time. They glorify the deeds of Louis XIV, who had also been depicted as Caesar on the three-axial projection of the central façade. After the Revolution his image was replaced by that of the goddess Minerva.

The east wing, planned to be symmetrical to the already completed west wing, was begun in 1720. But work did not progress at all for a long time. Finally in 1783 the magnificent portal was torn down and replaced by the front side of the east wing. As early as 1700, the Burgundian Estates had demanded an expansion of the rooms at their disposal in the west wing, but to no avail. In 1731, they turned to Parisian architect Jacques Gabriel. He made various sketches, one of which was accepted in May 1733. It is a two-story wing of ten axes, adjoining the west wing at a right angle. Gabriel placed a vestibule at the center, completely

in white, forming a passageway for wagons entering the court. Adjoining this vestibule to the east is an elegant and extremely stately stairway, the Escalier des Etats, leading up to the Salle des Etats. High niches for figures adorn the rounded corners, and the delicately framed wall panels and friezes are richly embellished with rococo decorations in flat relief. Artistically wrought iron railings accompany the flat marble steps. The typical rocaille forms can also be seen on both sides of the main portal and on its wooden door panels.

In 1712 a chapel had been built under the Salles des Etats for the members of the Estates. The desire for another chapel like it arose while the elegant stairway was being built, and in 1736 Pierre le Mousseux was commissioned to do the planning. A small court at the northern side of the front of the Salle des Etats seemed to be the right place. To honor the king, the chapel was placed under the patronage of St. Louis. Fluted Corinthian pilasters articulate the walls; between them, round arches give form to flat niches with portals or wall panels with reliefs. Rocailles, busts of angels, garlands, and liturgical instruments adorn the tympana, door panels, and wall panels. Antoine Spingola was commissioned to do the marble work in 1742. The woodwork, gilding, and coloration of the interior were done by Jacques Verberckt, while the sarcophagus altar of dark marble was the work of well-known Parisian architect Jean-Nicolas Servandoni. In 1745 the interior was completed and the Estates had a chapel that compared favorably with interiors that were being created in Paris at that time.

During these years of building activity, the "building bug" seems to have befallen the Estates. Proud and happy with their new wing and the beautiful chapel, they wished to continue their construction spree. Pierre le Mousseux was commissioned to make plans for more buildings to adjoin the new wing. There were suggestions and projects, but no decision. First the Estates bought the neighboring houses, and in 1769 they were finally in a position to begin new projects. This time they turned to Charles-Joseph Le Jolivet. He suggested closing in the court between the Salles des Etats and the new wing by adding two new wings. Work began in 1773, but after two years they had not proceeded further than the foundation. The Estates stopped the work and demanded less decoration in favor of expanding the building. Le Jolivet offered new suggestions and plans. In order to ensure the desired simplicity of façades and interior design, the work was finally given over to the *ingénieur en chef des Ponts et Chausées* ("chief engineer for bridges and roads"), Thomas Dumorey, and his colleague Emiland Gauthey. This is how the Cour de Flore came into existence. Le Jolivet was to complete the east

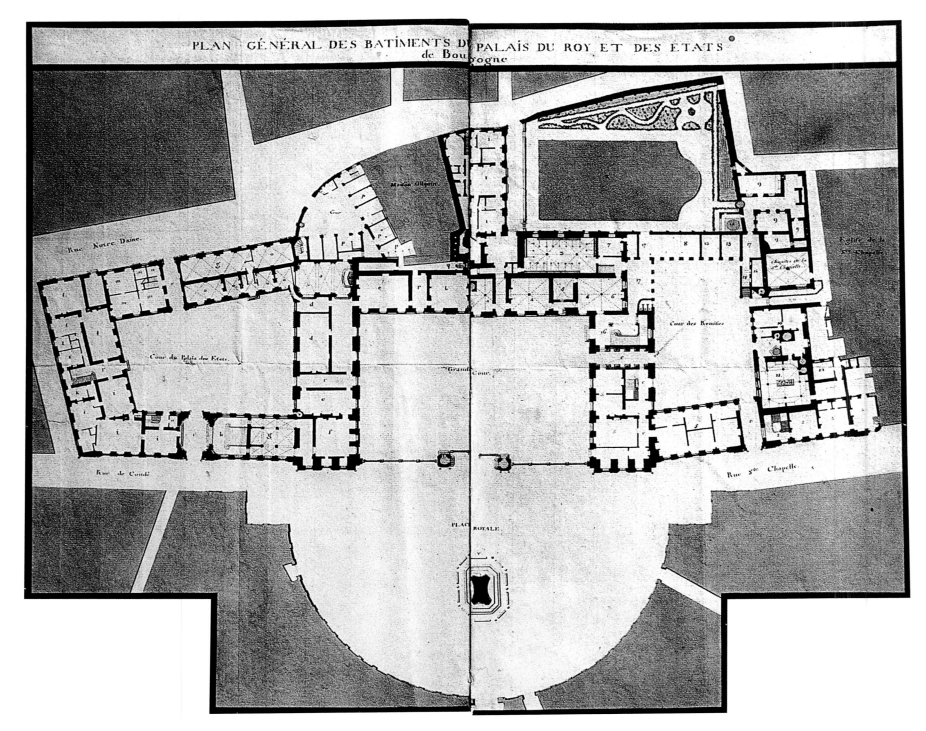

Dijon, 1786 plan of the Palais des Ducs/des Etats

a	Chapel of the Estates
b	Office of "Alcades"
c	Seat of the clergy
d	Chamber of the nobility
e	Chamber of the Third Estate
f	Administrative chamber
g	Archive
h	Stairway to the Hall of the Estates
i	Apartment for representatives of the clergy
k	Accomodation for the concierge
l	Quarters for representatives of the nobility
m	Quarters for representatives of the Third Estate
n	Accomodation for watchmen
o	Office of the "Vingtièmes"
p	Stables/carriage house
q	Latrines
r	Driveway
s	Office (modern construction)

Logis du Roi (royal tract)

1	Apartments
2	Garden
3	Stables
4	Offices
5	Laundry
6	Kitchens
7	Linen closet/cupboard/wine cellar
8	Carriage house
9	Roasting kitchen
10	Pâtisserie
11	Kitchen for the prince's household
12	New poultry coop
13	Slaughterhouse
14	Coal depot
15	New ice cellar
16	Main stairway (royal staircase)
17	Driveway
18	Secondary stairway

wing begun in 1720 according to the plans of Jules Hardouin-Mansart. Eventually, he added a building to the east wing to make it symmetrical to the wing of the Estates. He hardly altered Gabriel's plans at all. In fact, only the decorations hint at the influence of classicism.

The complex had barely been completed when the Revolution set about its destruction. The beautiful wood paneling of the Salle des Etats was destroyed, as were the interior decorations of the *logis du roi* (royal tract) in the main wing. In 1802, the Sainte-Chapelle was torn down, and in 1852/1853 the *pâtisserie* of Philip the Good followed. In its place, the architect Louis Belin erected a new wing for the Ecole des Beaux Arts, the Cabinet d'histoire naturelle, and the museum, among other

things, again closing the Cour de Bar. Since that time, stores and cafés have sprouted up in the arcades of the Place Royale, today called the Place de la Libération (illus. above).

City houses around the Palais des Etats

For centuries, the ducal palace, which later became the residence of the governor and the assembly house of the parliament, formed the center of Dijon. Court officials, merchants, members of the Estates, and people belonging to respectable professions settled around this complex. Too numerous to mention here, numerous houses and palaces, mainly from the 17th and 18th centuries, are located in the surrounding streets. In the rue des Forges, which leads between the Palais des Ducs and Notre-Dame,

Dijon, view towards the south from atop the Tour Philippe le Bon across the Place de la Libération and the Palais de Justice.

Dijon, Maison Maillard, ca. 1600.

Dijon, Hôtel Chambellan, end of 15th century, inner courtyard with stair tower.

there are an exceptional number of historical houses. Directly opposite the Cour de Flore the row begins with the Hôtel Chambellan. Erected at the end of the 15th century, it has an inner courtyard with splendid late Gothic tracery and half-timber galleries. The richly decorated windows with pointed arches and portals are reminiscent of the Loire châteaus, which were built during the same period. The most magnificent aspect of the house is the spiral staircase (illus. right). On its central column stands a somewhat squat figure with a basket on his shoulder. The ribs of the stellar vaulting, adorned with crockets, emerge from his basket.

The neighboring building, the Maison Maillard, dating from about 1600, is completely different (illus. above). Its strictly articulated windows and portals have segmental and triangular pediments adorned with the garlands typical of that time. The dormers are flanked by herma. In the axis of the portal, in the upper story, is a niche with a round arch housing a statue of the Virgin.

The Maison Milsand was built at approximately the same time as the Maison Maillard (illus. opposite bottom). Hugues Sambin is presumed to be the architect; he created his own style in his opulent decorations of the façade. Fruit garlands, trophies, animal and human heads, vases, and medallions in high relief encircle the gabled windows and fill in the wall areas between them. The façade was completely symmetrical until a storefront was installed on the ground floor sometime during the 19th century.

Standing wall to wall, the Maison Milsand is followed by the Hôtel Aubriot (illus. right), originally a 13th-century building. The man who owned it at the turn of the 20th century, the romantic poet Stephen Liégard, attempted to reconstruct the rather dilapidated building according to old pictorial sources as well as his own ideas of medieval decoration. In 1908 he commissioned the architect Louis Perreau and the sculptor Xavier Schanosky for the renovation. Two portals—one of which is a jamb portal, the other a magnificent portal in the style of the 17th century—and two simple biforiums on the ground floor correspond to four round-arched biforiums in the upper story. These are framed by numerous recessed archivolts resting on small, delicate columns. The overall effect makes the wall itself appear to dissolve into receding layers. The two dormers represent the Sambin style, popular around 1600.

Around the middle of the 15th century, at the same time the renovations and new constructions were going on in the Palais des Ducs, the Hôtel Morel-Sauvegrain was erected. The owner was Pierre Morel, *échevin et capitaine de Dijon* ("juror

RIGHT:
Dijon, Hôtel Aubriot, façade, end of 15th century/1908.

BOTTOM LEFT:
Dijon, Maison Milsand, façade, about 1600.

BOTTOM RIGHT:
Dijon, Maison Milsand, blind arcade of the inner courtyard.

Dijon, Place François Rude.

and commander of Dijon"), whose mother had been the wet nurse of Charles the Bold. Like the logis of the duke, the Hôtel Morel-Sauvegrain has an almost symmetrical façade with large, high, narrow windows whose molded frames curve in the middle of the lintel to form ogival arches. Splendid dormers adorned with crockets and finials complete the overall impression.

Another street within view of the ducal palace is the rue de la Chouette, with additional town palaces. Most noteworthy are the Hôtel de Voguë and the Maison Millière. The Hôtel de Voguë is another structure dating from the early 17th century (illus. right). It was built in 1607 as a three-wing complex around a small *cour d'honneur* enclosed by a wall with a rustic, gabled portal. Like the Maison Maillard, this building also has high, narrow windows with markedly protruding triangular and segmented pediments featuring decorative masks. The adjoining walls, on the other hand, remained undecorated.

Most of the medieval buildings in Dijon were half-timbered houses, and many of them are still standing. One of the loveliest is the Maison Millière, which the merchant Guillaume Millière and his wife Guillemette Durand had built in 1483 (illus. opposite, top). As in many city houses, the integrated store on the ground floor is original to the house's design. It was restored in 1926/1927. At that time the spaces between the beams were filled with bricks, the windows were changed, and the wooden pinnacles added.

From 1575 to 1580, the royal minister of finance, Bénigne le Compasseur (or his son), had a town palace built which has the same austerity as the Hôtel de Voguë. The magnificent bay window with opulent Sambin decorations is especially noteworthy.

The Maison des Caryatides is most surprising and unusual. It also belongs to the group of buildings surrounding the palace that were constructed around 1600. Ten life-size caryatids decorate both upper stories, and a row of animal and human heads

Dijon, Hôtel de Voguë, street façade, 1607.

which again enclosed the Cour de Bar. This wing was built from 1852 to 1856, parallel to the newly constructed theater. It was to house the Ecole des Beaux-Arts, the Cabinet d'histoire naturelle, the museum, and other institutions. Today it houses only the Musée des Beaux-Arts.

In 1765, on a small elevation above Dijon, the architect Charles de Wailly built the pleasure palace Montmusard in the typical Gabriel style. Destroyed during the Revolution, only three axes of the building remain. The center of the complex was a round, peristyle temple to Apollo, open at the top. It stood in the small court formed by the three cube-shaped buildings of the three-wing complex, which opened towards the entrance side. The raking cornice continued on the side wings, harmonizing the entire complex. Behind the peristyle was a round hall covered by a dome resting on a tambour. Parisian theories of Revolutionary architecture, based on exclusive use of cubic or circular forms, are evident in this hall. The façades are reminiscent of the Petit Trianon on the grounds of Versailles.

LEFT:
Dijon, Maison Millière, façade, 1483.

Dijon, theater, façade facing the Place du Théatre, after 1802.

forms the cornice of the roof like a metope frieze. The area between the windows of the first and second story is decorated with a gable bearing cornucopias and garlands. Only on the ground floor, which has a portal and two high round arches, has a strip of wall space remained undecorated.

Charles-Joseph Le Jolivet, the unfortunate architect of the Palais des Etats, built a town palace for Auguste Théodore Bazard in 1772. Colossal ionic pilasters and a stepped entablature articulate the elegant character of its façade. A broad, rustic portal visible on the left side of the ground floor is in strange contrast to the rather flat and conservative relief of the façade.

When the Sainte-Chapelle of the dukes was torn down in 1802, plans were made for a theater to stand in that location. It was begun in 1810 (illus. right). In front of the rigid, geometric, block-like building is a portico on a stepped base. Corinthian columns support the protruding roof that continues around the entire structure.

After the Sainte-Chapelle, the ducal *pâtisserie* next to the kitchen also had to be sacrificed to make room for new projects in 1852/1853. Here the architect Louis Belin planned and built a wing

Museums in Dijon

Dijon has a number of wonderful museums in historical buildings which are just as lovely to look at as the exhibits they house. The Musée des Beaux-Arts, for example, is located in a section of the Palais des Ducs/Palais des Etats. The chapter hall of the Sainte-Chapelle, removed in 1802, is now located on the ground floor of the Tour de Bar; in it Burgundian sculpture from the 14th to 17th centuries is on display. Particularly exquisite are two sepulchres by Jean Dubois, as well as some pieces of goldsmithing that originally belonged to the saints Robert of Molesme and Bernard of Clairvaux. On the landing of the large stairway is the old portal from the Palais de Justice, a work by Hugues Sambin of Dijon, whose mannered style can be seen on many city houses. The rooms of the upper story contain items including church implements, Renaissance and medieval ivories, furniture, and medallions. There are also paintings, including works by some 17th-century painters from Burgundy—among them a lovely rendering of the Château de Montmusard—and paintings from the 15th to 18th centuries displayed according to their country of origin.

At the southwest corner is the Salle des Statues, a high, bright room in which copies of statues from classical antiquity and 19th-century works can be admired (illus. opposite and below). The 19th century is primarily represented through the works of François Rude; there is another museum near Saint-Michel dedicated to his work, exhibiting terra cotta designs. Interestingly enough, the Joan of Arc on the

OPPOSITE:
Dijon, Musée des Beaux-Arts, sculpture room. This room was the first in the museum to be opened, in 1787, and was intended as a collection of models for the students of the Ecole des Beaux-Arts. The ceiling painting glorifying Burgundy and Prince Condé is a work of the classical artist Pierre-Paul Prud'hon.

Dijon, Musée des Beaux-Arts, sculpture room, *Amor as World Ruler,* a late work of François Rude.

main stairway of the Musée des Beaux-Arts is also a work of Rude's. Following the Salle des Statues is the Salon Condé, with wood paneling and stucco décor in the style of Louis XVI and corresponding 18th-century interior furnishings, including a bust of Louix XIV by Antoine Coysevox and one or Rameau and Piron by Philippe Caffiéri. The next room is the Salon Empire, which also contains valuable interior furnishings of the period.

The highlight of this museum is the Salle des Gardes. Here, where the dukes once staged their official appearances, the two sepulchres from Champmol now rest: the double sepulchre of John the Fearless and Margaret of Bavaria and the single sepulchre of Philip the Bold (illus. below). The enormous fireplace at the narrow end of the room is not a part of the original interior. It replaces an older fireplace that was integrated into the rostrum where the dukes often made their appearances.

On the north wall are three famous portraits showing Philip the Bold, John the Fearless, and Charles the Bold, the last of these from the hand of the famous painter Rogier van der Weyden. A fourth portrait in the group shows the duchess Isabelle. The large panel painting next to the portraits shows a wedding at the court of Philip the Good (illus. p. 35). This is one of the rare pictorial depictions of court ceremonies; written reports are far more abundant. Along the long interior wall with ogival-arched portals are three large retables and several small religious panel paintings. The right retable, the so-called Crucifixion, is a masterpiece of Flemish carving with wonderful scenes and opulent decoration (illus. left). The paintings on the exterior side of the wings are by Melchior Broederlam (illus. p. 80). In the room adjoining the Salle des Gardes, Flemish and Burgundian sculptures

Dijon, Musée des Beaux-Arts, Salle des Gardes, carved central panel of the Passion altarpiece by Jacques de Baerze from Champmol, gilded by Melchior Broederlam, ca. 1390.

Dijon, Musée des Beaux-Arts, Salle des Gardes, containing sepulchres, altars, and tapestries.

from the 15th and 16th centuries are displayed. The highlight of this exhibit is the masterful Nativity by Robert Campin, who is also known as the Master of Flémalle (illus. p. 81).

The Musée archéologique is located in the rooms of the former monastery of Saint-Bénigne. In the lower story, in dark vaulted cellars dating from the 11th century, are fascinating archaeological finds from the source of the Seine: votive offerings of metal and wood, often simple and reduced to essentials, but also the statuette of a young faun and another of Sequana, the goddess of the spring, standing upright in a bark (illus. p. 46). In addition, there are numerous Gallo-Roman steles with reliefs and pieces of broken stone figures. In the upper story lies what was once the dormitory of the monastery, an airy, elegant, three-aisled room with ribbed vaulting. It now serves as the exhibition room for medieval finds, where one can see not only

the head of the crucified Christ from Champmol (illus. p. 60), but also both of the surviving tympana from Saint-Bénigne (illus. p. 47) and some capitals from its rotunda.

The Musée Magnin, in an elegant city mansion dating from the 17th century, has retained the very private atmosphere of a stately but welcoming home. Most of its interior furnishings are original and have been well preserved, and an exquisite collection of paintings by lesser-known painters from the 16th to the 19th centuries (illus. above) is also on display.

Another trademark of Dijon is the cultivation of roses, an art that has been practiced here for centuries. This is apparent not only in the city gardens and parks, but even in the smallest villages surrounding Dijon. They are a pleasure to visit in May and June, when the small, gray, stone houses are almost hidden under blankets of blooming roses.

Dijon, Musée Magnin, exhibit room displaying 18th-century décor and lifestyle.

This depiction of Christ's birth is
the work of the Master of Flémalle,
identified as Robert Campin. His
most talented student was Rogier van
der Weyden, who painted the Last
Judgment altarpiece in Beaune, as
well as portraits of the two last dukes
and numerous court officials.

Dijon, Musée des Beaux-Arts,
right panel of the Passion altarpiece
by Melchior Broederlam with the scenes
Offering in the Temple and *Flight to Egypt*,
1394–1399, oil on panel.

The wings of the Passion altar—the
opposite side shows the *Visitation* and the
Annunciation—are the most significant of
Broederlam's works and among the major
works of Dutch painting before van Eyck.

Gentle Hills and Broad Plains between the Saône and the Seine – Dijonnais

The arrondissement of Dijon is defined by rivers. To the east it is bordered by the Saône and Vingeanne Rivers, in the south by the Dheune, and through its center the Ouche River flows in a wide arch. Within this area the varied landscapes of Burgundy are harmoniously combined, ranging from limestone plateaus in the north—the southernmost fringes of the Langres plateau—to gentle hills and extensive pastures in broad, tub-shaped valleys in the west, from flat alluvial plains in the east to the famous vineyards of the Côte d'Or region in the south.

The Canal de Bourgogne, meandering through the countryside west of Dijon in broad curves and tight bends, leaves the city heading southeast and makes a straight line towards the flat, somewhat monotonous landscape west of the Saône that runs into the Bresse further south. There are very few widely-known monuments here, but a visit to the small church of Saint-Jean-Baptiste in Rouvres-en-Plaine is worthwhile. Also worth visiting are Auxonne, the former border city that was once a fortification of the duchy against imperial Burgundy, and the châteaus at Talmay and Longecourt-en-Plaine.

Rouvres-en-Plaine

Saint-Jean-Baptiste was probably once the castle church of a fortress that Philip the Bold had renovated and expanded into a splendid residence shortly before 1370. Accordingly, it has a lovely interior. In 1148 a church dedicated to St. John is mentioned for the first time, but the present choir seems to date from an endowment made in 1223 by Alix de Vergy, Duchess of Burgundy. The transept and nave are later, probably from the late 13th and early 14th centuries. The three-aisle nave has the form of a basilica with high arcades on octagonal pillars with capital annulets, but no windows. The four-part rib vaulting rests on

Dijonnais countryside
near Savigny-sous-Mâlain, ca. 12 miles (20 km) west of Dijon.

Rouvres-en-Plaine, church of Saint-Jean-Baptiste, figures from the altar of the Machefoing chapel.
The elegant, graceful figures of the Virgin Mary with St. John the Baptist and St. John the Evangelist are attributed to Jean de la Huerta or his workshop.

OPPOSITE:
Auxonne, entrance gate to the city near Notre-Dame.

consoles. The transept has the same features, but two windows on the front and rear let in more light. The choir has a flat ceiling and is flanked on either side by a chapel. The southern chapel has retained its original appearance, while the northern chapel, a mortuary, received a new interior shortly before the mid-15th century by Monot de Machefoing, *capitaine chastellain de Rouvres, 1er valet de chambre et garde des joyaux de monseigneur le Duc de Bourgogne et de Brabant* ("castle commander of Rouvres, first chamberlain and treasurer to his Lordship Duke of Burgundy and Brabant"), and his wife Jeanne de Courcelles,

mère de lait du Duc Philippe le Bon ("wet nurse to Duke Philip the Good"). It seems that the tomb of the Machefoings lies in front of the altar. The large covering slab with incised figures, inscription, and marble incrustations is now located on the side wall. Also dating from this period are a large, richly ornate piscine and a stone altar that takes the place of a retable. It bears the figures of the Virgin Mary and the two St. Johns on a console (illus. left). The statues were certainly emulations of Claus Sluter's work and have been attributed to Jean de la Huerta or his workshop. They are masterpieces, with gracefully pleated robes and delicate, portrait-like facial features.

In addition to numerous tombstones, the interior of the church contains a larger than life-size statue of John the Baptist dating from the early 14th century, the very lovely figure of a clergy donor with a model of a church from the first half of the 15th century, a stone Madonna, and an Adoration of the Kings by Jean Dubois from Dijon. Dubois also created the fireplace reliefs in the *Logis du Roi* (royal logis) in Dijon in the early part of the 18th century.

Auxonne

As early as the late 12th century, Auxonne, the eastern outpost of the duchy of Burgundy, was the site of a castle of the Sires d'Auxonne and a parish church. Today, both have been replaced by newer structures. Duke John the Fearless had the castle renovated in 1414, probably as a square

River landscape near Pontailler (Vieille Saône).

complex with round towers at the corners. More changes and additions followed under the French kings Louis XII and Francis I before it was finally transformed into an arsenal under the direction of the famous fortification architect, Sébastien Le Prestre de Vauban.

The church of Notre-Dame is a good example of the early High Gothic style in Burgundy (illus. right and below). As was customary, the choir was built first, in 1235/1237. The existing church was torn down and the nave was completed in the mid-13th century. The three-aisle basilica has seven bays in the nave and side aisles, a transept of modest depth, and a five-sided apse behind a preceding antebay with chapels on either side. The elevation reveals a three-story structure with arcades, triforium, and a clerestory. Only the higher part of the nave opposite the crossing and choir has a walkway in front of the clerestory, a characteristic feature of Burgundian Gothic. The lower choir and the form of vaulting are slightly more old-fashioned than the nave, whose motifs resemble those in churches dedicated to the Virgin Mary in Dijon and Semur-en-Auxois.

In the 14th and 15th centuries, the nave was expanded with side chapels, and in about 1516, Antoine Le Rupt built the narthex in front of the

Auxonne, Notre-Dame, so-called Madonna of the Grapes, a Burgundian Madonna in the style of Claus Sluter.

TOP RIGHT:
Auxonne, Notre-Dame, arcades of the nave and side aisles.

RIGHT:
Auxonne, Notre-Dame, view of the choir, transept, and nave with lateral chapels.

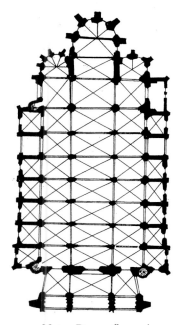

Auxonne, Notre-Dame, floor plan.

original simple, two-tower façade. Its rich décor is
still entirely late Gothic. With their unusually high
and elegant figural niches and splendid baldachins
(illus. right), the three entryways to the narthex
resemble portal jambs. Beyond them are the three
portals to the nave and aisles, dating from the
16th century. The original statues were destroyed
in the Revolution; the present sculptures were
probably created in the 19th century.

The most valuable of the interior furnishings of
Notre-Dame is the Madonna of the Grapes in the
southern side apse, a very graceful, slightly larger-
than-life alabaster sculpture clad in a magnificently pleated robe (illus. opposite, top left). She is
one of the figures created in the mid-15th century
under the influence of Claus Sluter, possibly in the
workshop of Jean de La Huerta. Next to this
Madonna is a second large Madonna with Child,
dating from approximately the same period, which
probably once stood on the façade above the
portal. Also noteworthy are a St. Anthony and the
women of a funeral, both from the late 15th century, as well as numerous epitaphs.

Southeast of Notre-Dame is one of the four
city gates dating from the second half of the 15th
century (illus. p. 85). On either side are vestiges of
the old city wall built in 1350, which was once
topped by 33 towers. In 1675, Sébastien le Prestre
de Vauban added eight bastions.

Talmay, 13th-century donjon adjacent to a château designed in 1762 by Jacques-Louis Daviler.

Talmay

North of Auxonne and also east of the Saône, the castle and donjon of Talmay (illus. above) stand in a large park. The five-story donjon, which was probably part of a square complex by Guillaume de Pontailler from the second half of the 13th century, was preserved. From the late 14th or early 15th century at the earliest, regularly placed latrines were added onto the upper story of the donjon. Its high roof with a lantern and dormers are additions from the 19th century.

The *logis*, or residence, added to the donjon is slightly off axis. The history of its construction is complicated and lengthy. Pierre I Filsjean commissioned the Paris architect Pierre Cottard to design plans for a logis that was probably meant to replace late medieval residences. The project remained unrealized until Pierre II Filsjean, who had likewise commissioned a series of eight architects with the planning, finally decided upon the design of Jacques-Louis Daviler in 1762. The actual construction of the two-story logis with seven axes built on a foundation with windows was carried out by Jean-Antoine Caristie. It is flanked on both sides by short wings, each with only one axis,

which probably meant that a *cour d'honneur* was intended. The corners of the wings are slanted and fitted with flat plates, and a beautiful wall of evenly hewn ashlars with broad supporting joints gives the wings and the central protruding façade bay an elegantly sophisticated appearance. On these elements the delicately profiled windows have round arches, in contrast to those on the other axes, which are rectangular, and set in slightly recessed rectangular frames. The interior furnishings of the château were completed around 1825 and are maintained in early classical style.

Longecourt-en-Plaine

Longecourt-en-Plaine, west of the Canal de Bourgogne, is a castle surrounded by water (illus. below). In the early 16th century the Baissey family initiated construction of the complex as it stands today. Its square plan fitted with round towers was determined by the foundations of an earlier fortification dating from the 13th century, of which the vaulted kitchen and the moat remain intact. In the 16th century, the four-wing complex built of different colored bricks—a feature characteristic of buildings in the Bresse—was added.

The richly ornate windows and portals that once articulated the façade disappeared when Nicolas-Philippe de Berbis had the architect Nicolas Lenoir le Romain apply delicate layers of rococo décor to the exterior of the building as well as to the interior. Only the dormers bear testimony to the original late medieval decoration. In the course of fairly extensive renovations in around 1690/1700, the entrance wing was torn down, the façades facing the courtyard were changed, and extensive gardens with tree-lined paths and viewpoints were designed.

Longecourt-en-Plaine, Château de Longecourt, view of the entrance side. The castle was built in several phases; the oldest dates back to the 13th century, the most recent to about 1700.

Gevrey-Chambertin

Further west, amidst the vineyards of the Côte-d'Or region, Yves de Chazan, who was the abbot of Cluny, had a monastic wine-producing estate built in Gevry-Chambertin between 1280 and 1289. It encompassed an *enceinte avec tours et porte fortifiée, un logis pour les moines, un pressoir et un grenier* (a "defensive wall with towers and a fortified gate, a residence for the monks, a wine press, and a storehouse"). It took the form of an almost square complex with a donjon on the southeast corner, a gate in the southwest, a surrounding moat, and a *basse-cour* (lower courtyard). Between the donjon and the gate stretched the residential and utility buildings; parts of these walls are still standing. After extensive destruction, the beautiful residence received its present façade—boasting a polygonal stair tower and windows adorned with ogival arches—around 1435/1445. During the first half of the 16th century, the corners of the encircling walls were fortified with towers; however, they soon collapsed and had to be removed. At the same time, the gatehouse received its present form with a small three-arched gallery on the ground floor. The interior boasts a vaulted wine cellar and numerous well-appointed rooms.

OPPOSITE:
Fixin, Parc Noiset, *Napoléon s'éveillant a l'immortalité*, monument by François Rude.

In reverence for Napoleon I, the imperial guard officer Claude Noiset had a small park designed in his native town of Fixin, north of Gevrey-Chambertin. At its center was the emotive, nationalistic sculpture *Napoleon Awakens to Immortality*. This late work by the sculptor François Rude of Dijon was created in 1846/1847, and captures the mood and expectations of the French at that time.

RIGHT:
Couchey
Renaissance cross.

Talant

Further to the north lies Talant, now a suburb of Dijon. Like Saint-Jean-Baptiste in Rouvres-en-Plaine, the Notre-Dame church in Talant was built in connection with a ducal castle. Just as construction began in 1210, Duke Eudes III donated a priory. The first provisional church was replaced by the present one in around 1240/1250. An inscription on the second pillar of the nave in the southeast that includes the date of consecration tells us that construction progressed only quite slowly: *Dimenche l'an mille cccc et xxx le II[e] jour de juillet* ("Sunday of the year one thousand four hundred and thirty, the second day of July").

The three-aisle nave (illus. left) stretches east with 11 bays directly adjoining the almost square choir. No transept interrupts the strong, longitudinal character of the nave. Two projecting walls separate small chapel-like rooms from the side aisles in the first and last bays. The elevation shows two stories. Above the arcade with pointed arches is a tall expanse of wall with exceptionally well-hewn ashlars, followed by a clerestory. Pillars and vaulting are not uniform, which indicates that the original plans were changed numerous times during the long construction period.

The richly ornate décor of the interior of Notre-Dame, especially in the northern side aisles, is rather unusual in churches (illus. opposite right). Some of the elements may have come from the castle, but this also emphasizes the significance of the church as a priory church. Among the most important pieces are a stone Madonna from the 14th century that was influenced by the

Talant, Notre-Dame, nave and side aisles, view towards the west.

Talant, Notre-Dame, burial group, early 16th century.

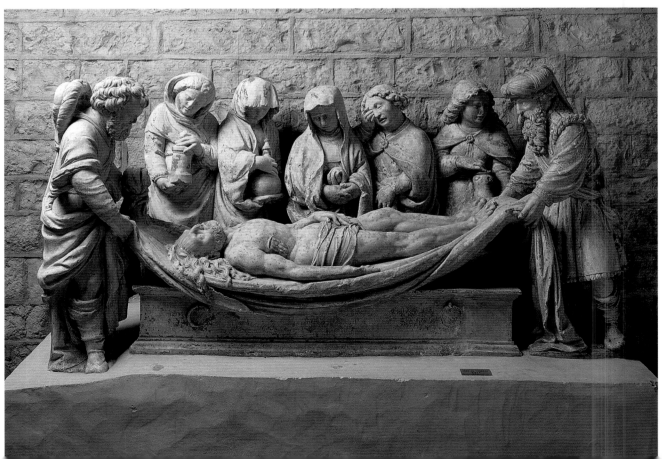

Talant, Notre-Dame, consecration inscription on the second pillar of the nave.

Talant, Notre-Dame, northern side aisle. Displayed here are numerous individual and group sculptures of high quality, among them St. Magdalene; a wall inscription informs about their creation.

famous Madonna in Fontenay, the Saints Margaret and Rochus dating from the 16th century, and a St. Stephen with donors from the same period. St. Magdalene is a masterpiece from the workshop of the Péchinot brothers from Talant. An inscription on the wall mentions 1570 as the date of its creation. In the southern side aisles is an Entombment from the early 16th century (illus. opposite bottom). This was a favorite motif among Burgundian sculptors during the late 15th and 16th centuries, and many churches have exquisite examples of such figural groups. In Talant, seven smaller than life-size, somewhat sturdy figures in Renaissance costumes surround the sarcophagus into which the dead Christ is being laid. Also from the 16th century is a Christ in Misery on the altar of the former Nicholas chapel. In the opposite chapel, we again encounter Jean Dubois of Dijon, who is thought to have created the painted stone Madonna.

Although panel paintings are rare in Burgundian churches, Notre-Dame is an exception. There one can see a panel of St. Clara from the 17th century, an Annunciation from about 1700, and a Baptism of Christ from the 18th century.

Another special feature is the series of inscriptions on columns referring to the sculptures and endowments, and also include epitaphs (illus. above). Beautiful tombstones complete the furnishings. Their range and form was characteristic of churches associated with ducal castles, few of which are as well preserved as Rouvres-en-Plaine.

Messigny-et-Vantoux

Following the road along the Suzon to the north, one finds the exquisite Vantoux château near Messigny-et-Vantoux. The view of the château from the gate seems like an 18th century painting (illus. left). Nicole de la Motte and her husband, Jean de Berbisey, who became president of the Burgundian parliament in 1716, began construction of this elegant residence in 1700. It was built on the site of an older building and completed in just four years. The plans probably stem from the circle of Jules Hardouin-Mansart, who had drawn numerous plans for the Palais des Etats in Dijon.

Jean de Berbisey rejected the idea of a building with long wings and instead chose a two-story cubic building with a relatively high-pitched roof. The façade has an exquisitely articulated and inventive décor. Triangular pediments emphasize the three-axis central façade bay on the main and garden sides. The interesting sculptural program features Jupiter, Juno, and Cybele on the corbels of the balcony over the entrance. Above the central window of the upper story is Apollo, framed by two panels that depict him accompanied by Daphne on one side and the python on the other. The garden side is dedicated to Diana—the ground floor to the goddess of the moon, and the upper story to the huntress—and Venus and Flora are depicted on the two lateral façades. A similar program repeats on the wood paneling of the reception hall in the upper floor (illus. below). The motifs are most likely a means of self-expression for the owner, reflecting his interpretation of the law as well as his goals.

LEFT:
Messigny-et-Vantoux, Château de Vantoux, 1700–1704, main façade and park.

Messigny-et-Vantoux, Château de Vantoux, festive reception hall on the first floor.

Beaumont-sur-Vingeanne, Château de Beaumont, built in 1724 as a *folie*, or private getaway, for Claude de Jolyot.

story building has a hip roof, trimmed with a graceful balustrade decorated with small figures and vases. The five axes of the façade facing the courtyard are articulated by flat, rusticated pilaster strips. The outer two axes protrude as façade bays. A pair of curved stairways lead to a gabled portal underneath a triangular pediment. On the garden side is a corresponding terrace with an equally graceful double stairway.

In 1754–1758, the architect Souhard from Paris built the three-wing Fontaine-Française estate for François Bollioud de Saint-Julien (illus. below), replacing the medieval castle that had previously stood on the site. Typical for the simple style of the period, this building has almost no articulation. Only the three axes of the central façade bay have flat rusticated bands at the corners, and the entrance is completed with a triangular pediment, above which the cupola with a belvedere rises atop the center façade of the main wing. The tall, slender windows are only gabled on the *bel étage* (main floor). The garden side is also lovely, with a stairway that is mirrored in a large natural pond. The two stone sculptures of Apollo and Pan found there may be the work of Jean-Baptiste Bouchardon.

Beaumont-sur-Vingeanne/Fontaine-Française

Two other structures document the lifestyle of the French nobility and the high clergy in the 18th century: Beaumont-sur-Vingeanne and Fontaine-Française, both in the extreme northwest of the arrondissement of Dijon, situated in a landscape characterized by extensive pastures and smaller woods. The very small Château de Beaumont in Beaumont-sur-Vingeanne (illus. above), one of the few *folies* (pleasure palaces, or private retreats) in Burgundy, was built by Claude de Jolyot in 1724 while he was prior at nearby Til-Châtel. The one-

Saint-Seine-sur-Vingeanne

In the near vicinity of Fontaine-Française lies a fascinating late medieval complex that should not be overlooked: the donjon of Rosières in Saint-Seine-sur-Vingeanne (illus. opposite). About 1430, Arnould de Saint-Seine and his wife built a two-story logis with an impressive five-story donjon towering above the southwest corner. The entire structure was encircled by a moat. A small portal with a drawbridge led from the west into a stately

Fontaine-Française, château, 1754–1758, view of the garden side with the large natural pond.

reception hall, from which one had access to a lovely spiral stairway. The entire space has been surprisingly well preserved.

Arnould's sons Pierre and Guillaume inherited the complex and added two stories to the logis in about 1465. The uppermost story received a battlement on stepped corbels, which widened at the corners into corner turrets called *échauguettes*. The majority of this defensive passageway is still extant, lending the massive donjon an unusually picturesque appearance. The charming gatehouse with an external spiral stairway is also an addition of the second construction period after 1465. Since the moat adjoining the donjon was no longer needed when the broad courtyard was walled in, a drawbridge leading to the entrance gate was never built. The small square pavilion was created between 1683 and 1685 at the behest of Claude Bernard-Maillard.

Grancey-le-Château-Neuvelle

In the northwest, where five or six springs flow together to form the Tille River, lies Grancey-le-Château-Neuvelle. A castle has existed there since at least 1113, and has been expanded and completed over time. In 1434, the duke ordered the fortifications removed, but in the late 17th/early 18th century, Jean-Louis de Médavy built a rectangular building on the remaining towers, the vaulted cellar rooms, and ground floor. This newer structure has a pitched roof and a balustrade along the eaves. The central façade bay, with a pediment above the entrance, as well as the side façade bays barely protrude from the façade and are framed by flat rusticated bands. The interior remained incomplete for a time and dates from the 19th century. A staircase with three flights of stairs at the rear of a brilliant white vestibule leads to the festive hall in the center of the upper story.

Saint-Seine-sur-Vingeanne, Château de Rosières, view from the west towards the entrance, which must be imagined as a small portal with a drawbridge. In front of it lay the moat, which once enclosed the entire donjon.

Saint-Germain-Source-Seine, Source of the Seine, an artificial grotto with the bronze figure of a spring nymph.

TOP RIGHT:
Countryside near Bèze.

BOTTOM RIGHT:
Bèze, spring basin of the small river, Bèze, at the outskirts of the town.

OPPOSITE BOTTOM:
Bèze, Grotto de Bèze.

Poncey-sur-l'Ignon, source of the Ignon.

River Sources

Extensive woods and pastures border the Dijonnais to the southwest. Many rivers and brooks have their origins in this hilly countryside, the most famous of them being the Seine, whose source is in a pasture at an elevation of 1500 feet (470 m). Above the main spring is a grotto with the reclining figure of a spring nymph dating from the year 1865 (illus. above). The statue is reminiscent of Antonio Canova's portrait sculpture of Paolina Borghese. Not far from the source, an extended sanctuary from antiquity was found that includes the vestiges of a Roman temple, foundations of numerous buildings, and many votive offerings of stone and bronze. The most famous of them are the river goddess Sequana standing in a bark (illus. p. 46) and a young faun, both now on display in the Musée archéologique in Dijon. A large number of wooden votive offerings were discovered in 1963, seeming to verify the assumption that the river goddess has been worshipped at this site since pre-Roman times.

The source of the Ignon, not far from that of the Seine, appears to have been a much quieter setting over the centuries. Numerous little springs emerge from between mossy boulders and shady ferns (illus. left) strewn about a hollow on a steep, wooded slope. The seclusion and stillness of this place evokes the emotion-infused landscapes of Romantic paintings.

The source of the Bèze is quite different from the others. It emerges at the edge of the town of Bèze in a walled-in basin in the shadow of ancient trees (illus. left). In rainy times the water output can be as much as 22 cubic yards (17 cubic m) per second. A few steps away is the Grotte de Bèze, first made accessible in the 1960s (illus. right). Two sources of the Tille River have formed a considerable underground lake here, with water so clear that one can see almost 60 feet (18 m) down into it. At its edges are stalactite and stalagmite formations, including the so-called "grenade" and the "Mexican hats." The water that forms the lake flows through an underground passageway and surfaces 4 miles (7 km) farther on.

The town itself has two beautiful 13th-century houses on the Place de Verdun, both richly adorned with large, profiled tracery windows and blind arcading (illus. above). The richness of their exterior décor sets these houses apart from other existing buildings of the same period, even from the logis façades of the castles. The only exception is the château of Brancion, which has an equally elaborate façade. These buildings were apparently part of a monastery.

Saint-Seine-l'Abbaye

The former abbey church of Notre-Dame in Saint-Seine-l'Abbaye, a town in a valley south of the Seine's source, bears resemblance to the church of Notre-Dame in Talant. Said to have been founded by St. Sequanus (Seine or Seigne) in the 6th century, the monastery is one of the oldest in Burgundy. In 774, Benedict of Aniane entered it as a novice. He later became a monastic reformer and advisor to Emperor Louis the Pious. The present church was begun in 1205/1209 under Abbot Olivier and is one of the earliest Gothic churches in Burgundy. The three-aisle nave is entered through a vestibule flanked by towers. It has just two twin bays with six-part vaulting, which lead to three transept bays and the three-aisle antebay preceding the choir. The corner between the tran-

sept and the side aisles of the choir is occupied by two small chapels, giving the transept a two-aisle look reminiscent of Cistercian churches. The elevation reveals two stories, with proportions similar to those of Notre-Dame in Talant. In typical Burgundian Gothic style, there is a walkway in front of the clerestory. There is no gallery towards the central nave, and the walkway is only visible from below where it cuts through the intersection of the vaulting arches.

After a fire in 1255, repairs were made to the southern transept, the vaulting over the crossing, and the nave, which was shortened by a double bay. The nave and southern transept were vaulted from 1375–1439. Then in the mid-15th century, the west façade, narthex, and two lower stories of the tower were completed, and upper stories were added to the north tower. A complete renovation followed in the 19th century. The crossing tower, removed in the 17th century, was not replaced.

Notre-Dame in Saint-Seine has rich interior furnishings. The choir screen with richly ornate ogival arches surmounted by a triforium was later moved into the choir. In style it is reminiscent of the architectural sculpture of Claus Sluter on the duke's sepulchre and the baldachins over the portal figures of Champmol. Sluter's influence extended into the 15th century, as is clear in the Annunciation group under the southern arch of the choir screen. The paintings on the exterior of the choir screen date from the early 16th century (1504 and 1521). On the north side are 23 scenes from the life of St. Sequanus, who commends the kneeling donor to the Virgin Mary, with commentary texts. On the south walls are additional donor paintings: left and right the Root of Jesse with donor and intercessor as well as St. Bartholomew and the Virgin Mary; at the center, again St. Sequanus with a donor and St. Christopher with the child Jesus. Most of the sculptures in the choir date from the 16th century.

LEFT:
Bèze, Place de Verdun, 13th-century buildings.

Bèze, view of the 18th-century church; church tower and entrance are from the 14th century.

Saint-Seine-l'Abbaye,
Notre-Dame, painting on the
exterior of the choir screen.

LEFT:
Saint-Seine-l'Abbaye, Notre-Dame,
view of the choir screen and choir.

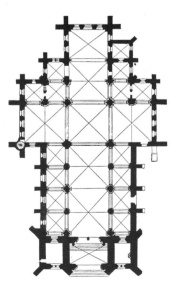

Saint-Seine-l'Abbaye, Notre-Dame,
floor plan.

Côte-d'Or   103

Grosbois-en-Montagne, Grosbois reservoir.

Val-Suzon, view of the village on the Suzon River from above.

Left and Right of the Seine –
The Plateaus of Montagne and Châtillonnais

The Montbard arrondissement, the northernmost of the department of Côte-d'Or, extends roughly between Châtillon-sur-Seine and Saulieu. The Seine, still small here, flows through the north, and in the far south the Serein, Armançon, Brenne, Oze, and Ozerain Rivers spring up, all of which converge into the Yonne. Between Châteauneuf and Montbard, the tree-lined Canal de

Bourgogne molds the landscape and offers ever-changing views. There are three Lower Burgundy plateaus, limestone areas at elevations of 1300–1640 feet (400–500 m) that drop off sharply to the southeast. Progressing geographically from southwest to northeast, the first is the Auxois, which like the adjoining Morvan lies on granite formations. It is followed by the Montagne, the

southern extension of the Plateau de Langres, and the Châtillonnais, the easternmost of the three. A dividing line seems to run through the arrondissement at the latitude of Montbard, separating the villages and small cities of the more populated south from the almost uninhabited north. Even if the expansive countryside north of Montbard may appear somewhat monotonous, the river valleys of the Brenne, Armançon, and Serein are thoroughly delightful (illus. below). Wide meadows lined with hedges are framed by wooded ridges, and the winding brooks and streams are often accompanied by magnificent old trees—this is a countryside which is left in the care of pasture animals and gives nature its space to unfold. Many areas here have the atmosphere of an English park, but this is primarily an historical countryside. Aside from some power lines, paved streets, and the occasional passing of a TGV cutting through the stillness like a ghost, this landscape has hardly changed over the course of the centuries. The small gray villages, which have no new housing developments but often include a noble's manor, fit naturally into the landscape.

Countryside in the Brenne valley.

the grave of a Celtic princess containing not only rich gifts of Greek and Etruscan origin, but also the largest preserved bronze krater of the classical world. It is 64 inches (164 cm) high, weighs 460 pounds (208 kg), and holds almost 290 gallons (1200 l). At its strongest point, the bronze is just .06 inch (1.5 mm) thick! The neck of the magnificent vessel is adorned with a frieze displaying chariots and foot soldiers, which were first cast using the lost-wax process and then riveted on (illus. p. 15 and opposite). It indicates that the krater was made in the late Archaic era, about 530 BC. The volute handles are decorated with delicate spiral vines, pearl staves, and leaf-like ornaments; between them is a gorgon with snakes and two lions. It has a bronze lid decorated with the figure of a standing nymph. The origin of the krater is still debated; both Sparta and southern Italy have been suggested as possible places of origin. The very size of the vessel seems to preclude the idea that it served a practical purpose; it was probably a representative gift to be displayed.

The grave site also yielded other finds, including a silver phiale (wide, shallow goblet) with a raised gold boss in the center, an Attic black-figured kylix (cup) depicting a battle between the Greeks and the Amazons, a second vessel with a transparent black glaze, and numerous bronze vessels, among them a unique beaked jug. The skeleton of the princess was wearing jewelry and lay on a funeral wagon. The most impressive piece is a diadem or collier of gold with a lion paw holding a sphere at each end (illus. below). Above them are tiny figures of Pegasus, the winged horse of the gods (illus. opposite, below right). The abundance of rich objects in this woman's grave attest to both the structure of this society and to the high position which women could attain in it.

Châtillon-sur-Seine
View of the town looking towards Saint-Vorles.

Châtillon-sur-Seine

The only larger settlement north of Montbard is Châtillon-sur-Seine. It is only a few miles away from Vix at the foot of Mont Lassois, on which an important oppidum was located in Celtic times. Settled since the Neolithic period, the 1000-foot (307-m) high hill alongside the Seine developed into one of the most important trade centers in all of Gaul (ca. 750–450 BC). The finds made here since the early 20th century have been correspondingly abundant. They provide evidence that the oppidum Latisco engaged in trade with areas from the Mediterranean to the Baltic Sea.

During an excavation campaign in 1953, Maurice Moisson, a farmer enamored of archaeology, made a sensational discovery outside of the official excavation area. Together with the archaeologist René Joffroy, called to assist, he unearthed

Châtillon-sur-Seine
Treasure of Vix in the archaeological museum/Maison Philandrier: gold diadem with lions' claws at the ends, ca. 500 BC.

LEFT:
Châtillon-sur-Seine
Treasure of Vix in the archaeological
museum/Maison Philandrier:
bronze krater (detail), about 530 BC;
height 64 inches (164 cm).

Detail of the bronze krater:
volute handles with gorgon.

Detail of the gold diadem:
Pegasus, winged horse of
the gods.

replaced semicircular transept apses, so that one might imagine a Benedictine choir similar to that of Cluny II. Choir and transept had barrel vaulting overhead; the windows are of a later vintage. The nave and side aisles must also have had barrel vaulting and were perhaps illuminated by small windows at the base of the barrel. The present vaulting originated in the 17th century (illus. below). The circular pillars, the groin-vaulting in the side aisles, and the vestibule with the gallery chapel, however, are original. The white plaster coating, which seems so archaic to visitors today, probably covers polychrome murals that must have made the room appear mystical and dark.

In the northern transept arm of the church hang two painted wood panels from the 16th century which originally may have belonged to a winged altarpiece. As background to the transferral of relics from Marcenay to Châtillon they depict the château of Châtillon, destroyed long ago. The entombment group in the crypt, dating from 1527, is a masterpiece of Burgundian sculpture (illus. opposite). The group of eleven life-size figures are depicted in contemporary clothes at the burial of Christ, as though in a snapshot. Their gestures are expansive and dramatic; their features, garments, and headdresses are carefully rendered and true in their details. At the foot of the group are the two kneeling donor figures.

The exterior of Saint-Vorles is also worth seeing, especially the east side (illus. left). Although later additions have marred the original composition of the structure, the staggering of basic

Châtillon-sur-Seine, Saint-Vorles, ca. 1000, view of the eastern side.

RIGHT:
Châtillon-sur-Seine, Saint-Vorles, southern side aisle looking west.

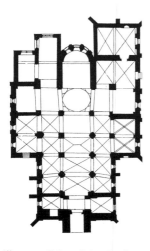

Châtillon-sur-Seine, Saint-Vorles, floor plan.

About 1,000 years after the burial at Vix, the first settlement in Châtillon-sur-Seine can be documented. On the site of the present church of Saint-Vorles, an oratory consecrated to St. Vorelius had been built by St. Deodatus (Didier) at the end of the 5th century. It was tended by the priests of the Cathedral of Langres, the same men who founded the Collège Notre-Dame here. It was already a first-rate institution in the first millenium, and Bernard of Clairvaux studied at the school around 1100. In 868, the Vorelius reliquaries were transferred, probably due to the construction of a church. This Carolingian church has been partially excavated; vestiges are perhaps preserved on the northeast side of the crypt. Around 1000, Bishop Bruno de Roucy had the Carolingian church replaced. Behind a westwork-like vestibule is a three-aisle nave with side aisles, the rectangular bays of the central nave run perpendicular to the nave, and the side aisles have square bays. The crossing is almost square, with projecting transept arms. The semicircular apse is preceded by a square antebay. The eastern extensions probably

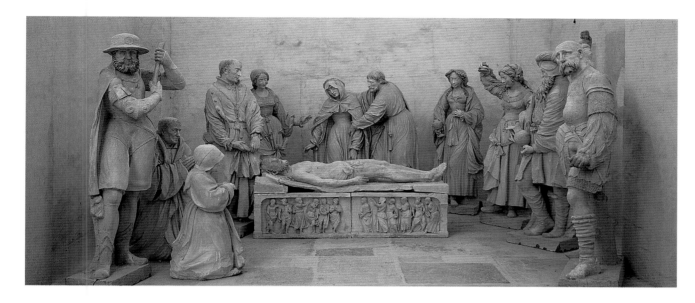

cubic forms decorated with arcade friezes is clearly visible.

Whereas Saint-Vorles once lay within the castle walls, Saint-Nicolas and Saint-Baptiste churches belonged to the city, which had its own walls and gates. Opposite Saint-Nicolas is the so-called Maison Philandrier, an enchanting Renaissance mansion that was built by Hugues Philandrier, prior of Notre-Dame from 1531, in the second quarter of the 16th century (illus right). The street façade receives its rich and sculptural articulation through engaged fluted pilasters between the windows. The façade facing the courtyard, with a round tower at its center, is also decorated with engaged fluted pilasters. Two gabled dormers crown the window axes. Some of the original interior fittings have been preserved, such as ceiling beams, a splendid Renaissance fireplace, and murals.

Today, the Maison Philandrier houses the Archaeological Museum and the Historical Society of the Châtillonnais. In addition to some medieval figures, abundant Celtic and Gallo-Roman finds from Mont Lassois and its surroundings are on display, including, of course, those from Vix.

Montigny-sur-Aube

Montigny-sur-Aube lies on a high plateau at the extreme northwest of the department. In the 9th century, a château with a moat was apparently built here, and a stone fortification was erected above it in the 12th century. Sometime after the middle of the 14th century, a square complex with round corner towers and a surrounding moat was built, a construction typical for the period of the Valois dukes in Burgundy. In 1501 it was acquired by Hélion d'Amoncourt; but it was Jean d'Amoncourt who, influenced by a journey he took to Italy between 1537 and 1552, built on to three sides of the old stone wall. A portico rose diagonally in front of one of the

Montigny-sur-Aube, Château de Montigny, 1537–1552, façade facing the courtyard.

Montigny-sur-Aube, Château de Montigny, chapel (far right) and portal of the chapel (right).

The square chapel tower, free-standing since the château fire of 1794, has stone masonry with pyramid-shaped rustication as well as a gabled, protruding façade bay with pilasters and a very lovely portal, displaying the coat of arms of the owner above the lintel. The chapel is roofed with a richly decorated, coffered barrel vaulting. It was donated by the owner, who had been the bishop of Poitiers.

Marmagne, sunlit woods near Fontenay Abbey.

FOLLOWING TWO PAGES:
Marmagne, Fontenay Abbey, church and monastic buildings viewed from the east.

corners; it was a hybrid structure, combining elements of the French late Gothic and Italian Renaissance. Flanked by round towers, it had two drawbridges; next to them were Doric and Ionic pilasters and gabled dormers. In 1794 a large part of the complex burned down. When the rest was razed in 1817, the debris was used to fill in the moat. The only part of the building that remained was one wing with a round tower at one corner. Its courtyard façade is a two-story structure built above a solid base of dark stone. Free-standing pairs of Doric and Ionic columns similar to those on the former portico articulate the façade into ten axes, every other one above a gabled dormer. Fluted Corinthian pilasters and beams articulate these dormers, each having two slender round-arched windows with a central column. The windows of the ground floor and upper story have delicate moldings. It can be presumed that the façades of the two lost wings resembled this one. The portal in the third axis is original, whereas the two French doors in the middle date from the 19th century. The rear side of the wing, the former main wall, was transformed into a garden façade during restorations that took place in the early 20th century.

Marmagne, Fontenay Abbey

One of Burgundy's most famous monuments is the Abbey of Fontenay in Marmagne, a little southeast of Montbard. Fontenay, together with Pontigny, are the only Cistercian monasteries in Burgundy that have survived, since only forlorn ruins of Clairvaux and Cîteaux remain.

St. Bernard of Clairvaux founded the abbey in 1118, and it was relocated to its present site in 1130. In 1139 a new church structure succeeded a temporary church building. It was consecrated in 1147 by the first Cistercian pope, Eugene III, and feverish building activity led to the completion of the essential monastic buildings by the end of the 12th century. Louis IX, the king of France who was elevated to sainthood, bestowed on Fontenay the title of "Royal Monastery," and from then on, the lily was a part of its coat of arms. Some 300 monks were living here around 1300, but even in the 14th century, stagnation became noticeable. Despite a brief flourishing at the end of the 15th century, the Wars of Religion that followed led to the decline of the monastery. In 1745 the large refectory was torn down. After the Revolution, the monastic buildings temporarily served as the production rooms of a factory.

Marmagne, Fontenay Abbey, so-called Madonna of Fontenay, about 1300.

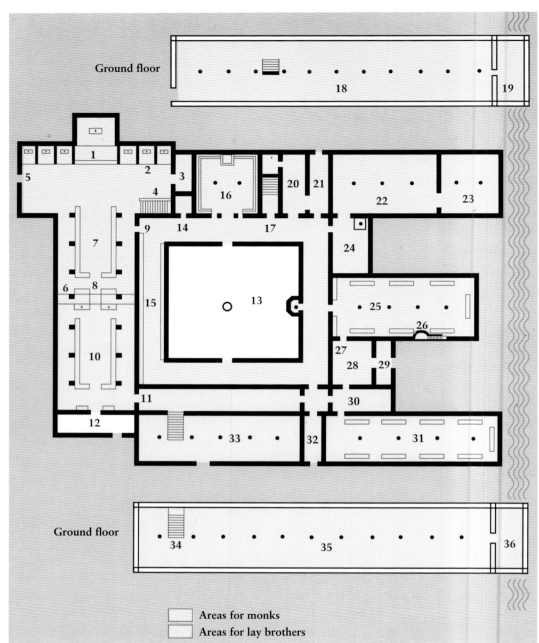

Ground floor

18   19

Ground floor

34   35   36

Areas for monks
Areas for lay brothers

The floor plan and elevation of the church are characteristically Cistercian, that is, clearly articulated and without ornamentation. The three-aisle, barrel-vaulted nave has stepped arcades on square piers with engaged half-columns and pilasters that continue into the vaults of the nave. Otherwise, there is nothing here, not even pews, which heightens one's original impression. Light floods into the nave and side aisles through round-arched windows in the west wall, four in the lower row and three in the upper one, of which the middle window is wider and higher. Light also enters through the small windows of the side aisles, which are groin-vaulted. The south transept arm connects directly to other convent buildings, extends for one bay to either side, and has small, square chapels in the east. The choir is also square, repeating the motif of the windows in the west wall in a somewhat different form.

The Cistercian Abbey according to Bernard of Clairvaux
(the ideal floor plan depicted here corresponds to a great extent to that of Fontenay).

1. Sanctuary and main altar
2. Side altars
3. Sacristy
4. Main stairway
5. Portal to the cemetery
6. Choir screen
7. Monks' choir
8. Choir for the sick
9. Monks' portal to the cloister
10. Lay brothers' choir
11. Lay brothers' portal
12. Narthex
13. Well of the courtyard
14. Armarium (library)
15. Cloister wing (collation walkway)
16. Chapter hall
17. Daytime stairway to the dormitory
18. Monks' dormitory

19. Latrines
20. Auditorium (consulting room)
21. Passageway
22. Scriptorium (monks' hall)
23. Room for the novices
24. Calefactory (warm room)
25. Monks' refectory
26. Seat for the monk reading during meals
27. Passage to kitchen
28. Kitchen
29. Supply rooms
30. Lay brothers' consulting room
31. Lay brothers' refectory
32. Lay brothers' passageway
33. Cellar
34. Lay brothers' stairway
35. Lay brothers' dormitory
36. Latrines

OPPOSITE:
Marmagne, Fontenay Abbey, view of the nave facing east, 1139–1147.

Marmagne, Fontenay Abbey, dormitory, second half of the 12th century, with a roof construction from the 15th century.

Marmagne, Fontenay Abbey, cloister courtyard looking north, second half of the 12th century.

The Madonna of Fontenay, a Virgin with Child probably dating from around 1300, is an especially lovely work (illus. p. 116). In this sculpture, the intimacy between mother and child that would become characteristic of late medieval religious paintings is already noticeable. In the choir is an altarpiece which can also be dated to about 1300. It depicts the Crucifixion with Mary, John, the holy women, and the soldiers. At the foot of the cross are Adam and the beginning of sin. Above the cross is an angel with the sun and the moon.

Like the church, the cloister to its south seems massive and heavy, but not awkward (illus. below and opposite bottom). Columns or pairs of semi-columns, with stout shafts and almost bare capitals, carry round arches that are topped both inside and out by large relieving arches. The masonry has been executed with particular care. The square chapter hall was once situated in the middle of the east wing, and four pillars divided the hall in three times three rib-vaulted bays. In the 15th century it was reduced in size by about a third. In keeping with the importance of the hall, its structural elements are more richly formed: bundled columns form the central pillars and support the richly profiled ribs (illus. right). The portal has five stepped jamb columns and archivolts; adjacent to them, double arcades open out on both sides.

To the south is the parlatory, an exit to the garden, and the so-called "hall of monks," a long, two-aisle room of six bays. Its original purpose is not known. Adjoining it is the calefactory, or warm room, used mainly by the scribes. Above it lies the dormitory with a roof truss dating from the 15th century (illus. opposite above). Some of the subsidiary buildings have also been preserved. The smithy is especially lovely. Here, too, the essential elements of Cistercian aesthetics—the exceptional masonry work and the clarity of the structural elements which make additional sculpture seem almost superfluous—are noticeable.

Marmagne, Fontenay Abbey, chapter hall, end of 12th century.

Marmagne, Fontenay Abbey, view of the east passageway of the cloister.

Bernard of Clairvaux and the Founding of the Cistercian Order

Molesme, view of the town. Molesme played a role in the early history of the Cistercian Order.

RIGHT:
Monks doing carpentry
Miniature from a manuscript from Cîteaux: *Moralia in Job* by Gregory VII, early 12th century, Dijon, Bibliothèque municipale, Ms 170, folio 59.

In 1070, Robert, a nobleman from Champagne, founded a monastery in Molesme under the rule of St. Benedict. It had close ties to Cluny without being legally subject to it. Robert himself became the first abbot. Until this point, Robert had searched continually for the true way of following Christ, for the *vita religiosa*. He had been a monk in Moutiers-la-Celle, abbot in Saint-Michel in Tonnerre, prior in Saint-Ayoul in Provence, and a hermit in the forest of Collan. These stations characterize Robert's restless, striving search for an ever stricter asceticism and an ever closer imitation of the ideals of the Gospels, a search that was in fact typical for his time.

Robert's newly founded monastery in Molesme quickly flourished, but this very success seems to have caused the abbot, the prior Alberich, and about twenty other monks to doubt the correctness of their way of life. About 28 years after the founding of Molesme—the Cistercian chronicles themselves named the year 1098—Robert departed his prospering monastery for a still more ascetic life. Twenty monks accompanied him into the wilderness, to a place in the Chalon-sur-Saône diocese by the name of Cistercium. They called their newly found place *novum monasterium*. There they settled to follow a life according to the original formulation of the rule of St. Benedict, that is, a life of personal poverty, rigorous asceticism, and work. They rigorously refused any later alleviations or additions to the rule in order to live exclusively by the work of their own hands.

For reasons that cannot be reconstructed today, the monks of Molesme soon laid claim to their former abbot by way of Pope Urban II. In 1099 at a church conference, the papal legate, Archbishop Hugh of Lyon, decided that Robert must return to Molesme and that the monks who wanted to could accompany him. In the future, however, both monasteries were to desist from wooing monks away from each other in a manner contrary to the rule. Robert submitted to this judgment, and more than half of his brothers accompanied him back. Those who stayed were Prior Alberich, who now took over the office of abbot, as well as Stephen Harding, who succeeded Alberich as prior, along with a few monks.

This was a great blow to the young monastery. Robert's recall is noted with bitterness and a lack of comprehension in later Cistercian chronicles. Since the Cistercians regarded their own community as the one that followed the rule most strictly, any transfer to another order or monastery to pursue a more dedicated life or for any other reason was simply rejected. In 1108 Alberich died and Stephen Harding succeeded him. Robert of

Molesme, on the other hand, entered Cluny towards the end of his life. He died there in 1111 and was honored by an annual mass to commemorate his death at Cluny. In the eyes of his former companions, this, too, must have seemed an affront, and the sharp attacks by Bernard of Clairvaux against Cluny a few years later were probably rooted in this disappointment.

Stephen Harding, also of noble family and well educated, had come from England. He, too, had sought the experience of the *vita religiosa* in various monasteries in England, Scotland, Ireland, France, and Italy, and had become acquainted with the leading religious and spiritual figures of his time. According to later Cistercian reports, it was Stephen Harding himself who gave *novum monasterium* its own rules, which were based solely on *ratio* (reason) and *auctoritas* (divine authority). The new abbot found both of these principles in the rule of St. Benedict.

In any case, Cîteaux seems to have flourished during his abbacy, because in 1113 he could already allow a group of monks to leave for La Ferté, where they founded a daughter monastery. In 1114 and 1115, three more daughter monasteries were founded in Pontigny, Morimond, and Clairvaux. It will become clear that this sudden flourishing was basically due to the arrival of Bernard of Clairvaux at the monastery in Cîteaux. Up to this point, the abbot had not kept a written chronicle of his monastery, and from the period of Stephen Harding only a few—albeit significant—illuminated manuscripts have been preserved. But now, it seemed important to have a charter. In strict rejection of the model of Cluny, which consisted of countless legally dependent abbeys and priories with differing legal conceptions and dependencies—Stephen Harding aimed at creating a homogenous union of equal and independent monasteries. In order to nevertheless guarantee the uniformity of religious life and absolutely strict adherence to the rule, he created the General Chapter and the Principle of Visitation. Each subsidiary monastery was independent and could elect its own abbot freely. Once a year, the abbot of the mother monastery visited each subsidiary to review their affairs and to remedy any problems. Moreover, once a year all the Cistercian abbots met for a General Chapter in which each one held an equal seat and vote in order to consult on mutual problems. In this way, each monastery was completely independent and free, but was at the same time safeguarded by the entire association.

It is no longer possible to reconstruct from existing sources how the charter fared under Stephen Harding, how it developed, and what

ABOVE:
Cîteaux, monastery, detail on the former library building façade. The rich decorative detail of the late Gothic structure is a stark contrast to the simple aesthetics of early Cistercian architecture.

BELOW:
Stephen Harding with a model of the church, miniature from the 12th century, manuscript from Cîteaux, *Commentary on Jeremiah*, Dijon, Musée municipale, Ms 130, folio 104.

St. Bernard of Clairvaux in the chapter hall; St. Bernard is tempted by the devil.
Miniature from the *Book of Hours of Etienne Chevalier* by Jean Fouquet, ca. 1450, Chantilly, Musée Condé.

"It is time for me to remember myself. May my monstrous life, my bitter conscience, move you to pity. I am a sort of modern chimera, neither cleric nor layman. I have kept the habit of a monk, but I have long ago abandoned the life. I do not wish to tell you what I daresay you have heard from others: what I am doing, what are my purposes, through what dangers I pass in the world, or rather down what precipices I am hurled. If you have not heard, enquire, and then, according to what you hear, give your advice and the support of your prayers."
(Letter 250.4, English translation from *The Letters of St. Bernard of Clairvaux*, translated by Bruno Scott James. Sutton Publishing, 1998.)

influence Bernard of Clairvaux had upon it. By the last third of the 12th century, at least three versions of this charter had been written: the *Summa chartae caritatis*, the *Charta caritatis prior,* and the *Charta caritatis posterior*. None of the three can be dated exactly. When the daughter monasteries themselves began founding monasteries—a third generation, so to speak—it was clear that the charter had to be modified. In these filiations, the abbot of Cîteaux no longer had visitation rights and no right to take action without a special assignment of the General Chapter. Sometime before the mid-12th century, the visitation rights of Cîteaux, which had no mother-house, were also given to the abbots of the first four daughter monasteries. This was surely done at the behest of Bernard, the abbot of Clairvaux, who was able to influence the course of the order through his important position in the church as a whole and his good relations with the pope.

Bernard was born in 1019 in the château of Fontaines near Dijon. Raised under the influence of his pious mother, he later came to the canons of Saint-Vorles in Chalon-sur-Saône. He decided on conversion early, perhaps as a result of the death of his mother. Although it was not unusual at the time for members of the aristocracy to choose a religious life, nor was it unusual to choose the strictest community in the area, Bernard distinguished himself from the outset through his missionary ardor and his pedagogical zeal. He persuaded 30 people closely connected to him, including all of his grown brothers and sisters, to take the monastic vows together with him. In time, his entire family followed his example.

In Cîteaux, where a group of monks had just departed for La Ferté, Bernard and his companions were most welcome. Their entrance allowed the monastery to found a second daughter, in Pontigny. Because of his strict asceticism and the profound seriousness with which he lived the *vita religiosa*, Bernard drew the attention of the abbot immediately after his entry into Cîteaux. In just his second year of monastic life, Stephen Harding sent the then 25-year-old to the fourth daughter

monastery, Clairvaux in the diocese of Langres, as its abbot. At this point Bernard took on the office that he was to keep for the rest of his life in this order; he died as abbot of Clairvaux. Nevertheless, he attained an importance in the ecclesiastical-political world unparalleled in the lives of other men of his time. In this way Bernard was able to continue in his order what the abbots of Cluny had begun for their own monasteries 200 years earlier.

In Clairvaux, a process repeated itself that had already characterized the beginnings of Cîteaux: the difficulties and drudgery of clearing and cultivating the land commanded the abbot's energies to a large extent for the first 15 years. At the same time, he was tireless in teaching his monks the virtues of monastic life. Bernard lived his ideal so strictly that he became seriously ill. His stomach suffered so much that he seems never to have recovered completely. In the short periods of free time allowed by the monastic rule, the abbot wrote or dictated tracts, sermons, and letters of missionary purpose. In his flowing, elegant style he attacked his readers and listeners, heaping reprimands, criticism, exhortations, and ridicule upon them. His writings were collected during his lifetime and he revised many of them himself. Almost 550 letters have been preserved and revised, at least in terms of content.

It is no wonder that Bernard's intense activity made his monastery and the young order famous.

Monks felling a tree,
miniature from a manuscript from Cîteaux: *Moralia in Job,* by Gregory VII, beginning of the 12th century. Dijon, Bibliothèque municipale, Ms 173, folio 41.

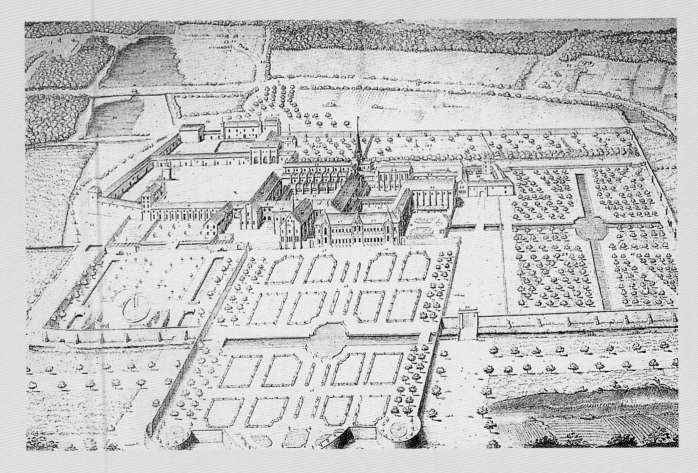

Cîteaux, Cistercian monastery, view of the complex from the south, between 1692 and 1712, engraving by Benoît Farjat. Dijon, Bibliothèque municipale.

Chauvigny/Vienne, former collegiate church of Saint-Pierre, capitals from the ambulatory.

TOP: A devil with a grimacing face shows his altar with the symbol of death. At his right is a mythical being with the head of a goat on a human body. It is holding a person. At the left is another mythical being.

ABOVE: A winged dragon with a human face holds a man captive in its mouth between two rows of sharp teeth and with two claw-like hands.

Bernard decidedly rejected such fantastical representations, as they distracted monks from their prayers.

The solemnity and severity of the rules engendered respect, and the order received many gifts and endowments. Increasing numbers of people entered the monastery. In addition, the cultivation of the land yielded high profits, which significantly increased the wealth of the monastery. In time, economic success began to thwart the religious program of the Cistercians, just as it had that of the monks of Cluny years before.

But at this time the order was still expanding, and the abbot of Clairvaux dedicated all his energy to the spreading and completion of his many filiations. In the 40 years in which he held office, Clairvaux founded or acquired 69 daughter monasteries, which again spawned 75 daughter groups, from which another 22 emerged. In fact, almost half of the Cistercian monasteries in existence were dependent on Clairvaux, which had 166 convents. By the time of Bernard's death, the number of dependencies had reached 344. Not all of these monasteries lay in lonely valleys and wildernesses, however, as the Cistercians had taken over many monasteries owned by the aristocracy or bishops for the purpose of reforming them. Moreover, the Cistercians now had to deal with older legal stipulations and inheritance laws.

Although the difficulties that resulted from these complications were obvious in Cluny, a monastic model the Cistercians had previously clearly opposed, Bernard nevertheless promoted the rapid tempo of his order's growth with great determination. The schism in Cluny surely influenced events in this respect. In 1124/1125, at a moment when Cluny was beset by the worst kind of financial difficulties, when it seemed impossible to guarantee even enough food for the convent and the abbot Petrus Venerabilis worried about the pitiable condition of the monks' habits, Bernard of Clairvaux attacked the luxuriant lifestyle of the monks of Cluny and their opulent menus in the many pages of his *Apologia*. He was disturbed by their resplendent clothing and the feudal manner of the abbot, whom he claimed to have seen with at least 60 horses in attendance, like a provincial prince. And of course, he found fault with the magnificence of Cluny III, its paintings and sculptures, the liturgical finery, and the furnishings of the libraries and dormitories. He remonstrated against the gilding, he called the chandeliers vain, and he admonished the church for displaying saints' images, as they distracted from prayer: monks should read books, not marble columns.

Petrus Venerabilis did not directly answer the attack on the massive church which his predecessor had begun, and which would fall to him to complete. But he did address a letter to Bernard in which he convincingly defended the *Cluniazensis ecclesia*, as he was in a position to know that the rule of St. Benedict was well adhered to in his monastery. He reminded the abbot of Clairvaux of the *caritas* which must be the measure of the monastic life and of the *discretio*, the ability to differentiate. Both were incorporated in the rule of St. Benedict, as Petrus Venerabilis emphasized. In any case, we have no concrete knowledge of the effect of this dispute between Bernard of Clairvaux and Petrus Venerabilis on the religious world of that time. Walter Map, who lived as a cleric at the royal court in England, described the dispute as a ridiculous quarrel between monks.

From 1130, a new challenge arose, to which Bernard devoted all his energies. In the papal election, two popes had been chosen in two separate elections, each of which was not entirely correct from a legal point of view. The result was that two popes, Innocent II and Anaclet II, opposed each other. Innocent fled to France by way of Italy and settled in Avignon: the papal schism had begun. The abbot of Clairvaux immediately took the part of Innocent, who was favored by the reformers in the committee of cardinals. Abbot Suger of Saint-Denis and Petrus Venerabilis followed his example, but no one defended the cause

of the reform pope as vehemently as Bernard of Clairvaux. The pope's cause became his own.

When Innocent was finally instated as the sole pope in 1139, Bernard's influence rose correspondingly. He was now one of the most important men of the church. In 1145, in the person of Pope Eugene III, a Cistercian monk even rose to the office of pope. Bernard's influence seemed to have reached its apex, like that of Abbot Hugh of Semur before him at the time of Urban II. At this moment, however, Bernard succeeded in making numerous enemies, not only among the cardinals. He was so resolutely in favor of the Second Crusade, winning over important figures in the Holy Roman Empire to his cause, that when the entire venture ended disastrously in the military debacle of 1147, Bernard of Clairvaux, its figurehead, lost much of his credibility. Despite his dismay in the face of this catastrophe, it would have been out of character for Bernard to give up his principles. In 1150, this time together with Abbot Suger, Bernard again attempted to win support for a new crusade, one that ended before it was begun.

Bernard now returned to his writings. In the form of a letter to Pope Eugene III, he wrote the tract *De consideratione*, in which he analyzed the world situation and the church from the papal perspective. And he would not have been Bernard of Clairvaux if he did not offer sharp criticism. Towards the end of his life—he died in 1153—he also turned his criticism against himself and his own life, calling it a *vita monstrosa*. He had to admit that his endeavors for the order and the monastic life had detracted from what he had wished to embody: a life of prayer and physical work in adherence to the monastic rule.

The Cistercian Order continued to flourish throughout 12th century, producing significant monastic buildings all over Europe. In the 13th century, when European cities began developing on their own, the situation changed. The Cistercian Order was edged out by the mendicant orders of St. Francis and St. Dominic, forming an entirely new ecclesiastical model.

Like every order, the Cistercians evolved with the needs of a certain period, its conceptions of life and faith. No order has ever sustained its relevance indefinitely. The Cistercian Order may have declined in prominence, but over the centuries the Cistercians have managed to meet the challenges of succeeding periods and survive by keeping on good terms with whatever order is prominent.

Marmagne, Fontenay Abbey, subsidiary building: the smithy.

Jours-lès-Baigneux and Bussy-le-Grand

As in Montigny-sur-Aube, the late medieval complexes of Jours-lès-Baigneux and Bussy-Rabutin—both square, walled fortifications with round towers and moats—were renovated in the 16th century. In the case of Jours-lès-Baigneux (illus. left), Claude d'Anglure and his second wife, Isabeau de Joyeuse, built a new wing with an integrated round tower between 1542 and 1566. The courtyard side received an elegant façade with rhythmic articulation, similar to that of Ancy-le-Franc. Blind arches over the French doors on the ground floor are framed by fluted pilasters, between which round-arched niches are set into the wall. The lintels of the upper-story windows have a décor of flat reliefs. All six of the axes are capped with gabled dormers. The asymmetrically placed entrance, probably determined by the structure that preceded the present one, has slits that indicate a former drawbridge. Garlands of fruit adorn the tall, rectangular windows, and broad cornices encircle the entire building. Two lead figures depicting Sultan Saladin and the owner are said to have once crowned the roof.

The château in Bussy-Rabutin is first mentioned in a document dating from 1348. At that

ABOVE:
Jours-lès-Baigneux, château, 1542–1566, courtyard façade.

Bussy-le-Grand, Château de Bussy-Rabutin, view of the inner courtyard with the Baroque main façade (1649) and the eastern gallery wing (1520).

time, the square stone fortification with round towers and residential buildings that can no longer be reconstructed belonged to Marguerite de Châtillon. The complex was modernized from about 1520 at the behest of Antoine de Roche-fort-Chandio. He had the southern main wall of the fortification torn down, adding two gallery wings of small depth with engaged pilaster articulation along the main east and west walls. The medieval round towers remained in place. One hundred years later, the old residence on the north side was also taken down, and François de Rabutin began building a wing that was completed in 1649 by his son, Roger. The elegant courtyard façade reveals the influence of Italian Baroque (illus. opposite). The windows are tall, crowned alternately with triangular and seg-mented pediments in the upper story. Between the windows are shallow, round-arched niches on the ground floor corresponding to oval niches in the upper story. The busts that once filled the niches have unfortunately been lost. A broad cornice separates the upper and lower stories, and the central axis protrudes just slightly. A split pedi-ment emphasizes the center of both stories. Gabled dormers adorn the edge of the roof. In addition, the large park is a lovely place to stroll.

The interior furnishings are strange and amus-ing. They are the work of Roger de Rabutin, a high-ranking officer who was banished from court for 16 years in 1666 due to various scandalous affairs. During this time he collected over 300 paintings, to which he affixed sayings fashionable at that time. Some are quotes, others he composed himself; almost all of them are unfriendly and directed at his rivals at court, testaments of his wounded pride and desire for revenge. The Salle de Devises on the ground floor exhibits views of royal châteaus as well as allegorical depictions of fruits, animals, and plants, all with commentaries; next to them are natural phenomena. Upstairs are portraits of generals and the French kings since Hugh Capet; in the Tour Dorée are the famed por-traits of women with commentaries (illus. above). The chapel in the southwest tower, visible from the outside through its windows, has a 16th-cen-tury stone retable depicting the miracle of Lazarus.

Bussy-le-Grand, Château de Bussy-Rabutin, portraits of women in the Tour Dorée, bearing the commen-taries of Rabutin, some of which are quite risqué.

TOP LEFT:
Bussy-le-Grand, Château de Bussy-Rabutin, portrait of Roger de Rabutin, who commissioned the main façade and the interior decoration.

Châtillonais landscape near Jours-lès-Baigneux.

Alise-Sainte-Reine
Statue of Vercingétorix.

Alise-Sainte-Reine

A visit to Alise-Sainte-Reine is a journey into a completely different era. This area was known to the Romans as Alésia, and here between the rivers Oze and Ozerain rises Mont Auxois, on which the Celtic tribe of the Mandubians once built their oppidum. This location gave the rebellious Gallic tribes, under the leadership of Vercingétorix, a commanding view of the entire surrounding area, which they controlled until 52 BC when they were decisively defeated by Caesar.

Vercingétorix, a young Gallic prince, temporarily united disparate Gallic tribes against Caesar and led the Gallic rebellion against the Roman occupation. After numerous armed conflicts the two forces faced off in Alésia for the decisive battle. The Gauls numbered 80,000 foot soldiers in addition to cavalry, opposing 50,000 soldiers on the Roman side. In his report of the Gallic Wars, Caesar described the Alésian battle in detail. In order to avoid an open battle, he laid siege to the

fortified city, erecting a double wall almost nine miles (14 km) long around it. This protected him from attack from both the front and the rear. He also correctly calculated the impatience of those under siege. The Gauls tried to break out before their reinforcements had arrived. They were trapped within the two encircling walls and mercilessly slaughtered by the Romans. Vercingétorix capitulated. He was taken to Rome, where he was displayed to the populace in Caesar's triumphal procession. After seven years of captivity, he was finally murdered in prison.

In order to put an end to a scholarly debate as to the location of Alésia, Napoleon III ordered excavations at Alise-Sainte-Reine, undertaken from 1861–1865. These corroborated Caesar's account, revealing the remains of a Celtic oppidum with a shrine for a spring and also the ruins of a Roman city (illus. opposite), including a large theater, a "monument with three apses"—perhaps a court of justice or market basilica—a temple with portico perhaps indicative of a capitol, colonnades connected to thermae, numerous single houses and housing settlements, including a Gallic quarter, a *monument à crypte*, a Celtic shrine, perhaps for the gods Ucuetis and Bergusia, and on the eastern plateau, a temple for the Celtic god Movitasgus, who is comparable to Apollo.

The archaeological finds (illus. right) are on exhibit in two museums, the Musée Alésia and the Musée municipal. Figures, vases, coins, utensils of everyday life, and the famous relief of the trio of gods—Jupiter, Juno, and Minerva—found in the vicinity of the Roman temple, as well as models and reconstructions, can be found here.

At the same time Napoleon ordered the excavations at Alésia, he also had a copper statue of Vercingétorix erected, 23 feet (7 m) high and visible from all the surrounding valleys and hills (illus. opposite). With an eye to the destiny of France, Napoleon gave the statue facial features similar to his own. The pedestal, equal in height to the statue, is the work of Eugène Viollet-le-Duc.

Flavigny-sur-Ozerain

On a rocky plateau opposite Mont Auxois, on the far side of the Ozerain, lies one of the most picturesque small cities of Burgundy, whose historical center has been almost completely preserved. Flavigny-sur-Ozerain (illus. pp. 130 f.) is grouped around the remains of a monastery dating from the 8th century. Widradus, the lord of Flavigny, founded an abbey here in 722 in honor of St. Praejectus (died 678 in Volvic), of which he himself was abbot until 745. Ten years later, Abbot Manasses was able to transfer the Praejectus relics

from Volvic to Flavigny. This year (755) is also associated with the completion of a first church. In 878 parts of a new building seem to have been completed as Pope John VIII consecrated seven altars, among them a certain Regina Altar. A few years before, the relics of St. Regina (Sainte-Reine) had been brought to Flavigny from Alésia.

Alise-Sainte-Reine, Celtic oppidum, excavation finds on display in the museum.

LEFT:
Alise-Sainte-Reine, Celtic oppidum, view into the excavation site.

FOLLOWING TWO PAGES:
Flavigny-sur-Ozerain, view of the town and surrounding hills.

The monastery now stood under the patronage of St. Peter. The eastern parts of the church, dating from the second half of the 9th century, have been excavated. Around a square encased apse with four supports and wall projections was a passageway leading to a three-aisle nave in the east that ended in a hexagonal chapel with six columns. On either side of the nave were oratories or *cryptae inferiores* (illus. right and bottom).

Above, following the same dimensions, was the sanctuary, connected to the nave below by stairs on either side. The ambulatory lay even higher and opened like a gallery in arcades to the choir. One looks through the columns from the main altar into the chapel. The excavations not only revealed the floor plan and elevation of the 9th-century abbey church, but also brought to light spoils from Alésia, which in some cases have even been identified and traced back to their original buildings. Moreover, Abbot Claude Courtépée documented the use of cut stone in his description of Burgundy. Around the middle of the 18th century, he saw Roman sculptures, among them gods, soldiers, and a wolf with Romulus in Flavigny. He also reported fragments of classical buildings that had been integrated into the foundations of houses only a few years before.

The complex in Saint-Germain in Auxerre, only a little older and in many respects related to that in Flavigny, seems to corroborate the 9th century as the time when the new building was erected, which perhaps integrated wall sections or columns from the previous building.

A Norman attack on the abbey in Flavigny in 887 caused substantial damage, which was re-

paired. Shortly before 1085 the building was reconstructed, and the wall projections and blind arches in the chapel date to this period. The *confessio* was abandoned and since that time the relics, enclosed in valuable shrines, have been preserved in the altar room. The sanctuary was probably also newly decorated. The reconstruction may also have included a new nave, whose dimensions were adopted by the later Gothic renovations in the 13th century. A three-aisle

Flavigny-sur-Ozerain, former Abbey of Saint-Pierre, about 878, capital in the crypt.

TOP RIGHT:
Flavigny-sur-Ozerain, former Abbey of Saint-Pierre, view into the chapel of the crypt.

Flavigny-sur-Ozerain, former Abbey of Saint-Pierre, interior of the apse of the crypt.

vestibule and two west towers were added, as well. The reconstructed nave comprised nine bays with compound piers, as depicted in the plan in the book *Monasticon Gallicanum*, a comprehensive collection of descriptions of French monasteries dating from the Baroque period.

The Maurins, owners of the estate since 1644, renovated parts of the monastic complex, which still houses the famous anise candy factory of Flavigny (illus. right and below). The church, however, was torn down and buried under rubble during the French Revolution. The production of anise candy in the monastery of Flavigny has a long tradition, going back to 1591 or further. One source mentions that the city of Semur handed out such pastilles as presents to guests, while another report cannot be verified: Pope John VII purportedly received three pounds (1.4 kg) of anise candy from the monks after the consecration of the altars in 878. In any case, the candy is still manufactured in gigantic copper cauldrons in the quarters of the former monastery and packed there, almost by hand. It is well worth a trip here to see the rooms and equipment.

Flavigny-sur-Ozerain, former Abbey of Saint-Pierre, production of anis pastilles in the monastic buildings of 1644.

Flavigny-sur-Ozerain, former Abbey of Saint-Pierre, packing room for the anis pastilles in the monastic buildings of 1644.

Flavigny-sur-Ozerain, Saint-Genès, main nave with bridge connecting the galleries of the side aisles on the north and south sides.

RIGHT
Flavigny-sur-Ozerain, Porte du Bourg.

The origins of the parish church of Saint-Genès date back to the first millennium, as bishop Valtarius placed it under the protection of an abbey, probably Saint-Pierre, in 997. Today Saint-Genès is a three-aisle, groin-vaulted basilica with six bays of varying depths, a perpendicular, rectangular crossing, and rib-vaulted transept arms that do not project (illus. above). The deep choir ends in a five-sided polygonal apse. The church is the result of repeated reconstruction and renovation. The deeply recessed jamb portal to the east, the arcades and galleries of the nave, and the floor plan of the transept seem to go back to a Romanesque emporium church with clerestory that was

taller than the present church. It may therefore have had a flat ceiling. The traces of blind arches above the galleries may have been part of an early Gothic vaulting which collapsed in the 15th century. New vaults were installed above the nave and transept with a far lower central nave and newly designed galleries—one can see where some of the old openings have been walled in. Laurent Pinon, the bishop of Auxerre, consecrated the church on May 6, 1434, the date which probably marks the end of the construction. A few years later, a fraternity formed in Saint-Genès, the Collège des Sociétaires, for whom the choir was extended. The peculiar bridge in front of the crossing dates from this time, and may have been connected to a choir screen. The side chapels, which date from the late 15th century onwards, are additions by private donors.

Just as appealing as the church itself are its interior furnishings, mainly from the late 15th century, which include richly adorned choir stalls—the work of a Flemish wood sculptor—a number of very fine statues, lovely *piscinas* and panel paintings in the side chapels, and many tomb slabs. A few years ago, one of the finest

Flavigny-sur-Ozerain, Saint-Genès, Annunciation Angel, recovered from a tomb (?) in the floor. Today the statue stands in the third chapel on the south side. Its hairstyle and robe reveal the influence of the Champagne region. It probably dates from the late 15th century.

FAR RIGHT:
Flavigny-sur-Ozerain, Maison au Donataire, today Syndicat d'Initiative, polychrome wooden Madonna with a small donor figure kneeling at her feet. Chronologically, the statue obviously belonged to the house, or rather in the niche in the upper story where it stood until the 1980s. The statue is slightly younger than the angel and follows the tradition of Burgundian Madonnas.

pieces was found underneath one of these grave slabs: the Annunciation Angel (illus. above), also a work of the late 15th century. Its hairstyle and posture point to the influence of Champagne. Notre-Dame in Semur-en-Auxois has an Annunciation Madonna that might be related to the angel in Flavigny.

More than almost any other town, Flavigny contains a unique ensemble of medieval and early Renaissance houses in an almost completely preserved labyrinth of streets, alleys, and squares. Among the most beautiful houses are the Maison au Donataire, with splendid late Gothic windows, ground floor openings of a medieval store and a

niche with a polychrome wooden Madonna (illus. above)—now kept indoors—plus two additional magnificent Renaissance houses. Close by, in the rue du Centre, are three late Gothic houses. In the rue de la Porte du Val is the 13th-century Maison Lacordaire, and nearby in the rue du Four are three houses from the 13th/14th centuries. In between are picturesque passages, stair towers, and arches. A section of the city's fortification wall is also still standing, as well as several late medieval gates with drawbridges and battlements over *mâchicoulis*, projecting stepped corbels with battlement parapets along the top of the wall (illus. opposite).

The *Maison Forte* – Family Seat of the Lower Aristocracy

Although late medieval aristocratic estates are not necessarily a specifically Burgundian invention, here they are our primary subject focus. Interestingly enough, this type of construction, commonly referred to as the *maison forte*, has only been recognized as an object of study in this particular part of France. Recently, this term has been defined anew in the course of a historical and architectural study of this phenomenon.

Jean Richard, a prominent historian of Burgundy, studied the source materials and made the first steps. Sociologically, the *maison forte* was a residence of the lower aristocracy, center of a small landowner's estate, endowed with the right and responsibility to keep peace, to protect and tax travelers; as well as the right to force subjects to use baking ovens, mills, and wine presses in exchange for payment of a fee.

Land distribution apparently began in Burgundy during the 10th century. At this time many strategic places seem to have been fortified for the first time by powerful feudal lords who had received large areas as fiefs. Their elevated châteaus were administrative centers, places of refuge, residences, and the seats of garrisons manned by the lower aristocracy—the *milites castri*—who lived there with their entire families. Around 1200 a new development began to evolve. The *milites castri*, whose wartime services were often paid in land due to the continual insolvancy of their lords, began to leave the elevated fortresses. As soon as a nobleman had earned, inherited or married into enough land to lead an independent existence, he settled there and erected a *maison forte* according to his means and privileges. These small, often positively tiny, land ownerships multiplied at the same time the garrisons of the large châteaus diminished.

In terms of form, a *maison forte* consisted of a house where the owner and his family lived, and a courtyard with an entrance gate and drawbridge, secured with walls, battlements, and moats. The utility buildings were located in an equally fortified *basse-cour* in front of or next to the main complex. The *maison forte* was not equipped to withstand a siege or a massive attack, but it did offer protection from various marauding groups and from essentially harmless, ill-equipped attacks. Far more important than security was the aristocracy's need to demonstrate its social standing.

From the outset, the *maison forte* was a square or rectangular complex. This form had become the norm about 1200, inspired by new buildings such as the Louvre, erected by Philip II August, and the château of Druyes-les-Belles-Fontaines (illus. p. 339), built by his cousin Pierre de Courtenay. A donjon, usually square, was placed at one corner of the walls and served simultaneously as living and defense quarters. Timber-framed buildings, which were both more comfortable and warmer, were built in some complexes. Beginning in the last third of the 13th century, circular towers made their appearance and were placed at the other three corners, giving the entire complex a stately and fortified impression. There are also a few examples in which a fourth circular tower is placed at the free-standing corner of the donjon, but in fact the era of the square donjon (illus. left) was coming to a close. From about 1340—Bussy-Rabutin and Savigny-lès-Beaune are the earliest examples—square-walled fortifications no longer had a donjon. Circular towers were placed at all four corners, and a gatehouse with drawbridge, or simply a gate with a *bretèche* and drawbridge, protected the entrance in the middle of the main wall. On the opposite side was customarily the logis, taking up the entire side, at times supplemented by a second living area. Many *maisons fortes* of this type have been preserved in surprisingly good condition. Still, probably about 50 percent of the buildings that once existed in Burgundy have disappeared.

Other types of construction, more rare, began to evolve through the modernization of the donjon structure in the 13th century. A good example

Semur-en-Brionnais, donjon from the 13th century.

RIGHT:
Corcelles-les-Arts, château, view of the garden side of the logis (18th century) and of the stair tower of the donjon (ca. 1460/1465).

is Corcelles-les-Arts (illus. opposite bottom). The donjons and wooden logis were no longer adequate to the needs, so living quarters within the square walls were expanded by the addition of a stone logis. The possibilities were limited. Most often a stone logis was added to the donjon, and the buildings were then connected through a stair tower. In the narrow courtyard of Corcelles-les-Arts, this solution was not possible. Instead, the logis was attached to a free wall and connected to the donjon by a covered passageway. This emergency solution gave rise to a new building type, found for example in Saint-André-le-Desert, where the donjon and logis were combined from the start.

The last building type is the most exciting in terms of the history of iconology and architecture: the four-tower donjon. Its roots in Burgundy can be traced precisely. Edward III of England had the first four-tower donjon built at Châtel-Gérard between 1359 and 1361 after his invasion of Burgundy. It is constructed of large, carefully hewn stone blocks. Four octagonal towers flanked the central structure, once four-storied. At the time, the construction was unmistakeably English and the intention of its builder obvious, seen in the context of his policies towards France after the disaster of 1356. Since Edward III had practically tied the hands of the young duke of Burgundy through a treaty of allegiance, England could mount its campaign to seize the French crown from Burgundian territory. The response of the equally young and inexperienced dauphin, who would later become Charles V, was the construction of a donjon at Vincennes that same year, despite extreme political difficulties.

In Burgundy, the four-tower donjon gained popularity from about 1390, no longer as a political statement, but as a comfortable residence as it had been originally in England. A four-tower donjon was a kind of compact castle. Towers, battlements, and moats were attached to the logis, and a simple encircling wall without towers sufficed for the courtyard. The most beautiful examples of four-tower donjons are the late structures in Rosières and Thenissey going back to the mid-15th century. In the course of the 16th century, the four-tower donjon evolved into the *manoir* in the Loire region and in the north.

All the complexes had wooden elements and painted surfaces that are largely missing today. Many of the battlements, of which only the stepped stone corbels have survived, were certainly built of wood, as were arcaded walkways on façades—recognizable by the beam pockets left in the walls—gallery-like protective roofs, interior or exterior shutters, gates, portals, and half-timber walls. These wooden surfaces were ideal for paintings or splashes of color, for coats of arms and ornamentation, as the few remaining examples prove. The moldings of portals and windows were accentuated with color. Coats of arms, stone rustication, and ornamental or figural décor enhanced logis façades and the entrance in the main wall, especially entrance gates and towers. On such elaborate complexes as Châteauneuf, Germolles, or the Hôtel-Dieu in Beaune, coats of arms, niches, and the statues to fill them—usually Madonnas—were sculpted. But most builders or lords—including Philip the Bold, because he initiated so many building projects—did not have sufficient funds for sculptures, and used painting for décor instead. The eaves and their fascias often show remnants of such paintings. Pictorial and written sources describe mainly interior painting, but also mention paintings executed on exteriors. For example, Philip the Bold had the Madonna and many saints painted on the towers flanking the entrance gates (a structure he introduced into Burgundian architecture) and the walls above it when renovating the châteaus of Rouvres and Argilly. The title page of a *terrier* (a description of all portable and immobile property) from the Chaussin/Jura estate indicates that the stone rustication on the main wall of the entrance side had a painting. A flower or a star was painted onto each stone block. The battlements, which served as a symbol of both the importance and the invincibility of the complex, were ideally suited for such décor, as they were clearly visible from afar.

The stone structures that have been preserved indicate how much care was taken in their ornamentation; good examples are Rosières, Posanges above the entrance gate (illus. right), and Rully, among others. The owner's painted coat of arms certainly adorned the wall under the formerets of wooden and stone battlements, perhaps accompanied by saints or beasts of mythological or heraldic significance. Of the once-abundant colorful décor, only the roofs with their colored glazed tiles remain. They, too, indicate the wealth of the owner—and all have been restored. Original tiles are only found in excavations.

The favored colors of the late Middle Ages were crimson red, ochre, royal blue, green, gray, black, white, and gold. In manuscript illuminations and textiles we encounter the same tones, which were applied with the same obvious love of color. In fact, since clothes signified rank, the colors of the garments of the dukes and their entourage have been described in great detail. The medieval world was enamored of color. Because pigments were expensive, color was a privilege of the aristocracy and the clergy, who used it to set themselves apart from the rest of the people.

Posanges, château, 1437–1453, gate with moat and large and small drawbridges.

Pouillenay, Château de Villiers, exterior view of the complex dating from ca. 1450 with one of the two corner towers still standing and a newer farm building.

Examples of Fortified Country Estates

Late medieval secular architecture outside of the cities—in other words, family estates of the aristocracy—are a specialty of Burgundy. Where else are there so many such estates, especially in a comparable state of preservation? Right at the foot of the hill in Flavigny is the *maison forte* Villiers in Pouillenay (illus. above). Its beginnings are tied to the monastery of Saint-Pierre: the duke granted the land to the monastery in 1239. A two-aisle cellar with heavy rib vaulting underneath the late medieval logis dates from this time, but nothing is known about how the estate looked at the time. In 1407 it belonged to Guillaume Damas, who perhaps undertook some renovations. The entire complex, a square stone structure with circular towers, a moat, entrance gate, and logis, seems to have been constructed after 1448, either as a new building or as a reconstruction on existing foundations. In 1554 the family Damas de Cormaillon added a gallery and several window axes in the towers, taking into account the form of the older

windows. Today, two circular towers, a part of the logis, and the exterior stair tower are missing. Only some of the original tall windows and dormers as well as both quadrant-shaped latrines protruding from the outer wall of the logis remain. But the external impression can be deceptive: very few of the noble estates in Burgundy retain as much of their original furnishings and atmosphere as Villiers.

Some miles further south, also on the bank of the Canal de Bourgogne and its companion stream, lies Marigny-le-Cahouet, a massive rectangular complex in an extensive park (illus. opposite bottom). Marigny is one of the early châteaus located in the plains; it is related to the *maison forte* of Lichères in Faulin and therefore very spread out. It was built about 1200 as an appanage for Alexander, a younger son of the duke, with a square donjon, battlements on the crown of the rectangular wall, and a wide moat. The two logis, the gate tower bearing a dovecote, and the stair tower are late medieval additions, probably from the 1460s. As a rule, gate towers divide a main wall at its center, but in this case the gate tower was moved off-center in order to make space for the southern logis. Still newer than the logis are the pavilions, which are placed diagonally at the corners of the rectangular wall. They may have replaced older circular towers, but that is only a conjecture; there may have been no corner towers originally. Finally, the 19th century brought a neo-Gothic interior and a gallery that was added or changed.

The donjon of Thenissey (illus. right) is an impressive example of the nobles' desire for security incombination with stately self-promotion. One feature of the era of the dukes is that they were, up to a point, benevolent towards their citizens— the cities of the Netherlands had forced this issue. As in the Netherlands, it was possible for Burgundian citizens to acquire a good standard of living, even genuine wealth.

In the early 15th century Guillaume I Poinceot, a sheep merchant, had begun to acquire control of Thenissey, site of a *maison forte* since the early 14th century. His son, Guillaume II, Seigneur de Thenissey, built a *forte tour*, a donjon, in about 1460/1470. The dimensions of the large rectangular building are about 33 x 66 feet (10 x 20 m), and it was once encircled by a moat. The entrance gate was positioned at the center, where a spiral stairway directly behind the outer wall led to the four stories and the enormous roof. Here alone the old layout is still clear: the high center wall reveals the former height and pitch of the roof, and in front of the stair tower are remnants of the

Thenissey, donjon, 1460/1470, view of the courtyard façade and the original central wall, with the top of the stair tower and vestiges of battlements.

LEFT:
Marigny-le-Cahouet, château, view of the entrance façade with gate tower and donjon.

Thenissey, château, 1718–1736, garden façade.

Vitteaux, Maison Bélime, 13th century, gable end with twin bifora.

battlements on stepped corbels that originally led around the entire complex. The donjon in Rosières, whose battlements are still intact, gives a good idea of just how imposing the donjon in Thenissey must have been. A few small windows placed in the axes, as in Rosières, two per story, allowed light to fall into the interior rooms. Only the upper stories had latrines, which were reserved exclusively for the use of members of the owner's family.

Between 1718 and 1736 the de Clugny family, who had in the meantime acquired control of Thenissey, had a new château built. Typical for its time, it is a strictly articulated building with a slightly protruding gabled central façade bay (illus. above). The landscape was altered to accommodate the building and the moat widened. The high foundation, complete with windows, supports three stories articulated by pronounced string cornices. The steeply pitched roof is devoid of dormers, and the slender windows have hardly any decoration. The garden side of the building is unusual, as here the edges of the protruding central bay of the façade are rounded. Its roof reaches to the ridge of the main building. Behind this façade is a two-story salon. The two sculptures in the moat in front of the southern façade are personifications of Day and Night.

Posanges is another noble manor from the era of the Valois dukes. It was commissioned by Guil-

laume du Bois, a favorite at court. After he had gradually acquired control of the widely scattered parts of the estate, he had a *maison forte* built about 1437 (illus. opposite bottom). When he died in 1453, the complex seems to have been essentially complete. From this period are the rusticated wall of excellently hewn stone blocks; the four circular corner towers with fireplaces, windows, and *niches-à-banquettes* (seating alcoves); as well as the chapel, the battlements on the crown of the wall, the wide moat, and the entrance with two drawbridges and a lovely gatehouse, projecting both inside and outside above a stepped *mâchicoulis*. The corbels are connected and decorated with ogival arches and coats of arms. Between the slits of the large drawbridge is a niche with an ogival arch for a sculpture: until a few years ago, a Madonna from the 17th century stood here. She probably replaced a Virgin that originally occupied that spot.

The residence definitely took up the entire west side, as windows have been preserved here in the main wall, and only by way of the main wall were the two towers accessible on this side. But by the 19th century, no traces of this building existed. This, along with the fact that construction lasted only 16 years, would indicate that the building was a half-timber construction. Apparently there were also two short wings on the entrance side, as the two east towers also must have been accessible. Moreover, there is a large niche here, one that only makes sense in connection with a building. Perhaps the residence had already been torn down towards the end of the 15th century, when Antoine du Bois had two stair towers built onto the east towers in order to make them accessible.

The small and lovely gatehouse, the large fire-places, and the carefully wrought masonry would suggest that Guillaume du Bois' estate was quite prestigious. The simple battlements along the crown of the wall do not seem to fit with the rest. Originally, there may well have been wooden battlements in splendid colors. On half-timber buildings as well, the beams and the wall areas between them were surely painted.

Arriving in Posanges, one reaches the Brenne valley, an especially charming countryside. For miles, the small river, whose spacious valley is bordered by woods and occasional limestone cliffs, accompanies the road. One passes Vitteaux with the Maison Bélime, a stately town mansion dating from the 13th century (illus. opposite bottom). In addition, the city wall, the moat, and a late medieval wooden market building are still intact.

Countryside in the Brenne valley.

Posanges, château, 1437–1453, view of the entire complex with the massive corner towers and the lovely gatehouse.

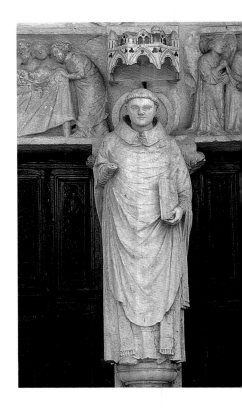

ture of a knight, probably a benefactor of the priory. The seated statue of the church patron is from about 1400; it might originally have been intended for this place. Portions of the church treasure are also preserved, including reliquaries and shrines from the 13th to 17th centuries.

In about 1280/1290, even before the choir, the Saint-Gilles Chapel was built. An elegant structure reminiscent of Gothic architecture from Champagne, it adjoins one side of the choir polygon. The oldest part of the complex, the north transept portal, still stands. It dates from about 1250/1260 and was surely influenced by the portal of Reims. In the jambs are four beautiful figures under baldachins, one of which is similar to the knight in the interior, and on the trumeau is St. Thibault in the habit of a monk (illus. right). His baldachin divides the lintel in two parts. To the left is the Death of the Virgin, to the right, her Ascension. The tympanum above is adorned with the Crowning of the Virgin; in the archivolts are depicted the wise and foolish virgins and pairs from the Old Testament. The wings of the wooden door date from around 1500 and show scenes from the life of the patron saint of the church.

Roads in this area are typically lined with trees, hedges, or woods and run in a straight line from one town to the next, rising and falling with the contours of the landscape. Just such a road leads from Saint-Thibault to Semur-en-Auxois. On the inclines along this road, numerous rest areas have been preserved. These are flat places where

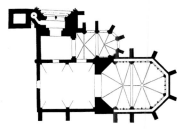

Saint-Thibault, floor plan.

TOP LEFT:
Saint-Thibault-en-Auxois, Saint-Thibault, ca. 1250 to ca. 1300, exterior view of the choir.

TOP RIGHT:
Saint-Thibault-en-Auxois, Saint-Thibault, sculpture of St. Theobald on the trumeau of the portal of the north transept.

LEFT:
Saint-Thibault-en-Auxois, Saint-Thibault, view into the polygonal choir.

Saint-Thibault

In Saint-Thibault one again meets the Canal de Bourgogne winding between ancient trees that line the streets. In about 1190, the lords of Saint-Beury founded a priory in honor of St. Theobald, whose relics were first brought here in about 1240. Soon afterwards, it appears, a new church was begun. After a collapse in 1712 and a fire 16 years later, only the choir, from around 1300, remained. After its repair by the architect Jean-Antoine Caristie, the church was consecrated anew in 1753. This 90-foot- (27 m-) high, very slender glazed polygon is the most daring achievement of Gothic architecture in Burgundy (illus. above and right). Between steeply rising vaulting shafts, the wall opens in four zones: the base with filigree blind arcades supports lit galleries with a narrow walkway, a triforium that echoes the foundation, and a high clerestory. As impressive as the choir are the interior furnishings, some of which are original: a triumphal cross in front of the central polygonal side, polychrome reliefs of the wooden altarpiece depicting the life of St. Thibault, a standing Madonna with Child and Bird, as well as the tomb sculp-

animals pulling wagons could rest after a strenuous climb and ready themselves for the next stretch. Modern road construction has evened out almost all of these old "saddle corners," but here they are still clearly visible.

Semur-en-Auxois

On the outcrop above the Armançon where Semur-en-Auxois now stands (illus. above) was once a Celtic fortification, later followed by a Roman *castellum*. In about 1300, the duke of Burgundy ordered a fortress built here, one of those early fortifications with a square floor plan and corner towers in the style of Druyes-les-Belles-Fontaines and the old Louvre. Today only the circular towers remain. In 1371/1372 Philip the Bold surrounded the city with a wall fortification with towers, one of which is still standing.

The former priory of Notre-Dame was founded by Girart de Roussillon, who placed it under the jurisdiction of Flavigny in 879. The first church was superseded in 1065 by a Romanesque structure; this in turn was replaced by a gorgeous rib-vaulted basilica about 200 feet (60 m) long,

Semur-en-Auxois, view towards the city with the towers of the château, dating from the late 13th/early 14th century, and the towers of Notre-Dame in the background.

LEFT:
Semur-en-Auxois, interior side of the city gate, 1371/1372.

Semur-en-Auxois, former priory church of Notre-Dame, tympanum of the north transept portal, the Porte des Bleds, from ca. 1250.

Semur-en-Auxois, former priory church of Notre-Dame, 1220/1225–16th century, north side aisle with the late Gothic and early Renaissance entrances into the side chapels.

Semur-en-Auxois, former priory church of Notre-Dame, burial group in the second side chapel in the northwest, Burgundian, 1490.

modeled on those in Auxerre and Dijon. The oldest parts are the choir ambulatory with three radiating chapels and the five-aisle antechoir (illus. opposite), corresponding to the five-part transept. The elevation is three stories high. The arcades support a double-arched triforium with figural heads in the spandrels and high, slender clerestory windows that are as tall as the arcades and triforium together. A walkway runs along here, adding depth to this zone.

In the nave, built about 1235, the elevation changes. The arcades were extended about 7 feet (2 m) and the triforium was abandoned; thus the clerestory rests directly on the arcades, completely changing the proportions: the central aisle appears much higher than the choir. In addition, the abun-

dant sculptural décor, numerous sculpted heads that enlivened the choir, is missing. The three western bays, the narthex with three portals, and the two towers date from the early 14th century. The side chapels, on the other hand, are 15th- and 16th-century additions. Their ornate late Gothic entrances set lovely accents in the northern side aisle. From 1844 to about 1854, Eugène Viollet-le-Duc carried out a general restoration.

The choir is also the most impressive part of the church from the exterior. Its structural elements are set one above the other in clear forms, peaking in a 184-foot- (56-m-) high, eight-sided tower. Here the consoles adorned with heads and figural motifs catch the eye. The spacious narthex was altered during the late Gothic period. Ori-

ginally it was open to three sides, possibly with free-standing arch supports instead of the smooth pier buttresses. Two chapel-like structures in front of the two west towers are also later additions.

The portals are still 13th-century in conception. Their sculptures were completely removed in 1793, and the Madonna with the Dove on the trumeau was placed here later. The Porte des Bleds in the north transept, however, dating from about 1250, has been preserved. The tympanum (illus. opposite) displays lively scenes from the life of St. Thomas in two panels: legendary scenes of his missionary work in India, and the doubter with Jesus. At the peak is a half-length figure of Jesus with worshiping angels and the world sphere. The same gestures and liveliness also characterize depictions of the months in the archivolt and the console figures; the jamb figures have been lost. The Porte des Bleds also has a two-story vestibule from which one could once step directly into the triforium. It was torn down in 1705.

Unlike most other churches, Notre-Dame was able to preserve a great part of its interior furnishings. The side chapels are especially opulently fitted, with richly adorned entrances, figural niches, altars, remains of gilded glass windows, and a

ABOVE:
Semur-en-Auxois, former priory church of Notre-Dame, choir capitals and arcades, about 1225.

TOP RIGHT:
Semur-en-Auxois, former priory church of Notre-Dame, one of the numerous small heads that adorn the choir inside and out.

RIGHT:
Semur-en-Auxois, former priory church of Notre-Dame, view into the choir.

Epoisses, fortress, dove tower in the courtyard with space for 3,000 pairs of doves.

Epoisses, fortress, logis, 15th to 19th centuries.

Epoisses

The gigantic castle complex of Epoisses, not far from Semur, is actually just at the edge of the Morvan mountain massif. Originally, the court of a Frankish king was situated here, with a very large fortified château that determined the dimensions of the structure now standing (illus. below). The duke of Burgundy, who had possessed Epoisses since 1189, granted it to the powerful Mello family in 1237. By 1421 they had added numerous logis into the irregular inner ring. After 1477 the castle changed hands numerous times, until it was occupied by the Catholic League in 1589 and fortified with bastions. In 1661 Epoisses went to Guillaume de Pechpeyrou-Comminges de Guitaut, who had a portion of the building renovated. During the Revolution, three of the original seven towers were destroyed as well as the wings that connected them, so that the former inner courtyard is now open to the south. The château has lovely late Gothic façades; however they are so even and regular as to be suspect. They would seem to be the result of restoration activities.

In the *basse-cour* are numerous utility buildings, a beautiful dove tower with an original ladder (illus. left), and the castle church. It was supposedly deemed a collegiate church and renovated by Rainard de Montbard in the second half of the 12th century. Further rebuilding took place in the late 15th century. The small, dark, unfortunately somewhat neglected church has many tomb slabs and epitaphs on its pillars, as well as a small pietà from the school of Jean de la Huerta.

stellar vault of many parts. The entombment group in the second chapel from the west (illus. p. 144) is famous. It dates from 1490 and was created in Burgundy; stylistically and in terms of motifs, it is comparable to the entombment scene in Tonnerre. In addition, there are a number of noteworthy panel paintings here. One, supposedly dating from 1299, depicts Christ standing, his hands in a gesture of blessing, with a sphere representing the world. Among the many others are one dated 1453 depicting the Tree of Jesse, and another showing St. Ann teaching Mary to read.

Saulieu, Saint-Andoche, from ca. 1125, figural capitals of the nave and side aisles, influenced by Autun with the motifs "Christ is Tempted by the Devil" and "The Devil hangs Judas."

Saulieu, Saint-Andoche, sarcophagus of St. Andochius in the northern side chapel.

Saulieu

In the year 177, St. Andochius supposedly was freed from a dungeon in Lyon, preached in Saulieu, and suffered martyrdom. At the beginning of the 5th century, a source reports the existence of an oratory over the grave of the saint; in 722 a first church was named Saint-Andoche, but it was destroyed by the Saracens in 731. Charlemagne apparently generously financed a rebuilding. A crypt, now inaccessible, is located under the apse and may date from this period. In the first half of the 9th century a monastery was built here; it was subordinated to the bishop of Autun in 843. In 1109 sources mention a festive *translatio* of reliquaries, followed in about 1125 by the construction of a new church building. Etienne de Bagé, the bishop of Autun who had overseen the start of construction of Saint-Lazare in Autun, also took charge of the construction here. Towards 1150/1160 the building was finished, but in 1360 the choir and transept were severely damaged. Finally in 1704 they were replaced by the simple polygonal choir standing today. An 1869 restoration was all too thorough.

Saint-Andoche was a successor to Saint-Lazare, the third church of Cluny. This can be deduced from the nave. Although it is shorter than that of Saint-Lazare and the bays of its central nave are more square, it has the three-zone elevation and rib vaulting of its prototype, albeit in much simpler form. The lateral aisles have groin vaulting. The (restored) capitals of the engaged demi-columns from 1140/1150 have some scenic ornamentation: Balam on the female donkey, the Flight to Egypt, the Temptations of Christ (illus. above left), Appearance to Mary Magdalene, and the Death of Judas (illus. top right). The capitals also show the influence of Autun. Originally a projecting transept and a three-part Benedictine choir extended the nave. In the choir are lovely late-14th-century pews; nearby are an eagle pulpit and a Gothic reliquary shrine. In the nave are numerous sculptures from the 15th and 16th centuries. In the northern side chapel now stands the marble sarcophagus of St. Andochius. Its short sides and covering slab are rounded, and it is richly adorned with incised ornamentation (illus. left).

Wine of the Côte and Haute-Côte – Beaunois

The arrondissement of Beaune adjoins the southern borders of Dijon and Montbard, stretching from east to west and forming the southern part of the Côte-d'Or department. To the east, Beaune is bordered by the Saône and its valley, and in the west are the granite heights of the Morvan. At its heart is the Côte d'Or, slopes rich with vineyards extending as far as Dijon in the north and almost to Chagny to the south. The hills are divided into the Côte de Nuits and the Côte de Beaune, and a further distinction is made between these Côtes and the Hautes-Côtes, hinterland of the Côtes, where it is not quite so warm and the ground is slightly less fertile. The former Côte de Dijon had to make way for the growing city, and vineyards remain only in Marsannay-la-Côte, where one of Burgundy's few rosé wines is produced.

Along with tools and such products as oil and wine, the grape vine probably came to Burgundy in Celtic times. According to written sources, however, viticulture only began in Burgundy in the third century, and it was the large monasteries that practiced viticulture on a grand scale. After the founding of the Cistercian Order, monasteries were founded all over Burgundy. The development of wine production in the Côte d'Or was also closely tied to the dukes of Valois, who promoted the cultivation and marketing of their "house wines." It is therefore no surprise that "wine from Beaune" was considered the very finest at the close of the Middle Ages. The first wine trading houses were not established here until the 18th century; they were followed by others in Dijon and Nuits-Saint-Georges. Even today, Beaune is associated first and foremost with wine, and secondly with its famous hospital, the Hôtel-Dieu.

Nicolas Rolin, chancellor to Philip the Good, whom history has largely credited with this duke's power politics, founded the hospital in 1443 with his third wife, Guigone de Salins, to ensure the salvation of their souls. Incidentally, the wealth of the foundation is still based on the original endowment, consisting essentially of 2000 acres (800 hectares) of vineyards, some of them in Burgundy's best locations. The original foundation

Vineyard countryside in the Côte d'Or
between Aloxe-Corton and Savigny-lès-Beaune.

FOLLOWING TWO PAGES:
Beaune, Hôtel-Dieu, from 1443, inner courtyard with view of the south wing and the west wing with the museum.

In the 15th century, the city already had three other charitable institutions: Saint-Pierre dating from the 12th century, the leper house founded by Duke Eudes III, and the Maison-Dieu, supposedly founded by St. Louis in 1254. In the 17th century, two of these were placed under the jurisdiction of the Hôtel-Dieu and the third disbanded.

Beaune

The four wings of the Hôtel-Dieu enclose a spacious, rectangular courtyard. The entrance wing with a splendid late Gothic portal depicting the patron saints of the hospital—Mary, John, and St. Nicholas of Bari—houses the enormous, wooden barrel-vaulted infirmary with 24 beds lined up in two rows (illus. left and opposite). At the end of the room is a not quite life-size polychrome statue of Christ in Misery. It once stood on a console in front of the wall giving the sick the comfort of the Redeemer. The opposite narrow side opens entirely into the chapel, visible from all the beds. Until the Revolution, the winged altarpiece of Rogier van der Weyden was here. The next rooms are the nurses' dining room and the Mother Superior's room. The south and east wings are connected to each other by way of a partly external polygonal stair tower and a two-story half-timber gallery. The windows are adorned with astragals and ogival arches, and the conspicuously colorful roofs are accentuated by two rows of large wooden dormers (illus. previous pages).

These colorful roofs are surely one of the most photographed motifs in Burgundy. Once there were many more of them. Like the colors and paintings on façades, which have all but disappeared, they were integral to every important building. Neither paint nor glazed tiles are very durable, and so those seen today can hardly be original.

The Hôtel-Dieu is of the same era as the ducal residences of Beaune and Dijon. The east wing houses a second infirmary, under which a brook flows. In the south are the kitchen—with life-size dolls in costumes and original kitchenware—and the pharmacy, where (as elsewhere) well cared-for tools and instruments are preserved from the long period during which they were used. The west wing, first built in 1659, now houses the museum, which contains the wonderful winged altarpiece from the chapel, one of Rogier van der Weyden's masterpieces from the period around 1450. During the Revolution the piece was hidden away and only rediscovered in 1836. It consists of nine wooden panels and, when opened, is 31½ feet (9.6 m) wide. The kneeling donor couple, with their coat of arms and their intercessors, is depicted on the exterior of the wings, not in a corner, as was customary at the time (compare to the portal in

Beaune, Hôtel-Dieu, beds in the large infirmary (*Salle des Pauvres*).

OPPOSITE:
Beaune, Hôtel-Dieu, view through the infirmary, which measures 46 x 236 feet (14 x 72 m), into the chapel, separated by a wooden screen.

charter stipulated not only the management of the financial resources and of the house down to the last detail, but also the way the sick should be cared for, as well as the clothing, education, and lifestyle of the nurses. The Hôtel was exempt from taxes or tributes. In addition, both the patients and those working there were freed from the jurisdiction of the bishop and of the chapter of Notre-Dame. Here, one can see how closely the court of Burgundy was affiliated with the Netherlands. The model for this hospital was the hospital of Valenciennes, and the chancellor had Flemish nurses come to Beaune.

Beaune, Hôtel-Dieu,
the Last Judgment altarpiece by
Rogier van der Weyden, with wings
open, about 1450, oil on panel.

Champmol, pp. 58/59). On the inside is the Last Judgment. It is a typical Dutch painting: unstintingly realistic, admirable coloring, almost unbelievable in the accuracy of its details and depiction of materials and skin. A multitude of figures and individual scenes join together into a single marvelous picture. Elevated at the center of the work is Christ, Judge of the World, seated on a rainbow in a shining crimson cloak, surrounded by gleaming light and bordered by rainbow-tinged clouds. At his side are angels bearing the instruments of the Passion: cross and crown of thorns, lance, vinegar sponge, and the scourging post. Beneath him is Michael, weigher of souls, a slender, courtly figure in a richly ornamented cloak. He is accompanied by trumpeting angels and must send those rising from the dead, the small figures at the lower edge of the painting, either into eternal damnation

on his left, or into Paradise, to his right. On the side panels the Virgin and John are depicted as intercessors, each accompanied by six apostles as witnesses of the Judgment, and finally by four men and three women, representatives of the medieval social classes. They are probably portraits of Pope Eugene IV, Jean and Nicolas Rolin, Philip the Good, and Rolin's wife Guigone. The composition itself is determined completely by symmetry. Although there is no spatial perspective, the painting is far from monotonous: it is full of life, dignity, and grandeur. The theme of the Last Judgment faced the patients, admonishing them to reform and do penitence, and extending the promise of paradise to the just. At the same time, it encouraged the patients to remember the donors of the hospital in their prayers, placing the donors unmistakably on the side of the blessed.

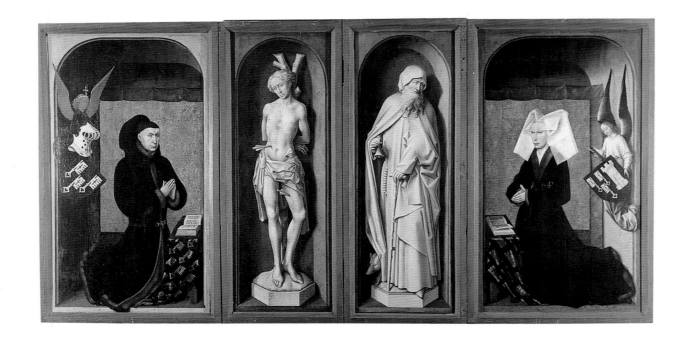

Beaune, Hôtel-Dieu, altarpiece of the
Last Judgment, outer side of the lower
wings. On the two external panels,
Nicolas Rolin and his third wife
Guigone de Salins, the donors, are
depicted kneeling. Between them stand
the two intercessors, St. Sebastian and
St. Antonius, a composition that is
similar to the somewhat older Ghent
altarpiece (illus. p. 63). There are also
similarities in the posture and coloring
of the figures.

OPPOSITE:
Beaune, Hôtel-Dieu, altarpiece of
the Last Judgment, detail. The
Archangel Michael employs scales
to weigh souls and decide between
salvation and damnation.

Beaune, Hôtel-Dieu, altarpiece of the
Last Judgment, detail. The damned
on their way to the gates of Hell.

Nicolas Rolin, the Chancellor of Burgundy

Nicolas Rolin was born about 1376, the younger
son of the lawyer Jean Rolin and his wife, Aimée
Jugnot from Autun, and was therefore *d'origine
modeste*. Like his father, he began his career study-
ing law, and later became a lawyer at the parliament in Paris. There he met the young Philip the
Good, who had become duke in 1419 under terrible circumstances. Philip must have been greatly
impressed by the much older lawyer Rolin, because he appointed him chancellor of Burgundy in
1422. Rolin has been accused of being personally
unscrupulous and politically glib; dishonesty and
cleverness are associated with his name. Therefore, it is not surprising that Rolin was often held
responsible for the opportunistic politics of Burgundy directed against France and the king, while
the image of Philip the Good as a statesman
remained intact. Even the betrayal of Joan of Arc
to the English has been blamed on Rolin. It is thus
likely that Rolin had reasons enough to sponsor a
hospital for the poor in Beaune for the salvation
of his soul, and so that the poor might pray for
him. Prior to that he had bought a large number
of estates and had repaired or renovated many of
their châteaus and fortresses. He was the owner of
palaces and hôtels in all the larger cities of
Burgundy, and had decorated many a church with
costly fixtures.

In 1443, Rolin (like the duke) commissioned
only the foremost artists of Burgundy to create the
hospital in Beaune: the Dutch architect Jacques
Wiscrère and the painter Rogier van der Weyden.
The building in general, but especially the interior,
was costly down to the smallest detail, indicating
the desire of the donors to be remembered and to
have the prayers of the patients and nurses.

Similarly, the portrait of Rolin with the Virgin,
painted about 15 years earlier, in which the viewer
looks through the window of a splendid palace
into the "world" beyond (illus. opposite), illustrates the desire of the donor for self-portrayal
and his claim to eternal salvation. Before him, the
one praying, the Queen of Heaven appears
directly with her divine Child, who holds up his
hand in benediction. He has come to free the
world of those stains that are depicted on the
capitals above Rolin's head: the Fall, Cain and
Abel, and Noah's drunkenness. And Nicolas Rolin
is the one who is to pass on this good news.

Jan van Eyck, *The Madonna of Chancellor Rolin*, ca. 1435, oil on panel, Paris, Musée du Louvre.

Beaune, Hôtel-Dieu, tapestry from the Eligius series, early 16th century.

Among the other exhibits in the Hôtel-Dieu are several sumptuous tapestry sequences, which were displayed on various special occasions, such as the *Tapisseries Roses* from the 15th century. Of this series, 30 are still in existence; they were hung in the infirmary on holidays. They depict pairs of doves alternating with monograms, coats of arms, and commentaries of the donors on a crimson background. Other treasures include the so-called Eligius tapestries from the early 16th century, a 17th-century Flemish tapestry depicting King David, two tapestries featuring St. Anthony, five tapestries with scenes from the life of the patriarch Jacob, and many others.

The logis of the chancellor and his wife no longer exists in Beaune, but an early 19th-century lithograph by A. Belin, today in the Bibliothèque municipale in Dijon, shows a view of the courtyard. At that time, a wing with a half-timber gallery ending in a polygonal stairway tower from Rolin's era was still in existence. Both of the other wings had been greatly altered by the time Belin

Beaune, view over the city from the tower of the former collegiate church of Notre-Dame.

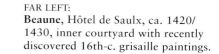

saw them. In 1843, the Hôtel Rolin was torn down. The duke also had a logis in the rue Paradis, a complex consisting of five half-timber buildings with carved beams, half-timber galleries, a polygonal stair tower, and lovely mullion windows. Today, some of these rooms house the wine museum where the history of wine is well documented. Among the exhibits are old wine presses, tools for the cultivation of wine, and everything pertaining to its enjoyment (illus. bottom and right).

In the rue Rousseau-Deslandes, two houses from the 13th century standing next to each other have been preserved. In the upper story they have lovely windows under lintels with trefoil reliefs. In addition, the so-called Maison du Chapitre at the cloister of Notre-Dame also dates from the 13th century (illus. top right). Its gable end is articulated by numerous bifora with delicate small columns, head consoles, trefoils, and sturdy cased arches (compare with the Maison Bélime in Vitteaux, illus. p. 140).

In the early 16th century the Hôtel de la Mare (or Rochepot) was built. On the ground floor, two shop arcades and a portal open to the street. In the two upper stories are two rows of tall windows with richly profiled frames. A surprising gallery façade with four rows of flat-arched arcades and medallions in the spandrels comprise the view from the courtyard.

The Hôtel de Saulx (illus. top left) was supposedly built in the early 15th century at the behest of the chancellor Jean de Saulx. In its layout, it is quite similar to the Palais des Ducs in the rue Paradis. Two wings adjoin two sides of a rectangular donjon; they have a stair tower in common that gives access to both. Two wings, both of which are only partially original, border the trapezoid-shaped courtyard to the south and east. An elaborate and very decorative 16th-century grisaille painting was recently discovered on the two half-timber courtyard façades. It had been hidden for centuries under old layers of plaster.

pointed barrel vault with transverse arches. This is similar to but less elegant than the construction in Autun. Horizontal cornices lead around strongly projecting vertical elements that give the room a firm sense of structure, but the fine effects of light and shadow created by the delicate profiling in Autun are not to be found here.

The 13th century also saw installation of the more modern clerestory in the high choir as well as High Gothic ribbed vaulting. On the outside, buttresses were added, making the choir seem steeper and more compact. The cloister—all that remains of it are two bays (illus. opposite top)—and the chapter hall also belong to this period. The recessed portal leading from the transept to the cloister, however, is Romanesque and part of the original building. Around 1300 the narthex was built, an airy structure open to three sides on a base of numerous steps. It has both the width and the basilica-elevation of the nave (illus. below), and recalls the churches of the Virgin Mary in Dijon and Semur-en-Auxois. The two supports dividing the central aisle from the side aisles are high and delicate, and the transverse arches and

Beaune, former collegiate church of Notre-Dame, from 1125/1130, choir, transept, and crossing tower.

Beaune, former collegiate church of Notre-Dame, view through the narthex dating from about 1300.

Notre-Dame in Beaune

About 1125/1130, the former collegiate church of Notre-Dame was begun. Like the church of Saint-Lazare in Autun and others, Notre-Dame is in the tradition of Cluny III. By mid-century the choir, crossing, and transept as well as four bays of the nave were already completed; the two deeper west bays were built according to the original plan in the 13th century. The three-aisle nave (illus. opposite bottom) is followed by a five-part transept with a square crossing, a bay preceding the choir, and an ambulatory with three semicircular chapels. The elevation is three-fold: arcades, a blind triforium, and a clerestory are topped by a

Beaune, former collegiate church of Notre-Dame, remains of the cloister from the late 13th century.

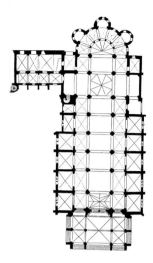

Beaune, former collegiate church of Notre-Dame, floor plan.

Beaune, former collegiate church of Notre-Dame, view through the nave and side aisles to the east.

ribs seem to rise up effortlessly from the goblet-shaped capitals. It is a great loss for the narthex that the statue ensemble of the three portals disappeared during the French Revolution.

The exterior of Notre-Dame—as simple as the interior—is primarily effective due to the stereometry of the structural elements, which peak in a lovely crossing tower (illus. opposite). The lateral chapels date from the late 14th century. Especially noteworthy are the Rolin Chapel in the north (the second from the west), and the Bouton Chapel in the south (first from the west). The former was donated in 1470 by Cardinal Jean Rolin, who had it painted with the Miracle of Lazarus and the Stoning of St. Stephen. The Bouton Chapel is a bit newer. Bouton, a canon, was captivated by the new style from Italy and had the chapel built in 1525–1533. It is fitted with a coffered ceiling of stone, revealing familiarity with Renaissance forms. The fine lines of the statue niches also belong to the new style, although the baldachins still show traces of late Gothic. The chapel entrance and its exterior decoration also are mainly Renaissance.

The interior of Notre-Dame also includes the stone slab with line engravings that belonged to the original main altar, two stone altars from the 16th century in the side chapels, and especially fine tapestries that depict the life of the Virgin Mary in a series of 19 scenes. They, too, were supposedly commissioned by Cardinal Rolin in Tournai in 1474. Measuring 20 x 6 feet (6 x 1.9 m), the tapestries were hung in the choir on holidays.

Savigny-lès-Beaune, view over vineyards towards the city and its château.

Savigny-lès-Beaune

In the Beaunois are several well-preserved late medieval aristocratic estates that number among the most beautiful in Burgundy. Their charm is irresistable. Because of the many additions and changes undertaken over the centuries, they embody a survey of the cultural history of Burgundy. Savigny-lès-Beaune, home of a wonderful white wine, is closest to the city. Approaching from the south through hills strewn with wildflowers, the buildings in the valley are visible from afar. The so-called Grand Château is a basically rectangular structure with four circular towers—two wide ones at the back and two more slender on the entrance side—and a moat (illus. below). A west main wall and a drawbridge once completed the complex. Jean de Frôlois had the structure built about 1340. The four round towers are crowned with battlements on stepped corbels that were added in about 1450. Battlements may have run around the entire structure at some point, but because the main walls were constructed of painted wood, they did not last. Jean d'Amboise destroyed the complex at the behest of Louis XI in

Savigny-lès-Beaune, Château de Savigny, 1340/ca. 1450, view into the inner courtyard, now open.

Savigny-lès-Beaune, so-called Petit Château, after 1617, entrance side.

Cîteaux, former Cistercian abbey, exhibit room in the late Gothic library building of the monastery.

1478. The three-wing building now standing was built on old foundations over the course of the 17th century, though parts of the cellar and ground floor were left in their original form. The entrance gate, the large barrel-vaulted hall articulated by engaged pilasters in the east wing, and the chapel in the northeast tower are 19th-century additions. The rooms, which are badly in need of renovation, now house an exhibition of old motorcycles. There is also a collection of war planes in the park.

A visit to the so-called Petit Château is more worthwhile. It was built by Bénigne Bouhier after 1617 in the Italian Mannerist style on the site of older subsidiary buildings (illus. above). The garden architecture is characterized by square porous stone blocks alternated with *mur vermiculé* around the windows and doors, and deep, angular blind arches and oculi above the French doors. A wine shop is now located here.

Cîteaux

Of the former abbey of Cîteaux, once the heart of the Cistercian Order, so little now remains that it is hard to find. There are, however, vestiges in the low-lying areas of the Saône on the small Vouge River. This is where Robert of Molesme (1029–1111) founded a monastery in 1098 as an alternative to Cluny, the *novum monasterium*. Cîteaux and its small community of monks thrived under abbots Alberich (1099–1109) and Stephen Harding (1109–1134), becoming the mother house and normative monastery to about 740 Cistercian monasteries all over Europe (see pp. 120 f.). Today a small community of Trappist monks lives on this site in modern buildings, and the plans of the church and entire complex can only be deduced from sources. Only a Romanesque chapel and a late Gothic library building remain; the latter is an impressive ruin with what was once a vaulted external gallery on the ground floor and a large vaulted hall with tracery windows in the upper story (illus. left). Although the architecture of the Cistercian Order was at first characterized by aesthetic austerity, they apparently could not entirely resist the general love of decoration at that time: the brickwork on the walls between the pier buttresses is laid in various patterns (illus. p. 121).

Vougeot, Château du Clos de Vougeot, view of the whole complex and the surrounding vineyards.

BELOW:
Vougeot, Château du Clos de Vougeot, from 1551 on, inner courtyard.

OPPOSITE:
Vougeot, Château du Clos de Vougeot, Renaissance hall in the upper story.

Château du Clos de Vougeot

One of the most famous wines is connected with the name Château du Clos de Vougeot, another 12th-century Cistercian monastery. Little more than the exterior form of the complex is still standing today. The sparsely decorated buildings around the trapezoidal court were commissioned by Abbot Jean Loisier from 1551 on (illus. right). The two residential wings are characterized by a mixture of Renaissance motifs, such as fluted columns and beams, and late medieval touches such as the windows. The three-aisle hall on the south side was part of the original building, except for some newer additions. It was given a wooden gallery in 1551, as was in fashion at the time of the dukes. Four old wine presses are still preserved in the pressing room in the west.

By way of a stone stairway with a coffered ceiling, one reaches the Renaissance rooms of the first floor. They still have their original interior fittings—wood paneling, fireplaces, floors—and today wines of the region are displayed and marketed here (illus. opposite).

The Wines of Burgundy

Vougeot, Château du Clos de Vougeot. Wine harvest: the hand-picked grapes are poured through a funnel into a harvester's hopper.

Pinot Noir grapes.

Some basic requirements

If some of the noblest wines of the world are grown in Burgundy, this is first and foremost due to the climate, the soil, and the type of grapes; but also to thousands of years of accumulated experience in cultivation and wine production.

Burgundy has a central European continental climate with winters that are often cold, and hot, dry summers. The vagaries of the weather result in marked differences among various vintages. The vineyards, at least those of the superior appellations, lie on well-drained slopes that face the sun, with their backs to the prevailing west wind that brings rain. The barren, stony soil is optimally suited for wine cultivation, as it forces the roots of the vines to grow deep down. The soil consists predominately of lime, clay, and silica; the mixture of these elements determines the character and aromatic expression of the wines. Lime promotes aromas, finesse, and volume; clay, the dark color, the distinctive structure, and tannin; silica, the lightness and palatability. Diverse minerals support the bouquet and lingering taste.

Climate and soil find their best expression in two outstanding types of grapes native to Burgundy, the white Chardonnay and the dark Pinot Noir.

Chardonnay vines sprout early, making them susceptible to late frosts, but they also ripen early and yield an especially sweet grape. Chardonnay is not a very aromatic type, but mirrors the precise site on which it is grown in the relationship of extract, acid, and sugar. Pinot Noir, also known as Savignin Noir or Spätburgunder, is sensitive and fickle. Only when the yield is kept low and the small grapes are allowed to ripen does it develop a delicious berry character, even when young. Through aging it gains a very complex bouquet and an incomparable finesse on the palate.

The heart of Burgundian wine cultivation is the slopes of the Côte d'Or. The red wines of the Côte de Nuits in general, and its 24 *Grands Crus* in particular, are famous for the excellent and differentiated expression that the Pinot draws from the soil. These lie in a narrow strip of land beginning in Gevrey-Chambertin south of Combe Lavaux, ending with La Tâche. When young, the wines are a dark, brilliant red. Their fragrance is distinguished by intense fruit aromas which suggest black, or sometimes red, berries. The *Grands Crus* fascinate the palate with a silky fullness, masking their robust structure. This derives from the fine tannins on one hand, and a certain touch of pleasant sourness on the other. Together they guarantee the long aging potential of the wines.

The *Grands Crus* of the Côte de Beaune present themselves in a completely different way from those of the Côte de Nuits. For one, these are two decidedly different zones, namely Corton and Montrachet, which lie comparatively far apart. For another, with one exception, exclusively white wines are grown here. Montrachet is the unrivaled champion of dry white wines. The slopes facing south and southeast receive maximal sun because the incline of the slope is so slight.

Chablis

Chablis, the world's most famous and most often imitated white wine, has a long history. In fact, it has had to surmount various hurdles before it could regain the fame it once enjoyed. In the early Middle Ages, Cistercians promoted the cultivation of wine in Chablis and its surroundings. In 1128, they built the estate Petit Pontigny, whose cellar had room for 53,000 gallons (2,000 hl) of wine—today it houses the headquarters of the wine-growers' association. Thanks to the monks, the wine pressed here from Chardonnay grapes was soon renowned. Proximity to Paris was also an important factor; the wine traveled from the neighboring town of Auxerre to Paris by way of the rivers Yonne and Seine. At the beginning of the

16th century, Chablis had almost 2,500 acres (1,000 hectares) of vines yielding fruit. Just over 100 years later the English took an interest in this dry white wine, and in 1770, Chablis was the first white Burgundy auctioned off at Christie's. In the 19th century it became truly successful, and this is the base on which its fame rests today. The approximately 70 communities producing Chablis exported not only to northern European countries, but also to Russia and the USA. At the same time, new vineyards were planted throughout the department of Yonne until they covered 106,000 acres (43,000 hectares). The phylloxera, or vine louse, brought catastrophe in 1893, putting an end to this mass production. Wars, economic depressions, and the migration of farmers to cities finished the job. By 1945, Chablis cultivation had shrunk to a mere 1,235 acres (500 hectares).

It was difficult to start anew. Vines were often damaged by late frosts in April and May, resulting in the loss of an entire harvest and discouraging the vintners. Finally, in the late 1950s measures were taken to protect the vines. First, *chauffrettes* were placed in the vineyards. At first these ovens were heated with petroleum, then with oil. Later a more ecological alternative was introduced, namely *aspersion*, or sprinkling. As soon as the temperature sinks to 32 °F (0 °C) sprinklers are activated. A fine mist then freezes on the vines, forming a shield of ice around the buds that protects them from severe damage. As frost protection measures and modern, mechanized methods of cultivation improved, the inhabitants' interest in wine growing also picked up. In 1970, 1,850 acres (750 hectares) were planted; this area doubled in the following decade. The area cultivated continued to increase throughout the 1990s, reaching about 9,900 acres (4,000 hectares) in 1998.

In 1938, Chablis was granted an *appellation d'origine contrôlée* that encompassed sites in 20 communities, with the stipulation, however, that the soil in which the vines were grown had to consist of the shell limestone that is best suited to Chablis. In 1943, the designation *Petit Chablis* included sites with other kinds of soil. In addition, improvements in wine production techniques were an important factor in the development of modern Chablis. Old wooden fermenting vats were abandoned, and cellars were equipped with hygienic steel tanks. Regulated fermentation temperatures and processes that prohibit any oxidation led to production of wines of reliable quality, with a predominantly fresh, fruity, and mineral character. In this way a method was created that led to the world-wide success of Chablis, a wine destined to be both an aperitif and the ideal companion to seafood and fish.

Chardonnay grapes on the shell limestone soil typical of the Chablis area.

Burgundy has a plethora of appellations that form a kind of hierarchical pyramid. The base consists of regional appellations, which make up more than half of all the Burgundy wines. A third is taken up by communal appellations, the *villages*. Finally, a little more than a tenth is classed as *Premier Cru*, but only 1.7% of Burgundy wines have been granted the highest distinction and are considered *Grand Cru*.

Vougeot, Château du Clos de Vougeot, an old wine press.

Châteauneuf-en-Auxois

Leaving the Côtes and the Hautes-Côtes heading west, you again meet up with the picturesque Canal de Bourgogne. High above it, on a rock plateau, lies the charming village of Châteauneuf with its spur château (illus. opposite). In 1175 Jean de Chaudenay set aside some of his estate, Chaudenay, for his youngest son, naming it Châteauneuf. On the peak of the spur, a small, irregular castle with a square donjon, a walled courtyard, and a trench was built. It probably extended to the present-day north gate. In the mid-14th century, the complex attained its current dimensions, that is, an enclosed not-quite-square courtyard was added in the east. Guyot de Châteauneuf had a small late Gothic logis added onto the donjon in 1420, and had a chapel built. His daughter, Cathérine, was the last of the family Châteauneuf. She was burned at the stake in Paris in 1456 for having poisoned her husband, Jacques d'Aussonville. Her property fell to the duke, who presented it to his chancellor, Philippe Pott. Pott had the château modernized. The circular corner towers, accompanied by slender stair towers, date from this time, as does the north entrance gate flanked by towers and decorated with the coat of arms of the Pott family. The east gate was also moved and decorations affixed, and both a splendid logis with large, richly profiled windows in the northeast and a second logis on the south main wall (illus. left) were built. The latter was added between the old logis and the chapel, and has a *Grande Salle* on the ground floor. The polygonal stair tower with its stately portal masks the seam

Châteauneuf-en-Auxois, château, main façade of the southern logis, after 1456. This logis is connected by a stair tower to the older building where the family lived (ca. 1420) and the donjon (ca. 1175).

Châteauneuf-en-Auxois, château, northern logis with stair tower set into the interior, after 1456, courtyard façade.

between the old building and the new, giving access to both buildings, but it is thus not centered in the façade like other stair towers of its time. The abundance of decoration on windows, portals, fireplaces, and dormers discloses the wealth of the powerful owner and his need to display his position; even the masonry consists of strikingly large and carefully worked blocks of stone.

The Pott family was succeeded in Châteauneuf by the de Montmorency family in 1543, who were followed by the Vienne family in 1597. Most likely, Charles de Vienne, who loved building projects,

was responsible for altering the small portal and the windows of the southern logis in the first half of the 17th century. Thereafter, the château was not consistently inhabited and fell increasingly into disrepair until the 19th century, when restoration put an end to the decline. Late Gothic fireplaces from Courcelles-lès-Semur found their way into the southern logis, while the wood paneling of the chapel can now be admired in Commarin. This haphazard method of monument preservation common in the 19th century has caused numerous difficulties for later scholarly research.

Châteauneuf-en-Auxois,
château, south side of the complex with donjon, main wall, battlements, and towers.

donjon built during the first half of the 13th century. It is a not quite perfectly square complex, with circular corner towers, a square gatehouse in the center of the south main wall, and inner constructions that only leave a narrow courtyard open. The north side has an angle at its mid-point and four bifora, almost symmetrically placed, which were renovated in the 19th century. The masonry is, as always in such cases, excellent. A deep moat ran along three sides of the donjon, ending on the north side in a trench, while the fourth side was protected by the steepness of the rocks. Only one model seems possible for this unusually well thought-out, symmetrical, and stately complex: Druyes-les-Belles-Fontaines (illus. p. 339), the château built by Pierre de Courtenay in order to compete with his cousin, Philip II August, who had the new Louvre erected in Paris

Mont-Saint-Jean, fortress, 10th century/first half of 13th century, view of the window façade framed by towers facing the valley.

Commarin

The château of Commarin (illus. right) in the plains north of Châteauneuf-en-Auxois has also existed since the 12th century, and was in the possession of the de Cortiambles family from 1346 onwards. When Jacques de Cortiambles was chamberlain to Philip the Bold and later standard-bearer to John the Fearless, he rebuilt the family estate. Around 1400/1410 it became a double square complex with six circular towers and had a gate tower and a system of moats that enclosed both courtyards, the logis, and the outbuildings. Extensive gardens also belonged to the estate. All that remains today are the two middle circular towers with double recessed windows from the façades that formerly faced the courtyard, part of the east wing, the chapel (without the wood paneling!), and the outer walls, which are marred by an early-18th-century façade on the south side. Jacques de Cortiambles' buildings seem to have been less durable than those in Châteauneuf, as many started to collapse as early as 1620; others were torn down. The towers and main wall were sacrificed in order to have a stately and modern *cour d'honneur*. In 1702 construction began on the façades of the southern wing, with its typical 18th-century motifs, and on the buildings in the northern part of the *cour d'honneur*.

Mont-Saint-Jean

The enormous hilltop château of Mont-Saint-Jean lies on an inaccessible rock plateau in the granite hills of Auxois, not far from Mont Tasselot (illus. above). This plateau seems to already have been fortified in the 10th century by a wall which then determined the dimensions of the later complex. Guillaume II de Mont-Saint-Jean, one of the most powerful men of Burgundy in his time, had the

shortly before 1200. Undoubtedly this type of structure was a symbol of power at the outset of the 13th century, one that only the most important families of France might make use of. The dukes of the House of Capet also built a number of square complexes with donjons in the 13th century. It is amazing to think that, aside from a few interior alterations, this enormous complex survived for centuries almost unchanged.

Still older than the donjon are the beginnings of the chapel. It had one nave, a projecting transept, and three apses. Its small crypt supposedly once held the relics of St. Pelagia. Today a grave there bears the inscriptions of a bishop from around 1200. In the 16th century, the chapel was given side aisles. Its remarkable interior fittings include a stone retable and a wooden reliquary box, as well as numerous Burgundian sculptures.

LEFT:
Mont-Saint-Jean, entrance side.

Commarin, château, ca. 1410/18th century, view into the inner courtyard with the two late medieval towers and the Baroque façades of the logis.

La Rochepot

La Rochepot is also a complex dating from the High Middle Ages. Alexandre de Bourgogne, for whom the château of Marigny-le-Cahouet was built a short time later, supposedly had La Rochepot erected shortly before 1200 on the spur above the road leading from Basel to Moulis. In 1403 the castle was in the hands of the duke's chamberlain Régnier Pott, who left it to his son Philip on his death. The striking similarity between La Rochepot and Châteauneuf is not due to their having the same owner or the same architect. La Rochepot was renovated and repaired in 1669 and in 1741. During the Revolution it burned down and its ruins were sold. Not until the early 20th century did the Carnot family commission the architect Charles Suisse and the sculptor Xavier Schanosky to rebuild the castle. Where should they look for prototypes but to Châteauneuf and the Hôtel-Dieu in Beaune? The two logis in the south and west of the approximately triangular complex are furnished in a primarily neo-Gothic style. Next to the entrance gate with drawbridge and barbicans stands the chapel, which was erected in the 13th century.

LEFT:
La Rochepot, château, ca. 1200/20th century, view of the entire complex and the surrounding countryside.

La Rochepot, château, view from the battlements into the inner courtyard.

DÉPARTEMENT
SAÔNE-ET-LOIRE

S aône-et-Loire is the southernmost department in Burgundy, and it consists of four arrondissements: Chalon-sur-Saône in the northeast, Autun in the northwest, Charolles in the southwest, and Mâcon in the southeast. It is bordered in the southwest by the Loire, which departs from the border of Burgundy north of Bourbon-Lancy in a northwesterly direction, and by the Saône to the southeast.

Limestone Ridge and Floodplain of the Bresse – Chalonnais

One glance at a map of the Chalon-sur-Saône arrondissement makes clear the distinction between this region and the landscapes already introduced. Here the Saône River divides the department almost in half, and the Bresse, the alluvial plain in the east, is only sparsely inhabited with isolated farmsteads. There is not much in the way of art to be found here, but the abundant woods and water of the Bresse have other qualities. Just as grapes in

PREVIOUS TWO PAGES:
Pierreclos, château, view from the west of the old donjon and tower of the castle chapel, second half of the 12th century, and of the newer donjon (right), from 1434.

LEFT:
River scene in Bresse: the Doubs.

Free-roaming Bresse poultry.

TOP RIGHT:
Saint-Trivier-de-Courtes, Ferme de la Forêt, 16th/17th centuries, now an open-air museum, well.

Countryside near Pourlans
in the north of Bresse.

Côte-d'Or and the famous vineyards of Yonne have been cultivated since the Middle Ages, the highest quality poultry has been bred and cultivated here. Bresse chickens were served to the dukes, according to records. Architecture in the Bresse is almost exclusively half-timber with brick; buildings tend to be small and carefully placed, without plaster coating or chalk priming, giving the landscape a unique character. An especially charming *maison bressane* is the Ferme de la Forêt in Saint-Trivier-de-Courtes, dating from the 16th

and 17th centuries. Today it serves as a cultural museum (illus. above, opposite). There are some 30 additional complexes of this type in the surrounding area, all dating from the 17th and 18th centuries. Typical is not only the construction material, but also the enormous free-standing fireplace inside, its chimney ending in a so-called *cheminée sarrasine*, a one or more story turret modeled on the bell towers of churches. Years ago, they also had a bell whose ring regulated the course of the day on these isolated farms.

Saint-Trivier-de-Courtes, Ferme de la Forêt, residential and farm buildings.

Saint-Trivier-de-Courtes, Ferme de la Forêt, farming implements.

Pierre-de-Bresse, Château de Pierre, from 1680, view into the expansive, stately inner courtyard.

Pierre-de-Bresse, Château de Terrans, from 1765, main façade and subsidiary buildings.

Pierre-de-Bresse

One of the few châteaux in Bresse, far to the north, is Château de Pierre in Pierre-de-Bresse (illus. above). Claude de Thyard began building an enormous Baroque complex here about 1680 on the site of a medieval castle. Three brick wings form a spacious *cour d'honneur*, enclosed in the west by a wrought iron gate. In Burgundy this type of structure—the even square surrounded by a moat with circular corner towers—had a long tradition and was not easily relinquished. On the east side, the towers even had battlements on stepped corbels. The well-proportioned main façade has few adorn-

ments, but the effect of its protruding two-axis bay, with split pediment and columns joined by arches, is very pleasing. At the side wings the arcades become a blind articulation.

In the same town, Château de Terrans (illus. below) is a small private château begun in 1765 for Jean-François-Guillaume de Truchis by the architect Edme Verniquet. The slightly protruding one-axis portal on the façade of the two-story building is framed by attached pilasters or ashlars. Pillars joined by arcades articulate the ground floor of the detached wings, and an iron gate with two portal pillars frames the *cour d'honneur*.

Louhans

The only small city in Bresse is Louhans, on the banks of the Seille. Here one finds a number of markets with traditions reaching back to the Middle Ages, for example butter, egg and poultry, cattle, and pig markets. Trading brought wealth to Louhans early on, as can be seen in the medieval houses on the Grande Rue with their arcaded passageways built on columns and pillars of stone and wood. The wares could be spread out under their protective covering. Like all important medieval cities in Burgundy, Louhans had a Hôtel-Dieu, now a building dating from the 18th century, whose infirmary hardly differs in its partitionings from those in medieval times. The pharmacy with its 18th-century wooden paneling is especially lovely, and a considerable collection of hand-blown glass vessels and faience works are on display. In addition, the pharmacy has a pietà dating from the 16th century—perhaps from the infirmary. It is one of the rare depictions of Mary kneeling and lamenting her dead Son.

Chalon-sur-Saône

The banks of the Saône are more densely settled. With the founding of Massalia by the Greeks in the 6th century BC, the course of the Rhône and Saône became an important trade route. Chalon-sur-Saône, once Cabillonum, was founded by the Romans. It was a harbor city and a supply center for Caesar, but nothing remains from that time today except for a few vestiges of a city wall. In the 6th century, during the period of tribal migrations, Chalon was intermittently the capital of a Burgundian realm situated along the Rhône and Saône, extending almost to the Mediterranean in the south, up to the vicinity of the Upper Rhine in the northeast, and including Savoy to the east.

From the 5th century on, the city was a diocese and had a cathedral, Saint-Vincent, whose wealth of columns, marble sheathing, and mosaics were praised in accounts by Gregory of Tours. Saint-Vincent was destroyed by the Saracens, giving rise to a new building in the Carolingian era which, as was the practice everywhere, made ample use of the previous structure. In the early 12th century, a three-aisle basilica with transept and three apses was built here. With the exception of the central apse, the entire ground floor and the groin vaulting in the side aisles have been preserved. From 1230/1235 the main apse and the upper stories were renovated in High Gothic style; the triforium in the nave (perhaps unfinished until then) was only completed in 1310. In front of the clerestory, as in the choir, runs "a Burgundian walkway" (illus. right). The church ceiling was not vaulted until 1374. In the 15th and 16th centuries, the

side chapels in the nave and southern choir area were added, which is characteristic of the prospering middle class of the late Middle Ages.

The spatial impression of the church is thoroughly Gothic, even if the arcades seem rather massive and the pillars and capitals recall the cathedral of Autun since their 19th-century restoration. The transept, on the other hand, retained its original pointed vaulting with a late Gothic window beneath each segment, and the side aisles of the choir with apsidals are also original. In the choir you can see the baldachin of a wall-niche tomb, which once bore a Crucifixion group, and

Chalon-sur-Saône, view across the Saône towards the city.

BELOW LEFT:
Chalon-sur-Saône, former cathedral of Saint-Vincent, early 12th century to 1374, nave and side aisles.

Chalon-sur-Saône, former cathedral of Saint-Vincent, capital in the nave, 12th century.

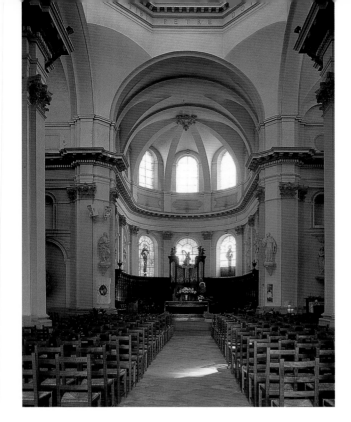

Chalon-sur-Saône, Place Saint-Vincent, half-timber houses.

RIGHT:
Chalon-sur-Saône, Hôtel-Dieu, founded 1528, 18th-century laboratory.

FAR RIGHT:
Chalon-sur-Saône, Hôtel-Dieu, 18th-century pharmacy.

the so-called Crozier of St. Lupus, a 12th-century reliquary with an ivory cross. Late Gothic sculptures, doorways, and screens, including some of superior quality, adorn the side chapels.

At one side is an adjoining cloister from the late 14th century, an elegant and delicate structure that has unfortunately been somewhat disfigured by ungainly newer buttresses. The construction of the double-tower façade was delayed until 1844. It is one of the earliest neo-Gothic façades in France. Although it is perfectly executed, it nevertheless lacks strength and seems frail.

The Place Saint-Vincent and the streets leading from it are to a large extent lined by medieval gabled houses adorned with carvings and medallions (illus. left)—a lovely example of historical

city planning and design of city squares, even though the paving stones currently in place do not work well. Here in Chalon, Nicolas Rolin also had a town house called La Chancelière, consisting of a tower and one wing. Shortly before this ensemble burned down in 1791, it was depicted in an engraving from 1780, published in 1841/1842 in the *Album historique et pittoresque du département de Saône-et-Loire*. The donjon, probably four stories, was divided at the center on one long side by a polygonal stair tower whose upper stories were accompanied by a second turret on a corbel. Apparently there were also battlements on a stepped corbel on this side, but it was already missing on the long side by the 18th century. The pitched roof is in all probability not original. The logis adjoined the donjon next to the stair tower, which surely provided access to both buildings, and apparently two circular towers stood at the free end of the logis. The windows can no longer be discerned. As this residence was built at the same time as the new wing of the Palais des Ducs in Dijon, this is a likely model.

While Nicolas Rolin's residence in Chalon was being built, his son Jean was the bishop of the cathedral from 1431 to 1436. Nicolas donated memorials there to his father and to his mother, Marie de Landes.

The former Saint Peter's Abbey, today located near the river, is said to have been founded by Bishop Flavius. On an elevation above the city, facilities for a small community of monks were erected in 584 in the vicinity of an older oratory. This complex was destroyed in an onslaught by the Saracens in 887, then later renovated by Bishop Gilbod and placed under the rule of St. Benedict. During the 12th and 13th centuries, the

Chalon-sur-Saône, Hôtel des Messageries, Niepce Museum, projector.

RIGHT:
Chalon-sur-Saône, Hôtel des Messageries, Niepce Museum, exhibit.

As the son of an advisor to the king, Niepce was wealthy enough to be able to devote himself entirely to his research. In addition to developing photography, he invented an internal combustion engine together with his brother. He was not able to make a commercial success of either invention and died in poverty.

Chalon-sur-Saône, Hôtel des Messageries, Niepce Museum, bust of Nicéphore Niepce (1765–1833).

monastery was converted into a castle with walls, towers, moats, and a donjon. Francis I extended the fortification in the 16th century, but in 1562 it was captured by the Calvinists during the Wars of Religion and expanded into a citadel. After the conquest, the monks left their abbey. Unsuccessful in their attempts to find shelter in other monasteries of the city, they erected a new church and monastic buildings, which were consecrated by Bishop Pontus de Thyard in 1580. These were probably only temporary quarters, as new monastic buildings arose again from 1684, and a new church, begun in 1693, was consecrated in 1713. Saint-Pierre is one of the few Baroque complexes of this area, a cruciform building with monumental pilasters supporting a high encircling entablature with a sturdy cornice. Above, in the transept arms, are round-arched windows above a delicately profiled balustrade and groin vaulting; in the choir is a semidome with curved molding above lunettes (illus. opposite). The choir stalls date from the 17th century. The crossing is crowned by an octagonal dome and a tambour resting on pendentives. In the early 20th century, the façade was renovated and the northern transept arm widened.

In 1528, the jurors of the city founded a hospital on the island, the Hôpital Saint-Laurent. Like the one founded by Nicolas Rolin in Beaune, it was based on Flemish models. It once had a lovely late Gothic façade towards the river and steep, colorful roofs. Continually in use and exclusively financed through the donations of citizens, the hospital is still used as a clinic today. Some of the buildings and furnishings are preserved: for example, the original building with stepped gables and mullion windows on the river side with the mother superior's room, a private sick room, and a small oratory; the old 17th-century refectory with wonderful wood paneling in the style of Louis XV and a passageway to the vaulted kitchens with cupboards full of pewter dishes; and the somewhat unsuccessful chapel of Emiland Gauthey from 1770, in which the furnishings of torn-down buildings are on display. They include wooden paneling, a rare pietà from Sluter's workshop, a pulpit and the three choir portals from the older chapel, a basin for consecrated water, and many other pieces. The pharmacy and laboratory are set apart as a museum in a small, separate pavilion. These are interesting rooms, wood-paneled with faience pieces and historical laboratory instruments (illus. opposite).

The Tour du Doyenné, which once stood near the cathedral, is now nearby. This building was taken down in 1907 and reconstructed on the island. On the opposite riverbank, the Roseraie Saint-Nicolas was established in a bend of the

Saône, a botanical garden where primarily roses are grown in a mild micro-climate.

Two famous names are associated with the city of Chalon: Vivant Denon and Nicéphore Niepce. Each has a museum dedicated to him. Denon, the sketcher and engraver, was artistic advisor to Napoleon I. He founded and furthered many museums in addition to introducing lithography to France and is considered co-founder of the science of Egyptology. The Musée Denon is in a subsidiary building of the former Ursuline convent. On the ground floor are regional prehistoric finds. Upstairs is a collection of paintings from the 17th to the 19th centuries, including important works of the Italian, Dutch, and French schools; numerous medieval pieces; objects of historical and cultural interest from Chalon—shipping items, furniture, tools, ceramics, models—and finally works by Denon and his contemporaries.

The Niepce Museum in the Hôtel des Messageries near the Saône is a museum of photography, as Niepce is the inventor of the art (illus. left). It was made popular, however, by Daguerre (daguerrotype), who, far more business-oriented than Niepce, marketed his invention. In lovely rooms, the museum exhibits instruments that project light, the development of the camera, historical photographs, and much more (illus. above).

Rully, château, last third of the 13th century, view of the east side of the complex with the wing and battlements from the 15th century, and 17th-century windows.

Rully, château, view through the 18th-century *basse-cour* to the entrance of the inner courtyard, protected by a trench, drawbridge, and battlements.

Rully

In the Chalonnais are also a number of very old and picturesque aristocratic estates. The northernmost of these is the Château de Rully, located in a famous wine-producing area. The complex arises out of the rows of vines as though standing on a tray. The promontory over the Saône and Agneux rivers has been fortified since at least the 10th century, but the oldest parts of the square complex with donjon and circular corner towers only date from the last third of the 13th century. In the mid-15th century, the complex was modernized and extended through the addition of wings—on which a few mullion windows are still original—the impressive battlements on stepped corbels that run along the fortification walls, and a moat on the south and east sides that forms a plateau for the enclosure. There was probably a gallery on the west side, indicated by traces on the walls of the donjon. In the interior, some of the rooms are still late medieval, untouched by the 17th-century renovations, including the groin-vaulted kitchen (illus. above). The old *basse-cour*, which lay outside the original defensive trench to the south, was straightened out in the 18th century. Since then, symmetrical rows of farm buildings have lined a straight entrance driveway. The trench was filled in and the logis modernized once again. The neo-Gothic additions to the donjon were among the last projects to be completed.

TOP RIGHT:
Rully, château, 15th-century kitchen with fireplace and groin vaulting.

RIGHT:
Rully, château, inner courtyard with façades that were altered in the 17th and 19th centuries.

Mellecey

Farther south where the hills of Côte-d'Or continue by the name of Côte Chalonnaise, one finds the Château de Germolles in the vicinity of Mellecey. Visiting this rather modest complex, one would hardly suspect that it has one of the most interesting histories of all the castles in Burgundy. At the time it was completed, no other complex could rival its exquisite beauty. About 1380, Margaret, the wealthy Flemish wife and heiress of Philip the Bold, had her private residence built here, which was in no way inferior to the residences of her husband or his brothers, neither in architecture nor interior decoration. The architect was Drouet de Dammartin, whose brother, Guy de Dammartin, was famous as the *général maistre des œuvres du Duc de Berry* (the master architect for the Duke of Berry). The interior paintings were executed by Jean de Beaumetz, and Claus Sluter created a Madonna for the gatehouse, numerous fireplace settings, and a flat relief—probably a tympanum for the main portal of the logis. The subject of the relief was programmatic: the duke and duchess under a tree, surrounded by a herd of sheep. The ducal couple as shepherd and shepherdess—almost 400 years before Marie Antoinette's *Trianon*! The idea of making space for a simple pastoral life was Margaret's own, for as a young girl she had had the opportunity to become acquainted with the writings of Petrarch, who praised a secluded life in the countryside.

Thanks to surviving accounting records, it is possible to reconstruct the entire complex, which combined a residence with a model estate run in an exemplary economical manner, as well as the interior furnishings and décor down to the smallest detail. The buildings formed a long, rectangular courtyard, enclosed by a double-tower entrance gate in the northeast that took up the entire width of the courtyard. This structure is thought to have resembled the entrance gate to Mehun-sur-Yèvre, the favorite residence of the Duke of Berry. Wings adjoined the towers on both sides, flanked at the corners by elegant turrets on corbels. Only the largely intact southeastern wing is still standing today. The once richly ornamented two-story chapel (illus. opposite) was adjacent to the apartments of the duke and duchess and their

Mellecey, Château de Germolles, capitals at the fireplace in the Salle des Gardes (by Claus Sluter?).

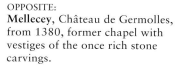

OPPOSITE:
Mellecey, Château de Germolles, from 1380, former chapel with vestiges of the once rich stone carvings.

Mellecey, Château de Germolles, late medieval painted walls: P stands for Philippe le Hardi (Philip the Bold), M for Marguerite de Flandre (Margaret of Flanders).

Saint-Ambreuil, former abbey of La Ferté, palace of the abbot, late 17th/early 18th century, and 1760 main façade.

Saint-Ambreuil, former abbey of La Ferté, palace of the abbot, vestibule with the grand staircase, 1760/1770.

children. The so-called *grande vis* (grand spiral staircase), whose portal was adorned with Sluter's pastoral relief, was undoubtedly inspired by the *grande vis* of the Louvre, and served to connect the chapel with the residential rooms. It is most unfortunate that these parts of the building have been lost. The splendid painted walls covered with monograms, flowers, and stars (illus. p. 189) and the colored façade design, which was not recorded but can be assumed, might yet exist under later coats of plaster. Two fireplaces attributed to Claus Sluter have also been preserved. At the center of the long sides arose two square towers: one contained the steam baths of the duchess and had *fenêtres flamenches*, Flamboyant windows. The narrow southwest side was enclosed by a shallow wing, of which almost nothing remains.

Germolles, Margaret's favorite residence, allows us to look deeply into the mentality and self-image of this exceptional woman, who was able to realize her own vision even at the side of an ambitious and powerful husband.

Saint-Ambreuil

In Saint-Ambreuil, near the Saône, is another Baroque complex that goes back to the abbey of La Ferté, first daughter house of Cîteaux. Since that time, the complex has had an eventful history. The first renovations of the convent buildings were made in the 13th century. Beginning in 1415, the complex was fortified with walls, moats, and an entrance gate, but in 1570 it was captured by Admiral de Coligny. Only the church, sacristy, and chapter hall remained; the dormitory and the church interior were reconstructed in the late 16th century. A century later, Abbot Claude Petit began construction of a new abbey palace and a cloister. The damaged fortifications were removed and the moats were filled, making space for a building typical of the late 17th/early 18th century, with rows of slender rectangular windows connected by vertical bands of plaster that culminate in dormers (illus. above). At each end of the building, a two-axis façade with exposed corner ashlars protrudes; in the center is an elegant, protruding three-axis façade. Above the rusticated ground floor and pilaster articulation on the upper story is an enormous segmental pediment adorned with the coat of arms and flanked by floral décor and vases. The articulation and layering of the façade is subtle and harmonious. The protruding center façade may have been created under the direction of Abbot François de Filsjean, who is known to have commissioned changes to the logis in 1760. The interior design, including the festive vestibule and grand staircase (illus. left), was executed at a later time, during the abbacy of Antoine-Louis Desvignes de La Cerve.

Tournus

Farther south, directly on the river and at the border of the arrondissement, lies the former abbey of Saint-Philbert in Tournus. The origins of Saint-Philbert lie in Noirmoutier/Vendée, where a Philbert monastery was founded in the 7th century. Frequent Norman attacks forced the monks under Abbot Hilbod to leave their monastery in 836 and search for a new home. The first stop on their long journey was Déas, now called Saint-Philbert-de-Grand-Lieu after the church they erected there, which still stands today. In 875, after several interim stations and under the leadership of Abbot Geilo, they arrived in Tournus, where the small abbey of Saint-Valérien was located. Its monastic community apparently integrated the wanderers and their relics. Under the influence of their new members, the small existing church was probably expanded or rebuilt; its remains indicate that the new church must have had a striking resemblance to Saint-Philbert-de-Grandlieu. Over the next 200 years, the present church, Saint-Philibert, evolved in several construction phases (see pp. 194 ff. for the history of its construction).

A two-story narthex in the west almost forms a preceding church. The low, dark ground floor has narrow side aisles spanned with transverse barrel vaulting and dates to about 1020/30. It has an archaic and mysterious feel, while the upper story, with strikingly wide arcades and twin windows in each bay, creates a light, and in comparison almost elegant, impression. From the front bays of both side aisles one has a good view into the west tower. In the east wall, the so-called Gerlannus arch opens onto a box-like wall projection. The two ashlars with reliefs, which carry the arch, date from the first half of the 11th century, and are among the oldest sculptures in Burgundy (illus. right). They were probably moved to this site from elsewhere. The main nave is considerably broader than the narthex. Tall circular pillars, constructed of small cut stones and unplastered, support the arcade arches, followed higher up by the transverse arches with a décor of alternating masonry blocks. These do not carry a round barrel vault, as might be expected, but pointed transverse barrel vaults whose arcade walls contain the clerestory windows (illus. p. 195). For this reason, the groin vaulting of the side aisles rising towards the central nave is unusually high. Everything about this nave is unusual: the exposed masonry of small cut stone, the proportions, and the vaulting. In the east is a five-part barrel-vaulted transept with two apses and a crossing

Tournus, former monastic church of Saint-Philibert, relief from the Gerlannus arch, first half of the 11th century.

Tournus, view of the city on the Saône with Saint-Philibert in the center.

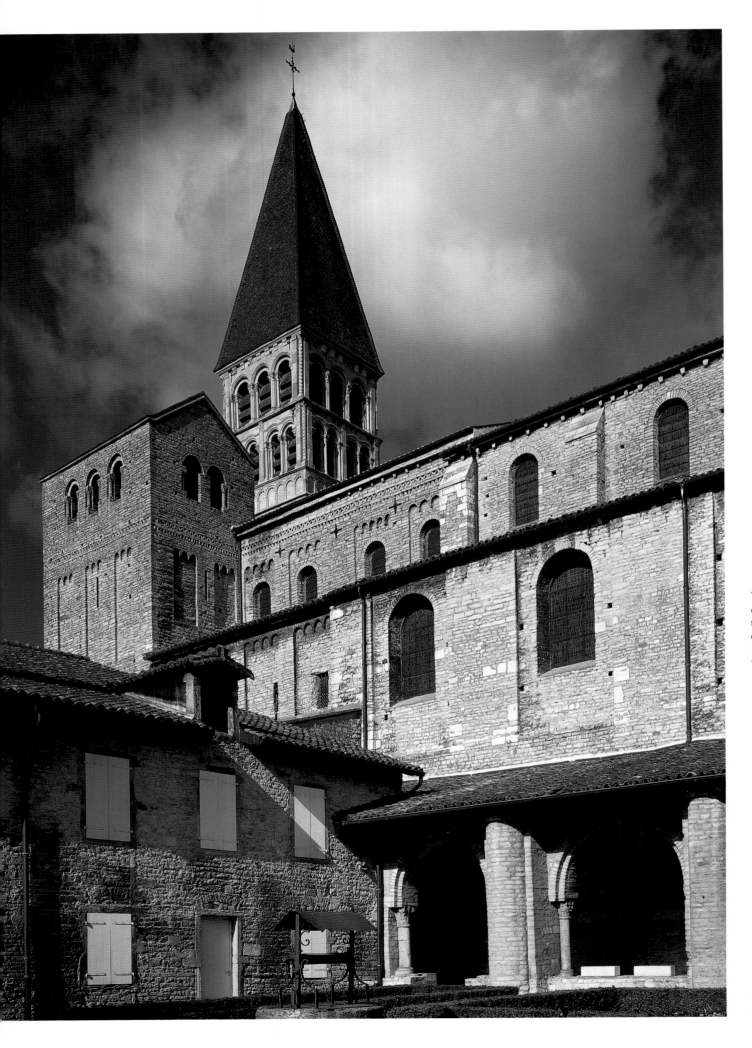

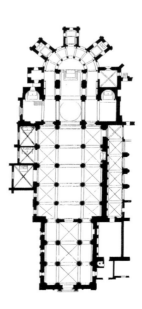

Tournus, former monastic church of Saint-Philibert, south side of the nave, second half of the 10th century; west towers, from ca. 1020/1030 on; and northern cloister wing, 11th century.

Tournus, former monastic church of Saint-Philibert, floor plan.

tower as well as an ambulatory with three rectangular radiating chapels and two different annexes off the antechoir. Underneath the nave is a crypt which follows much the same floor plan. It was probably built during the second half of the 10th century, as its external walls reveal remnants of masonry in the typical herringbone pattern. The ambulatory makes a half-circle around the three-aisle crypt containing the *confessio*, which is covered by a groin vault resting on four pairs of columns; there are no transverse arches. The shafts of the columns might be spolia, whereas the rather archaic capitals date from the original period of construction.

The external walls of the narthex and the towers are articulated by lesenes with rows of blind arches. On the external walls of the nave (illus. opposite), which are among the oldest parts of the church, the original flat lesenes are still visible; they may have originally been part of a large arched articulation. The apsidal choir and the two upper stories of the crossing tower date from the 12th century.

To the south is the cloister (illus. below), in which Abbot Ardain, who was later canonized, was buried in 1056. Of the 11th-century building only the north wing remains; the chapter hall in the delicate High Gothic form was built under the direction of Abbot Bérard in 1237. At the same time, the dormitory and other monastic buildings were also reconstructed, but they were torn down shortly before the French Revolution.

Abbot Jean de Toulonjon had a residence built behind the choir between 1471 and 1494. Pier buttress-like vertical responds with pinnacles spaced at regular intervals articulate the long façade. Between them are tall, six-part mullion windows with delicately profiled frames. In the last bay, which is not centered, is the lovely portal, surmounted by an ogival arch crowned with a finial and flanked by pinnacles (illus. above).

Tournus, abbot's residence, 1474, detail of the façade with portal.

Tournus, former monastic church of Saint-Philibert, north cloister wing, 11th century.

Saint-Philibert in Tournus and the Problem of Vaulting in the 11th Century

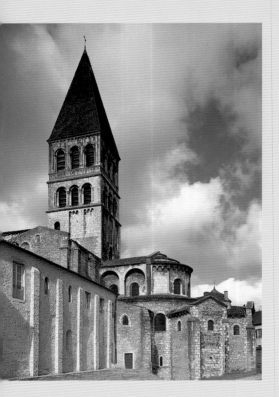

Tournus, former monastic church of Saint-Philibert, view of the ambulatory circling the choir with rectangular chapels, second half of the 10th century/1008–1019; and crossing tower, early 12th century.

RIGHT:
Chapaize, former priory church of Saint-Martin, ca. 1030, nave and side aisles with massive circular pillars and the transverse barrel vault (renovated in the 12th century).

OPPOSITE:
Tournus, former monastic church of Saint-Philibert, central nave with transverse arches and transverse barrel vaulting, 1040/1050 and 1070/1080.

The complex history of the construction of Saint-Philibert in Tournus is a good illustration of the problems of church construction between the 9th and 12th centuries, illustrating both the aims of the builders and their attempted solutions. At the outset of this long history is a small monastic church consecrated to St. Valerianus, and a community of monks that came here bringing their accumulated experience in construction. They had been forced to leave their church in Saint-Philbert-de-Granlieu. Under their influence, the Valerianus church was altered or built anew.

Apparently, an unvaulted basilica was erected first. The crypt was surrounded by a recangular ambulatory from which small, parallel, semicircular or rectangular chapels extended, as in Saint-Philbert-de-Grandlieu. This church, the monastery, and the city were destroyed by the Hungarians in 937 and dire famine followed. A new building was begun about 950, an unvaulted three- or five-aisle basilica with transept that one might liken to their excavated or surviving counterparts in Clermont-Ferrand and Saint-Maurice-d'Agaune. This means that at least the floor plan of the extant eastern section and the external walls of the nave originate from this same period. Along the external walls are flat vertical lesenes that could continue into an arcade arrangement.

In 1007/1008 the entire monastic complex and much of the church furnishings were lost to fire, but enough survived that repairs made the church usable again, at least for a time. In 1019 it was reconsecrated, but changes were in the planning: a few years later, a new building was begun to the west. It was narrower than the old nave and side aisles, about the width of the choir, which had been renovated a few decades earlier. The massive circular columns were doubtlessly meant to support the barrel vaulting of the central nave. Shortly before, about 1000/1010, construction of a barrel vault with windows at its base had been successfully completed in Cluny II. The intended height of the barrel vault in Saint-Philibert can be deduced from the crossing tower windows, which today open into the nave and side aisles.

Three bays of the new nave with side aisles were built—with square bays in the nave and narrow rectangular bays in the side aisles—connecting the new part to the old naves and side aisles. Again, plans changed: instead of continuing the narrower nave and side aisles, an attempt was made to transfer the new vaulting concept onto the existing wider nave and side aisles. Keeping the width of the old central aisle, five pairs of circular pillars were erected, bordering the bays of the central nave and the side aisles.

Here, the practical experience of the monks of Tournus with Saint-Martin in Chapaize, a priory church of Saint-Philbert, became tangible. There, from about 1030, a new building modeled on Cluny II had been erected. The nave had transverse rectangular bays spanned by round barrel vaulting with windows in the base of the vault (this later collapsed and was replaced by vaulting with pointed arches; illus. below), and the side aisles had square bays with groin vaulting. This concept was more advantageous, and only needed to be applied to the old nave and side aisles of Saint-Philbert. Vertical elements on the external walls carried the transverse arches for the groin vaulting, and the central nave was given barrel vaulting with windows. The nave and side aisles begun in the west became the cellar of a narthex. The square bays of the central nave were groin-vaulted, and the side aisles received transverse barrel vaulting. For this reason the imposts of the circular columns were set visibly lower.

light in the central nave; the barrel vaulting begins high above the windows. Groin vaulting spans the side aisles. Both façade towers were part of this construction project, as well.

Even during construction of the upper story of the narthex, it may have been a concern that the central aisle of the nave was probably too wide for barrel vaulting; it had originally been part of the flat-roofed 9th-century basilica. It is not clear whether a collapse led to a change of plans. Perhaps cracks in the vaulting were enough, as the transverse arches of alternating masonry bands in the western bays are completely preserved. In about 1070/1080 the barrel vault of the central nave was replaced with an unusual transverse barrel vaulting (illus. below left), about which there has been much speculation among experts. The solution is unique and has not been imitated, with the exception of Mont-Saint-Vincent, where it was implemented as an emergency measure.

Not much later the crossing tower seems to have collapsed, damaging the choir and the two eastern bays of the nave and side aisles, because the alternating bands of masonry of the transverse arches is missing in these two bays. The choir was rebuilt according to the former floor plan and reconsecrated in 1120.

About 1070, the bright, airy narthex upper story was built (illus. above). It is a perfect vaulted basilica that profited from the practical experience in vaulting just gained from Saint-Etienne in Nevers (Saint-Etienne was begun in 1063). Two large windows in the broad zone over the arcades provide

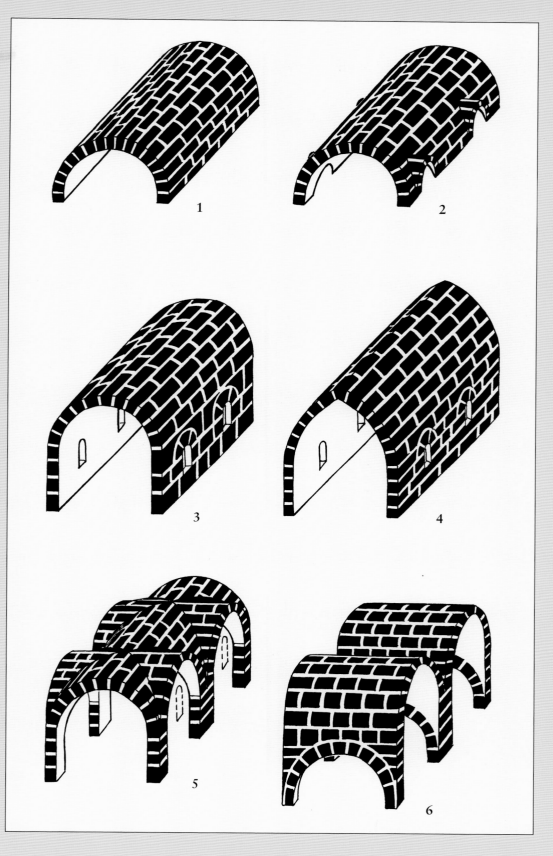

From about 1070, plans for the construction of a new church were made in Cluny; it was begun in 1088. What emerged is one of the major buildings of the Romanesque period—certainly the most perfect—and at the same time already almost an anachronism. Cluny III was consecrated in 1131/1132. After many attempts, a master achievement succeeded here: a 46-foot- (14-m-) wide nave was spanned with a barrel vault, giving the building a sense of spaciousness previously unknown. In Normandy and in England, however, building experts had already developed a new wall concept and experimented with rib vaulting. As early as 1140/1144, Abbot Suger of Saint-Denis had succeeded in spanning the first early Gothic building, Saint-Denis in Paris, with rib vaulting (illus. opposite). This form of vaulting was ideally suited to the new sense of space. Burgundy alone remained true to the old barrel vaults, and numerous churches were still spanned with barrel vaulting throughout the 12th century. At the same time, prior to 1100, other buildings—Anzy-le-Duc (illus. above), Avallon, Vézelay—had already profited from the advantages of groin vaulting over the central nave which, like four-part rib vaulting, forms large arches in the walls of the central nave. The structural concept behind these solutions varies, but neither barrel vaulting nor groin vaulting had a future once the Gothic period dawned.

Forms of vaulting during the 11th and early 12th centuries:

1 Round barrel vault without clerestory (Tournus, Saint-Philibert, narthex cellar).

2 Round barrel vault with curved molding in the lunette or windows at the base of the barrel (Cluny II?; Romainmôtier, Saint-Pierre-et-Saint-Paul; Chapaize, Saint-Martin?; Charlieu, Saint-Fortunat).

3 Round barrel vault above the clerestory (Nevers, Saint-Etienne; Tournus, narthex upper story; Cluny III before the collapse).

4 Pointed barrel vault above the clerestory (Cluny III in the second attempt and all successors).

5 Groin vault (Vézelay, Sainte-Madeleine; Avallon, Saint-Lazare; Anzy-le-Duc, Sainte-Trinité).

6 Transverse barrel vault (a special solution for the central nave in Tournus).

Countryside near Sercy.

Sercy

Farther to the west, the land contains mineral resources, hard coal and ores that once determined the industry of this region. The names of towns such as Montceau-les-Mines, Sanvignes-les-Mines, and Perrecy-les-Forges still testify to this past. The landscape is hilly, at times even steep, and woods and extensive meadows abound (illus. opposite). They form the backdrop for an exceedingly picturesque aristocratic residence. Sercy (illus. below) is a large castle set in the plains dating from the first half of the 12th century. It has a donjon with a small irregular courtyard wall, a *basse-cour* with a chapel, and a moat. The lower stories of the donjon in the northwest, its round-arched entrance, numerous windows, parts of the courtyard wall, the moat, and a one-aisle Romanesque chapel outside the moat enclosure are all that remain from the original structure. The irregular complex was first fortified with circular towers during the 13th century; one of them was later transformed into a pigeon tower. It is not known whether residential buildings existed at this time. Jean de Sercy had the complex thoroughly modernized in the last years of the 15th century. The height of the courtyard was raised one story. Both stair towers were erected then, as well as numerous logis with half-timber façades, the donjon, and the circular tower with *mâchicoulis*. The part of the courtyard in the northeast that was closed off by the construction of a staircase and a new, very unusual entrance became the kitchen. The entire complex, whose entrance façade is mirrored for the visitor in a pond, has an almost romantic, 19th-century air. Architects and builders seem to have had châteaux such as this one in mind when reinventing medieval castles and city houses. Nor did Sercy remained unscathed by attempts at repairs and "beautification" in the 19th century. Among them are the entrance stairway and changes to the interior and the courtyard façade of the western logis. The 12th-century donjon burned in 1929. Since then its eastern half is gone, and an interior courtyard now occupies that spot.

Sercy, Château de Sercy, view over the pond-like moat to the entrance of the complex, 12th to 16th centuries.

Messey-sur-Grosne, *maison forte*, donjon and corner tower of the complex from the second half of the 13th century, logis from ca. 1400, and square corner tower from the 16th century. The masonry of small, carefully layered bricks is typical for Bresse.

Messey-sur-Grosne

If you follow the course of the Grosne River a bit to the northeast, you come upon the *maison forte* of Messey-sur-Grosne (illus. left). The dukes of Burgundy had a hunting mansion here, between Goutteuse and Grosne, for duck hunting. It is a small, square, stone structure with a donjon and three circular towers, enclosed by a moat. The complex is constructed of small brick. About 1400, the duke apparently wished to enlarge the living area. The complex was then expanded into a double square by adding a logis on the outside of the donjon—the two were joined by a round stair tower—and by adding two additional walls and towers. In the 16th century, the southeastern tower was replaced by a pavilion and large windows were set into the donjon.

Autunois – Bordered by the Morvan and the Foothills of the Côte

The heart of the arrondissement of Autun is the Autun basin, through which the Arroux River flows. In the northwest it is bordered by southern Côte-d'Or and the foothills of the Haut-Morvan, whose highest elevations are also the highest peaks in Burgundy—namely Mont Préneley, Mont Folin, and Mont Beuvray (illus. below), attaining heights of 2600 to 3000 feet (800 to 900 m). The Morvan is a massif of bedrock, largely granite, the foothills of the Massif Central. Thick woods cover the hilltops. Due to abundant rain and slow-draining soil, many lakes have formed.

The Morvan is a quiet, barren countryside. At its edge, isolated from the rest of the massif and bordering the department of Saône-et-Loire, Mont Beuvray arises, thickly wooded and with numerous springs on its gently rounded peak. It seems the perfect place for an early fortification and settlement, and in fact, from the second century BC it was the site of the Celtic oppidum Bibracte. This was the main site of the Aeduia, who attained wealth and fame through their skill in handicrafts. Apparently this wealth was closely connected to the iron-ore reserves in the basin at the foot of Mont Beuvray. These mineral resources also made the region famous later on as the smithy of Burgundy. From the 19th century, industry began to settle here. This development was spurred by the relocation of glass manufacturing from Sèvres

Morvan countryside near Mont Beuvray.

to Le Creusot in 1784 at royal behest, as the coal necessary for glass smelting could be mined there. The *manufacture des Cristaux de la Reine* continued until the year 1833, when the business was sold.

The writings of Caesar are the most important historical source as far as the early history of the area is concerned. After the Battle of Alésia in the year 52 BC, Caesar spent the winter in Bibracte and began writing his *Gallic Wars* commentary. He described Bibracte as the largest and wealthiest settlement in Gaul. It encompassed 135 hectares (335 acres) and was enclosed by a wall built of wood, earth, and stones that was 3 miles (5 km) in length. Its traces are still visible today.

Autun

Shortly after their victory in Alésia, the Romans began the colonization of Gaul. At the foot of Mont Beuvray they founded the city of Augustodunum (Autun, illus. above) in about 10 BC. Its rapidly increasing wealth and luxury soon persuaded the inhabitants of the mountain to leave their higher dwellings in favor of the city.

Augustodunum also had a city wall. It was 3.7 miles (6 km) long, was fitted with 54 defensive towers, and enclosed an area of 200 hectares (500 acres). Traces of the wall and towers still exist, as well as a typical Roman city plan. Cardo and Decumanus, the two main streets, intersected at right angles, and at their ends four main gates

secured the city's entrances. Each of the smaller streets also led to a watch tower. Today, the Porte d'Arroux (illus. above) in the northwest remains, an imposing two-story gatehouse with two high, barrel-vaulted passages in the center and a lower one at each side, as well as a delicate columnar arcade with protruding fluted pilasters in the upper story. The Porte-Saint-André (illus. below) also remains in the northeast, differing from the Porte d'Arroux only in details. Its upper story was added to in the 19th century by Eugène Viollet-le-Duc, using material from the classical era. The Porte Saint-Andoche in the west and the Porte de Rome in the south exist only as excavation sites; remains of a marble facing were found at the Porte de Rome. This suggests that the emperors probably

entered the city through this gate; hence it was distinguished by especially ornate décor.

Excavations have uncovered the orchestra and a few stepped rows of a sizeable theater with a diameter of 485 feet (148 m) and 15,000 seats (illus. p. 16). The amphitheater in the northeast, known only from sources, was the second largest theater of the Roman Empire after the coliseum in Rome. In addition, writings report of a capitol, a forum with temples for the triad of gods Jupiter, Juno, and Minerva, and of magnificent columned halls in which the famous schools of Augustodunum were held. The city was rightly known as "the Rome of the Gauls," and its important remains lie buried beneath the present-day city.

Two monuments outside the city wall are puzzling. The so-called Pierre de Couhard (illus. below) is about 10 feet (3 m) high, a funerary pyramid lying on a southern junction of the road built by Agrippa. Its original form cannot be determined today as large parts are missing. The outer surface, which probably consisted of cut stones, has been carried off completely. The so-called Temple of Janus is also a ruin (illus. right); the roof and outer sheathing of cut stones are missing. All the walls were articulated in the same manner, by flat niches on the ground floor and three windows per side in the upper story. A colonnaded ambulatory encircled the entire structure. The interior walls, supposedly once covered with a coating of red plaster, were again articulated by niches, which were painted. In the center of the room was apparently a block of stone with mosaics, perhaps the base for a religious statue of Mars or Janus.

Autun, so-called Temple of Janus, after the first century AD.

Autun, funerary pyramid outside of the ancient city walls, known as the Pierre de Couhard.

ABOVE AND RIGHT:
Autun, cathedral of Saint-Lazare, north wall of the nave, from 1119/1120.
On the capitals: God questioning Cain (above), the flight to Egypt (top right), the death of Judas (bottom right).

OPPOSITE:
Autun, cathedral of Saint-Lazare, wall of the central aisle of the nave.

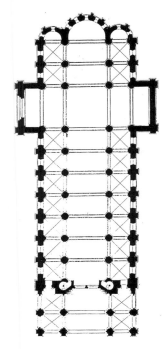

Autun, cathedral of Saint-Lazare, floor plan.

Inscriptions on graves confirm that Christians were already living in Autun in the late second century. Legend has it that Symphorianus founded a Christian community here at the time of the Apostles, and according to records, the city was a diocese from the third century on. After 420 Autun became a part of the lands owned by the Rhineland Burgundians; in 534, after a bloody battle before the city walls, Autun became a part of the Frankish Empire. Saracens and Normans attacked and ravaged the city several times.

South of today's cathedral stood the old cathedral dedicated to its patron saint, Nazaire, until the 18th century. Little is known of its form or age, but it seems logical to assume that there were numerous buildings, both in succession and interconnected, as in other cathedral constructions.

In 1119/1120, Bishop Etienne de Bâgé (1112–1136) began construction of a church dedicated to Lazarus, intended to be a pilgrimage church, and modeled on the nearly completed Cluny III. The unfinished building was consecrated in 1130 during a visit of the pope. Even when the ceremonial *translatio* of the relics of Lazarus from Marseille to Autun took place in 1146, the narthex was still not completed. Despite some damage inflicted to the church by the English in 1379 and during the Wars of Religion, Saint-Lazare survived the centuries in good condition and, at least in the interior, is an impressive example of the Clunian sense of space. Only the choir is not in keeping with this. Its upper story was renovated in the late Gothic style, making it much too bright.

Walking through the three-aisle narthex, two bays deep, you enter the three-aisle pillar basilica. A five-part transept separates the nave and side aisles from the Benedictine choir, which continues in three aisles. The floor plan reveals the incredible clarity of and strict adherence to the design, which even before the Gothic made use of small modules, steadily repeated.

In the central aisle of the nave, pointed arches on fluted piers, a blind triforium, and one window per bay combine to form the steep vertical elevation (illus. opposite). Above, as in the transept, is a pointed barrel vault; the side aisles have groin vaulting. The knowledge of classical construction in this age is quite apparent in the details. The fine treatment of surfaces produces a very subtle light-shadow effect, transforming the church interior into a veritable festive hall.

The exterior is determined by late Gothic additions: the customary side chapels, a high choir, and the crossing tower. The sacristy at the southern transept arm was built in 1520.

The architectural sculpture, created under the direction of Master Gislebertus, is justly famous.

There are over 100 capitals in the nave, side aisles and narthex; 49 of them are figural. Scenes from the New and Old Testaments, mythology, and fables are depicted with outstanding workmanship. They are impressive, easily understood, moralizing and admonishing *exempla* (illus. above). The canons themselves had the sculpture of the former main north portal destroyed, but the program is known: victory over death, and rebirth to salvation. In the tympanum one could see the Awakening of Lazarus; on the lintel, the Fall from Grace. The most famous sculpture from Autun, the enchanting Eve from this lintel, has been preserved and is in the Musée Rolin (illus. pp. 210/211). The capitals of the jambs and columns

elucidate this program, one along the edge of the mandorla: *omnia dispono solus meritos (que) corono quos scelus exercet me judice poena coercet* (I alone dispose all things and reward the deserving. Those whom crime binds are punished according to my judgment), the other above the lintel: *Quisque resurget ita quem non trahit impia vita et lucebit ei sine fine lucerna dei—terreat hic terror quos terreus alligat error nam fore sic verum notat hic horror specierum* (Thus shall rise again everyone who does not lead an imious life, and endless light of day shall shine for him—here let fear strike those whom earthly error binds, for their fate is shown by the horror of these figures) [Transl. by Don Denny in "The Last Judgment Tympanum at Autun" in *Speculum*, 1982]. At the feet of Christ, the master artist left his name in the inscription *Gislebertus hoc fecit* (Gislebertus made this). Sculpted medallions depicting the animals of the zodiac, the months, and 18 of the 24 Elders of the Apocalypse can be seen in the archivolts. The central jamb, necessary because of the extreme width of the portal (21 feet/6.5 m), carries the figures of Lazarus and his two sisters, Martha and Mary, all completely restored.

Numerous pictorial themes merge in this immense and impressive composition: the recurrent *maiestas domini* (here without the symbols of the Evangelists, gestures of blessing, and the book). The angels of the Ascension accompany Christ, who points to the blessed and the damned. Their fates are clearly depicted. The 24 elders of the Apocalyptic vision surround these scenes, pointing to the Judgment that will take place before the final reign of God will begin.

It is due to the genius of Master Gislebertus that he abandoned a composition of parallel bands in favor of a clearer pictorial message. In this way he could contrast the greatness and majesty of Christ with much smaller figures; Christ's serenity and stasis are set against the dynamic movements of individual scenes.

The surface treatments also reveal outstanding workmanship. The fine texture of the stone is not "natural," but reveals a heightened reality. As is true of many extraordinary artistic personalities, Master Gislebertus' artistic roots are not entirely clear. He was certainly familiar with the sculptures at Cluny III, but his artistry involved so much personal creativity that speculation about his sources of inspiration becomes less important than acknowledgement of his own achievements. His artistry clearly lies in the unusual emotive power of gestures, the subtle ones as well as the vehement, that make the pictorial program of the tympanum—which was surely determined by the canons or the bishop himself—so unforgettable.

Autun, cathedral of Saint-Lazare, detail of the tympanum of the west portal: Archangel Michael with the scales to weigh souls, the Devil, and the damned.

OPPOSITE:
Autun, cathedral of Saint-Lazare, west portal with the depiction of the Last Judgment by Master Gislebertus and his workshop, ca. 1150.

FOLLOWING TWO PAGES:
Autun, Musée Rolin, Eve from the north portal of the cathedral. The former main portal in the north was removed by the canons themselves. This is the only remaining figure.

are also still extant. They depict the rich man on whose door a desperate Lazarus knocked in vain, and the same rich man in Hell. On the opposite side is Lazarus in the lap of Abraham. Above the columns is the awakening of the young man from Nain and the Return of the Prodigal Son.

The tympanum of the west portal is preserved under the roof of the narthex (illus. opposite and above). Completed around 1150, it was covered by a wall in 1766 and uncovered and restored in 1836. Here, on 29 stone tablets, is a depiction of the Last Judgment. At the center—over 10 ft/3 m high—is Christ in Majesty in the mandorla. At his right are Paradise with Mary, the Apostles, Peter as the guardian of the gate, and the approaching blessed. At his left are the Archangel Michael with scales for weighing souls as well as the Devil, the damned, and the gates of Hell. There are more blessed and damned on the lintel. Two inscriptions

The lapidary in the south part of the cathedral houses detached figural capitals as well as original foliage capitals, but the famed Eve from the north portal and the remains of the Shrine of Lazarus are in the Musée Rolin. The latter was a monumental, two-story-high reliquary (20 ft/6 m high, 10 ft/3 m wide, and 15 ft/4.5 m long) that once towered behind the main altar, its west side probably serving as the altar retable. A few steps led from there into the crypt, where the sarcophagus with a supine figure was kept. Mary and Martha stand at their brother's head, with Christ, Peter, and Andreas at his feet. Three of the diminutive figures are still extant (illus. opposite).

Aside from some of the cathedral furnishings, the Rolin Museum also preserves numerous finds from Bibracte and Mont Beuvray as well as from the Roman city Augustodunum. In addition, it has high-quality late Gothic sculpture, painted altars, the famous donor painting of Cardinal Rolin that is attributed to the Master of Moulin, and the so-called Madonna of Autun, a painted stone figure from the 15th century characterized by its modesty and delicacy (illus. left).

The house itself is also definitely worth seeing (illus. right). It was the home of the Rolin family, where future chancellor Nicolas Rolin was born in about 1376 as the younger son of a citizen of Autun, Jean Rolin, and his wife, Aimée Jugnot. Nicolas studied law and then began a career as a lawyer that was so successful that he came into contact with the duke. He made his fortune in the service of the Valois dukes. Philip the Good appointed him his chancellor, and it is said that Philip gladly left many important decisions to his discretion. Indeed, Philip's policies are thought to have been essentially those of his chancellor. In any case, in his second marriage Nicolas Rolin married a noblewoman, Marie de Landes. His third marriage was to Guigone de Salins, who was also of noble birth and had considerable holdings.

He himself bought estates—in the 16th century Barthélemy de Chasseneuz mentioned 25—usually with older castles, which he renovated and updated. One example that is still standing is the 13th-century castle of Epinac, about halfway between Autun and Beaune, which Rolin bought in 1430. He built a new logis here with an external stair tower that divided the façade at the center, as well as an imposing entrance tower. At the same time, he also bought the neighboring Laizy estate. At its center was a castle dating from the 13th century, which Rolin adorned with a new logis and encircling battlements. In fact, the list of his possessions is long. He owned city houses not only in Beaune and Chalon, but also in Dijon. There alone he had a palace, a courtyard complex

LEFT:
Autun, Musée Rolin, the so-called Madonna of Autun, stone, painted, 15th century.

OPPOSITE:
Autun, Musée Rolin, Shrine of Lazarus.
Martha and Mary, Lazarus' two sisters (who once stood at the head of the sarcophagus), and the apostle Andreas, sculpture from the foot of the sarcophagus, stone, about 4 feet (1.25 m), ca. 1140/1145.

BELOW:
Autun, Hôtel Rolin, now a museum. Nicolas Rolin, the famous chancellor of Burgundy, was born here in 1376. After he had earned high honors and enormous wealth in the service of Duke Philip the Good, he had his parents' house in Autun rebuilt and newly furnished, among other projects. The building has a circular tower with battlements over stepped corbels facing the street; in the courtyard is a stair tower. The beautiful mullion windows with ogival arches are typical of the period.

with wings that later housed the town hall and then the archive of the department. Numerous reconstructions and renovations have altered the buildings beyond recognition; all that remains of the original are a few small windows and walls. Like the magnificent buildings of the dukes, so too the residences of Nicolas Rolin have all but disappeared, with only a few exceptions. In addition, Rolin outfitted numerous churches with costly furnishings and decorations. A large number of these still can be admired today in the Musée Rolin. That building, the Hôtel Rolin in Autun, is one of few among his vast former real estate holdings still in existence. Rolin also had his parents' house altered: the late Gothic building has a round tower facing the street, while a polygonal stair tower and lovely mullion windows grace the courtyard side.

Château de Sully

East of Autun, where the plain gives way to soft hills dotted with woods, lie the noble estates of the Autunois. Sully is the northernmost of them. The estate of Sully, which was owned by a succession of powerful noble families, is mentioned beginning in 1180. Today one finds a Renaissance complex that resembles Ancy-le-Franc. The marshal Gaspard de Saulx-Tavannes, "le Grand Sully," began a new building there in about 1570.

Its dimensions were possibly determined by one or more previous buildings on the site. He commissioned a renowned architect, Nicolas Ribonnier of Langres, who had already built the castle Le Pailly for him near Langres, with the project. When Gaspard died in 1573 his widow continued the project with much energy, but it only seems to have been finished around 1610.

Four wings, accented by diagonally placed corner towers on the exterior, enclose a square inner

courtyard. A stone bridge leads over the moat encircling the complex to the main entrance on the west. This is the only original external façade. It has rusticated masonry at the foundation and large, squarely hewn stones in the almost entirely closed ground floor. The living area is the upper story with large mullion windows, double pilasters, and a wall relief. The middle of the façade is emphasized by a triangular pediment with tutelary spirits that once held a coat of arms. Much of the

inner courtyard, with strongly sculpted articulation, is also in its original condition. Above the rusticated ground floor, Ionic attached pilasters frame windows and flat niches (formerly painted) alternately. In the 18th century, the north façade was pushed farther out, giving the space greater depth, and the building was lengthened by five window axes. In 1808 the Maréchal de Mac-Mahon, Duc de Magenta, was born here. In 1873 he became the president of the Third Republic.

Sully, Château de Sully, main façade, 1570 (planned) until 1610.

Morlet

Morlet is a typical late medieval *maison forte* with donjon and elevated plateau, moats, an entrance building, *basse-cour*, *avant-cour*, and a chapel. In the late 13th century the de Loges family became vassals of the duke in exchange for this estate. The form of the entire complex, the donjon, and the moats date from this period. In about 1470/ 1480 the complex was expanded by a logis, which was adjoined to the donjon, which was then fitted with mullion windows and dormers. Only a few remnants of the entrance and drawbridge have been preserved. In the 18th century, the logis was restored. It was given new windows and a diagonally placed corner tower was added. At this time the plateau was still enclosed by walls on all sides, and it is likely that such towers were intended for the other two corners. There may even have been an overall plan. Simon de Loges had a gatehouse erected at the entrance to the *avant-cour* in the Mannerist style, a martial structure of rusticated masonry (illus. below). Two broad, square towers project out from the façade, framing the two different-sized portals in the style of late-medieval gatehouses. Corbels for battlements (that were perhaps never built) carry reliefs of lions' heads. There are also traces of a rusticated wall that seems to have once enclosed the entire complex.

Saint-Emiland

The estate of Epiry in Saint-Emiland is also on record since the 12th century. In the 14th century it was in the hands of the Rabutin family, who had a new complex built about the mid-15th century. The *maison forte*, of which significant elements still exist (illus. right), was a double square with circular corner towers and flanking towers centered in the long sides. A moat enclosed the rectangular plateau, but did not divide it into a *cour d'honneur* and a *basse-cour* as in Commarin. A chapel or an apsidal chapel is located in the southern flanking tower. It could be reached by way of a logis at the southern main wall. The west main wall collapsed in the 19th century and was replaced by an iron gate that still closes off the courtyard today. A second logis lay in the north and battlements on stepped corbels crowned the main walls. Several latrines still remain in the northwest tower.

In the first half of the 16th century, the north wing was rebuilt. Its rhythmic articulation, simple portal, and stairway with two interior flights of stairs plainly show Renaissance influence, although the mullion windows belong to an older style. In 1717, the Magdelaine de Ragny family commissioned the Baroque wing. The second courtyard in the east was sacrificed, and the east side became

Saint-Emiland, Château d'Epiry, mid-15th century, view of the inner courtard with the main façade renovated in the Baroque style; the side wing and the west main wall were torn down in 1824.

Morlet, Château de Morlet, gatehouse of the forecourt in the Mannerist style, 1584.

the garden side. The entrance—until then in the east—was moved to the west, and the new wing overlapped with the logis in the north by one axis. During the Revolution, the Magdelaine family was dispossessed. They bought their estate back in 1800, only to sell it to Antoine de Loisy in 1824. He had the south wing and the west main wall torn down, and may have had the old mullion windows moved to the exterior side of the north wing. He also reconstructed the courtyard façade of the north wing and the west side of the chapel, which used to be part of the southern wing.

Another noble estate with a similar history is Couches-les-Mines, although here only the foundation of the complex and the donjon remain. The residential buildings date from the 19th century.

Issy-l'Evêque

In the sparsely settled region at the southern edge of the Morvan lies Issy-l'Evêque. Saint-Jacques-le-Majeur (illus. right) is a typical Romanesque country church, following the example of Charlieu in its groin vaulting. Built in the first third of the 12th century, it has a three-aisle central nave of six bays and three semicircular apses. Above the arcades, with rounded arches in the east and pointed ones in the west, are small windows; above these is groin vaulting in all three aisles.

Issy-l'Evêque, Saint-Jacques-le-Majeur, first third of the 12th century, view to the east through the groin-vaulted central aisle of the nave.

Pastures in the area surrounding Issy-l'Evêque. Typical of this countryside are the *bocages,* or hedges, dividing the pastures from each other.

RIGHT:
Charolais cattle.

Fertile Pastures between the Loire and Grosne – Charolais

The boundaries of the arrondissement Charolles are largely identical to those of the old county of Charolais. This is the region the Valois dukes customarily gave to their eldest sons, who then bore the title Count of Charolais. On its south side, Charolles borders on the Morvan and the Côte d'Or. This is a gentle, hilly area whose fertile, marly soil produces magnificent meadows. On the west it is bordered by the Loire, and in the east by the Monts du Beaujolais and the Monts du Mâconnais. The southern part of Charolais is known as Brionnais; this is the more interesting region from a cultural standpoint.

The wealth of this region comes from its cattle, and in fact, white, woolly Charolais cattle dot the landscape in many areas (illus. opposite). These resilient and undemanding animals, bred from a cross between native animals and the Durham cow in the 19th century, were first put to pasture in Nivernais. In the meantime they have become a trademark of Charolais, but they are also bred in Auxois, the Morvan (where they have to be fed a supplement), and Puisaye. Because they are bred exclusively for meat, they can be seen on their pastures from spring well into the fall. In October of each year, a cattle market, a loud and busy affair, is held in Charolles.

During the Carolingian era, Charolles was the seat of a viscounty. Over the years it changed hands several times, becoming a possession of the duke of Burgundy in 1237. He elevated Charolles to the status of a county for the sake of his niece, Beatrice of Bourbon. Beatrice's son, Jean de Clermont, supposedly erected a nine-towered castle here between 1310 and 1317, which was bought back by Philip the Bold in the course of his efforts to expand territorially. He gave it to his eldest son, John, as an appanage. In 1471 the castle was destroyed by the king's armies, then annexed by the crown in 1477. Today, only the so-called Tour des Archives, or Tour Charles le Téméraire, remains. Marie of Burgundy acquired the county once again in 1493 as wife of Maximilian of Hapsburg. Only in 1761 did the county finally become a part of France.

A Clarissa nunnery was built directly beneath the castle in the first half of the 16th century. Some of its rooms are used today by the *Syndicat d'initiative* (tourism office). The buildings, among them a lovely two-story galleried structure, are grouped around an irregular courtyard. A stair tower with an insignia relief above its portal gives access to the gallery and the adjoining wing, which has lovely mullion windows.

Pastures around Château de Nobles in the hills near Brancion.

Philibert in Tournus or Saint-Bénigne in Dijon—were much like those of Saint-Nazaire. It is probably their simplicity that makes these interiors so immensely dignified. Moreover, Saint-Nazaire is in excellent condition and houses a museum with Roman and Merovingian finds, as well as numerous valuable pieces from the 19th century.

The city itself seems to have originated as a Celtic site on which the god Borvo was venerated. Later the Romans called the settlement Borvoniae or Aquae Nisineii because of its hot springs. From about 921, a landowner is recorded by name, possibly because at this time construction was begun on a castle that was expanded, little by little, before being completely razed in 1775. The only remains are the so-called *Beffroi*, an entrance tower from the late Middle Ages (14th century) and the Maison du Bois, a half-timber house with ogival-arched windows and an ogival-arched portal from the early Renaissance (illus. opposite). Wooden houses can also be found in other cities, but they are comparatively rare, as Burgundy has a wealth of stone quarries.

Perrecy-les-Forges

Like Saint-Nazaire, Saint-Pierre-et-Saint-Paul in Perrecy-les-Forges is a priory church dating from the 11th century, but it has not been as completely preserved. A chapel to St. Peter stood here as of 836. It came into the possession of the abbey Saint-Benoît-sur-Loire in 876, and the Benedictine monks of Saint-Benoît built their third priory on the site. The oldest remaining parts are the unvaulted, pillared nave and side aisles, which are

Bourbon-Lancy, former priory church of Saint-Nazaire, after 1030. The nave and side aisles are now used as a museum.

RIGHT:
Perrecy-les-Forges, former priory church of Saint-Pierre-et-Saint-Paul, 11th century/ca. 1120/1130, view through the southern side aisle.

OPPOSITE:
Bourbon-Lancy, *Beffroi* ("belfry"), 14th century, and Maison du Bois, late 15th/early 16th century.

Bourbon-Lancy

Southern Charolais has a number of famous Romanesque churches. One of the oldest and largest churches still standing in Burgundy is Saint-Nazaire in Bourbon-Lancy, near the Loire in the north. The occasion for the founding of a new priory seems to have been a donation made to the Cluny monastery by Anceau de Bourbon in 1030. Construction began immediately and, as in Cluny II, the church was given a Benedictine choir with five barrel-vaulted apses closed off from each other. Engaged semicircular columns, most with renovated capitals, carry the transverse arches. The high transept has a flat ceiling and is divided by one transverse arch in the middle of each arm. The crate-like form of the nave and side aisles was apparently too broad for a vault. Wide, round arches on square piers support the arcades, above which are large, high windows. The wall area between them was probably painted. Purportedly the naves and side aisles of other large structures of the late 10th and early 11th centuries—Saint-

Palinges, Château de Digoine, 1709 to 1770, main façade.

Palinges, Château de Digoine, view into the white foyer dating from the late 18th century.

now missing the northern side aisle, the crossing, and the groin-vaulted north transept. In about 1120/1130 the two-story, three-aisle narthex was added, bearing a tower with richly decorated open stories. The architectural sculpture of the main portal is significant: Christ enthroned at the Last Judgment with a book in one hand and the other raised in blessing, while two seraphim from Isaiah's vision hold the mandorla. On the lintel are scenes from the Passion: the Mount of Olives, the Kiss of Judas, the Captivity, Christ before the High Priest, Peter's Repentance. The capitals show the hermits Antonius and Paulus, battling angels, and much more. Lintel and tympanum are not of the same material, nor by the same hand. While the Passion scenes show a wealth of lively, emotional figures forming a pictorial narrative, both the composition of the tympanum as well as the individual figures are completely symmetrical. Here a different, perhaps more old-fashioned, pictorial conception is at work. In this way, perhaps unintentionally, a sharp contrast exists between the dignified severity of the Judge of the World and the lively, busy activity of the crowded human world, striving for ornament and decoration.

Palinges

Near the brook Bourbince and the Canal du Centre, which flow parallel to one another, François de Reclesne des Regard bought the Digoine estate with its remains of a medieval castle in 1700. His son Claude-Eléonore had the old walls removed and began a new building in about 1709. Its construction dragged on, occupying the next generation, until it was finally completed in 1770. Short

ABOVE RIGHT:
Palinges, Château de Digoine, garden theater for private performances, about 1840. Such names as Constant Coquelin and Sarah Bernhardt are associated with it.

Palinges, Château de Digoine, view into the interior and onto the stage of the garden theater.

wings at each end of the two-story main building suggest a *cour d'honneur*, whereas at the back two circular towers frame the garden façade between them (illus. above left). The design of the courtyard side is typical of the period: two rows of simple rectangular windows, a central protruding façade bay of three axes with a triangular pediment, simple profiling between the stories and at the eaves, the usual repertoire. The free-standing columns, the slight outward swing of the entablature, and the iron balcony railing on the central bay lend the garden façade a kind of rococo serenity. This protruding central bay is slightly too tall; sculpted ashlars adorn the windows and delicately profiled panels are attached to the wall. Trophies take the place of the final gable. All of these surely belong to the last period of construction, which was completed in 1770.

The large foyer inside is pure white except for the floor of white and black marble tiles. This, too, suited late 18th-century taste (illus. opposite). In 1825 a neo-Gothic library was installed in one of the towers. In the park is a theater for private performances of the de Reclesne family, with an unusual, opulent ceiling (illus. above and left).

Saint-Bonnet-de-Joux

The theater was a modest hobby in contrast to the passion for horses that beset Philibert de La Guiche. His wife, Henriette de La Guiche, Duchesse d'Angoulême, had a magnificent stable built by François Martel from Charolles in the courtyard of her castle, Chaumont-La-Guiche, near Saint-Bonnet-de-Joux. Built from 1648 to 1652, it was Henriette's gift to her husband. There was

Saint-Bonnet-de-Joux, Château Chaumont-la-Guiche, stately horse stable with two magnificent stairways and an equestrian statue of the owner, Philibert de La Guiche, 1648 to 1652.

Saint-Vincent-des-Prés, Saint-Vincent, second third of the 11th century, exterior from the southeast showing semicircular apse, crossing tower, and the south side of the nave and side aisles.

room for 99 horses, as only the king was allowed to own 100. There was, of course, a 100th horse in Chaumont: an equestrian statue of the owner in a niche above the main portal (illus. above). This portal is flanked by four monumental stairways made of stone. At the center of each pair is another portal with engaged pilasters and cartouches. The low upper story was kept simple, so the dormers and the two enormous chimneys seem all the more elaborate by comparison. The dormers are ornamented with volutes, pediments in the shape of segmental arches, acroterions, and cartouches—most of the dormers have circular windows called *œuils-de-bœuf,* or bull's eyes. The chimneys, encased in rusticated masonry, display the coat of arms of the de La Guiche-d'Angoulême family in their segmental pediments.

The logis looks neo-Gothic. Built between 1500 and 1514 by Pierre de La Guiche, it was altered in the 17th century. In order to keep up with contemporary fashion, two wings with pavilions were added onto the main building; they were removed in 1805. In 1840/1850, the 16th-century façades were redesigned. One side received a portal from the castle of Saillant, the other a faux façade in neo-Renaissance style. Its articulation is absolutely regular, with pinnacles framing the windows, a central portal, and enormous dormers. The polygonal stair tower is also new, as is the pavilion meant to suggest a donjon. Chaumont-la-Guiche is one of the best examples of how the Romantic age viewed—and recreated—the Middle Ages.

Saint-Vincent-des-Prés

Not far from Saint-Bonnet-de-Joux, in the center of the village Saint-Vincent-des-Prés, is the small church of Saint-Vincent (illus. opposite bottom). A chapel stood on this site in the 10th century, and probably belonged to the cathedral chapter of Mâcon. The building currently standing is just slightly newer than Saint-Nazaire in Bourbon-Lancy and Saint-Pierre-et-Saint-Paul in Perrecy-les-Forges, i.e., from about the second third of the 11th century, but is of a different kind. The three-aisle nave has three nearly square barrel-vaulted bays in the central nave and extremely narrow side aisles with groin vaulting. Strong circular pillars carry the arcades; the clerestory at the base of the vaulting was covered later, probably for reasons of structural engineering. The crossing of the non-protruding transept is covered by a dome resting on a tambour with a tower above it. In its plain solidity, this three-story tower seems bulky on the small church. The apse is ornamented within and without with engaged semi-columns and blind arcades. The architectural dependence on Tournus and Chapaize (compare p. 194) is obvious here.

Bois-Sainte-Marie

Bois-Sainte-Marie, now a village, was a small fortified city in the Middle Ages. Its church of Notre-Dame, perched high above the town square, is a more advanced example of a barrel-vaulted basilica (illus. below). Built in the first half of the 12th century, it adopted structures from Cluny III in its nave and side aisles; it may have been served the monastery as a priory. The three-aisled, pillared nave of four bays is joined by a non-protruding transept and an ambulatory around the choir without chapels. The arrangement of four T-shaped columns under the choir arcades, corresponding to double columns on the outside wall, are striking. The groin vaults of the ambulatory have no transverse arches, almost like an annular barrel vault with curved molding above lunettes. In the nave, the capitals of the semi-columns carrying the transverse arches are partly figural and some recall Anzy-le-Duc (illus. right). But due to their restoration in the mid-19th century, they are not completely reliable. The capitals in the ambulatory with stylized leaf décor and the table altar with five supports may stem from a preceding building.

Bois-Sainte-Marie, Notre-Dame, first half of the 12th century, capital from the nave or side aisles.

LEFT:
Bois-Sainte-Marie, Notre-Dame, view through the nave to the choir.

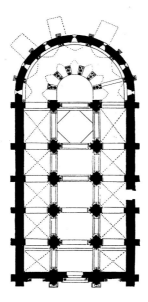

Bois-Sainte-Marie, Notre-Dame, floor plan.

Cattle grazing in countryside near Curbigny with solitary trees typical of the area.

Curbigny, Château de Drée, from 1620, view into the inner courtyard.

Curbigny

Not many buildings in Burgundy dating from the 17th century are still in good condition, and most of the exceptions are city palaces in Dijon (Maison des Caryatides, Maison Maillard, Hôtel de Voguë). Examples in the country are the main wing of Bussy-Rabutin, as well as the Cormatin and Drée châteaux in Curbigny (illus. opposite). The latter was begun at the behest of Charles de Blanchefort de Crécqui in 1620. It was finally completed in the second half of the 17th century. Four pavilions, wider than the wings, mark the corners of the stately three-wing complex, serving to enliven the roof and the façades. They are articulated by dormer, segmental, and triangular pediments as well as flat horizontal and vertical bands. A protruding three-axis façade bay marks the center. It has full columns and a projecting cornice; the decorative top is a later addition from 1838. The rococo interior was created after 1748 for Etienne or Gilbert de Drée. The white salon is especially spectacular. It is named for its white ceiling and walls, enhanced by sparse use of gilding on the rococo stucco and the grisaille paintings over the doors and the fireplace. The effect is unequalled nobility and elegance. Happily, the room's delicate furniture has also been preserved.

Oyé

Chaumont in Oyé is a younger château by two decades. Hector Andrault de Laugeron, Marquis de Maulevrier, acquired the Chaumont estate from Cluny in 1636 and built a Baroque palace a few hundred feet from the old one. His is a three-wing structure with high mansard roofs. In the 19th century, the front part of the complex was Gothicized. The large hall from the château of Moulin-l'Aronce was brought here stone by stone and integrated.

La Clayette

La Clayette (illus. above) lies farther to the south where the small Genette river forms numerous small lakes. In 1380, Philibert de Lespinasse modernized an older manor, preserving the plateau and the moat; he built a long rectangular wall with circular towers, a logis, a protected entrance, and two courtyards. In 1435 ownership went to the de Chantemerle family, who belonged to the inner circle of the ducal court. This is probably when the encircling battlements on stepped corbels and one or more logis were added. The château's present appearance, however, derives from Gothic remodelling in 1830 so extensive that it might as well have been a new construction.

La Clayette, château, late Middle Ages and 19th century, view from the river across the moat towards the 19th-century logis. The slender corner turrets and battlements and the large, regularly placed windows are typical.

Saint-Julien-de-Jonzy

All that remains of the church of Saint-Julien in Saint-Julien-de-Jonzy, first mentioned in 1106 and renovated in the first half of the 12th century, is the crossing with a dome on a tambour, a richly articulated tower, and an especially beautiful portal (illus. left). These vestiges make the loss of the church particularly painful. Columns bear the powerful gable into which the round arch of the tympanum, framed by a band of leaves, has been set. On the lintel is a depiction of the Last Supper with the washing of the feet in front of a wall of ashlars with an ornamental band. In the tympanum is Christ enthroned with a book, making the gesture of blessing (the Judge of the World) in a mandorla held by angels. The soft modeling of the bodies and the ornamental treatment of the garment pleating and surfaces are striking. They date the tympanum to the end of the Burgundian Romanesque, or about 1150.

Saint-Julien-de-Jonzy, Saint-Julien, portal, ca. 1150. In the tympanum is Christ in the mandorla with a book, his hand raised in blessing; at his side are angels. The Last Supper is depicted on the lintel. The ornamentation of the archivolts is typical for the period.

Semur-en-Brionnais, view of the town. To the right is the donjon, left the church of Saint-Hilaire with its crossing tower.

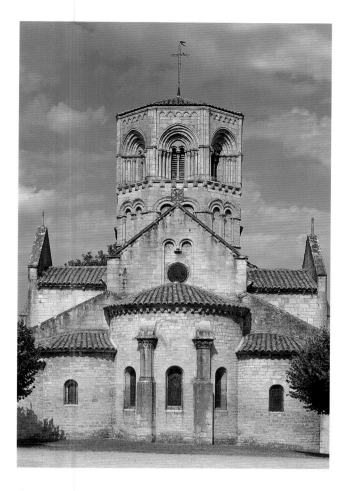

Semur-en-Brionnais, Saint-Hilaire, west portal, detail of the scenes from the life of Hilarius.

LEFT:
Semur-en-Brionnais, Saint-Hilaire, west portal, 12th century.

FAR LEFT:
Semur-en-Brionnais, Saint-Hilaire, 1120/1130 to late 12th century, view facing the choir, transept, and crossing tower.

Semur-en-Brionnais

In Semur-en-Brionnais (illus. opposite) the connection between castle and church is clear. This is the birthplace of Abbot Hugh of Cluny, also known as Hugh of Semur (1049–1109). The rock plateau on which the town rests was fortified no later than the 9th century, and was remarkable for its 10th-century donjon. The present donjon is a 13th-century construction with a *chemise*, or crenelation, that shielded the most vulnerable part of the tower. The original raised entrance, possibly connected to other parts of the castle by a drawbridge, is still recognizable: its round-arched portal lies in a rectangular indentation in the wall.

Saint-Hilaire (illus. above and right), one of many successors to Cluny III, was begun during the abbacy of Hugh of Cluny. At his place of birth, a new building was erected from about 1120/1130, surely replacing an older castle chapel or church. It was completed towards the end of the 12th century. In 1274 the owner of Semur, Jean de Châteauvilain, and the Bishop of Autun endowed a college for 13 canons under the patronage of St. Hilarius. Like so many churches in Burgundy, the complex was damaged by the English in 1364. Two hundred years later, in 1576, the Huguenots wreaked havoc. Repairs and restoration were carried out in the 19th century.

Saint-Hilaire is a three-aisle basilica with the typical Cluny elevation: a slightly protruding transept, a three-aisle choir bay, and three apses. A round barrel vault was constructed in the 19th century, replacing the original pointed barrel vaulting. In comparison to Cluny III and other churches influenced by it, Semur has less décor. Only the elements that carry transverse arches are fluted on the ground floor; higher up they become twin columns. The ashlars in Semur were very carefully hewn. Only the octagonal crossing tower is distinguished by blind arcading in the first story and by deeply recessed acoustic arcades in the second free story. There is a recessed Romanesque portal at both the north and south sides, one with a quatrefoil, the other with an ansate cross in the tympanum.

The west portal (illus. above) has figural ornaments on the lintel and tympanum; small geometric patterns are incised around the columns and archivolts. The lintel was reserved for scenes from the life of St. Hilarius. In the tympanum is again Christ enthroned with the book, his hand lifted in blessing. Seraphim hold the mandorla; beside them are the symbols of the Evangelists. As in Autun, the depiction combines the motif of the Judge of the World with the subject of the *Maiestas Domini*, connecting two events occurring successively in time. The lamb at the apex of the outermost archivolt, incidentally, is quoted from Charlieu (see p. 235), to which the portal sculpture of Semur is heavily indebted.

Semur-en-Brionnais, Saint-Hilaire, view through the nave to the west.

Brionnais countryside, view from the Montagne de Dun.

Winter landscape near Bois-Sainte-Marie.

View from Semur-en-Brionnais onto the **church of Saint-Martin, in a valley near Marcigny.**

Anzy-le-Duc

The former priory church in Anzy-le-Duc, consecrated to the Trinity, the Holy Cross, and the Mother of God (illus. left and below), was founded by the monastery of Saint-Martin in Autun, which was abandoned long ago. The first abbot was Hugh of Poitiers (died 930), a friend of Abbot Berno of Cluny. His grave became a pilgrimage site during the 11th century, necessitating the building of a church in the second half of the century. This church also documents the various efforts at vault construction made by Burgundian builders during the 11th century. The once colorfully painted Benedictine choir above the crypt, the chapel at the vertex of the sanctuary, and the projecting, barrel-vaulted transept were elements adopted from the mother church in Autun and can thus be traced to Cluny II. But all three aisles of the five-bay, pillared nave are groin-vaulted. The central nave's stepped vertical responds and the transverse arches they carry (illus. below) suggest that barrel vaulting was originally intended in the nave as well, but groin vaulting allowed for taller windows in the formerets. The spatial impression is largely the result of the magnificently hewn ashlars. The 40 sculpted capitals (illus. p. 234), which pre-date those in Autun and Vézelay, are also remarkable. Most of them have stylized leaf décor, and the figural sculpture often

Anzy-le-Duc, former priory church of Sainte-Trinité, Sainte-Croix et Sainte-Marie, second half of the 11th century, view of the monastic buildings dominated by the tall crossing tower.

BELOW:
Anzy-le-Duc, former priory church of Sainte-Trinité, Sainte-Croix et Sainte-Marie, southwest view of nave and side aisles, transept, and tower.

Anzy-le-Duc, former priory church of Sainte-Trinité, Sainte-Croix et Sainte-Marie, nave and wall of north side aisle.

depicts scenes from the Old and New Testaments as well as moral instruction. The heads and bodies are still rather awkward and the pictorial composition schematic. The recessed portal in the west (illus. bottom right) is more recent, from about 1130/1140. Small, free-standing figures representing the 24 Elders encircle the tympanum with Christ in a mandorla held by angels. Depicted on the lintel are the Virgin and Apostles from an Ascension. The figures are definitely more slender and emotive, with more natural proportions of heads and bodies. In the southern wall of the monastery is a second, contemporaneous tympanum that is very weathered. Here we see the Temptation of Adam and Eve and the Adoration of the Magi; on the lintel, Heaven's Gate and the Vengeance of Hell. The exterior, dominated by a beautiful crossing tower with three open stories, was also surely inspired by Cluny III. Unfortunately, the steep stone spire is missing. The monastery was abolished during the Revolution and the church was sold. Since 1818 it has been a parish church. The first restoration attempts were made in 1852, and as in so many cases, they do not meet the scholarly standards of our time.

Charlieu and Montceaux-l'Etoile

Sainte-Trinité in Anzy-le-Duc has a twin structure in Charlieu: Saint-Fortunat. The similarities between their floor plans are so striking that a period of common planning seems likely. In Charlieu a barrel vault over the central nave was in fact completed, another argument for the assumption that this was also intended in Anzy-le-Duc. Saint-Fortunat, incidentally, is a ruin; only the foundations and western bay with the west wall and (rebuilt) narthex are still standing (illus. p. 235).

The church of Saint-Pierre-et-Saint-Paul in Montceaux-l'Etoile is a little older than Anzy-le-Duc. It is a modest country church with a semicircular apse, a barrel-vaulted nave, and an antechoir topped by a tower. It is interesting to note that the capitals and the recessed portal (illus. p. 134) are related to the sculptural work of Anzy-le-Duc and Charlieu, as well as to the sculpture on the lateral tympana in Vézelay. Simple astragal archivolts surround the tympanum, which, together with the lintel, is carved out of one block. Below are the Apostles, the Virgin, and angels witnessing the Ascension of Christ, who stands upright in a mandorla and is being transported heavenwards by angels. In flight, his robe and those of the angels are waving in a breeze one can almost feel. Here too, the themes of the Ascension and the *Maiestas Domini*, parting and return, have been connected. The capitals and consoles portray angels and saints as well as battle scenes.

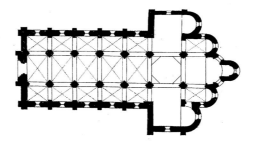

Anzy-le-Duc, former priory church of Sainte-Trinité, Sainte-Croix et Sainte-Marie.

TOP: Fresco in the calotte of the main apse with depiction of Christ's Ascension; below, in a semicircle, the Apostles (12th century).

ABOVE: West portal from 1130/1140

LEFT: Floor plan.

LEFT:
Anzy-le-Duc, former priory church of Sainte-Trinité, Sainte-Croix et Sainte-Marie, capitals from the nave and crossing, about 1080/1090. The capitals in the choir and nave of Anzy-le-Duc were begun about the mid-11th century and are among the oldest figural sculptures in Burgundy. They depict male caryatids, lions, eagles, a dove, jesters— all suggestive of Christian themes, yet without any specific connection to scenes from the Old and New Testaments.

Montceaux-l'Etoile, Saint-Pierre-et-Saint-Paul, west portal, second quarter of the 12th century, Ascension of Christ.

Charlieu, former monastic church of Saint-Fortunat. Lintel, tympanum, and archivolts from the portal and windows of the north side of the narthex, ca. mid-12th century.

Framed by the abundantly ornate archivolts, the tympanum depicts Christ in Majesty with book, his hand raised in blessing. He is accompanied by angels and the symbols of the Evangelists. On the lintel is the Virgin Mary, flanked by two angels and the Apostles. Very special features are the lamb on the crown of the arch, and two of the 24 Elders of the Apocalypse on the springer. Rosette nimbuses on the outer archivolt point to the remaining 22 Elders. The tympanum of the window depicts the Wedding at Cana; the lintel, a sacrificial scene. On the archivolt are five fields with figures: at the top is Christ with Moses, to their right Elijah and Peter, and to their left Jacob and John.

Charlieu, former monastic church of Saint-Fortunat, tympanum of the west portal, late 11th century. This is one of the earliest monumental depictions of this type, and the oldest sculpture in Burgundy.

Paray-le-Monial

One of the most significant successors to Cluny III and one of the major churches of Burgundy is the former monastic church of Notre-Dame in Paray-le-Monial. Count Lambert of Chalon founded his own monastery there in 973, and his son Hugh, bishop in Auxerre, gave it to Cluny in 999. Abbot Odilo consecrated a church here in 1004; in the first half of the 11th century the still extant narthex with a double-tower façade was added. In about 1090, almost two decades after planning for Cluny III had begun, Abbot Hugh began a new church in Paray-le-Monial, considered the "pocket edition" of Cluny III. Here a broadly projecting five-bay transept with two apses in the east connects to the basilical choir ambulatory with three radiating deep chapels via a connecting bay that adjoins to the bays of the nave and side aisles. In the nave only three bays were completed (illus. right). The old narthex was not torn down as planned, but remained. Apparently, the plans for the choir were changed: the ambulatory is both narrower and lower than the rest of the structure. The elevation of the choir has only two zones. Eight columns carry arcades with round arches, above which is a smooth wall instead of blind arcades. Above that a row of closely spaced windows is topped by barrel vaulting. These characteristics and the form of the chapels at first seem to suggest Saint-Etienne in Nevers as the source of inspiration. Saint-Etienne was redesigned according to the concept of Cluny III: a basilica-like choir, broad nave and side aisles accessed through a connecting bay, a barrel-vaulted transept with apses, and an octagonal crossing tower. The vertical, light-flooded nave with its few bays resembles the model and—until computer simulation began to enhance the imagination—provided an authentic impression of how Cluny III must have looked (except for its five-aisle structure). The portals are richly ornamented; the tympana are not sculpted but may have once been painted. The exterior, with a double-tower façade and a pointed crossing tower, as slender and steep as the interior, is beautifully reflected in the Bourbince River (illus. opposite). Notre-Dame was completed about 1130/1140. The monastery was closed during the Revolution, and in 1876 the church was re-dedicated due to a resurgence of worship of the Sacred Heart in Sacré-Coeur. After the visions of Marguerite-Marie Alacoque, the movement was centered in Paray-le-Monial (see p. 239).

The present town hall was the palace of textile manufacturer Pierre Jayet (illus. p. 239). On closer inspection, its richly decorated Renaissance façade (1525/1528) clearly shows Gothic elements. Between the engaged pilasters, medallions with heads adorn the balustrades.

Paray-le-Monial, former monastic church of Notre-Dame, central nave and choir, 1090 or later.

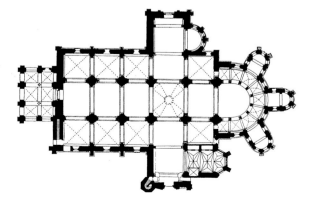

Paray-le-Monial, former monastic church of Notre-Dame, floor plan.

OPPOSITE:
Paray-le-Monial, former monastic church of Notre-Dame, view across the Bourbince to the narthex and double tower façade from the second half of the 11th century, as well as to the nave, transept, and crossing tower from the late 11th century.

Paray-le-Monial, former monastic church of Notre-Dame, choir and transept from the northeast.

The French mystic Marguerite-Marie Alacoque was born in 1647 and entered the Order of the Visitation in Paray-le-Monial in 1671. It had been founded by St. Francis of Sales and St. Jane de Chantal in 1610. The Salesians, or Visitandines, devoted themselves to contemplation, caring for the poor and the sick, and to youth education and welfare. Soon after she entered the monastery, Marguerite-Marie experienced a number of apparitions of Jesus, who showed her his heart. The most significant appearance took place on the feast of Corpus Christi in 1675; on this occasion, she was given the task of establishing a separate feast for the Heart of Christ. Marguerite-Marie became mistress of the novices and died in 1690. In 1864 she was beatified, and canonized in 1920. At this time the worship of the Sacred Heart began to grow rapidly, especially in France where it took on a nationalistic flavor after the lost war in 1870/1871. Paray-le-Monial is still an important pilgrimage site today; the former monastic church of Notre-Dame has been re-consecrated to Sacré-Coeur. In 1873, the pope elevated the church to a Basilica minor. The mortal remains of Marguerite-Marie Alacoque are buried in the Chapelle de la Visitation in the monastery of the Visitandines.

Paray-le-Monial, façade of the town hall, 1525–1528.

Green Hills along the Saône – Mâconnais

The Mâcon arrondissement—in terms of area, the smallest in Burgundy—lies at the extreme southeastern corner of the province, its eastern border formed by the Saône. Its geological profile and terrain are determined by the southernmost foothills of the Côte d'Or, which taper off much more gently here than in the north. The agriculture of the region is a diverse mixture of everything cultivated in neighboring areas: farming, viticulture, poultry and cattle breeding, as well as forestry. The region is also geologically diverse. In the east near the Saône, limestone dominates in the soil, while further west in the Grosne valley, granite formations from the Morvan move in. Industry has developed in the fertile alluvial land east of the Saône, especially near Mâcon. But that area belongs to the Ain department, and is not a part of Burgundy.

Mâcon

Mâcon is the southernmost city of Burgundy, connecting north and south in terms of both climate and culture. Situated close to the river, which has been a very significant trade route since antiquity, Mâcon's origins seem self-evident. Nevertheless, archaeological finds of tools near the cliff of Solutré, 7.5 miles (12 km) southwest of the city, indicate that this area was already comparatively densely populated by around 20,000 BC. Prehistoric finds near the cliff were so significant that the place gives its name to the era between 20,000 and 15,000 BC: the Solutrean. The most spectacular and oddly touching of these prehistoric finds are certainly the thousands of horse skeletons (estimations range from 30,000 to 100,000 horses) found in piles up to 6 feet (2 m) high at the foot of the rock. When they were discovered by Adrien Arcelin in 1866, the phenomenon was interpreted in the romantic fashion typical of the time: it was supposed the wild horses had been chased up the gentle side of the rock and were then forced by the use of noise and fire to jump from the steep cliff to their deaths. Today the site at the foot of the unusual limestone formation is regarded as a place of slaughter where not only horses, but also mammoths, bisons, aurochs, and elks were butchered. Since 1967 this grave site has belonged to the French government, which erected a museum to house the finds here that had previously been taken to Chalon.

LEFT:
Mâconnais countryside near Matour (ca. 18 miles/30 km west of Mâcon).

ABOVE:
Hilly countryside near Cluny.

Mâcon, view of the city from across the Saône. At the right are the towers of Vieux-Saint-Vincent, to the left the towers of Saint-Pierre.

During the Celtic period, this region was inhabited by the Aedui. They were a tribe friendly to the Romans and did not object to the founding of the *castrum matisconensis*. Trade, mainly in oil and wine, formed the basis of their growth and wealth. In 443, Aetius moved the Burgundians, whom he had defeated, from Worms and resettled them along the Rhône and Saône. The *castrum matisconensis* became a part of the newly founded kingdom of Burgundy, which was conquered by the Franks by 527. In 1435 Mâcon was again annexed to Burgundy, and remained part of the ducal fiefdom until it eventually fell to the crown for good in 1477. The city itself has preserved

astonishing little from all of these centuries. A civil war between the Armagnacs and the Bourguignons, and then the Wars of Religion destroyed many buildings, and the Revolution wreaked greater destruction here than elsewhere. Many churches were completely destroyed, leaving the cathedral only a sad ruin, a testament to neglect and vandalism. The diocese of Mâcon was abolished at that time and has not been re-established. In 1799 Saint-Vincent began to be dismantled.

The diocese purportedly had been in existence for almost 200 years when the Frankish king Childebert transferred the relics of St. Vincent from Spain to Mâcon in 543. This occasion most likely

prompted the construction of a new building, but nothing is known of it now. Of the succeeding building as well, which was begun in the 10th century and finally vaulted in 1096, only a few ornamental pieces are preserved. Apparently it had two west towers, whose cellars still exist. After 1147 a three-aisle narthex—which is still standing (illus. p. 244)—was placed between these two towers. Despite extensive damage, its rich articulation comprising lovely figural capitals is evident. The tympanum depicting the Last Judgment in five narrative bands is rather unusual. The bottom band is Paradise and Hell; above that the Awakening of the Dead, followed by the minor and major

prophets of the Old Testament. In the third band is Christ in the mandorla accompanied by the Apostles as witnesses to the Last Judgment, and Mary and John as intercessors. Finally, seraphim and cherubim symbolize the sphere of Heaven. The tympanum has no lintel and was (perhaps later?) carved at its base to form an arch.

From 1239 the cathedral was renovated in High Gothic style. Although the damage inflicted during the Wars of Religion was severe, the years of neglect afterwards seem to have been worse. Repairs were not initiated until the early 17th century, and then undertaken hesitantly, without conviction. It is therefore not surprising that by

Mâcon, former cathedral of Vieux
Saint-Vincent, northern exterior of
the narthex, after 1147.

Mâcon, Saint-Pierre, 1860/1870,
central aisle of the nave and high choir.

1799 the cathedral was so dilapidated that hardly
any protest arose when it was finally dismantled.

About 60 years later, in the 1860s, a student of
Viollet-le-Duc named Jean-Baptiste Berthier was
commissioned to design a church dedicated to St.
Peter, to be built in line with the Hôtel Montrevel
(the present town hall), which had been built
in 1750. Drawing on stylistic elements of various
Romanesque monumental buildings, Berthier
created a composite floor plan and elevation that
surely never existed in the 11th century. Behind
the rather bland, academic, three-story exterior
façade framed by two octagonal towers is a
surprisingly pleasant interior, with a three-aisle
galleried nave adjoined by a transept and a choir
ambulatory with chapels (illus. above). As a docu-
mentation of an era, Saint-Pierre is an impressive
structure, indeed.

Mâcon, hospital on Square de la Paix, formerly Hôtel-Dieu, after 1760, pharmacy.

St. Vincent of Paul (1576–1660) had founded a hospice, the Charité, at the corner of rue Carnot and quai Lamartine, which was recognized as a public hospital in 1682. Badly in need of repair by the 18th century, renovations to it were begun in 1750 by Jacques-Germain Soufflot, the architect of the Pantheon in Paris. His attention focused particularly on the chapel (illus. left), which was still a basic component of all hospices. It is oval and roofed with an elliptical dome on colossal pilasters. Groin-vaulted galleries, from which the patients on all levels could participate in the mass, form the two upper stories.

At the Square de la Paix is a second hospital, the old Hôtel-Dieu, dating from the 12th century. Soufflot was again asked to draw a plan for its renovation in 1747, but this time declined. Finally, in 1760, an architect from Lyon, Melchior

ILLUS LEFT:
Mâcon, Charité, rebuilt by Jacques-Germain Soufflot from 1750 on. View into the chapel with three consecutive stories of arcades; at the left is the altar.

ground floor of stone once had open arcades that served as merchants' stalls. Above are three half-timber stories richly decorated with wood carvings and wood-framed windows (illus. left).

The Hôtel Senecé is a building from around 1750 with typically rounded corners on the *cour d'honneur*. Pilasters and wrought iron balcony railings articulate the façades of the main building. The interior contains flat stucco reliefs depicting the seasons, as well as carved doors and wood paneling. Since 1896, this has been the seat of the Académie de Mâcon, founded in 1805. Today most of the rooms serve as a museum essentially dedicated to the Romantic poet Alphonse Prat de Lamartine, born in Mâcon in 1790. The museum houses numerous portraits of Lamartine, documents of his political career, drawings from his private collection, as well as art works by his wife, Marianne (see pp. 248/249). Finds from prehistory and antiquity, paintings, and objects from the cultural history of the city and its environs are exhibited in the city museum, which is housed in the former Ursuline convent (illus. opposite).

Mâcon, Maison du Bois, early 16th century, façade facing Place aux Herbes. On the ground floor, the once open arches are still visible on one side; they formerly served as a store and a workshop. Above are the living quarters.

Munet, a student of Soufflot, was commissioned for the work. He based his designs directly on the new Charité, which was still under construction. Like many hospitals, it has an especially lovely pharmacy, a room with wood paneling in the style of Louis XV with a collection of pharmaceutical faiences from the period (illus. p. 245).

One of the last early Renaissance half-timber houses, which were once commonplace in the city, is the Maison du Bois on the Place aux Herbes. The

Mâcon, Hôtel de Senecé, seat of the Académie de Mâcon since 1896 and now primarily the Musée Lamartine. Caritas, first half of the 18th century (property of the Académie).

ABOVE LEFT AND RIGHT:
Mâcon, former Ursuline convent, today city museum, archaeological finds from Roman times and even earlier, including household items and a mosaic depicting a gladiator.

BELOW:
Mâcon, former Ursuline convent, today city museum, room in the upper story housing the cultural-historical department (pictures, furniture, rugs, sculpture).

Alphonse de Lamartine – A Romantic in the Country

Mâcon, Hôtel de Senecé, now the Musée Lamartine, enfilade of the exhibition rooms with scenic paintings over the doors.

Alphonse-Marie-Louis Prat de Lamartine was the son of a country nobleman of Burgundy. He was born on October 21, 1790 amidst the turmoil of the French Revolution, in a house next to the Ursuline convent in Mâcon. At the age of seven he came to Milly, today Milly-Lamartine, where he spent most of his youth. Like many country aristocrats, Lamartine began a diplomatic career after his formal education with the Jesuits, but the July Revolution of 1830 put an end to those plans. In 1833 he was elected deputy to the chamber of representatives. The Revolution of 1848 followed, after which Lamartine did not manage to re-establish himself in politics. He died in Paris in 1869.

Lamartine was born as a landowner, which at that time still meant that he was feudal lord of an estate. His land consisted mainly of vineyards. Contemporary paintings portray him as elegant, sophisticated, and confident; a typical representative of the French nobility, dressed according to fashion and surrounded by the requisites of luxury. He was often seen with a pair of greyhounds who accompanied him like a trademark (illus. right). This was only one aspect of his life and his character, however. His other side, his literary penchant, was rather untypical for a person of his rank. Nevertheless, his poetry was incomparably more influential than his political endeavors.

In 1820, the year of his marriage, he published his first volume of poetry, *Méditations poétiques* (Poetic Meditations). In it he evoked the natural world, essentially the landscapes of his native southern Burgundy, in lyrical, sentimental language. His verses captured the mood and longings of the time and found resonance throughout Europe.

Romanticism influenced the spirit and art of an entire era. It had its origin in Germany in the last quarter of the 18th century. Creative imagination and subjective and individual experience were given priority over classical notions of humankind and the world, and the ideals of Romanticism began to pervade philosophy, religion, poetry, music, and art as well as the natural sciences and politics. The one-sided image of man—and the stifling rules and etiquette associated with rationalism—were displaced by a greater awareness of history (especially an idealized Middle Ages), religion, the quest for "the soul of the people" as manifest in folk poetry, and the subconscious world of dreams; as well as sensitivity towards nature, the night, and things dark and hidden.

In England, Romanticism was not based on a systematic, philosophical-scientific endeavor as it was in Germany, but rather on the experience of nature and the rediscovery of the folk song and folk tale. From here, Romanticism moved to France, where as early as 1802 François René de Châteaubriand had rekindled sentimentality for the Roman Catholic faith and heightened interest in the Middle Ages with his writings. In addition, Jean-Jacques Rousseau had paved the way for the rediscovery of nature in the mid-18th century. During her two journeys to Germany, Madame de Staël forged links to German Romanticism, expressing her views and impressions in the treatise *De l'Allemagne* (On Germany), published in 1810 and 1813. The sensitive, nature-loving Alphonse de Lamartine absorbed these impulses and transformed them into sentimental and sublime verse. By 1825, just five years after its publication, his first volume of poetry had appeared in 12 editions! Lamartine's programmatic intentions are evident in the vignette of the frontispiece, where nature is symbolized with attributes pawned from Romantic and religious fantasies—such as the cross, harp, book, chalice, and wreath—evoking a sentiment or atmosphere similar to the *memento mori* images of a previous age.

Alphonse de Lamartine, painting by Belgian artist Henri Decaisne from 1839. The portrait shows Lamartine at the age of 49 against the backdrop of a Romantic landscape. Mâcon, Musée Lamartine in the Hôtel de Senecé.

Saint-Point, Château de Lamartine. The château of Saint-Point was thoroughly renovated in neo-Gothic style in the 19th century. This was the point of departure for the movement that inspired literature and the visual arts equally, indeed, the entire intellectual life of the period, and is now known as Romanticism. Alphonse de Lamartine's father gave his son Saint-Point as a wedding present. After restorations to repair the damage inflicted during the Revolution and the addition of generous extensions, Saint-Point became one of Lamartine's preferred residences. Today the building is a museum in which Lamartine's study and living quarters can be seen. In addition, it houses letters of famous contemporaries and paintings by Lamartine's wife, Marianne. In the park is the ancient oak tree that has become famous in literature through the lyric novel *Jocelyn*. Lamartine had a neo-Gothic chapel erected on the cemetery next to the church, a kind of mausoleum in which he, his mother, his wife, and his daughter are buried. The church is a beautiful small building dating from the first half of the 12th century, surmounted by a two-story bell tower decorated with lesenes and blind arcading.

Alphonse de Lamartine, bust by Brian, 1843. Mâcon, Musée Lamartine in the Hôtel de Senecé.

In 1823 Lamartine published his sequel, the *Nouvelles méditations poétiques* (New Poetic Meditations), followed in 1836 and 1838 by the lyric epics *Jocelyn* and *La chute d'un ange* (The Fall of an Angel). Today they are difficult to read; the slowly evolving, contemplative plot can only be comprehended through an understanding of the rhythm of life in the French countryside. Incidentally, Lamartine remained, on the exterior, completely correct and elegant. Not one of his many portraits depicts him as a Bohemian with wild hair or with the large, softly falling poet's shirt that so appealed to his literary friends.

Despite a considerable income from his estates, Lamartine was nearly ruined financially by 1848, whether by the thorough renovation of the château of Saint-Point (illus. above), his unsuccessful election campaign after the 1848 Revolution, which supposedly devoured enormous sums, or perhaps simply due to an overly extravagant lifestyle. Disappointed by the reality of politics, he devoted himself to historical and political writings. In a pavilion in the vineyards near Montceau, called *la Solitude*, he composed the *Histoire des Girondins*.

Lamartine's influence on French Romantic literature is uncontested, but far greater and almost entirely unrecognized is his influence on architecture. The architecture of southern and central Burgundy was inundated, as it were, by a wave of Gothic and Romantic revival. Following the example of Eugène Viollet-le-Duc, who magnificently resurrected the Gothic in both his writings and his buildings, countless castles in Burgundy were Gothicized, re-Gothicized or built in neo-Gothic style. Moveable architectural elements such as fireplaces, wood paneling, and portal casings were moved to new places in order to re-create a medieval style that had never been or no longer existed. Some examples are La Rochepot, Rully, Commarin, Saint-Point, Saint-Bonnet-de-Joux, the Hôtel Aubriot in Dijon, Berzé-le-Châtel, and many others. Churches were equally affected by the new trend, especially in places where sculpture damaged by the Revolution had to be restored or completed, or where entire buildings had to be renovated. New construction was invariably executed in the new "style." Eclecticism dominated the architecture and interior design of an entire century, often in an academic, dry manner and in dark, dull colors that are easily recognizable. As Modernism emerged, these "Gothic" buildings were soon considered to be in bad taste. Only recently has *néo-style* come to be appreciated as a document of its era.

Brancion

Atop one of the rock formations of the Monts du Mâconnais, between the Saône and the Grosne, is the famous Brancion castle (illus. right). According to legend, this site had already fortified been and settled during the era of the Burgundian kings, but the first verifiable lord was Warulf de Brancion (died 927). Four rings of walls, partly fortified with gates and towers, enclosed the village and church, a first and second *basse-cour*, and an inner courtyard with a donjon. In 1259 the duke of Burgundy acquired Brancion. Odo IV, a frequent visitor, purportedly had a logis added to the donjon in the first half of the 14th century. Vestiges of large tracery windows facing the courtyard and two large halls on each story can still be recognized. The mural above the fireplace of the large hall from the late 15th century shows Josserand III of Brancion at the side of Louis IX (St. Louis) with the castle as a backdrop, including the outer fortification wall and main entrance, the church of Saint-Pierre, the Maison de Beaufort, as well as the inner gate and donjon.

BELOW:
Brancion, Saint-Pierre, 12th century, exterior view from the southeast.

BELOW RIGHT:
Brancion, Saint-Pierre, detail of the murals of the Saint Anthony chapel. Pilgrim scene, 1325–1335.

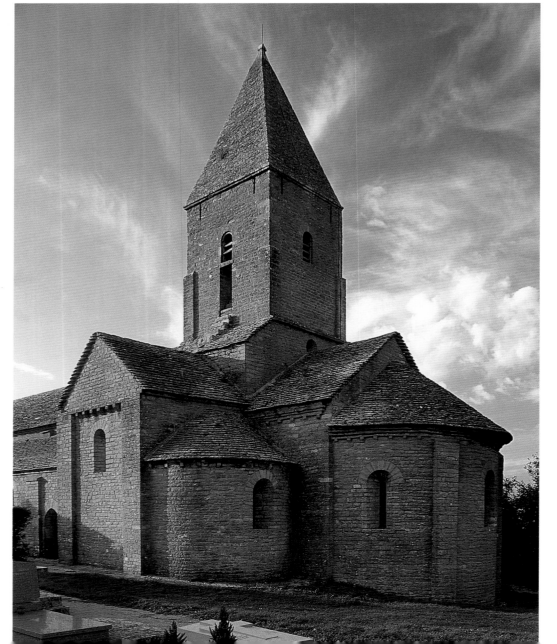

A castle church, dedicated to St. Peter and under the supervision of Cluny, belonged to the 10th-century castle. The present building was supposedly built in the second half of the 12th century (illus. opposite). However, its appearance suggests an earlier date or the work of a conservative architect. Simple rectangular piers with engaged columns divide the interior into a nave with five transverse oblong bays flanked by side aisles. The groin vaulting of the side aisles and the windowless barrel vault of the central nave rest on heavy arcades. Adjacent in the east are the rather low, short transept, also spanned by groin vaulting, and three apses; the central apse is preceded by an antebay. The external walls are articulated by engaged flat pillasters and a square tower crowns the crossing. In concept it resembles the narthex basement of Tournus, thus assigning it to the first half of the 11th century. The arcades, however, already have pointed arches.

The interior painting probably dates from around 1325/1335. In the choir apse is a depiction of the Last Judgment, on a choir column is a holy bishop or abbot, and in the chapel of St. Antonius to the south are images of a pilgrimage (illus. opposite) and a sermon. The north chapel bears a Christmas scene and in the adjacent side aisle are two death scenes, in which the souls are received into Abraham's lap. Next to them is a figure from a 13th-century grave that was moved to Saint-Pierre in 1959 from a tomb in the park of the castle of Uxelles. Purportedly, the figure portrays Josserand III de Brancion, who was killed on crusade in 1250 in Mansourah.

Brancion, castle, at the top right are the donjon and logis from the first half of the 14th century. In the middle is a logis from the 15th century and on the left, the town which developed within the castle walls and the church of Saint-Pierre.

Mâconnais countryside with a view of La Chapelle-sous-Brancion.

Chapaize, former priory church of Saint-Martin, about 1030, nave with side aisles and square crossing tower seen from the southwest.

OPPOSITE TOP:
Cormatin, Château de Cormatin, early 17th century, exterior view of the wings.

OPPOSITE BOTTOM:
Cormatin, Château de Cormatin, interior view showing the original furnishings and paintings.

Chapaize

Saint-Martin in Chapaize (illus. above), in the hills northwest of Brancion, is a significant structure contemporary with the Tournus tradition. No construction dates are known, but the small church can be dated to around 1030 following the chronology of Saint-Philibert. The floor plan and the shape of the pillars as well as the overall measurements correspond to those of the narthex basement of Tournus. Interestingly, they also correspond to those of Romainmôtier in Switzerland and to the reconstructed measurements of Cluny II. This would suggest close connections among the monasteries and their builders, who certainly collaborated on the realization of their spatial conceptions.

The bay structure in Chapaize corresponds to that of the nave and side aisles in Tournus, already signifying progress in the knowledge of vaulting techniques. A perpendicular bay structure in the central nave was spanned by a barrel vault with windows—it apparently collapsed in the 12th century and was replaced with a pointed barrel—and flanked by side aisles with square, groin-vaulted bays. To this day, the upper walls of the nave still have a slight, seemingly precarious outward slant to them (illus. p. 194).

In keeping with the more modest demands of the priory, Saint-Martin had only a low transept and three apses. The crossing tower, however, is slender and tall and articulated with a décor of lesenes and blind arcading. This structural arrangement of architectural forms became typical for the Romanesque churches of Burgundy, and it is interesting to note the role of the crossing tower in this connection. At first, it was square and opened into more or less ornate, bell towers of several stories; later it often took an octagonal shape. Its belfry arcades are often decorated with richly ornate recessed molding. The crossing tower makes the church visible from afar, whereas the nave and choir disappear behind the woods or surrounding structures, or before the backdrop of cliffs. Nonetheless, crossing towers served mainly as belfries, and their appearance in Burgundy seems related to the founding of the monastery at Cluny. Apparently, the sound of bells became a significant element in the liturgy of Cluny, which engaged the senses to a high degree. The sound of the bells ringing is a festive and solemn language, loud and dominating without being noisy, and their sound helps connect places that lie far apart.

Cormatin

Proceeding upstream along the Grosne, one reaches Cormatin lying in a broad valley, where Antoine du Blé d'Uxelles built an expansive three-wing château on the site of a medieval castle (illus. opposite) in the early 17th century. The complex had changed owners frequently, and its southern wing was turned into a cotton weaving plant in 1809. Today only two wings are preserved, in rather decrepit condition: on a slightly banked foundation of rusticated ashlars, rising directly from the moat, are two stories articulated by wide horizontal bands. The corners are accentuated by rusticated ashlars that echo the foundation. The tall mullion windows are devoid of décor. Slightly more elaborate are the gabled dormers, the slender turrets over engaged pavilions on ringed corbels, and the protruding façade bays, vertical elements that add some relief to the façades. Several features are typical of early 17th-century French architecture that sought to replace Renaissance preoccupation with classical antiquity. These include the structure's articulation in wings and pavilions with individual hip roofs, the accentuation of the corners and window axes with contrasting stone décor or protruding bands, the horizontal articulation of stories through intermediate cornices, and the use of stone décor. Although Jacques Androuet du Cerceau has been credited with the design, this has not been reliably substantiated.

Today the château of Cormatin houses a comprehensive collection of Baroque paintings, primarily portraits, attributed to important masters such as Rigaud, Nattier, Mignard, Lesueur, and Velásquez. The rooms, featuring original trabeated ceilings and richly ornate fireplaces, are quite remarkable (illus. opposite).

Softly rolling hills of the **countryside near Bonnay.**

Bonnay, former priory church of Saint-Hippolyte, late 11th century, view of the ruins of the nave and into the choir. The extension of the crossing tower dates from the 13th century.

Bonnay

Farther west, in the gently rolling foothills of the Côte d'Or, lies Bonnay. From the 11th century, it was the seat of a priory of Cluny and center of a feudal estate with an extensive castle. The priory apparently had been endowed by Hugh of Semur (the later St. Hugh of Cluny). The church of Saint-Hippolyte, built in the 11th century, was a three-aisle basilica (originally?) with a pointed barrel vault spanning the central nave and groin vaulting over the side aisles. Adjoining in the east were a high transept with a crossing tower and a semi-circular central apse flanked by side apses with a preceding bay—in short, a typical late 11th-century Cluny church. During the 13th century the transept was raised and converted into a kind of donjon in which the belfry arcades of the crossing tower remained in place as windows. Nave and side aisles seem to have carried battlements. Under the weight of the tower, however, it soon collapsed. The eastern part of the church with the original altar and parts of the nave wall have survived as a picturesque ruin (illus. left).

Bonnay / Besanceuil

All that remains of the castle of Besanceuil (illus. above and right) are a few sections of wall, two circular towers, and a chapel from the 12th century. It is a one-aisle building with a low transept, a semicircular apse articulated with lesenes and blind arcading, and a crossing tower. The nave walls still show traces of black mural painting, a *lit de mort* (death bed), which was always applied when a deceased member of the feudal lord's family was laid out in the church before burial.

In one of the castle courtyards, a four-tower donjon was built in about 1465. It had an external stair tower with a beautiful portal, windows with ogival arches, and an inscription bearing the date they were built: *En 1466 fut faitte cette visse*. Subsequent additions, installation of windows, and dismantling of the battlements have unfortunately disfigured the building. The complex nevertheless has an unusual atmosphere. Without visible traces of restoration, buildings stemming from several centuries are combined and form an ensemble of rare intensity.

Bonnay / Besanceuil, view of the hamlet and the castle.

Bonnay / Besanceuil, Château de Besanceuil, 12th century/1465.

ABOVE:
Countryside near Taizé.

RIGHT:
Hilly, misty landscape near Cluny.

Taizé, the town and its Romanesque church.

Taizé

Back on the Grosne is Taizé, set on a rocky promontory (illus. left). Few come here to see the Romanesque village church Sainte-Marie-Madeleine: visitors seek community, rather than art! Roger Schutz founded the first Protestant monastic community here, near his native Switzerland, in 1940. The rules of the community are similar to those of Roman Catholic orders. At first the monks were devoted to helping fugitives. Roman Catholic monks joined later, and one of the first centers of the ecumenical movement began to evolve. Growing numbers of visitors necessitated a new church, and in 1962 the Church of Reconciliation was built outside the village. Today it is at the heart of a whole town with some permanent buildings and many temporary structures, where believers from all over the world, especially young people, congregate to meditate and pray.

Cluny

The atmosphere of Taizé can perhaps give us a faint impression of the aura surrounding Cluny in the 11th and 12th centuries, when the monastery prospered and attained the height of its power. Taizé doesn't have the influence within the church and government that Cluny once enjoyed, but the presence of countless pilgrims, accomodating such large numbers of people in an atmosphere of silence and devotion to God, might have been similar. And yet Cluny remains incomparable—its history, its artistic and political achievements, its devotion to the poor and the dead, its community.

William, duke of Aquitaine and count of Auvergne, founded a monastery here in 910; it was dedicated to the apostles Peter and Paul and placed directly under the authority of the pope. The first abbot, Berno (910–926/927), consecrated a small church, Cluny I, in 915. Excavations on the Carolingian estate that formed the foundation for the monastery have revealed that this church was a hall church.

By 948, construction of a second church had already begun; its floor plan and elevation can be reconstructed from excavations and numerous buildings for which it was the prototype. Cluny II was a three-aisle basilica consisting of seven bays with a broadly projecting transept adjoined by a symmetrical seven-part Benedictine choir with radiating chapels (visible in the illus. of Cluny III,

Cluny, former monastic church of Saint-Pierre-et-Saint-Paul (Cluny III), view of the church from the east in a 16th-century lithograph by Emile Sagot (after 1789). Paris, Bibliothèque nationale, engravings collection.

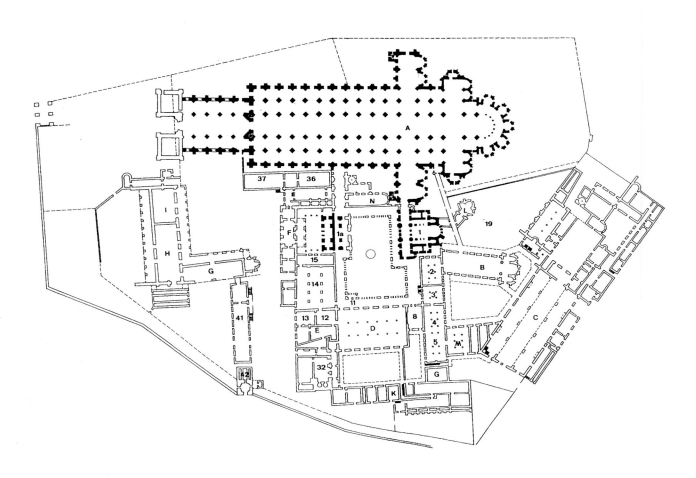

Cluny, former monastic church of Saint-Pierre-et-Saint-Paul, floor plan of the entire complex; reconstruction as it would have appeared around 1150 (according to K. J. Conant).

Cluny, former monastic church of Saint-Pierre-et-Saint-Paul, 1088 to 1131/1132, view from the axis of the lost nave towards the west; in the background are the remains of the southern transept.

left). This sequence of seven rooms of varying widths and depths began with the main apse in the center and grew shorter, ending with the two transept apses. The second and fifth "apses" were closed rooms with straight rear walls, penitential rooms for the monks. Three arcades on each side connected the elevated choir with its side aisles. This floor plan called for 15 altars, as noted in the so-called *Consuetudines* (Habits). In the west the basilica was preceded by an atrium and a galilaea (narthex). This church was consecrated in 981 under Abbot Majolus (963–994). Abbot Odilio (994–1048) purportedly ordered the vaulting of the nave and side aisles—most likely a barrel vault with windows at its base.

Although the actual construction of Cluny III did not begin until 1088, Abbot Hugh (1049–1109) had been involved with its planning since at least 1070. It was to meet the needs of the expanded liturgy and especially to provide enough space for the growing numbers of monks. In 1095 Pope Urban II consecrated the main altar, which is now on exhibit in the museum. Records mention that the barrel vault over the central nave collapsed in 1125; it was replaced by a barrel vault with pointed arches. The final consecration

took place around 1131/1132, but the completion of the three-aisle rib-vaulted narthex took almost another 100 years; it was consecrated in 1225. In 1790 the monastery was abolished and after 1811 almost completely torn down.

The liturgy in Cluny evolved into an enormous theatrical performance of songs, light, and colors, a complex drama giving form to the Heavenly Jerusalem. Prayers, masses, and choral music took up a great part of the daily activity of the monks at Cluny. The third church, whose architecture developed for and with the liturgy over many decades, became a complete work of art, surpassing anything that people had seen and experienced before. All that remains is a portion of the southern transept arm with one of two symmetrically placed octagonal towers (illus. p. 263).

At 613 feet (187 m) long and almost 100 feet (30 m) high , the nave of Cluny III had five aisles and 11 bays, two transepts with four east apses each, two crossing towers, and a choir ambulatory with five radiating chapels. At the time even the old Saint Peter's Church in Rome was not as large! Compared to Cluny II, the number of altars was more than doubled—an absolute necessity for the approximately 300 monks. The elevation had

three zones in all secions, familiar from Autun, Paray-le-Monial, Saulieu, and others. Over the arcades—still with round arches in the choir, but pointed in the nave and side aisles—ran a triforium of three blind arches per bay surmounted by the clerestory, with three windows per bay. A pointed barrel vault spanned the central nave, which was more than 46 feet (14 m) wide! The overabundance of architectural sculpture recalls classical antiquity. The remaining capitals are masterpieces, now on display in the Musée du Farinier (illus. pp. 265 and 268/269). For the first time in the then young history of Burgundian sculpture, the figures—though still engaged—are almost free standing, and seem to move although they are not yet physically accurate. This made it possible to recount admonishing stories on the capitals—certainly a major intention of the abbots. The capitals of the chevet depict the Fall, Abraham's Sacrifice, the notation of Gregorian chant, the four rivers of Paradise and its trees, the theological and the cardinal virtues, the seasons, and the elements.

The recessed portal of the double-tower west façade has also been preserved. On the lintel are scenes from the Resurrection; on the tympanum is Christ enthroned in the mandorla. These scenes are also on display in the Musée du Farinier.

In Cluny III, Abbot Hugh separated the monks' church from the lay church. The broad nave with five aisles, lending it the character of a hall church, was for the lay brothers; the eastern parts—two transepts with two intermediate bays, the apses, and ambulatory choir—were reserved for monks.

Cluny, former monastic church of Saint-Pierre-et-Saint-Paul, 1088 to 1131/1132, interior view of the southern transept.

Cluny, former monastic church of Saint-Pierre-et-Saint-Paul, model, Musée du Farinier.

Cluny, former monastic church of
Saint-Pierre-et-Saint-Paul, 1088 to
1131/1132, southern transept.

LEFT:
Cluny, former monastery of Saint-Pierre-et-Saint-Paul, *le farinier* (granary), second half of the 13th century, two-aisle groin-vaulted hall on the ground floor. The mill once stood here.

OPPOSITE:
Cluny, former monastery of Saint-Pierre-et-Saint-Paul, *le farinier*, upper story with wooden barrel vault. Since 1949, the remains of the monastic church have been on display here. Among them are the eight capitals of the choir in their original sequence, reconstructed according to Conant. Each capital measures 31 in (80 cm), and the column shafts were 29 ft (8.85 m) tall. Incidentally, during the Middle Ages the number eight was a figure that symbolized perfection, the Resurrection, and universality because of its recurrence in the story of the life and resurrection of Jesus Christ. There is also a Romanesque altar slab with an arcade ornamentation—perhaps the altar that was consecrated by Pope Urban II in 1095—a marble urn that allegedly once contained the heart of Abbot Hugh, two models, and numerous other artifacts. One of the two models shows not only the entire sculptural décor, but also the chapel of St. Michael above the west wall lof the church, which, as in Vézelay and Semur-en-Brionnais, was accessible only through the gallery of the narthex.

The eastern sections of Cluny III realized various ideas from other sources. The two successive transepts recreated the Benedictine choir of Cluny II with its numerous altar spaces. The choir ambulatory clearly derived from pilgrimage churches, which had ambulatories surrounding their sacred relics. In Cluny III, the ambulatory not only provided room for numerous altars, but also optimal passages for Cluny's elaborate ceremonial processions. The idea of a double transept supposedly stems from experiments with this form in Saint-Benoît-sur-Loire. The vaulting is Burgundian: since the construction of Cluny II builders had experimented with barrel vaults above the clerestory. This concept had first been successful in the gallery church of Saint-Etienne in Nevers (ca. 1065). In Cluny III, it became possible to flood the clerestory of a monumental church with light under a stone barrel vault without galleries.

Compared to Gothic churches, the interior of Cluny III was certainly still dark; but one must imagine the church filled with the shimmering of countless candles on wide round chandeliers, creating an illumination that blurred the contours of the room and plunged the more distant parts into darkness. Today it is hard to imagine the feelings that must have overwhelmed the pilgrims and the countless poor who were regularly cared for and fed at Cluny—who were accustomed only to natural colors and light—when they entered the nave and peered into the vault soaring almost 98 feet (30 m) high, accompanied by the angelic chants of choirs of monks. It was the very image of heaven towards which every believing soul strived.

Cluny, Palace of Abbot Jacques d'Amboise, ca. 1500, today the city hall.

Cluny, former monastery of Saint-Pierre-et-Saint-Paul, so-called Pope Gelasius II façade, ca. 1310/1320; since 1873 this has served as the entrance to the monastery complex.

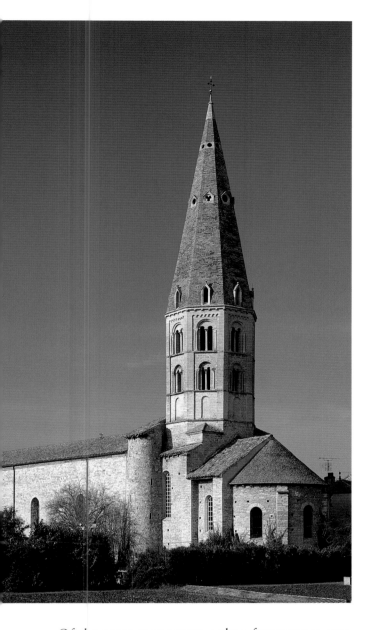

Of the great monastery, only a few towers, vestiges of the walls, and a few residential buildings have survived. The oldest structure is the *farinier*, an enormous granary dating from the 13th century (illus. pp. 264/265). It has a two-aisle ground floor and once housed the mill. The upper story is roofed with a lovely wooden barrel vault, and since 1949 has housed the museum. The so-called Pope Gelasius façade is a wide façade with windows from around 1310/1320; behind it—since renovations in 1873—are the rooms that lead into the monks' quarters (illus. opposite).

The logis of Abbot Jean de Bourbon, today the Musée Ogier, is a late medieval construction from about 1460. A little later, around 1500, the palace of Abbot Jacques d'Amboise was built; it is now the town hall (illus. opposite top). The only late Gothic elements are two engaged square pavilions with rich blind tracery décor on the three exposed sides. The castle-like monastic buildings, which Grand Prior Dathoze began in about 1750, differ little from château constructions of the period.

The sheer size of the complex accentuates the rather monotonous architecture. Today the rooms house the Ecole Nationale des Arts et Métiers.

In the second third of the 13th century, the parish church of Notre-Dame was erected in the *burgus* (village) of Cluny. It is a slender, three-aisle, columned basilica with rib vaulting, a low choir, and a non-protruding transept crowned by a tower. The elevation is distinctive. Above the pointed arcades runs a "Burgundian walkway" along the narrow windows of the clerestory, making the springers of the vault appear lighter. Typical of the period are also the round pillars with engaged semi-columns and crocket capitals (illus. above). With the exception of two consoles, all of the west narthex and portal sculptures were destroyed in the Revolution.

From the church of Saint-Marcel, first mentioned in 1159, only the octagonal crossing tower (like that of Cluny III) and the choir bay with a semicircular apse remain. The wide nave received a flat ceiling during a renovation (illus. above left).

Cluny, Notre-Dame, second third of the 13th century, arcades of the nave with the typical "Burgundian gallery" in front of the high windows.

TOP LEFT:
Cluny, Saint-Marcel, after 1159, view of the apse, crossing tower, and the barn-like nave.

The Community of Cluny

Cluny, former monastic church of Saint-Pierre-et-Saint-Paul, choir capitals. Top, the Fall; bottom, the discovery of the first sinful couple.

In order to understand the history of the monastic community of Cluny, its impact and radiant fascination in its own time, and its religious and social achievements during the 10th and 11th centuries, there is no better source than the writings of Joachim Wollasch. His years of extensive research recreate a surprisingly detailed picture of Cluny.

The community's history begins on September 11, 910, or possibly 909, in Bourges, where Duke William the Pious of Aquitane established a monastery dedicated to the apostles Peter and Paul, placing it directly under papal jurisdiction. He endowed the foundation with the Cluny estate in Burgundy, an inheritance from his sister Ava.

At this time, the reign of the Carolingians was coming to a close. Their power had declined and France was plagued by Hungarian, Saracen, and Norman invasions. Monasteries suffered greatly from repeated attacks and destruction (compare the history of the monks of Saint-Philbert on p. 191). If strong secular protectors or a bishop's troops did not come to their defense, monasteries were helpless and vulnerable. Even when defense was provided, they did not always fare better, since the secular powers were often the owners of the monasteries, ensuring their own power and high standard of living through the monasteries in their possession. To this end, they instated abbots who furthered their interests. Feudal lords and their families often lived in the monastery, making it difficult or impossible for the monks to observe the rules of their order. Times were hard, and many voices expressed a desire for reforms, a wish to return to the origins of a Christian life, to asceticism and apostolic poverty. New foundations sprang up in many places in response. An endowment like Duke William's was not unusual for his era, but driven by the personalities of its first abbots, his monastery attained previously unimaginable greatness.

The foundation deed includes an urgent plea for the protection of the young community with no secular lord in the form of a prayer, an invocation: "I entreat you, o holy apostles and glorious princes of the earth, Peter and Paul and you, Bishop of the bishops of the Apostolic Chair, that you may, through your canonical and apostolic authority which you received from God, keep away from the community of the holy Church of God and from participation in eternal life those who rob these goods that I gladly and freely present to you, who invade and take them away.

May you be the protective lords of those servants of God living there and of all their possessions, for the sake of the kindness and mercy of the Redeemer who looks upon us in His goodness."

William placed his endowment under the protection of the apostles Peter and Paul, addressed as glorious princes of the earth, and of the pope, the Bishop of bishops, as there was no other defender. At the same time, he relinquished it completely, both for himself and for his heirs. That was something new. A few years before, Girard de Roussillon and his wife Berta had endowed the monastery in Vézelay, also placing it directly under papal protection, but Girard had retained the use of all rights as well as the duties of protection and defense during his lifetime.

The foundation deed of Cluny also specified the purpose of the endowment, namely the attainment of salvation, an entirely common procedure throughout the Middle Ages. Cluny was not only the guarantor of the salvation and physical health of its donor and his family, the deed also included his feudal lord, the king, and those who are "faithful to us in their service and attached to us," and—this is completely astonishing—"the continued existence and prosperity of the Catholic religion and of all believers in Christ in the past, present, and future." New also was the detailed description of the monks' tasks. They were to perform "daily acts of compassion towards the poor, the needy, and travelers as well as pilgrims who asked for shelter."

Finally, William appointed the first abbot for Cluny; his successor, however, was to be elected freely by the monks. William chose Berno, who apparently was an aristocrat from Burgundy and had already founded a monastery in Gigny from his own wealth, and had become abbot there. But Berno's monastery was not a private cloister typical of the time. He had become a monk himself, and the monastic life in Gigny was so ascetic that it attracted monks who had left their monasteries and hadn't been able to find another one that provided the opportunity to live according to the Rule. Berno thus already had the reputation of being a reformer when William appointed him abbot of Cluny. During the 17 years of his abbacy, six additional monasteries were offered as donations to Cluny and Gigny.

After Berno's death in 927, the Benedictine monk Odo succeeded him. He took office with the vow to pursue the duties specified in the charter, that the community of monks should serve for the salvation of all living and deceased Christians. His conception of monastic life was based on the apostles' reports of the life of the original church in Jerusalem. Everything had been communal property; those who had owned property laid it at the apostles' feet, so that the poor received their share in the community. Convinced that the end of the world was nearing, Odo wanted to save souls. Even before he had entered the monastery he had lived the life of a monk and had convinced even his parents to join the monastic life. His biographer, the monk John of Salerno, called him a lover of poverty and wrote of him, "Never did a poor man leave the lap of his mercy empty-handed; for whenever I set out with him, he would always inquire carefully whether we had enough to feed and care for the poor." This generosity and compassion burdened the church to such an extent that the prior of Cluny finally objected. But Odo went a step further and demanded the same acts of compassion of the lay people that the Benedictine Rule imposed on monks. In his description of the life of Count Gerald of Aurillac he established the ideal of the "holy layman," a count who in the pursuit of his secular obligations secretly lived the life of a monk, refraining from the use of force and giving generously to the poor.

"Incomparably more highly regarded than a monk who breaks his vows is the compassionate layman," he wrote, appealing to lay people as few had before him. According to the reports of John of Salerno, kings had heard of Odo, bishops were familiar with him, and the important secular powers favored him. "Monasteries that were built in their sphere of influence were dedicated into the legal possession of our father that he might teach them our monastic way of life and lead, improve, and guide them on the right path."

Monasteries were not always given into Cluny's possession. The abbot was often called to other monasteries in order to reform them, even if they were not placed under Cluny's jurisdiction. These tasks kept Odo far from his own convent for long periods of time, and when he could no longer meet the demand on his own, he began sending out his students.

Odo was the abbot of a steadily growing group of monasteries. Around the year 930 he reformed the abbey of Saint-Benoît-sur-Loire despite initial difficulties. His biographer reported what Odo demanded of the monks: voluntary poverty, to eat no meat, to refrain from owning private property and to give away any hidden property. In addition, the monks must dedicate themselves to the duties of the liturgy, which determined the course of their entire day.

Since Odo aimed at the creation of a single large Christian community that would unite monks and laymen, as in the original Christian church, he must have been deeply satisfied with the growing number of monasteries that formed around Cluny. In fact, he vigorously promoted them. In order to closely integrate and unify the monastic communities, he sent his monks to negotiate affiliation contracts with monasteries that were not under Cluny's jurisdiction and had not yet been reformed. In 942 he negotiated such contracts with the abbeys of Saint-Benoît-sur-Loire, Saint-Martial in Limoges, and Saint-Pierre in Solignac; in the future, there was to be no difference between the monks of these monasteries, and they were to consider themselves as one. At the center of this association was Cluny.

Odo's greatest achievements, however, were his endeavors to ensure the safety of the monastic communities. More than ten papal documents and five royal documents were issued during his abbacy. Soon after Odo took office, Pope John X issued a document in which he bade King Rudolf of France, Archbishop Wido of Lyon, the bishops of Chalon-sur-Saône and Mâcon, Duke Hugh the Black of Burgundy, and Count Giselbert of Autun to give protection and help to Cluny. In the same year, the king of France confirmed the property and rights of the abbey as well as the monks' right to freely elect their abbot.

Apparently, Odo had already established personal contact with the pope and with the king in 927, and by means of his integrity and powers of persuasion managed to negotiate these privileges for Cluny. Further donations were confirmed and freedoms ensured during the papacy of John XI. At the same time, the pope distinguished Cluny from all other monasteries by granting it permission to accept monks from other monasteries if a life according to the rule was not possible at their own. The pope also allowed Cluny to legally acquire monasteries whose owners wished to have them reformed. This document gave Cluny the legal right to head the group of monasteries that had already formed. From then on, existent or newly founded monasteries could legitimately be placed in the possession of Cluny by their owners, clearing the road for Cluny's enormous expansion. Through the reciprocal confirmation of the royal and papal documents and the fact that each quoted the other, Abbot Odo had succeeded fabulously in creating a dense network of support and protection for Cluny by secular and clerical powers, ratifying the demands formulated in the foundation charter. In fact, there is reason to believe that Odo himself is the learned author of this contract.

Cluny, former monastic church Saint-Pierre-et-Saint-Paul, two views of a choir capital with depictions of two sounds of Gregorian chant.

When Odo died in 942, Aymard, his successor, had already been his representative for several years. In free election, the monks confirmed him as their abbot. During his 12-year term as abbot, the monastery expanded tenfold to include about 130 monks. Documents of this period mention that Aymard no longer needed to petition the emperor, the king, or the pope in person; instead, princes and counts performed these tasks for him. This shows how Odo's efforts to protect and promote Cluny through the most powerful men on earth had begun to bear fruit. He no longer needed to ask for protection; others considered it an honor to act on his behalf.

Twelve years after becoming abbott, Aymard went blind and resigned from his position. This is the first confirmed instance of an abbot of Cluny chosing his own successor, asking the monks to confirm his decision. Aymard's choice was Maiolus, who had been an archdeacon of the diocese church of Mâcon before entering Cluny, where he served as librarian and apocrisiary (in charge of the reliquary treasures). The monks confirmed Aymard's choice. Like his predecessors, Maiolus was often absent from the convent, either conducting reforms at other monasteries, visiting other monasteries of the order or traveling to Italy. The fact that these long absences caused no internal disruptions attests to the strong bond of mutual trust between the abbot and his monks.

Maiolus was also the one who established a good relationship between Cluny and the imperial court of the Ottonians. He did so with the help of the empress Adelaide and the count Heldricus, who was a confidant of Otto the Great. Heldricus later became a monk in Cluny; afterwards perhaps abbot of Saint-Germain in Auxerre, Saint-Pierre in Flavigny, and Saint-Jean-de-Réôme.

Syrus, the abbot's biographer, recounts that Maiolus was highly respected at Otto the Great's court. He notes that Otto the Great had wished to entrust the direction of the imperial monasteries in Italy and Germany to Maiolus, while Otto II and Adelaide would have preferred to suggest him as the first candidate (the emperor's right) for the impending papal election of 974. Maiolus, however, declined both offers, not wanting to desert the monks entrusted to him, and in the genuine sense of the Benedictine rule, placing his obligation to represent Christ in his monastic community before the office of the pope. What loyalty and unity in the monastery of Cluny!

Since both of Maiolus' parents came from southern France, he had good connections in this region, and many monasteries in Provence came into the Cluny fold during his tenure. In Rome he established close ties with the monastery of San Paolo fuori le mura; he instructed its monks about a consistent way of life and supported them financially. When the monks of San Paolo had to leave their monastery in 981, they brought their most valuable treasure, the ashes of the apostles, with them to Cluny where they were preserved in a column under the high altar after the consecration of Cluny II. From then on, St. Peter could be worshipped in Rome and in Cluny.

In Burgundy, too, a growing number of monasteries belonged to Cluny. At this time, Paray-le-Monial became a priory of Cluny. Moreover, the priory of Saint-Marcel-lès-Chalon, the Germanus monastery in Auxerre, and the abbeys Saint-Pierre in Flavigny-sur-Ozerain and Moutiers-Saint-Jean were reformed by Cluny; and the bishop of Autun signed an affiliation contract with Cluny.

In or before 987, during a journey to Rome, Maiolus made the acquaintance of young William of Volpiano, who was discontent with the lifestyle practiced in his monastery of Lucedio. He asked the abbot of Cluny for permission to enter his monastery. William became one of Maiolus' most influential students, eventually reforming 40 monasteries, as is documented by his biographer, Raoul Glaber. The most famous of these is Saint-Bénigne in Dijon where, ten years after he was appointed abbot, William built one of the most unusual and puzzling large monumental structures of the Middle Ages (see pp. 42-47).

Despite Cluny's obvious success, ensuring the Cluniac monastic freedom for monasteries that had been entrusted to Cluny for reform, but not been placed entirely under its jurisdiction, remained difficult. Maiolus was very much aware of this problem, and therefore had never undertaken efforts to reform these monasteries. William of Volpiano, however, received with Saint-Bénigne a monastery that was under the jurisdiction of his uncle, the bishop of Langres. Not all of the other monasteries that he reformed in Normandy and in Lotharingia were placed under the jurisdiction of Saint-Bénigne or Cluny. William executed the reforms, but afterwards only exercised as much authority as the bishop or secular owner of each monastery granted him.

The continued and rapid growth of Cluny and the long absences required of the abbot and the most trustworthy and capable monks may be among the factors that led Maiolus to set down the rules and regulations of monastic life at Cluny in writing for the first time. This text reveals the great intensity with which the entire daily routine of the monks was focused around liturgy—in fact, it focuses almost entirely on the communal liturgy. An essential part of this liturgy apparently was the compassionate care of the poor, not only of the twelve poor who lived permanently in the monastery, but also of the countless impoverished people who came to the monastery every day. Bread and wine was set out for them, as stipulated in the original community charter. Just as important as care of the poor was the veneration of the deceased. All deceased brothers of all monasteries belonging to or affiliated with Cluny, as well as their benefactors, patrons, and all those buried in their cemeteries, were invoked in prayers of remembrance every day. Their names were documented in long necrologies which were recorded in Cluny and then copied in the other monasteries. The monks' strict adherence to their monastic duties so deeply impressed people living near Cluny that the number of donations, especially for a funeral in Cluny, greatly increased.

In 992, two years before his death, Maiolus made Odilo his coadjutor. In 994 he died on the journey to Saint-Denis, where he had been summoned by Hugh Capet, king since 987. Very soon after his death, people everywhere began to revere him as a saint. The monks confirmed Odilo, designated by Maiolus, as abbot in an election. Duke Henry of Burgundy, his stepson Otto William, Rudolf III—King of Burgundy, and numerous bishops and archbishops signed the election document, confirming and strengthening Cluny's right to a free and impartial election of its abbot.

Odilo, also of aristocratic birth and highly educated, understood himself as preserver of Cluny's monastic tradition as well as Maiolus' spiritual successor. He wrote Maiolus' biography and four hymns to be sung on Maiolus Day in his remembrance. He also supported Maiolus' burial monastery, the priory of Souvigny, in every way possible. These details are significant because Maiolus and Odilo determined the development of the monastery for an entire century, from 954 to 1048.

Odilo's first years in office were overshadowed by difficulties. A frightful disease called the fire of St. Anthony (ergotism) began to spread like an epidemic, and the people sought relief and healing at the graves of saints, especially the grave of St. Maiolus in Souvigny. Here, according to Raoul Glaber, many found healing. In 1005/1006 Burgundy, as well as the rest of Europe, was hit by a famine. These disasters were interpreted as resulting from sin and guilt, and seen as the just punishment of God, signaling the end of the world. In response, synods were called in order to restore peace with God and renew Christian life.

About this time, the Abbot of Cluny complained that nobles had built fortifications on Cluny's land and taken cattle from Cluny and the adjacent *burgus* (village). He appealed to the king and the pope for protection and support. He himself resorted to a measure related to Odo's earlier idea of the layman-saint: Odilo leased monastery land to aristocrats for life. While the income from these fiefs was less than the profit generated from cultivating the land themselves, it did grant the monastery the protection of these vassals, who became *fideles s. Petri* (vassals of St. Peter). The aristocrats not only received land to build up their power, but were also promised *memento mori*, prayers of remembrance, in Cluny after their deaths. Growing numbers of men from noble families in the vicinity of Cluny now entered the monastery. The connection, even solidarity, of the aristocracy with the monks of Cluny increased. As a result, not only powerful nobles but also lords of castles entrusted their more modest estates to Cluny as priories. The ranks of the protecting powers in state and church, which the pope regularly called upon, were now joined by the middle and lower lords, especially those in the immediate vicinity of the monastery. During Odilo's abbacy the number of monasteries in Cluny's possession rose from 38 to 70, plus the priories, dependent members of the association.

During the abbacy of Maiolus, Cluny had begun to provide uncultivated land to farmers for clearing and cultivation. In exchange, half of the cultivated land transferred to the possession of the farmers after five years. Free landowners could

Cluny, former monastic church of Saint-Pierre-et-Saint-Paul, choir capital without figural décor.

LEFT:
Cluny, former monastic church of Saint-Pierre-et-Saint-Paul, remains of the former west portal and the bases of the central nave pillars.

of Maundy Thursday was the *mandatum*, the washing of the feet, which the monks performed on every one of the poor. In addition, the poor were supplied with food and money that would safely take them to the next monastery. For in the poor, the monks encountered Christ himself.

Odilo's major concern was not the physical well-being of those in his care, but the salvation of their souls. Back in the 6th century, Gregory the Great had reported the fate of a monk who was damned because it came out on his deathbed that he owned property, which was strictly forbidden. After some time, Gregory had been seized by pity and celebrated masses for him for 30 days, upon which the deceased appeared to him and announced that he had experienced substantial relief in his sufferings. This event was the basis of the belief that the prayers of the living, especially the 30-day memorial, could save souls. As the abbot of a monastery that was already considered exemplary in its care for the dead, Odilo nevertheless tried to improve by introducing All Souls' Day, a new day to remember the dead, one day after All Saints' Day, on which all the poor were fed bread and wine as on Maundy Thursday. All monasteries under Cluny's jurisdiction had to celebrate this day festively. As early as the 11th and 12th centuries this celebration had spread to other monasteries, until this day of remembrance was eventually adopted by Rome in the 14th century, becoming an integral part of the church year.

The deceased monks of a monastery and of its affiliated monasteries, as well as deceased benefactors and donors, were commemorated with prayers, celebration of mass, and acts of compas-

transfer their property to Cluny but retain use of it for the duration of their lives by paying a tax, thereby securing not only their property against hostile attack, but at the same time, the salvation of their souls.

Cluny's treatment of serfs was exceptional in medieval society. Abbot Odo had urged the freeing of bondsmen in his biography of Count Gerald. In exchange for their services, bondsmen in Cluny were either given their freedom or they were permitted to enter the monastery as monks. Laymen who worked for the monastery in agriculture or in construction received the same care as the monks. They received daily *praebenda*, which in the second half of the 11th century consisted of a measure of wine and a pound of bread, to which beans were added on four days. The twelve poor who lived permanently in Cluny were given the *praebenda*; in addition the poor received vegetables from Cluny's gardens as well as meat and fish on specified days. At Easter they were given nine ells of woolen cloth, and new shoes at Christmas. In return, they had to participate in the monks' choir prayers.

Numbers regarding the poor that came to Cluny on any given day and were provided with necessities are only available from the second half of the 11th century. At the outset of Lent they numbered 17,000! One permanent part of the liturgy

Cluny, former monastery of Saint-Pierre-et-Saint-Paul, model of the entire complex by François Gueugnon, 1855.

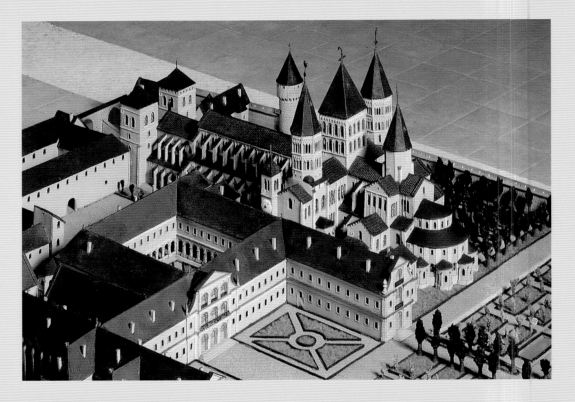

sion every day of the week except Sunday, the day reserved for the Lord. Each deceased was entered by name in comprehensive necrologies and mentioned publicly on her or his own day, so that a close relationship evolved between the living and the dead. This compassion in the care for the dead at Cluny, which reached its zenith under Odilo, had transformed the monastery into a greatly desired place of burial and remembrance for emperors, kings, the aristocracy, and ordinary citizens—for clergy and laypeople alike.

Like his predecessors, Odilo continued Cluny's traditionally good relations with the imperial court, the kings, and the pope. Emperor Henry II supposedly entrusted Cluny with the imperial insignia and the golden scepter immediately after his coronation, as well as some of his robes, a golden crown, and a golden crucifix. Odilo had the crown, which had hung over the altar, and the insignia melted down during the great famine of 1031/1032 in order to sustain the poor.

Despite pressing needs and problems during his abbacy, Odilo managed to replace the first monastic church, which had become too small, with Cluny II. Its original elevation can be reconstructed less from descriptions of the church than by comparing it to the priory church of Saint-Martin in Chapize and to elements of the monastic church of Saint-Philibert in Tournus (see p. 194), which evidently adopted the ideas of Cluny II. The foundations of this church have been excavated.

Odilo had not designated a successor before he died, but he had appointed a number of monks of exceptional abilities to be the electors. Odilo had, however, excluded Hugh of Semur, his young prior, from this group. The convention inferred that Hugh had been designated as the next abbot, and acted accordingly. Hugh came from Burgundian high nobility and had taken the habit of a monk against his father's will. He was a highly intelligent and educated man with great ambitions. He had wanted the position of abbot, but had not campaigned for it. He delayed the date of the election for several weeks so that it would coincide with the celebration of St. Peter's Chair, the day that commemorated St. Peter's acceptance of the papal office, an event celebrated as a high feast in Cluny. He thus created a parallel between St. Peter, who acceptance of responsibility for the church made him Christ's representative on earth, and the abbot of Cluny, who according to the rule was the representative of Christ within the monastery. The community of Cluny emerged as nothing less than an image of the Church, calling itself henceforth *Cluniacensis ecclesia*—the Church of Cluny, also the Holy Church of Cluny. During his abbacy, the monastery expanded to 300 monks in

Cluny alone. The number of donations and especially the number of new foundations in favor of Cluny, who received protection under the jurisdiction of the abbot, increased considerably in all of Europe until his death. Cardinals and bishops, princes and counts took the vows under Hugh's care, and the powerful of the world sought his advice.

Shortly before 1055 Hugh founded the first priory for women in Marcigny, 99 women to be precise, who were of aristocratic descent and at least 20 years old. At the top of the list of those seeking entrance were Hugh's own mother and sister, later followed by two more sisters and two nieces. A few years later, Hugh's brother, Gaufred II of Semur, also took the habit together with his son Gaufred III, his wife, and their three children. In the process, the estate of Semur was gradually integrated into Marcigny.

The increasing importance and the growing number of monks at Cluny required construction of a third church, begun around 1088. The planning stage had already taken some time, perhaps due to experiments with the elevation and vaulting. Although the abbot's biographer, Gilo, justifiably rated the establishment of the *Cluniacensis ecclesia* as his highest achievement, it is certainly true that the construction of Cluny III provided the appropriate framework for this extraordinary

Consecration of the high altar of Cluny III by Pope Urban II in 1095. Manuscript illumination, 12th century. Ms. lat. 17716, fol. 91r. Bibliothèque Nationale, Paris.

community. The architect was Gunzo of Baume-les-Messieurs, a monk of Cluny. After only seven years, the main altar was consecrated by pope Urban II, a former monk of Cluny. In 1125 the central nave was vaulted for the first time. When it collapsed and was repaired, the final consecration took place in 1131/1132. At the time, Cluny III was unequalled anywhere in the world both in terms of its enormous size and the magnificence of its interior design. One of the most generous patrons of Cluny III was King Alfons VI of Castille-Léon, whose donations were surpassed only by those of Henry I of England.

Hugh's greatest achievement in increasing the influence and significance of Cluny was his role as mediator between the emperor and the pope in the investiture controversy. Hugh was held in the highest regard by both men. During the papacy of Leo IX, Hugh had been a papal legate, and on Easter Sunday 1051 he became godfather of the future Emperor Henry IV in Cologne. Hugh was able to maintain the trust of both parties, and he was present in the castle of Canossa in January 1077 when Henry pleaded with the pope to rescind his excommunication.

The abbot was not able to help his godson have the ban lifted, and he did not live see the end of the investiture controversy. However, despite the pope's threat to excommunicate him, as well, due to his friendship with Henry IV, he courageously maintained this relationship, demonstrating the compassion of the *Cluniacensis ecclesia*.

It is not surprising that the monks of Cluny rose to high honors, and that Odo, a monk from Cluny, eventually ascended to St. Peter's chair as Urban II in 1088. As Odilo had once made Hugh of Semur a prior soon after he entered the monastery, so did Hugh quickly elevate Odo to the posi-

Malay, former collegiate church of Notre-Dame, late 11th century, exterior view looking towards the southwest with apse, transept, crossing tower, and nave.

tion of head prior. The relationship between the two men was characterized by profound trust even after Odo's election as pope. And it was this pope who—in analogy with Christ's words to his disciples—called the monks of Cluny "the light of the world" and granted his monastery even greater privileges. During the time of Urban II alone, Cluny was granted 16 papal decrees. In 1095 Urban II was the first pope to travel to Cluny, where he consecrated the main altar of Cluny III. Afterwards he visited several priories, performing consecrations and granting privileges. Finally, he extended the privilege granted Cluny in 931 that permitted monks from any other monastery to enter if they had not been given the opportunity to pursue life according to the Rule. He also extended a privilege—one that allowed any repenting sinner, even the excommunicated, to be buried in the cemetery of Cluny—to apply to the cemeteries of all monasteries and priories belonging to Cluny. This accounts for a decline of burials in Cluny itself after this decision.

It is impossible to overlook the fact that by the abbacy of Hugh at the latest, the *Cluniacensis ecclesia*, with all its duties and privileges, had evolved into a major political power that influenced the emperor, kings, and the pope in their decisions. At the same time, Cluny had reached the height of its power with Hugh of Semur and Pope Urban II. Having been a monk in Cluny, the pope continued to be absolutely loyal to his former abbot, even seeking his advice.

Nevertheless, a crisis began to emerge. On his deathbed, after 60 years in office, Hugh appointed Pontius, who had been elected by the monks, as his successor. Like Hugh, Pontius came from Burgundy's high aristocracy and was still young at the time of his election. His godfather, the later Pope Paschal II, had recommended him to the abbot of Cluny. Unlike his predecessor, however, Pontius had not been a member of the convent of Cluny before his election, but came from Saint-Martial in Limoges. Since extremely capable men belonged to the monastery at the time, it is likely that factions had formed within the community, but no one candidate had been able to muster a clear mandate. In spite of this, it seemed at first as though Cluny's tradition would be maintained with customary brilliance. Pontius, a relative of Emperor Henry V, helped settle the investiture controversy. Moreover, he received from his godfather, Pope Paschal II, an extension of the privilege granted Abbot Hugh by Urban II, namely, permission for the abbot of Cluny to wear the robes of a bishop at certain high holidays. The pope even presented Pontius with a dalmatic that he himself had worn. Pope Calixt II, who had

come to Cluny in 1120 at Abbot Pontius' instigation in order to sanctify Abbot Hugh, reconfirmed this privilege, adding the right that allowed the abbot of Cluny to assume the office of a Roman cardinal forever and everywhere. This privilege granted Cluny independence from all bishoprics, but outraged the bishops of France.

In 1122, the discord within the community of Cluny became manifest for the first time. Monks from Cluny had sent a written complaint about Pontius to the pope. When the abbot was told the content of the letter, he immediately laid down his office and traveled to the Holy Land. The convent elected Hugh II as his successor, a monk who until then had been a prior in Marcigny and an "outsider," who died after just three months in office. At that time, the monks elected Petrus of Montboissier, the prior of Vézelay, who became known as Petrus Venerabilis.

Two years after these events, Pontius returned to Cluny, and with the support of the inhabitants of the *burgus* forced his way into the monastery, demanding to be reinstated. He apparently still had followers among the monks. Pope Honorius II called both parties to Rome, but Pontius was neither willing to compromise nor to repent. He was imprisoned and died in captivity without having repented in 1126. Nevertheless, he was granted a ceremonious burial and received the prayer of remembrance due an abbot of Cluny.

Attempts have been made to explain this discord within Cluny as the result of confrontations with the bishops, increasing competition from the Cistercians that highlighted necessary reforms at home, and the changed political role of the monks of Cluny after the resolution of the investiture controversy.

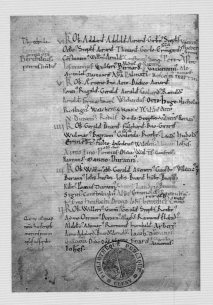

Page from the Cluniac Book of the Dead from Macigny-sur-Loire, begun by Elsendis. Nouv. Acq. Lat. 348, fol. 134. Bibliothèque nationale, Paris.

Cluny, former monastic church of Saint-Pierre-et-Saint-Paul, choir ambulatory, watercolor drawing, first half of the 18th century.

However, it seems more likely that economic and internal political problems caused the deterioration of the community's once unswerving unity. This had begun to affect the convent during Hugh's abbacy, but became increasingly severe with the election of Pontius, an outsider. The enormous construction site of Cluny III must have strained the convent emotionally and especially financially to an extent that we could only truly comprehend if we had seen the full magnificence of the church. Ample financial support from Spain, which probably induced Hugh to increase expenditures, declined in 1113. The funds necessary to feed the monks and the many poor could no longer be obtained, partly because the liturgy and the care of the dead and the poor occupied all the monks' time. This, in fact, was the Cistercians' main criticism. Others felt the monks' lifestyle had become too comfortable.

Another reason for the personal and political difficulties in Cluny may have been that during Hugh's abbacy, growing numbers of noblemen from the environs of Cluny had taken the habit. When they were given important offices within the monastery, the risk of conflict between monastic and family interests arose. Furthermore, Pontius, being an "outsider," had had no advocates within the monastery who would have supported his appointments to important offices. It is also reported that he did not display the same sensitivity and tact within the monastery as he did in the negotiations between the pope and the emperor while serving as the papal legate in Spain.

With Petrus Venerabilis, a successor worthy of his renowned predecessors once more assumed leadership of Cluny. He maintained the office for 34 years. Praised as a man of great patience, kindness, and exquisite diplomatic talents, he managed not only to guide the *Cluniacensis ecclesia* safely through the beginning papal schism, but also to end the schism within Cluny by reconciling the convent and the *burgenses* (the inhabitants of the *burgus*) after the latter had supported efforts to reinstate Pontius. Petrus Venerabilis was able to reestablish trust among the parties and formulated three documents that were approved by the entire monastery. They concerned the relationship of the *burgus* to the monastery, the monastic economy, and reform of the regulations that determined the daily service. The abbot proceeded with great sensitivity and wrote the documents between 1145 and 1147. Only when he was absolutely certain that he had the support of all the brothers and all the convents did he venture to act. It must have been an enormous task, considering the size of the convent and the number of monasteries and priories belonging to Cluny, all of which were just as hurt by the leadership schism as the mother house. In spite of his successes, Petrus Venerabilis was not able to restore the full importance that Cluny had once enjoyed; the difficulties were too great. The economic problems of the monastery also resisted his best efforts: the expense of the innumerable feasts at the memorials for the dead and the new church weighed too heavily on the monastery's endowment, especially without financial support from Spain.

In addition, the Cistercians were enjoying rapid growth and increasing popularity, and had even won the support of the emperor. Bernard of Clairvaux, the famous Cistercian abbot, attacked the *Cluniacensis ecclesia* sharply, criticizing its daily routine and construction of a new church. Conflicts arose where Cluniac and Cistercian properties bordered one another. Only with the unflagging support of Abbot Bernard of Clairvaux had Pope Innocent II been able to vanquish the usurping pope, and in the process Bernard had gained enormous influence. In 1145, Pope Eugene III was elected. A former Cistercian monk, he maintained the same ties to his monastery that Urban II once had to Cluny.

Petrus Venerabilis died on Christmas Day in 1156 and was laid to rest in the choir of the new abbey church. He was the last in the succession of great abbots of Cluny who had been able to maintain the authority of the monastery, and the last to preserve unity and peace in the convent.

Immediately after his death, factions among members of the powerful noble families in Cluny resurfaced. Petrus Venerabilis had not designated a successor, and therefore the party of Robertus Grossus at first asserted itself at the abbatial election. The pope refused to recognize Robertus, who died while returning to Cluny from Rome. Hugh de Frazans then became Abbot Hugh III. Unfortunately, he possessed neither the persuasive powers nor the courage of his predecessors. During the papal schism, which particularly burdened Cluny with its widely scattered property, he sought the advice of his convent, but was abandoned. Hugh III and his followers were banned from the monastery in 1161; he sought refuge at the imperial court. In Cluny the abbots now followed one another in rapid succession. The *Cluniacensis ecclesia* lost the abbeys of Vézelay and Baume-les-Messieurs. The immunity and protection of the monastery, which for 200 years had been ensured by the great secular and ecclesiastical powers, was lost. After various attacks, the monastery placed itself under the protection of the French king in 1169. Cluny became a *commenda*, which was given to cardinals, among others to Richelieu and Mazarin. After 1790, it was torn down except for minimal vestiges. Cluny shared the fate of so many famous buildings that had symbolic significance in their time, and they were destroyed by later generations.

Hilly countryside near Cluny, outside Bergesserin.

Berzé-la-Ville, Château des Moines with Romanesque chapel, second half of the 11th century, view to the west.

Berzé-la-Ville

Tradition has it that Hugh of Semur (1049–1109) had an estate built as a retirement seat for himself several miles south of Cluny. What actually remains is a chapel that has two stories, probably because of the steeply sloping terrain. The prayer room is a small hall with a semicircular apse. Above a high base are blind arcades on slender columns, and murals that originally covered the entire chapel. As the frescoes show a strong Byzantine influence, they have been dated to the time of Petrus Venerabilis (1122–1156). In the calotte of the apse, executed in soft olive, blue, vermilion, and ochre hues, is a painting of Christ in the mandorla, blessing the apostles with his right hand and giving Peter the writ of his calling with his left. Underneath are two saints on each side, supposedly Berno and Hugh, the first and sixth abbots of Cluny, as well as Benedict, founder of the order, and Desiderius of Montecassino. This fresco has also been seen as an attempt to equate the founding of the Benedictine Order with the establishment of the monastery of Cluny—an interpretation which seems plausible in light of Cluny's sense of its own great mission and importance. In the spandrels the Wise Virgins are depicted. On the base, above painted drapery, are saints in rectangular fields, while in the blind niches we see the martyrdoms suffered by St. Blasius and either St. Laurentius or St. Vincentius. These tall, slender figures with delicate limbs and large eyes, and richly pleated robes covering lively and animated bodies, are contemporaneous with the sculptures in Autun and Vézelay.

Berzé-le-Châtel

Many decades before Abbot Hugh built Berzé-la-Ville, Geoffroy de Berzé fortified a nearby rock plateau that falls off sharply on all sides, so that he could overlook the entire valley. Here he built the donjon of Berzé-le-Châtel. The castle could be reached only by means of a narrow, rocky path. In the course of time, the castle was expanded through the addition of concentric walls built

around the original donjon. A small chapel dating from the 12th century is preserved, and the circular towers were added in the 13th century.

In the war between the Bourguignons and the Armagnacs, the entire complex fell into the hands of Philip the Good, who gave it to his master of stables, Macé de Rochebaron. He in turn had the old main entrance widened into a two-towered gate. Battlements on *mâchicoulis* connected the towers; between the slats of the drawbridge, a plate bearing a coat of arms proudly proclaimed the owner. In a similar manner, Philip Pot in Châteauneuf renovated the entrance to a castle he had received from his sovereign. Two further entrances to the inner courts have similar forms. It is likely that Macé de Rochebaron also had other living quarters renovated, but the 19th-century Gothicization made most of them unrecognizable.

Berzé-le-Châtel, castle, 12/13th century and 15th century. At the right of the picture is the gate with two towers bearing the coat of arms of Macé de Rochebaron. Behind it are the two courtyards and the living quarters, which were Gothicized in the 19th century.

Berzé-la-Ville, Château des Moines, frescoes in the chapel, second quarter of the 12th century.

ABOVE:
Martyrdom of St. Blasius (detail).

FAR LEFT AND LEFT:
Details found under the mandorla of the *Maiestas Domini*.
At the far left are the two abbots, opposite them the two bishops.

OPPOSITE ABOVE:
Apse calotte with *Maiestas Domini*. Beneath the mandorla are two bishops and two abbots (Berno and Hugh of Cluny?). At both sides of Christ are the apostles, whom he is blessing with his right hand; with the left, he is giving Peter the *traditio legis*, the writ of his calling.

OPPOSITE BOTTOM:
Two of the Wise Virgins. They have been compared to Byzantine princesses.

DÉPARTEMENT
YONNE

The department of Yonne forms the north-western part of Burgundy. To the east and the south it is bordered by the Côte-d'Or and Nièvre departments, and in the north and west by Aube and Loiret. The northernmost district of Yonne, the Sens arrondissement, was not traditionally a part Burgundy, but was added later when the province was divided into departments.

Geologically, the southern part of Yonne, up to about Auxerre, is located on the so-called Lower Burgundy Plateau, the limestone plateau that rises towards the northwest and falls off steeply towards the southeast. The lively Yonne River, which often floods its banks, and the Serein and Armançon Rivers have dug deeply into the limestone, creating wild and picturesque valleys. On the more gentle slopes, wine grapes have been cultivated for centuries, most famously in Chablis. The arrondissement of Sens, once called Sénonais, is flatter and reminds one of Brie. The varied types of soil make its diverse agriculture possible.

The countryside in Yonne is primarily quiet, with thinly settled, bare, and karstic plateaus. In its narrow river valleys are deciduous trees and mixed forest with occasional steep scarps. The Renaissance flourished here in the north as nowhere else in Burgundy. Some of the most famous early Renaissance châteaux are here, as well as numerous churches with splendid interiors.

PREVIOUS TWO PAGES:
Chablis, village and surrounding vineyards.

RIGHT:
Cliffs of Saussois along the Yonne.

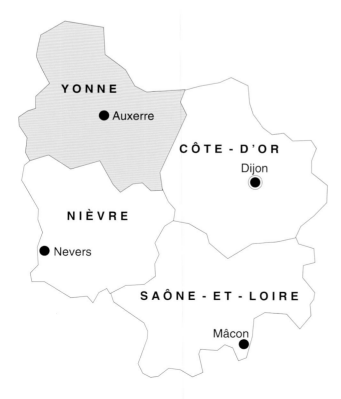

Deep River Valleys between the Yonne and Serein and Vast Woodlands – Avallonnais

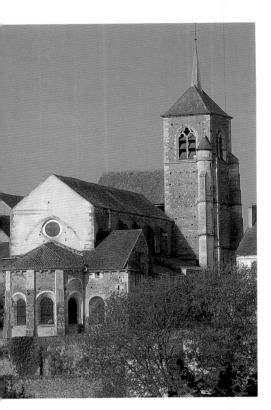

Avallon, Saint-Lazare, late 11th century, view of choir and nave.

Let us begin in the southeast with the Avallon district. It runs in a north-south direction and its entire length borders on the arrondissement of Montbard. In the south, it encounters the Morvan. Two rivers, the Cure and the Cousin, both of which have their sources in the Morvan and are often quite torrential, flow through ravines and extensive wooded areas to join the Yonne.

Avallon

In Celtic times, only two settlements existed in what is now the department of Yonne: from them the cities Auxerre and Avallon emerged. Avallon, known to the Celts as Aballo, was situated on a rocky terrace and isolated from its surroundings by deep gorges. With a good view over the Cousin valley (illus. below), it was easy to defend. Until the 6th century, it was the main settlement of the *pagus Avallensis* or *pagus Avalisio*, and was supposedly already well fortified then. In the year 731, a Norman rampage that stormed Tournus, Chalon, and Saulieu also destroyed Avallon. A 10th-century castle was taken and destroyed during the warring over inheritance between King Robert and Count Ott-Henry of Burgundy, and apparently never rebuilt.

The most important church of the city is the former collegiate church Saint-Lazare (illus. left). Its origins are obscure, but like the castle, it seems to have been built during the 10th century; an inscription on the portal supposedly testified that a relic of Lazarus was given to the church in the year 1000. The church had until then been consecrated to the Virgin, so it enjoyed the dual patronage of Mary and Lazarus. Duke Hugh I gave this church to Cluny in 1077, under whose leadership a new building was begun. It was consecrated by Pope Paschal II in 1106. Ten years later the church was turned over to the Bishop of Autun.

That church, begun in the late 11th century, is a three-aisle basilica with upper nave walls resting on piers. The nave drops off nearly 10 feet (3 m) from west to east, following the very steep hillside. An integrated transept with a transverse rectangular crossing opens into three apses. Despite the great incline of the nave, there is a crypt under the choir, parts of which surely belonged to the previous church. The elevation reveals two stories. Compound piers with engaged semicircular columns support the pointed arches and the clerestory under a groin vault. A cornice that runs above the engaged columns on the wall, following

Avallon, view over the Cousin River towards the city.

Avallon, Saint-Lazare, right jamb of the central west portal, about 1150/1160, detail.

FAR RIGHT:
Avallon, Saint-Lazare, right portal of the west façade, tympanum, about 1150/1160.

RIGHT:
Avallon, Saint-Lazare, central nave with groin vaulting and apse, late 11th century.

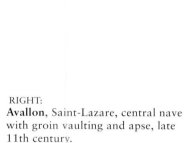

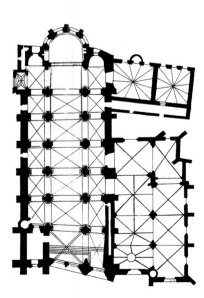

Avallon, Saint-Lazare, floor plan.

the incline in right-angled steps, divides the two stories and carries the slender columns under the formerets of the vault. Although the nave of Saint-Lazare is not of the same quality as that of Sainte-Madeleine in Vézelay, the affinity between the two cannot be overlooked. Even their consecrations, which in both cases probably only concerned the choir—not preserved in Vézelay—are chronologically close together. Saint-Lazare is therefore a church built immediately after Sainte-Madeleine, and should be dated accordingly. The Carolingian nave in Vézelay burned in 1120 and was immediately renovated. The nave of Saint-Lazare (illus. right) may thus be a construction from around 1130. A restoration done in 1859 seems to have focused mainly on the choir. Impressive, though not planned concurrently with the church, is the west façade with portal, once in three parts. It was built shortly after the middle of the 12th century. As in Vézelay, here too was a narthex. Unfortunately, the lintel and tympanum of the central portal have disappeared. Records indicate that there were once depictions of Christ in the mandorla with angels and the symbols of the Evangelists, the meal of Bethany with Lazarus, and the Crucifixion. Angels, the 24 Elders of the Apocalypse, and depictions of the months and the zodiac decorated the archivolts. On the jambs stood the prophets, one of whom is preserved: a

tall, narrow, almost bodiless figure who seems to consist entirely of the narrow, straight folds of his robe (illus. left). The richly carved classical patterns woven masterfully over jambs and archivolts and appearing on every free space are exceptional. Their variety allows for almost no repetition. The north portal no longer exists, but the south portal still has a lintel—depicting the Resurrection and the Harrowing of Hell as well as scenes from the life of Lazarus—and a tympanum with the Adoration of the Magi (illus. above).

The militarily advantageous position of the city also makes it extremely picturesque and airy. Today almost nothing is left of the fortifications that once defended the city against attacks. After

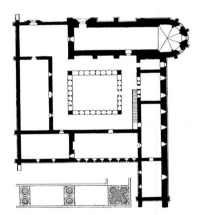

Avallon, Maison des Sires de Domecy and Tour de l'Horloge, both 15th century.

Sauvigny-le-Bois, former priory Saint-Jean-des-Bonshommes, floor plan.

Sauvigny-le-Bois, former priory Saint-Jean-des-Bonshommes, late 12th/early 13th century, cloister arcades.

tower above the portal. The Grande-Rue Aristide Briand runs into the Place Saint-Lazare from the north. If you follow it, you come to the Tour de l'Horloge, which was also erected during the 15th century over the Porte de la Boucherie at the city's highest elevation. This was once the office of the jurors of Avallon. The Ursuline convent and *collège*, both from the 17th century, are located on either side of the tower. The continuation of this street, which has always been the main road through the city, is lined with beautiful houses from the 16th to 18th centuries.

Sauvigny-le-Bois

The priory of Sauvigny-le-Bois, just outside Avallon, was a settlement of the Bonshommes from the Grammontensian Order, whose rules were close to those of the Cistercians. Between 1174 and 1192, Anséric IV of Montréal gave them land on which a small monastery was constructed. All that now remains are a few arches from the cloister and a chapel, a hall with brick barrel vaulting, and a semicircular apse. Columns articulate the apse both inside and on the exterior.

Pontaubert

West of Avallon beyond the Cousin valley lies Pontaubert, with the light, airy Nativité de Notre-Dame church, often pleasantly empty. It is part of a *commanderie*, a commenda of the Order of St. John of Jerusalem, endowed by Jocelin du Vault in

these fortifications were sold to the city by Louis XIV, terraced gardens and avenues were created on the steep slopes, which afford a wonderful view far into the Cousin valley and to the mountains of the Morvan. On the Place Saint-Lazare is the Maison des Sires de Domecy (illus. above), a 15th-century urban house with a projecting stair

Pontaubert, La Nativité de Notre-Dame, from 1167 on, tympanum with Adoration of the Magi and Ascension of the Virgin.

Pontaubert, La Nativité de Notre-Dame, view through the nave into the apse.

1167. Besides the church, a leprosery, the *maladière* Saint-Michel, and a Hôtel de la commanderie belonged to the complex at that time. The Order of St. John was active here until 1658, caring for the sick and for pilgrims en route to Vézelay.

The three-aisle columned nave (illus. left) is entered through a small, late Gothic narthex. Four of the five bays are square, while the easternmost is shallower and adjoined by the three-sided polygonal apse. The two-story elevation of arcades and clerestory, the piers-and-arches design, and the groin vaulting in all three aisles indicate that Nativité de Notre-Dame is a latecomer in the Vézelay-Avallon group. Oddly for this region, the façade has a central tower. Below it is a Gothic recessed portal. Noteworthy is that instead of a trumeau and lintel beam, it has only a slender pillar with an engaged semi-column and narrow, profiled molding. The sculpted figures, depicting the Adoration of the Magi and the Ascension of the Virgin, seem isolated in front of a background of smooth stone blocks. The Virgin, who is seated, is noticeably larger than the standing figures. Holding her child on her lap, Mary faces forwards, towards the viewer (illus. above).

Three figures of considerable quality have been preserved from the old interior: St. Barbara, who greatly resembles another depiction of her in the Musée Rolin in Autun; a St. Syra in the robes of a pilgrim; and St. Eutrophius, all 15th century. The seated Virgin with Child comes from the chapel in Saulce d'Island, a chapel which also belongs to the order of St. John.

Lichères-sur-Yonne, Château de Faulin, ca. 1200 to ca. 1500, view of the entire complex. In the front are the courtine, the rectangular gate tower, and both corner towers of the original complex, to which the donjon on the left also belongs. Next to it is the four-tower donjon from 1389, now missing the two front circular towers. Farther to the right is the *basse-cour*; in the foreground is the pigeon tower.

Lichères-sur-Yonne

A complex dating from the same time period is the Château de Faulin in Lichères-sur-Yonne—but this is a secular building. Here in the remote, extreme southwest of the arrondissement is a colossal rectangular wall dating from about 1200 (illus. below). A small square donjon is situated in the northeast corner; the circular towers are probably not original. In 1389 the estate came into the possession of the Le Bourgoing family. The long rectangular enclosure was apparently later divided into two courts (and fitted with circular towers?). The south courtyard, reserved for service buildings, was fitted with a gate tower; in the northern one, the *cour d'honneur*, a pleasing four-tower donjon was built, one of the earliest of its kind. Originally, it had four stories, circular towers at each corner, and probably a circular stair tower in front of or behind the main façade. In or shortly after 1500 it was modernized and expanded.

The desire for a stately main stairway with a late Gothic, richly decorated portal meant that the two corner towers in the west had to go. So the square stairway tower was built, typical for the period around 1500. The windows, too, were renovated, and instead of small openings with ogival arches on the lintels, large mullion windows with fishbone profiling were installed. The façade was clad with ashlars, and cornices were added to highlight the new division of stories. At the same time or shortly thereafter, the donjon was apparently enlarged by the small two-story building.

An inscription above the gate is still legible—*Deo conscientiae et honori* 1577 (For God, Conscience, and Honor)—disclosing the date of the last renovations. They concerned the defensive structures: the donjon, walls, and entrance gate were fitted with *bretèches* and regularly spaced openings for canons.

Vézelay

Turning back to the southeast, you can see from afar Sainte-Madeleine, the Magdalene church of Vézelay, rising from a hilltop (illus. opposite). This is justly considered one of the most beautiful churches of Burgundy, and is one of the most often visited sites in the region, perhaps even in all of France. No matter how often you have been to the church, the spatial effect and the impact of the incredible sculpture is majestic and overwhelming.

In 858, still prior to the founding of Cluny, Girart of Roussillon endowed a nuns' convent at the foot of this hill, placing it directly under the jurisdiction of the pope. Shortly thereafter it was

destroyed in a Norman invasion. In 878, sources report the consecration of a church in a monastery on the hill. As to the form of this building, which was constructed at the same time as the crypts preserved in Saint-Germain in Auxerre and Saint-Pierre in Flavigny, only speculation is possible; nothing is known for certain. William of Volpiano, the abbot of Saint-Bénigne in Dijon, reformed the monastery here according to the ideals of Cluny in the early 11th century. Although nothing is known about the origins of the Magdalene relics, it does seem that the cult of Mary Magdalene began at this time—coinciding with the Lazarus cult in Avallon, where the relics of Mary Magdalene's brother, Lazarus, arrived about 1000. Here, too, Mary, together with the apostles Peter and Paul, had been the first church patroness. A consecration in Vézelay, dated in the year 1104, probably related to the renovated eastern sections of the Carolingian nave, conceivable as a three-apse choir, analog to the east parts of Avallon. On the other hand, however, increasing numbers of pilgrims surely necessitated an ambulatory around the choir. It is also possible that the older choir had already included a kind of ambulatory (as did Saint-Pierre in Flavigny and Saint-Germain in Auxerre).

In 1120 the nave burned down and was immediately replaced by the one now standing (illus. opposite). Its consecration by the pope in 1132 does not necessarily indicate that the building was finished at that time. The rebuilding was probably not completed until 1140 due to delays caused by the need for an exceptionally long nave (for processions). The three-bay narthex was built next, in which an altar to St. Michael was consecrated between 1145 and 1151. In 1152 the west towers were under construction. In 1165, another fire destroyed the crypt, and a new choir was planned but not begun until late in the 12th century.

This period of successive construction, in which one part of the building—apparently without design alterations—was immediately followed by the next, creating an immense need for sculptures, all seems to indicate that the many pilgrims brought the church an enormous income. The interior must have been equally rich as a result of the pilgrims' gifts and donations. Unfortunately, nothing has been preserved.

But in the 13th century, Vézelay had to take second place in the cult of Mary Magdalene. Pilgrimages turned increasingly to Provence, to the churches of Saint-Maximin-la-Sainte-Baume—in whose ancient cemetery Mary Magdalene relics had been sought and found—and to Les Saintes-Maries-de-la-Mer. The prominence of Sainte-Madeleine in Vézelay waned decidedly. In the 15th

century it was placed under the jurisdiction of the king, and after 1537 only a few canons still lived here. In 1569, the Magdalene relics were lost to Protestant attacks.

A narthex of three bays, three-aisled and of the same breadth as the nave, formed the entrance, or reception hall, of Sainte-Madeleine (illus. p. 294). Three portals open out from the ground floor; above, at the sides, the west towers rise up, only one of which is complete. Originally planned to be lower (see the springers on the west wall of the nave), the narthex is higher than the nave. Its elevation has two zones—arcades and galleries—whose vaulting supports the groin vaulting of the central nave. The third bay has a false ceiling, giving the impression that the galleries surround three sides of the room. Here stands the altar to St. Michael, in sight of the central nave. A series of ten bays make up the three-aisle nave—in Cluny there were eleven—and they meet a five-part transept with a square crossing. Behind lies the ambulatory around the choir, consisting of two antechoir bays and a five-sided main choir surrounded by nine ambulatory bays and nine chapels, which are interconnected. The central

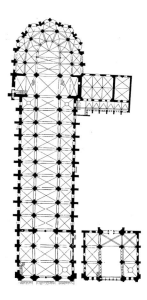

Vézelay, former monastic church of Sainte-Madeleine, floor plan.

OPPOSITE:
Vézelay, former monastic church of Sainte-Madeleine, nave (1120 on) and raised choir (late 12th century).

Vézelay, former monastic church of Sainte-Madeleine, view of the exterior from the southwest.

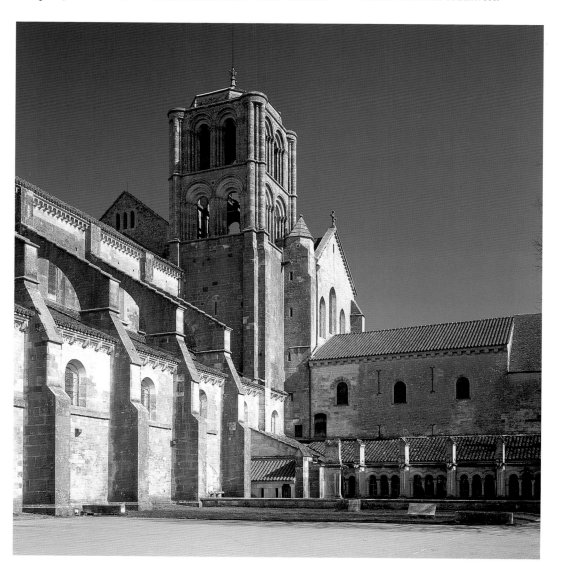

Vézelay, former monastic church of Sainte-Madeleine, narthex, ca. 1140 to ca. 1151, view to the southwest of the southern lateral portal.

nave also has two stories: round-arched arcades between recessed pillars with engaged semicircular columns (above which runs the cornice articulating the stories), and a high clerestory. Above this is groin vaulting. All the arches, arcades, transverse arches, and formerets—as well as imposts and cornices—are adorned with ornamental bands. The capitals that made Vézelay famous are sculpted with highly artistic figures. The transverse arches in the main nave were constructed of alternating bands of ashlars. The lively, finely worked reliefs and the interplay of light and shadow combine to give the interior a festive aura. Like Cluny III, the nave of Sainte-Madeleine displays a high level of artistry and is the work of an uncommonly wealthy builder. There is no indication here of the experimentation one sees in Tournus; here, everything is certainty and clarity. Every possibility to increase the desired effect was identified and used to advantage. The transept, of the same date as the choir at least in its upper reaches, has three stories and a gallery between the arcades and the clerestory. Slender vaulting shafts with shaft rings support the arches of the ribbed vaulting. In the choir the arches are pointed; above are the two-part gallery arches and windows without tracery. In the choir vaulting, the certainty that characterizes the nave is gone. The first choir bay is vaulted in six parts; the second, in the western half, in four parts; and the eastern bay continues the fan ribs of the chevet vaulting. This made an additional support in the second choir bay necessary. The directly adjacent

Vézelay, former monastic church of Sainte-Madeleine, view down the northern side aisle, from 1120 on.

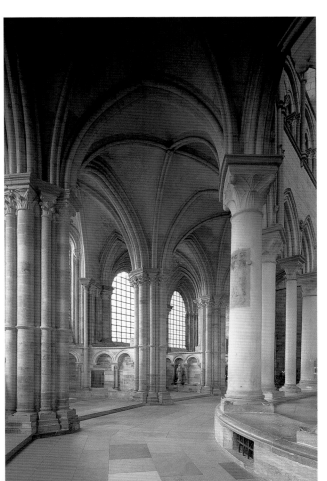

chapels are separated only by low partitions (illus. left). The attempt to connect the radiating chapels into a second ambulatory had already been made at the start of early Gothic in Saint-Denis (1140). This arrangement and the planned, but only partially completed, six-part vaulting link the choir of Vézelay with the buildings of the early Gothic.

Like Cluny III, Sainte-Madeleine contains a rich treasure of sculpture. Portals and capitals were decorated at great expense. While the outer portals lost most of their ornamentation in the Revolution—the neo-Romanesque Last Judgment tympanum dates from a restoration under Viollet-le-Duc in 1840–1861—the inner portal façade under the emporium is completely preserved (illus. p. 297). This portal is immensely impressive, almost frightening in its domination of the narthex and entrance due to its greater height and breadth. John the Baptist, a large figure reaching into the lintel, stands on the trumeau of the central portal. Smaller figures of the apostles stand at the sides—Peter and Paul immediately to the right and left, the others on the jambs. On the lintel are a

Vézelay, former monastic church of Sainte-Madeleine, ambulatory around the choir, late 12th century. The adjoining chapels are striking. Only a low wall with blind arcades separates them.

Vézelay, former monastic church of Sainte-Madeleine, two of the many figural capitals.

procession of peoples: on the right Panotians, Pygmies, and the peoples of Europe; on the left Romans, Scythians, and Parthians. The outer of the two archivolts enclosing the tympanum is decorative, while the inner one depicts the labors of the months and signs of the Zodiac. The tympanum itself consists of the pictorial area with a raised center crowned by an arch divided into four small "picture boxes" on each side. Here more peoples are depicted: Greeks, Jews, Cappadocians, Arabs, people from India, Ethiopians, Armenians, and Cretans. In the center sits Christ in Majesty in the mandorla, rays streaming from his fingers towards the heads of the apostles at his sides. This might be an attempt to combine the themes of the coming of the Holy Ghost and the sending forth of the apostles, that is, the beginning of the church into which all the peoples of the world are to be gathered. Depictions of the months and the Zodiac represent the course of the year and human activity, which is always a part of the process of salvation. In short, all the peoples of the world find their salvation in the universal church! The images seem almost like snapshots: the slender figures are lively and in motion; their robes flutter and flow around the anatomically accurate bodies in closely gathered and encircling folds. Especially the procession of peoples on the lintel seems almost classical. The ornamental decoration on arches and capitals is also in a classical vein.

Above the side portals are small, two-zoned tympana, placed directly above the capitals.

Strongly sculpted bands with high-relief foliage and flowers form the archivolts. The pictorial area on the south portal bears the Annunciation, the Visitation, the Adoration of the Shepherds, and the Adoration of the Magi; the north portal has the encounter on the road to Emmaus and the Ascension.

In addition to these portals, Sainte-Madeleine has one of the most comprehensive cycles in France, including over 150 capitals (illus. above). Almost two-thirds of them are of a quality, in figures or scenes, that surpasses those of Cluny. The truly plentiful columns touch on almost every important subject of the medieval world, including stories of the Old and New Testaments, classical mythology, church fathers, saints, angels, and demons. As on the tympana, the virtuosity of the sculptors is remarkable: the figures free themselves ever more visibly from their background. They are vivid and their movement is dynamic, even if the stone surfaces have not always been finished with the same care. Determining whose hand created what figure has occupied art historians for more than a hundred years, as has the iconology of the sculpture. None of these complex questions has been completely resolved.

The south transept adjoins the full width of the chapter hall, which is supported today by the cloister wing designed by Viollet-le-Duc. The two-aisle room includes three bays and a rib vault with sculpted bosses, which correspond to relief medallions in the vault cells. It was built before the reconstruction of the choir in 1161/1171.

OPPOSITE:
Vézelay, former monastic church of Sainte-Madeleine, narthex and inner west portal with the formidable tympanum. It is perhaps a combination of two themes: the Descent of the Holy Spirit and the Sending Out of the Apostles, that is, the founding of the church. Both the figure of Christ in the field below the arch and John the Baptist on the trumeau break through their architectural field, towering into the next pictorial area. This creates an impression of monumentality that had not been achieved before.

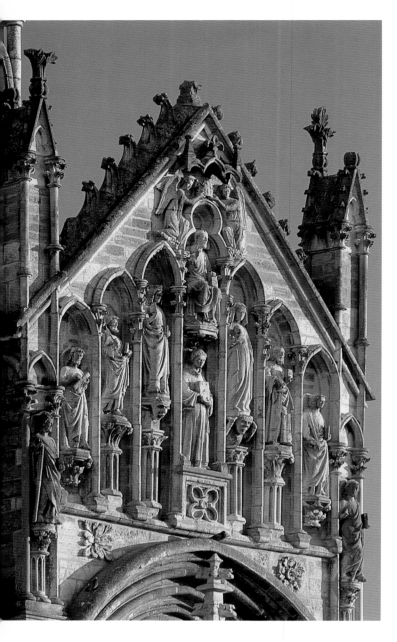

slender vaulting shafts and bundled shafts that rise into ribs and arches with much articulation. At the back wall are the older west portals with a Last Judgment tympanum at the center. The sculpture of the narthex is also striking, as are the sarcophagus of Guibour (wife of Hugh of Gaudri), the incense angels on the jamb of the central portal, the Crucifixion of the south portal with the Wise and Foolish Virgins in the archivolts, as well as the relief of a donor holding a model of the church and a woman with a book.

Above the narthex, the rose tracery and the gable, which is richly decorated with figures in the blind arcading, become visible (illus. left). Delicate bundled columns serve as bases for the lovely jamb figures. Their heights vary with the stepped heights of the arch frames. The same delicately elegant articulation that distinguishes the entire building is repeated here and on the tower. Figures beneath baldachins decorate the pier buttresses between the portals and the archivolts of the central portal.

For reasons that remain unclear, a choir, a shallow five-aisle antebay, and a choir ambulatory with radiating chapels were rebuilt during the first half of the 14th century. After damages incurred during the Hundred Years' War, the vaulting was reconstructed in 1449.

The parsonage dates from the 17th century. It has been converted into a small museum that houses almost exclusively finds from the area, documenting the settling and history of the area from prehistoric times to the Middle Ages. A very beautiful, large statue of a spring divinity was found during excavations in Les Fontaines-Salées.

Saint-Père-sous-Vézelay

At the foot of the pilgrimage mountain, in Saint-Père-sous-Vézelay, the monks built a church consecrated to the Virgin Mary, now one of the most important examples of Burgundian High Gothic. About 1225–1230, the eastern sections and the three-aisle nave (illus. right) were built. It has two stories—arcades, clerestory with walkway—and four-part rib vaulting, but the slender vaulting shafts that absorb the ribs and arches only extend down to the ground in every other bay. The others rise from consoles in the spandrels of the arcade. An epitaph on the west wall cites the year 1258— by this time the nave was completed. The first bay of the northern side aisle bears a tower 165 feet (50 m) high.

About 1300 the narthex was added. It is three-aisled and two bays in length, but has only one story. To the north and south it is light, with large tracery windows; to the west are three lovely recessed portals. The interior is articulated by

ABOVE LEFT:
Saint-Père-sous-Vézelay, Notre-Dame, 1225/1230 to 1258 and first half of 14th century, figural decoration on the gable of the west façade.

LEFT:
Saint-Père-sous-Vézelay, Notre-Dame, nave central aisle and chevet.

Chastellux-sur-Cure

At the edge of the Morvan, on the jagged cliffs of the Cure valley, rises the château Chastellux-sur-Cure (illus. pp. 300/301). Its origins date back to the 11th century, and it has been expanded and rebuilt multiple times since then. Sources note that Artaud III rebuilt the original castle in 1240; the Tour des Archives and a logis were added in the first quarter of the 15th century; in 1551 an entrance gate with drawbridge to the *cour d'honneur* was built, and the Tour d'Amboise and a further logis were added in the late 16th century. A cloister in the inner courtyard was built in the early 17th century. This late medieval-early Renaissance complex, which probably had an elaborate logis with tall mullion windows, generous fireplaces, and polygonal turrets, was thoroughly redecorated in Baroque style between 1749 and 1771. Very little remained from this building which, under the influence of Romanticism, was thoroughly restored in the neo-Gothic style beginning in 1820.

View from the hilltop monastery overlooking **Saint-Père-sous-Vézelay and the surrounding countryside.**

LEFT:
Saint-Père-sous-Vézelay, Notre-Dame, statuette of St. Peter.

FOLLOWING TWO PAGES:
Chastellux-sur-Cure, Château de Chastellux, 11th to 19th centuries, view of one side of the château. At the right is the entrance court where the courtine is missing, left is the *cour d'honneur* whose buildings were Gothicized in the 19th century. Near the center are the peaks of the two towers that flank the entrance.

Montréal

Northeast of Avallon, Montréal dominates the valley of the Serein. Supposedly, the *mons Regalis* (royal mountain) was settled as early as the 6th century, although land ownership is not documented with certainty until the 12th century. The castle consisted of three concentric stone walls that followed the natural terrain and surrounded three expansive courtyards on different levels. Both the size of the complex and its exposed location are indications of an early settlement. In the 13th century, flanking towers and gates with pointed arches were added. The walls and defensive fortifications as well as the living quarters were renovated again in the 16th century before Henry IV had the fortifications of the complex dismantled in 1597.

No later than the 11th century, the lords of Montréal had endowed a collegiate church, which lay opposite the inner castle. Around 1160, Anséric I of Montréal—who in the mid-12th century had repaired the castle following a Norman attack—fulfilled a vow and had the collegiate church of Notre-Dame de l'Assomption rebuilt, probably in the same place. Work on the church dragged on, ending only in the early 13th century. The small three-aisle basilica has three nave bays, a high, three-story transept with almost square arms, and a rectangular choir that is two bays deep and accompanied by two small square chapels. The elevation has two levels and was influenced by Vézelay; around 1300, the building was given rib vaulting throughout. In the west is an emporium for the lords or owners of the estate. Notre-Dame has two valuable works: a 15th-century, tripartite, partially gilded alabaster relief from England that depicts scenes from the Virgin's life (illus. above), and choir stalls with 26 seats created by the Rigolley brothers from Nuits-sur-Armançon (illus. opposite). They are dated 1525. The realistic, detailed scenes from the Old and New Testaments, complementing each other typologically, are framed by filled pilasters, medallions, and seashell-shaped niches that clearly reveal the influence of the Italian Renaissance on French art. The triptychs from the 16th century and a Madonna from the 17th, as well as the lovely tombstones, are well worth seeing. The terrace behind the church offers an expansive view over the Serein valley, the Auxois, and the Terre Plaine. Also beautiful are the medieval and early Renaissance houses that were originally built within the protection of the outer stone wall.

Noyers

Following the course of the Serein River, which flows north in countless windings and curves before turning northwest, and finally west to join the Yonne near Auxerre, you travel through thinly settled areas of abundant forests and meadows. A curve of the river encircles Noyers (illus. below), a small, quiet, old-fashioned city that was preceded by a Roman settlement dating back to the second century AD. When the Normans were terrorizing the area, a castle was built on a naturally protected cliff around 860. After it had fallen into disrepair, the castle was rebuilt in 1195 by the lord Hugues de Noyers, who was also the bishop of Auxerre. That castle consisted of an encircling wall—perhaps already fitted with towers—surrounded by a triple moat, a square donjon, a fortified gate, and many buildings for living quarters and auxiliary structures no longer clearly identifiable today. This was the imposing center of an estate on which 80 vassals depended. As befit his position, Hugues de Noyers had a house chapel built with a splendid interior. Not long after, he also had the growing city, which was dependent on the castle for protection, fortified with walls, gates, and towers. He endowed a parish church that later became a priory.

OPPOSITE TOP: **Noyers**, circular towers of the former city fortification. In between them, where walls once stood, are now houses and gardens.

OPPOSITE BELOW: **Pastureland in the Serein valley**, tucked against a wooded hill.

LEFT:
Noyers, small Renaissance palace in the rue de la Madeleine, 16th century.

Noyers, View over the small city; in the center is the church of Notre-Dame, 1489 to 1515.

In 1419, the last surviving male of the Noyers family died, and with him one of the great and powerful noble families of Burgundy. Agnès and Isabeau de Noyers sold the estate to Margaret of Bavaria, the widow of Duke John the Fearless. When the city became a part of the duke's estate, a period of economic prosperity ensued. Streets and squares were built, lined with half-timber houses with lovely carvings and open arcaded walkways. From the Place de l'Hôtel-de-Ville, where the 17th-century city hall stands between older wooden houses, one reaches the spacious, three-cornered Place du Marché-au-Blé, the former grain market, and from there, the church. In the early 16th century, the Renaissance also came to Noyers. Dating from this period are stone houses, small city palaces with walls articulated by pilasters and typical Renaissance décor. Henry IV had the fortifications of the castle of Noyers dismantled in 1599, just as in Montréal, but left the city walls standing. Sixteen of its towers still exist (illus. above).

Following a referendum, the parish church of Notre-Dame was begun in 1489 and consecrated in 1515. The church itself is plain, but elaborate Renaissance forms adorn its westwork. Abbot Claude Courtépée (see also p. 132) criticized the church for these embellishments in his 18th-century account of Burgundy.

Nuits-sur-Armançon

Somewhat further to the east, the Canal de Bourgogne flows beyond the borders of the department of Yonne. Almost parallel to the Armançon, it meanders through hilly countryside. Several Renaissance châteaux were built in the 16th century along the river: Nuits-sur-Armançon, Ancy-le-Franc, Tanlay, and further north, Maulnes in Cruzy-le-Châtel. The smallest of these is Nuits-sur-Armançon (illus. above, below and opposite). Claude de Chenu, whose father Pierre bought the estate in 1533, probably had it built in order to fortify the border with Champagne in the 1550s.

The small, one-wing building has only one story on the garden side, necessitated by the slope of the terrain towards the river. The entrance side, however, framed by two square towers, has two stories. Fluted Corinthian pilasters articulate the garden façade, creating an elegant effect. The façade facing the courtyard, on the other hand, was intended to be defensive. A fortified wall with towers, which might have originated from an older structure, has largely disappeared today. The kitchen on the ground floor still has the old well; the rooms in the upper story were newly furnished in the 18th and 19th centuries.

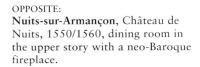

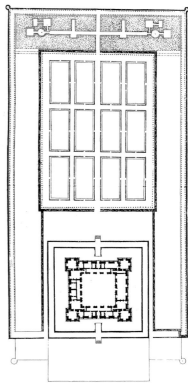

Ancy-le-Franc, château, from 1543/ 1544, exterior (left) and floor plan (above) according to J. A. du Cerceau.

Ancy-le-Franc

Ancy-le-Franc is one of the purest examples of Italian architecture in France. Antoine III de Clermont, General Water and Forest Master of France and friend of King Francis I, began construction of the château in 1543/1544. A plains castle dating from the 12th century had previously stood here. Plans for the square complex were included in Jacques Androuet du Cerceau's collection of the *Plus excellents Bastimens de France* (Most Excellent Buildings in France). Four two-story wings enclose an inner courtyard with four square towers at its corners. The external façades are almost identical: nine engaged Doric pilasters frame simple rectangular windows and one central portal. This articulation continues around the towers, which have only one window axis on each side. The motif of the rhythmic travée—an alternating sequence of a broad axis with a round arch followed by a narrow axis containing a small niche topped by a rectangular panel framed by engaged pilasters—determines the articulation of the courtyard façades. The same principle of articulation reappears later in Bussy-Rabutin and Sully. By 1552 the complex was habitable. It is surmised that Antoine de Clermont had the interior furnished, and in this case painted, (illus. above, below and opposite) after he had fallen out of favor at court, indicating that he withdrew to Ancy-le-Franc. This behavior was typical for nobility,

and not only in France: social or political difficulties or thwarted ambitions often resulted in artistic ventures, whose iconological message expressed self-justification or claims. Decoding these puzzles is among the most exciting and difficult tasks of art history, because the early modern age attached meanings to events and representations from classical mythology or the Bible—their preferred vehicles for expressing statements and messages—quite different from those that modern philology has given them.

OPPOSITE:
Ancy-le-Franc, château, *chambre des arts* with depictions of the liberal arts and the muses who inspire them in the medallions above the wood paneling.

Ancy-le-Franc, château, entrance façade of the interior courtyard with the famous rhythmical travée décor, an alternation between windows and pilaster-framed niches.

Ancy-le-Franc, château, Medea gallery with grotesque figures above the wood paneling base; in the oval areas are scenes from the Argonaut saga.

This also applies at Ancy-le-Franc, where one can assume that the interior pictorial program at least in part expresses the owner's desire to vindicate himself; this is corroborated by the many Latin and Greek inscriptions. Still preserved is the Hall of Cult Offerings, or of Judith and Holophernes, (who bear the features of Diane de Poitiers and Francis I), the cabinet of Pastor Fido adorned with scenes from the pastoral play of the same name, the Salle des Gardes, the Pharsalus gallery, the flower chamber, the chamber of the arts, the Medea gallery, and the chapel.

Three great Italian artists are associated with Ancy-le-Franc: the architect Sebastiano Serlio, and the painters Francesco Primaticcio and Niccolò dell'Abbate. The discovery of two manuscripts of the unpublished sixth book of Serlio's treatise *On Architecture* allows us to say with some certainty

that the conception of the floor plan is his. The original views of the complex as preserved in du Cerceau's plans, however, are not identical with Serlio's plans, even though the Italian's manuscripts contain annotations about the progress of construction of Ancy-le-Franc. Serlio also made remarks in which he praised the owner's knowledge of art. This would indicate that the two had a congenial relationship, even if the plans that are preserved do not correspond with the plans of the present structure. Of course, there may have been plans other than the ones that have survived. Of all these variations, Serlio published his ideal plan, and ideal plans are rarely identical with actual buildings, for in all time periods contingencies make compromises inevitable. The drawing by a French architect—perhaps Pierre Lescot—also shows a variant of the Ancy-le-Franc views,

Ancy-le-Franc, château, Salle des Gardes. The largest room of the castle, it measures 65 by 30 feet (20 by 9 m). It was furnished in 1580 for a visit of King Henry III, and later used as a theater.

but one that is still further removed from the completed building. It seems best to assume that a French architect oversaw the construction in Ancy-le-Franc, and tried to influence its planning. Serlio did not mention him in his tract on architecture, and the French architect was probably only able to exercise influence over the dormers and the pitch of the roofs.

*No one has ever seriously doubted that the frescoes (illus. pp. 309 and 311) are the work of Francesco Primaticcio or members of his atelier. It is likely that Antoine de Clermont made the acquaintance of Primaticcio at Fontainebleau during his soujourn at court, and that he then commissioned him or his atelier with the interior decoration of Ancy-le-Franc. The similarity between the paintings at Fontainebleau and those in Ancy-le-Franc is unmistakable.

In 1580, de Clermont's grandson, Charles-Henri de Clermont-Tonnerre, had the terrace that surrounded the château removed. He also had the drawbridge replaced by a standing bridge, two further entrances added, and the solid wall areas between the windows to the inner courtyard opened. The latter step changed the façades as much as it affected the interiors. In 1683 the complex was sold to Louis XIV's minister of war, François-Michel Le Tellier de Louvois. He commissioned André Le Nôtre to design a park. He created two long axes flanking the château with three nearly square garden spaces between them and to each side. These garden squares, with clear borders on their exterior sides, were precisely and geometrically subdivided. In 1747 interior changes were planned, and in 1836 the moats were filled in.

Ancy-le-Franc, château, Galerie de Pharsale (Pharsalus gallery). Frescoes depicting Caesar's decisive victory over Pompeii on large rectangular surfaces above the high base.

Ancy-le-Franc, château, dining room.

Cruzy-le-Châtel

Apparently the stern yet harmonious façades of Ancy-le-Franc, which so differed from traditional French façades, inspired Antoine de Clermont's brother-in-law, Antoine de Crussol, to a still more daring, even curious, complex. In 1556 he replaced a hunting castle of the counts of Tonnerre that stood on a broad hilltop north of Cruzy-le-Châtel with the château of Maulnes (illus. below). It is hard to overlook: Maulnes is an experiment, a playful conglomeration of architectonic building elements which, given the raw climate of northern Burgundy, must have made the château uninhabitable for most of the year. Goethe once said of Palladio's Villa Rotonda in the Veneto that it was "habitable but not livable." What might he have had to say about Maulnes!

Nevertheless, the castle is enchanting. Its pentagonal tower is five stories high, with pentagonal pavilions on the four corners and a square gatehouse with a drawbridge on its fifth side. It rose up from a broad moat, more than half a circle, which continued as a low-lying parterre with an exedra to the south. Directly in front of the southern façade is a nymphaeum, with steps leading to it from three sides. A wide rectangular wall with bastions on the long sides and at the corners enclosed the complex. An arched gallery led from the entrance in the north to an oval *avant-cour*. One half, the inner one, also consisted of a one-story arcaded walkway, while the other, which curved in a semicircle from the outer wall, consisted only of a wall. Du Cerceau documented this complex as well in his tract on architecture. The façades seem to have been intentionally plain and without any articulation; only the pavilions have gables on two sides.

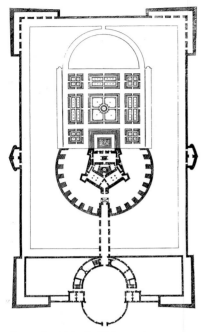

Cruzy-le-Châtel, Château de Maulnes, plan of the entire complex according to J.A. du Cerceau; less than half of the entire plan was actually carried out.

Cruzy-le-Châtel, Château de Maulnes, from 1556, exterior.

The residential tract with its nymphaeum was completed and survives. The moat has been filled in, making the building today seem out of proportion. A part of the surrounding wall as well as a wing of the oval *avant-cour* still stand as well, but the entire complex is in a pitiable condition. There is a well at the center of the pentagon, which was fed by several springs under the main building. A stone pentagonal pipe rises above the pool, around which a splendid stairway winds upward. It rises above the roof and adjoins a dome that opens up through an oculus. From the stairs you can see through numerous windows into the basin of the well. The rooms are ordered around this inner pentagonal form, three parallel to each other in both the south and north sides of the pentagon, as well as behind the north tower. On the third story, the complex could be entered by way of the drawbridge.

The interior was just as bare as the exterior of the building. Apparently the complex was based on a philosophy and not merely an architectural experiment. This philosophy had to do with water, the inclusion of the elements and nature into the building, and probably also with the exposed and isolated location. The architect is unknown, but the château's unusual shape is reminiscent of Giacomo Vignola's pentagon in Caprarola. It is conceivable that Sebastiano Serlio, caretaker of Ancy-le-Franc, also contributed. Even though Maulnes seems more exotic than Ancy-le-Franc when considering French châteaux of this period, its design nevertheless reveals clear Burgundian roots: it is unmistakably a donjon, even though it has been cast in the architectural language of Italy. Towers, pavilions, or corner fortifications, moats and drawbridges are the elements of a donjon, here offered in a different disguise.

Tanlay

The last and most conservative building of this group of châteaux is Tanlay (illus. pp. 314–317). François de Coligny, Seigneur d'Andelot, had it begun in about 1555, around the same time as Maulnes. Of the 13th-century castle which had existed here, part of the foundation and the moat were incorporated. Coligny remained true to Burgundian tradition: the nearly square complex has circular towers, moats, a gatehouse, a main building opposite the entrance, small wings at the sides, and a stair tower in the corner between two wings. Only the decoration was modern. By the time of Coligny's death in 1569, the southern part of the main building, the south wing, and the two circular towers were completed. Work did not resume until 1643, a year after Michel Particelli d'Emery, the *surindendant des Finances* (chairman of finances), acquired the estate. He commis-

OPPOSITE:
Tanlay, château, 1555-1648,
bridge between the entrance court
and the *cour d'honneur* with two
obelisks.

Tanlay, château, entire complex.
To the left are two circular towers,
to the right a one-story side wing as
well as the roof and a stair tower of
the main building.

sioned the architect Pierre Le Muet, who by 1648 had completed the main façade, created the interior furnishings for a number of the rooms, and erected the large gatehouse. Stylistically, this still belongs to the 15th century, but its décor is already Mannerist. A stone bridge with two obelisks, whose massive bases serve as gatehouses, connects the plateau with the outer courtyard. Today a low balustrade closes off the plateau, but in the 17th century, a wall with blind arcades and battlements stood here—another reminder of 15th-century castle architecture.

In designing the main façade, Le Muet seems to have followed the already completed decoration of the south wing. The windows of both stories, set far apart, are framed by flat, engaged double pilasters, so that these areas have four pilasters each. Here, as in both pavilion-like wings as well, the architect drew on the concept of François Mansart in Maisons-Lafitte. Still, Mansart's plan is incomparably more modern.

Visitors to Tanlay first enter the Vestibule of the Caesars (illus. p. 316). Four Doric double columns divide the room into three segments times

three. Here, too, one can see the finely wrought profiling of the flat relief. Replicas of antique sculptures are placed along the walls. On both stories, the rooms are richly furnished with fireplaces, furniture, and contemporary pictures. The Galerie des Grisailles (illus. p. 316 bottom) is in the upper story; it is completely clad in grisaille frescoes. Tanlay is famous for the frescoes in its southeast tower, called the Tower of the League. They were commissioned before 1569 by François de Coligny and are probably works of the Primaticcio school, which was also active in Ancy-le-Franc (illus. pp. 316/317).

In 1558, work was begun on the Petit Château in front of the moat. It was to be a kind of monumental gatehouse with short wings, which, like two protruding façade bays, framed the entrance on the ground floor level. The decoration suited the taste of the time: above a rusticated base was the ground floor with ashlars at the corners and frames, followed by the upper story with pilasters between windows with pediments, an ornamental frieze, and ornately adorned dormers. At the back, the Petit Château borders on the *cour verte*.

RIGHT: **Tanlay**, château, Vestibule of the Caesars.

FAR RIGHT:
Tanlay, château, southeast tower, so-called Tower of the League, dome fresco of the upper story (detail), school of Primaticcio, before 1569. The subject is the justification and glorification of Protestantism. Clad in the robes of classical gods are representatives of the Catholic League and the Huguenots. King Henry II, the double-headed Janus, looks upon the representatives of the Catholics in a friendly manner but angrily at the Protestants, to whom François d'Andelot, commissioner of the painting, belonged. Mars, Venus, and Vulcan are on the side of the Catholics, pictured here; Neptune, Hercules, and Minerva (representative of Reason and Cleverness) embody the Protestant virtues.

Tanlay, château, Galerie des Grisailles, paintings according to the designs of Pierre Le Muet.

Tonnerre, view over the city, above left the square west tower of the former collegiate church of Saint-Pierre.

OPPOSITE:
Tonnerre, former hospital Notre-Dame-des-Fontenilles, view through the large infirmary with the enormous wooden barrel vault to the east into the chapel, which is brightly lit through the large tracery windows. This room was completed in 1295.

Tonnerre

The only city in the arrondissement besides Avallon is Tonnerre, located in the far north. It lies on the banks of the Armançon and is surrounded by vineyards, forests, and meadows. In 1556 a fire destroyed almost all the buildings. One of few exceptions was the former hospital Notre-Dame-des-Fontenilles, which is one of the oldest hospitals in France. Tonnerre belonged to the domain of Margaret of Flanders, sister-in-law of Louis IX (St. Louis), and founded the hospital in 1293; the enormous infirmary was completed in 1295. Without the entrance hall, which is no longer standing,

the room measures 260 by 60 feet (80 by 18.3 m) and is 27 feet (8.3 m) high under the massive, continuous wooden barrel vault (illus. opposite). As in Beaune, patients' beds were lined up along the long walls, 40 to each side, so that each of them could see the three rib-vaulted chapels at the east short end. A wooden gallery encircled the entire hall, allowing access to the windows. The richly appointed interior is also characteristic of a hospital. Wooden figures in the niches at the western end of the hall depict the benefactresses, Margaret of Flanders and Margaret of Beaumont, Countess of Tripoli, who retired here together with Margaret of Flanders. Both date from the 13th century. Over the main altar, slightly newer and larger than life, are stone figures of the Virgin with Moses in the Bush of Thorns. The famous Entombment of Christ is in the Chapelle du Revestiaire (illus. pp. 320/321). It was executed in 1454, making it one of the earliest depictions of this subject in Burgundy. The seven figures standing around the stiff body of Christ merge into a dramatic scene. They are reminiscent of the Sluter school, although the facial expressions don't have the intensity that distinguished Sluter's figures.

The marble double tomb of Louis XIV's minister of war, François-Michel Le Tellier de Louvois, and his wife (illus. p. 323) arrived from Paris in 1819. It is one of the main works of the sculptor François Girardon (1628–1715), who also created Cardinal Richelieu's tomb. Made between 1693 and 1699, it is surprising for this period. Despite the social importance of the deceased, the tomb is

Tonnerre, former hospital Notre-Dame-des-Fontenilles, founded in 1293, view of the exterior from the northeast. In the east is the chapel at the end of the expansive infirmary.

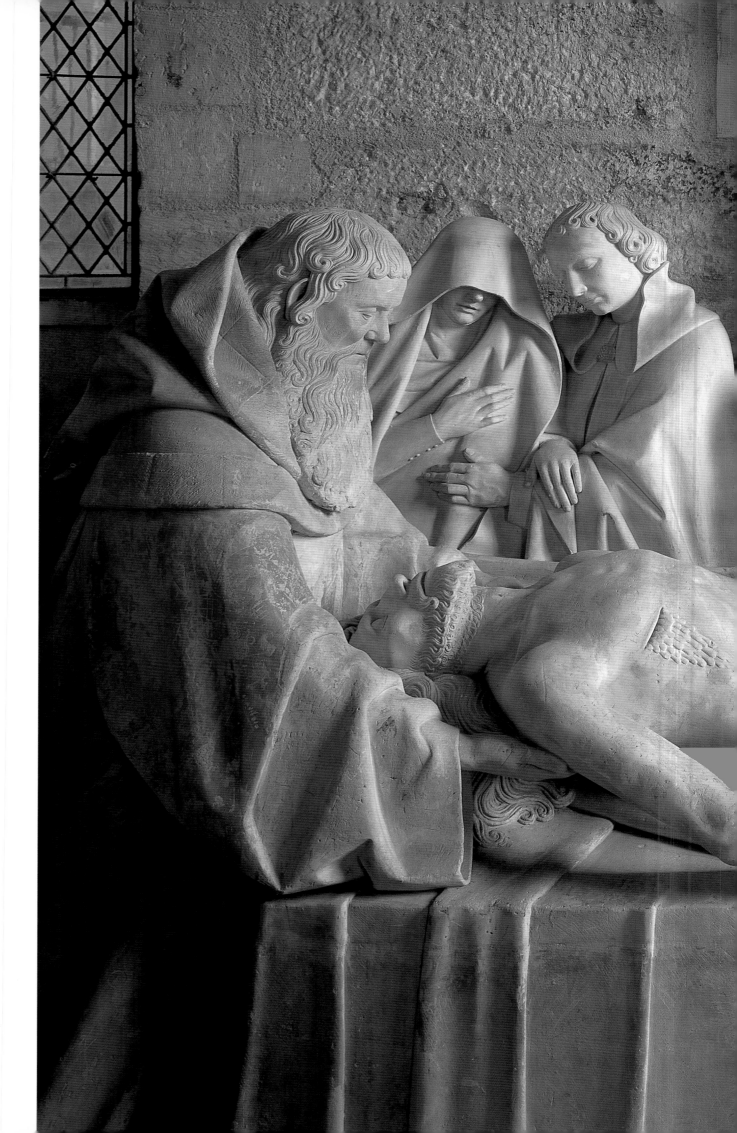

Tonnerre, former hospital Notre-
Dame-des-Fontenilles, Chapelle du
Revestiaire, entombment group,
1454, limestone, about life-size.

plain and desists from the customary trophies and allusions to victories and successes. The pose of the marquis is also unusual. Instead of facing upwards, as expected, his gaze seems to be expecting the visitor. His expression is neither serious nor sublime nor festive; these apply only to the face of his wife. It is also quite remarkable that he is turned away from her, and that no relationship or parity exists between them. Some have said that this is the marquis' revenge on his wife for her infidelity, something he could not forgive even in death. François Girardon also created the bronze figure *Wisdom*; the figure *Vigilance* is from the hand of Martin Desjardins. The tomb of Margaret of Flanders was lost, but it was re-created in 1826 and can be found in the central chapel.

The former collegiate church of Saint-Pierre lies above the city on a rock outcropping. The city fire destroyed a building which must have seemed curious even to its contemporaries. Between a west end with a double portal dating from 1110/1120 and a polygonal choir from the early 14th century lay a small, three-aisle church just 16 to 20 feet (5 to 6 m) in length. It burned down and was replaced by a double antechoir, a five-part transept, and two bays of the nave. Apparently, destruction of the old façade was planned but never executed. Instead, an elaborate Renaissance façade was finally erected in the south.

Right next to Saint-Pierre is the Fosse Dionne (illus. opposite), an ancient well consecrated to Divona, goddess of the springs. The present enclosure was made in 1758 along with the lovely semicircular wash house. At the base of the spring basin is a funnel through which the water flows after it has fallen down a steep, 145-foot-long (45-m) gallery in the rock. A small canal links the romantic Fosse Dionne with the Armançon.

Tonnerre has a number of magnificent town houses dating from the Renaissance. The Hôtel d'Uzès, today a bank, is worth seeing, especially the lovely portals of the east façade (illus. right). Incidentally, the Hôtel d'Uzès is the birth house of Charles-Geneviève-Louise-Auguste-Andrée-Thimothée Eon de Beaumont, who was known simply as Chevalier or Chevalière d'Eon. Today he would be considered a transvestite. In the 18th century, he managed to leave his contemporaries completely bewildered as to his sexual identity. Born in 1728, he first embarked on a brilliant military and diplomatic career, in the course of which it was apparently necessary for him to appear in women's clothing. Later he was exiled to England, and was only allowed to return to France dressed as a woman. Not until his death in England in 1810 was the mystery of this person's identity finally resolved: he was a man.

Tonnerre, former hospital Notre-Dame-des-Fontenilles, left lateral chapel (symmetrical with the Chapelle du Revestière), tomb of the Marquis de Louvois and his wife by François Girardon, 1693 to 1699, marble, about life-size.

OPPOSITE:
Tonnerre, Fosse Dionne, well spring basin and wash house, 1758.

ABOVE:
Tonnerre, Hôtel d'Uzès, late 16th century, inner court with two elaborate portals and a polygonal stair tower.

Along the Yonne – Auxerrois

The arrondissement of Auxerre, called Auxerrois, shares its eastern border with Avallonnais. In the north it borders on Sénonais, and in the west and the south it is enclosed by the regions of Gâtinais and Puisaye, both in the Loiret department. The Yonne River flows through the entire length of Auxerrois. It is bordered by the limestone ridge of the Lower Burgundy Plateau, which in some places reveals sheer cliffs of blinding white rock. The high areas that were once covered with forests have been cleared long ago, and the ground is karstic. In many places efforts are being made to reforest the land.

The Auxerrois is a traditional wine-producing area—grapes are grown in Chablis, in Irancy, and in Auxerre itself. In addition to the vineyards, cherry cultivation also has a long tradition here.

Auxerre

Auxerre, the capital of Lower Burgundy, spreads out over a small rise on the banks of the Yonne (illus. right) and is surrounded by vineyards. Like other cities in the department of Yonne, Auxerre was originally a Celtic settlement, named Autricum by the Senone people. Under Caesar in around 54–52 BC it became Autissiodorum, one of the stations on the way from Lyon to Boulogne-sur-Mer. The past several hundred years have wiped out most traces of these early settlements; a city wall from the third century and some towers are known only through excavations. Since that time the history of the city has been full of vicissitudes. Following the conquests of Chlodwig, the city belonged to the Frankish Kingdom beginning in 486. Later it became a part of the Carolingian Empire. Saracens plundered the city in the 8th century, as did the Normans in the 9th. After that Auxerrois was successively in the possession of the duchy of Burgundy (until 1005), the county Nevers (until 1358), England (until 1371), the French crown (until 1435), then of Burgundy again, and from 1477 onwards the city reverted once again to the crown.

Auxerre, view across the Yonne towards the city. At the right is the former monastic church of Saint-Germain with its southern façade tower from the 12th century, which remained standing when the western parts were torn down in 1811; left, the cathedral with the former bishop's palace beneath the choir.

Saint-Etienne Cathedral

Auxerre has been a diocese and had a cathedral, Saint-Etienne, since the early 4th century. It has stood on this spot since about 400, but nothing at all from the first millenium has been preserved. In 1023, the city and its cathedral burned down. The hall crypt, with ambulatory, of the building that arose in its place are the oldest part of the cathedral (illus. p. 330). The chapel at the vertex of the sanctuary still has its original coat of paint from about 1100/1120. On the barrel vaulting, in front of the backdrop of a large cross, one sees Christ on a white horse surrounded by four angels, also mounted. The painting on the calotte of the apse reveals Christ enthroned between candelabra and the symbols of the Evangelists; it was executed during the 13th century.

In 1215, Bishop Guillaume de Seignelay began the High Gothic building that measured 360 feet (110 m) from its portals to the chapel at the vertex of the sanctuary. The nave and choir are of roughly equal length, with a five-part transept between them. The bright three-aisle choir with four straight bays, a polygonal chevet, a five-sided ambulatory and—because of the older foundation—only one chapel in the vertex, were all completed by 1234. Slender arcades, a delicate grillwork in front of the triforium walkway and large, three-part tracery windows form a finely proportioned, bright space reminiscent of the early Gothic. The vaulting, too, was first planned as six-part.

Auxerre, Saint-Etienne Cathedral, ca. 1100/1120 to mid-13th century, central nave and southern transept, at the front the first bay of the choir, built above the 11th-century crypt.

BELOW:
Auxerre, Saint-Etienne Cathedral, exterior from the southeast.

OPPOSITE:
Auxerre, Saint-Etienne Cathedral, view into the choir and transept, ca. 1215.

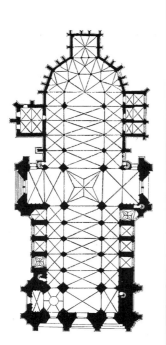

Auxerre, Saint-Etienne Cathedral, floor plan.

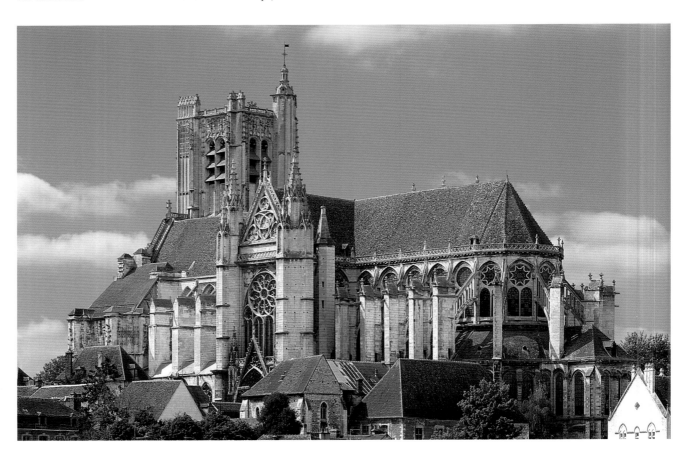

OPPOSITE:
Auxerre, Saint-Etienne
Cathedral, stained glass windows
in the choir, 13th century.

Auxerre, Saint-Etienne
Cathedral, ambulatory and
easternmost chapel, ca. 1215
to 1234.

Auxerre, former Bishop's palace, today a prefecture, gallery wing, 1120/1130.

Auxerre, Saint-Etienne Cathedral, crypt, after 1023, southern ambulatory tunnel.

FAR RIGHT:
Auxerre, Saint-Etienne Cathedral, crypt, painting on the vault of the vertex chapel, ca. 1100/1120.

It seems the Romanesque nave remained useable for a long time, because as soon as the choir was completed, construction of the double-towered façade modeled on famous prototypes began. The work dragged on. Nevertheless, in 1309, work began on both the nave and the transept. In 1334 the high altar was consecrated—perhaps an indication that the transept had been completed.

In the meantime, France found itself embroiled in the Hundred Years' War, and most projects were curtailed. The nave was finally finished in the late 14th century, and the vaulting in the next. Even though the nave was modeled on the east sections, it is far more plain and rigid in its individual forms. Gothicism in cathedrals had in the meantime become a kind of mannerism, and original creative impulses had become extremely rare.

Throughout this period the western sections also grew. The entire right portal on the west façade, the Baptism Portal depicting scenes from the life of Jesus and John the Baptist on the four zones of its tympanum and in the archivolts, was probably completed by 1260 (illus. opposite). The trefoil niches of the upper zone of the base show David and Bathsheba as symbols for Christ and the Church. Above are personifications of philosophy and the *septem artes liberales*, the liberal arts—grammar, dialectic, rhetoric, arithmetic and geometry, music, and astronomy. In these depictions the influence of Reims is clear, both in the plasticity of the bodies and in the realism of the narrated scenes. The lower portions of the central portal were probably done together with the Baptism Portal. Recognizable, but badly disfigured, are the seated figures in a series of closely spaced blind niches—perhaps prophets with angels above them. The upper zones of the portal date from the 14th century. The lintel and tympanum record the Last Judgment, while the surrounding figures

typologically intensify the central depiction: the prophets at the base, the Wise and Foolish Virgins on the door jambs, the (now missing) apostles in the jamb niches, as well as the stories of the Lost Son and Joseph of Egypt on the jamb.

The left portal, dedicated to Mary, also dates from the 14th century and points out a clear typological relation of Adam and Eve to Jesus and the Virgin. On the plinth base reliefs are scenes from Genesis: the Creation of Heaven and Earth, Separation of Land and Water, Creation of the Animals. On the jamb are the Creation of Adam and Eve (receiving the commandment in a scroll), the Fall and Expulsion from Paradise, the Sacrifices of Cain and Abel, Fratricide and Cursing, and finally Cain's Death and Noah's Ark. On the lintel is the Crowning of the Virgin; on the archivolts, scenes from Mary's life. The north tower was finished in 1543; the south one remained incomplete.

The transept, too, has charming figural portals. The St. Stephen Portal at the south end is a 14th-century work. St. Stephen's life is depicted in three bands on the tympanum, on the lintel is a row of small niche figures, and in the archivolts are angels, patriarchs, and prophets. The Germanus Portal at the north end depicts, of course, the story of the saint from Auxerre.

Many of the interior fittings were lost in the Wars of Religion, so it is all the more surprising that the cycle of windows survived. Along with those of Bourges, Chartres, and Troyes, it is one of the most significant in all of France. These windows date from the 13th century (in the choir, illus. p. 328) to the 16th century (west window and window in the transept). Unfortunately, two thorough restorations in 1576 and 1866 to 1873 marred them by exchanging some panes and by replacing others incorrectly. Among the themes depicted are portrayals of Christ, the martyrs, patrons of the church, virtues and vices, apostles and prophets, Old Testament scenes, legends, and donors.

The former bishop's palace, today the prefecture, is below the cathedral, near the river. The oldest part of this complex is the gallery wing, built by Bishop Hugh of Montaigu (1115–1136) on the east wall of a previous building after it was destroyed by fire. Plain double columns with leafy capitals bear 18 windowed arcades (illus. opposite). The roof terrace above dates from the 19th century. Perpendicular to it is the Salle Synodale, which has large windows with pointed arches at the front of the gables. It was built by Bishop Guy de Mello in 1257. Beneath it is an older wine cellar. Two portals are also original, one late Gothic and the other a Renaissance portal that has been walled in. The other buildings date from the 19th century and display various neostyles.

Saint-Germain

The High Gothic cathedral of the former Benedictine monastery of Saint-Germain was built over one of the most important pre-Romanesque architectural monuments of France, the crypt of Saint-Germain. St. Germanus, born into a noble family in Auxerre in 378, studied in Autun and Rome, and first tried his hand at politics. When he felt himself increasingly drawn to the Church, he left his family and began the life of a hermit, endowing several churches and monasteries from his fortune. In 418 he was appointed bishop of Auxerre; he died in Ravenna in 448. After his death, his successor Mauritius, also later canonized, buried his remains in a small oratory on the family estate in Auxerre. Soon, reports of miracles at his grave drew pilgrims to the site. Queen Clothilda (died 544, also later sanctified) endowed a small monastery and had the oratory replaced by a new, larger structure. The saint's remains were enclosed in a reliquary of gold that pilgrims could view into the 9th century, as reported by Gregory of Tours. In his 876 writings *De Miraculis sancti Germani*, the monk Hericus mentions a new Carolingian building by Count Conrad, the lay abbot

Auxerre, Saint-Etienne Cathedral, tympanum of the south portal on the west façade, completed ca. 1250, so-called Baptism Portal with scenes from the lives of Jesus and John the Baptist.

Hericus does not say. Two fires in 1064 and 1075 necessitated initial repairs, and in the 12th century further renovations were done on the west building and west bays. The north tower and the chapter hall date from this period of construction.

After four centuries, the Merovingian-Carolingian building was apparently so dilapidated that a decision was made to erect a new building, incorporating the crypt with the tombs of the saints and early bishops. Construction began in 1277. Work at first progressed quickly, but was then discontinued intermittently for longer periods. The reason was, as almost everywhere in Burgundy, the Hundred Years' War. When construction finally ceased, in 1398, the choir and nave, as well as the portions of the nave belonging to the monks' choir, were complete. In the west, the Carolingian and Romanesque parts were left standing. After this, almost all accounts are of its undoing: plunderings by the Huguenots in 1567, crumbling, small repairs, Napoleon's donation of the complex to the hospital in 1810, dismantling of the west nave bays and the west building in 1811 except for the south tower. Only a few years later, a neo-Gothic façade was erected for the east nave bays.

The layout of the pre-865 crypt is a confusing four-part combination of a tunnel crypt (one consisting of individual chambers) and an ambulatory crypt. At the center is a short, three-aisle room with three parallel barrel vaults supported by

Auxerre, former monastic church of Saint-Germain, crypt, ca. 840 to 863, murals in the northern part of the ambulatory, scenes of St. Stephen.

RIGHT:
Auxerre, former monastic church of Saint-Germain, crypt ambulatory.

who was an uncle of the emperor. This new building, to which the crypt belonged, must have been begun shortly after 840, as Hericus reports the miraculous healing of Count Conrad after he spent a night at the grave of St. Germanus. In the following year, the saint's remains were temporarily exhibited elsewhere, probably due to the construction. They were brought to the new confessio in 860. Three years later, the remains of martyrs and the bishops of Auxerre were also brought here and laid in the aisles leading to the saint's grave. In 865, the *cryptae inferiores* were consecrated, and later the same year, the west building and *cryptae superiores*, and probably the high choir. The church was now more than 325 feet (100 m) long! Was there also a Carolingian nave? Or did they keep the Merovingian one?

chapel and of two unidentified bishops on the slanted corners. It seems certain that the models for these paintings were miniatures from the school at the court of the emperor.

The Gothic upper church has a delicately articulated chapel at the vertex of the sanctuary built over the foundation of the crypt. The church and the remaining buildings of the convent are used today by the archeological museum. Here you can see primarily prehistoric pieces, as well as finds from the Gallo-Roman settlement in and around Auxerre (illus. left).

The city itself is an inviting place to take a stroll. Besides many lovely streets and lanes with an almost intact ensemble of 16th-century houses, it boasts an entrance gate from the 15th century with a splendid clock tower (illus. below).

LEFT:
Auxerre, former monastic church of Saint-Germain, today an archaeological museum, Gallo-Roman equestrian torso.

Auxerre, city entrance with clock tower, 15th century.

oaken architraves, each on two columns, behind which is the tomb of the saint. Two pillars on the eastern exterior of this central hall complete this three-sided polygonal structure to form a rectangle. Around this rectangle is an ambulatory that originally had only one aisle, was partly groin-vaulted and connected in the east to a three-aisle passageway leading to the chapel at the vertex of the sanctuary, renovated in Gothic style. The resemblance to the crypt of Saint-Pierre in Flavigny is unmistakable. Constructions of this type were ultimately the ones that prepared the way for an ambulatory with radiating chapels around a choir.

In 1927 frescoes were discovered in the northern arm of the ambulatory that are among the most important surviving examples of early medieval painting (illus. opposite). Above a painted base with columns, floral patterns are discernable in the intrados of the arches and on the transverse arches, and scenes of St. Stephen are under the formerets. There is also a depiction of the Adoration of the Magi on the vaulting of the Laurentius

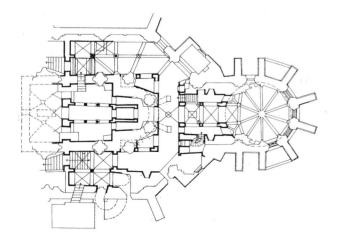

Auxerre, former monastic church of Saint-Germain, floor plan of crypt.

The Puisaye

Southwest of Auxerre lies the Puisaye, a land of brooks, ponds, and lakes, of extensive woods and meadows. The contours of the countryside are softer than those to the east; the valleys do not cut so deeply into the earth. The longest river is the Loing, originating not far from Treigny. The Puisaye is thinly settled and has the reputation of being a monotonous, even a stern place. The damp climate allows splendid forests to thrive, and a rich variety of flora can be found along the lakeshores and riverbanks (illus. left and below). The *bocages*, those dense, impenetrable hedges that have been a feature of Burgundian country-side for centuries, trace lines through meadows, opening views far into the distance. The sandy soil contains silex and flint embedded in white and red clay. This clay has been made into pottery since the High Middle Ages, but only in the 17th cen-tury did an industry develop around production of the famous Bleu de Saint-Vérain. Later, dishes for daily use were made here until artists dis-covered the clay as an artistic medium in the late 19th century. Saint-Amand-en-Puisaye is a center of pottery and earthenware workmanship today. Saint-Sauveur-en-Puisaye is the birthplace of au-thor Gabrielle-Sidonie Colette (1873–1954). The main city in the Puisaye is Saint-Fargeau.

Parc natural Saint-Hubert de Boutissaint, forest with ferns (above), and one of the many lakes (right).

Saint-Fargeau

Jacques Cœur of Bourges, immeasurably wealthy merchant and chancellor to Charles VII, bought the estate of Saint-Fargeau in 1450. He then renovated the 10th-century castle, a not-quite-regular pentagon with corner towers and two towers flanking the gatehouse, a moat, and what was likely a splendid logis. In 1453, he fell into disfavor at court. He was forced to flee and died soon thereafter, completely impoverished; so little separated fortune and misfortune, power and misery at that time. Saint-Fargeau first fell to the estate of the king, then in 1566 to the possession of François de Bourbon. His great-grandchild, Anne-Marie-Louise d'Orléans, a cousin of Louis XIV, was a supporter of the Fronde and was exiled to Saint-Fargeau from 1652 to 1657 and 1662 to 1664. A clever and charming adversary of the king, she was better known as the *Grande Mademoiselle* (illus. p. 336). During the years of her exile, she had the old castle renovated and rebuilt by the Parisian architect François Le Vau (the brother of Louis Le Vau). A fire in 1752 devastated all the roofs and large parts of the interior, but the façades of the four Le Vau wings were able to be salvaged. They are typical for their age: *brique et pierre*—a mixture of dressed stones and bricks—and give the façade a lively, slightly rustic appearance. Above the fenestrated base is a ground floor with high windows under flat blind arcades,

Countryside near Saint-Saveur-en-Puisaye.

followed by a mezzanine with windows that are framed by dressed stones and coat-of-arms cartouches on a red brick wall. The high mansard roofs allow light and air to enter through regularly placed *œuils de bœuf*. Unlike the more ornate dormers, these windows do not affect the articulation of the façade. A round pavilion in one corner cleverly replaces a protruding entrance bay, which would not have been effective in this medieval complex with its comparatively short wings. The stairs, with 20 steps, form a quarter-circle wedge (illus. opposite). Three arches that continue the articulation of the ground floor façade open into the domed vestibule (illus. below). Behind it, in the old east tower, lies the chapel. Here the young Louis-Michel Le Peletier de Saint-Fargeau, known by the name "Le Saint-Fargeau," was buried. In 1793 he was a deputy of the National Assembly and had voted in favor of the execution of Louis XVI. On the eve of the execution, Louis-Michel Le Peletier was murdered by the king's guards. The Revolution and the populace celebrated in him the first martyr of Liberty.

The northwest wing was not completed by Le Vau. Not until 1715 did the great-grandfather of Le Saint-Fargeau acquire the complex, and he drew up a new design for the wing. The interior decoration dates from 1829 and later, but the English park, replacing a French garden, had already been laid out in 1809.

Saint-Fargeau, château, portrait of Anne-Marie-Louise d'Orléans, better known as *La Grande Mademoiselle*.

RIGHT:
Saint-Fargeau, château, ca. 1450 and 1652–1664, vestibule, mid-17th century.

OPPOSITE:
Saint-Fargeau, château, main entrance with stairs in the form of a quarter circle and the adjoining wings, mid-17th century.

Treigny

Château Ratilly (illus. below) is also a late medieval complex. It dates from about 1400 and is an example of a castle based around two courtyards with circular corner towers, and moats encircling both courts. Jean de Beaumont was the builder. Today the only original elements remaining are the walls surrounding the inner courtyard and their towers. At the center of the entrance side is a gate flanked by mighty half-round towers, once protected by a drawbridge and battlements. On the southeast side, traces of a defensive platform and the beam pockets for the battlements are still visible. The southwest tower was used at the same time as a dovecote. The windows, placed at regular intervals on the entrance side, are all Renaissance, as are the inner buildings, whose sloping gables meet the southern towers. The original wings were lost at the beginning of the religious wars, when Ratilly was a base for the Jansenites. The wings were replaced in 1587 and 1617.

Today, ceramics are made here. Some rooms contain exhibits of old earthenware and pottery of the Puisaye, while others show contemporary art in exhibitions that are continually changed.

Druyes-les-Belles-Fontaines

The castle of Druyes-les-Belles-Fontaines, which stands on a steep, long, drawn-out ridge with a view of the Yonne, is in terms of the history of its development one of the most important medieval secular buildings in France. A fortress called Drogia is known to have been located on this rocky plateau from the 6th century on. In the 12th century, the estate belonged to the Count of Nevers, whose daughter Agnès was a ward of King Philip II August as well as one of the wealthiest heiresses in France. In 1184 Agnès married the king's cousin, Pierre II de Courtenay, a grandson of Louis the Fat, thus contributing numerous estates to his wealth, including Druyes-les-Belles-Fontaines. In time it became clear that Pierre II was just as ambitious a man as the king. When both returned from the Third Crusade in 1193, each of them—surely spurred by competitiveness—began building castles that greatly resembled each other: the Louvre and the castle of Druyes-les-Belles-Fontaines. What was completely new was the architectural type: a walled square with bold circular corner towers, a strong gatehouse, and one or two residential wings. There has been much

Treigny, Château de Ratilly, about 1400 and late 16th century, entrance side with two corner towers and two U-shaped towers flanking the entrance.

speculation as to the origins of this type of structure: did it come from the Holy Land? Was it an "invention" of the king, modeled on oriental castles that are no longer known? Whatever the origin, the king built it on flat land in Paris and thereby created the prototype of the plains castle of the High Middle Ages. Pierre II transposed this plains castle type onto a rocky ridge. Built of excellent square ashlars, the castle measured 175 feet (53 m) square. Circular towers protected the corners and a massive gatehouse with a wreath of *mâchicoulis* guarded the gate behind the moat. In its current form, this is probably all that remains of the renovations and beautification undertaken by Margaret of Flanders in 1375 with the financial resources of the ducal treasury, as the castle was a part of the duke's estate from 1370 on. The rib-vaulted chapel in the center of the southwest side, whose apse is in a square flanking tower, and the logis with the splendid Romanesque windows facing the valley, belong to the initial building period (illus. above). The interior wall of the logis is articulated by a blind arcade on delicate columns and testifies to the wealth and power of the duke. Incidentally, Pierre II left Burgundy shortly after 1216, as he had been offered the crown of the Latin Empire established by the crusaders. However, he failed to reach Constantinople. While on the journey there, he was taken prisoner and died shortly afterward, without ever seeing Burgundy again.

Walls also surrounded the enormous, irregular *basse-cour*, which had its own gatehouse and later became an entire village. Still preserved is the former castle church of Saint-Romain, which originated in the 12th century. Directly next to it is the spring of Druyes.

Cravant

Farther to the north, at the confluence of the Cure and Yonne Rivers, an older fortification, Cravant, developed into a village in the late 13th century. Remains of a city wall, a tower, and a square donjon are still preserved from this era. The three-aisle pillared nave of the small 13th-century church of Saint-Pierre-et-Saint-Paul, which was probably part of the castle, was given a choir ambulatory between 1551 and 1598 with radiating chapels and a choir tower in the north, corresponding to a two-aisle sacristy in the south with the same area, probably a re-planning of the second tower (illus. p. 340). The three long choir bays with six-part rib vaulting in the central nave and stellar vaults in the side aisles open into a five-part chevet with trapezoidal, stellar-vaulted ambulatory bays. The chapels, directly adjacent to each other, have coffered barrel vaulting. The structure of the building is definitely Gothic, but the impression inside is created by the Renaissance décor. Because of its decoration, the massive tower as well can only be classified as a Renaissance work (illus. right).

Cravant, Saint-Pierre-et-Saint-Paul, nave and side aisles, 13th century, sacristy, second half of 16th century, and floor plan (right).

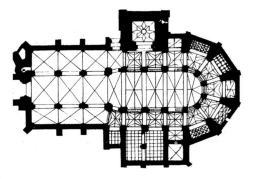

Saint-Bris-le-Vineux

The Saint-Prix-et-Saint-Cot church in Saint-Bris-le-Vineux is another disparate mixture of Gothic and Renaissance. Its origins, however, reach far back into the first millennium. In the first half of the 5th century, the remains of the martyr Priscus of Auxerre were found here, and the famous bishop Germanus had a church erected on the site. In 1103, the powerful Dreux de Mello family took over the estate. The remains of the tower on the southern side between the nave and choir date from this time. Then, in the first third of the 13th century, the three-aisle, rib-vaulted nave was built. Simple windows open above profiled arcades that rest on compound piers. Here, too, a tower flanking the choir rises over the last northeastern bay of the side aisle. As in Pontaubert, a rectangular choir seems to have directly adjoined the nave. The chapels between the pier buttresses are late Gothic. About 1370 a two-bay chapel, which later became the southern side aisle of the choir, was erected in an eastern extension of the Romanesque tower remains. The central nave and northern side aisle followed only in the early 16th century. Both end in a three-sided polygonal apse and have rich Renaissance décor. To the north, the side aisle of the choir (illus. opposite) was expanded into shallow chapels with coffered barrel vaulting similar to the ambulatory chapels in Cravant.

The most extraordinary pieces in this church are the 15th- and 16th-century stained-glass windows (illus. opposite), a monumental fresco of the Tree of Jesse, and a richly decorated pulpit from the early 16th century.

Saint-Bris-le-Vineux, view over the town and vineyards; at the back right stands the church of Saint-Prix-et-Saint-Cot.

Irancy

In a charming side valley of the Yonne lies Irancy. Despite its diminutive size—only 370 inhabitants—it is worth a visit. The plan of the village is round, evident especially when looking down on it from surrounding hills. This is the birthplace of Jacques-Germain Soufflot, born in 1713, who was one of the most important architects of classicism. Irancy is surrounded by vineyards offering lovely views of the surrounding countryside (illus. p. 343).

Chablis

Chablis is famous for the wines that have been cultivated here for centuries, but the town also has a lovely, spacious, and bright church (illus. below right). The previous building on this site was founded by St. Martin of Tours, but around 1212 a new one was erected. It is a three-aisle basilica with three six-part vaulted double bays, an alternating system of supports in the nave, and an ambulatory around the choir without chapels. There is no transept. The vaulting of the nave, the alternating system of supports, and the three-story elevation with galleries give the impression of an early Gothic building. The closely spaced columns in the chevet, windows without tracery, and individual forms reminiscent of Pontigny and Vézelay all point to the early Gothic era as well. The originally planned double-tower façade was redesigned in the 17th century; in the 19th century, it and the interior were restored. The sculpture of St. Peter with book and key (second half of the 13th century) and the somewhat newer sculpture of a pope may be original furnishings.

Saint-Bris-le-Vineux, Saint-Prix-et-Saint-Cot, stained-glass windows in the choir, 1559.

FAR LEFT:
Saint-Bris-le-Vineux, Saint-Prix-et-Saint-Cot, northern side aisle of the choir, early 16th century.

Chablis, Saint-Martin, from 1212, central nave and choir.

Préhy (near Chablis), church of Sainte-Claire in the vineyards.

Préhy (near Chablis), church of Sainte-Claire, next to a modern wine-producing estate.

Irancy, view of the town with its surrounding vineyards.

Pontigny

One of the four subsidiary monasteries founded by Cîteaux even before the order was confirmed in 1119 was Pontigny. Although founded in 1114, construction of the large monastic church was not begun until 1145. Ten years later the choir was finished. From 1186 on, that is, soon after completion of the nave, the rectangular choir typical of Cistercian buildings was replaced by a broad ambulatory around the choir with nine radiating chapels. After an eventful history, the monastery was disbanded during the Revolution. The abbot's palace, which had just been completed, and all the monastic buildings were torn down and sold off. Only the monastic church remained standing.

The church has a three-aisle nave of seven bays entered through a three-part narthex. The lower transept is seven-part with rectangular chapels on all free sides and a long choir three bays deep with an ambulatory and chapels, joined in a wide semicircle on the exterior (illus. below). The original rectangular choir, by contrast, only took up the western bay of the long choir. The elevation is also characteristic for Cistercian buildings: cruciform piers with engaged semicircular columns carry the pointed arches and the supports for the arcades,

above which are simple windows. Instead of the usual pointed barrel vaulting, the church in Pontigny has four-part rib vaulting between canted piers. The builders refrained completely from decorative ornamentation. Its very absence, however, serves to emphasize the few clear architectural forms of the Cistercian church, melding them with inimitable harmony and suffusing the entire church with dignity and solemnity. The light is also spectacular: on sunny days the stone shimmers a wonderful shade of golden yellow.

The two-story choir (illus. p. 346) is rib-vaulted as well, and although the wall articulation of the nave was continued here, it is more richly articulated through vaulting shafts and engaged columns. Although it has no sculptured ornamentation, it seems more subtly articulated, more delicate. The choir expansion added no fewer than 13 new altars and extended the church's length by more than a third. Visually, the exterior of the monastic church of Pontigny became very unusual. With no towers, strong horizontal division of the elevation, and an unusually long ambulatory around the choir, the horizontal axis clearly predominates at Notre-Dame. In fact, the flying buttresses on the choir are one of the only vertical elements.

OPPOSITE:
Pontigny, former monastic church of Notre-Dame-de-l'Assomption, nave, central aisle, and southern lateral aisle, 12th century.

Pontigny, former monastic church of Notre-Dame-de-l'Assomption, from 1145, southern side with low transept and wide choir ambulatory, from 1186.

Appoigny

West of Pontigny lies Appoigny, once part of the domain of the bishops of Auxerre. It is thought that Guillaume de Seignelay, bishop of Auxerre from 1207–1220, endowed the collegiate church dedicated to the apostles Peter and Paul just as the choir of Pontigny was being finished. In fact, the church of Appoigny is closely modeled on its neighbor. A rectangular choir and a non-projecting

transept are followed by a broad nave with galleries from the 1230s (illus. below). Although its proportions are somewhat bulky, the delicacy and wealth of its profiling and the lovely flower buds on the capitals maintain its elegance. This impression is enhanced by the Renaissance choir screen that separates the nave from the eastern parts of the church like a kind of three-arched triumphal gate. In addition to architectural ornamentation such as fluted pilasters, architraves, niches, and gables, it is also adorned with flat relief panels depicting scenes from the life of Jesus and St. Peter. The choir screen was a donation of Bishop François de Donadieu from 1606/1610.

La Ferté-Loupière

The small country church of Saint-Germain in La Ferté-Loupière from the 12th and 15th centuries (nave and choir respectively) is not an outstanding example of Burgundian sacred architecture. Nonetheless, in 1910, well-preserved murals from ca. 1500 were found above the nave arcades depicting the legend of the Three Living and the Three Dead and a multi-figured Dance of Death (illus. above). In lovely, soft colors—white, gray-blue, ochre, and red—people of all stations of life and professions are accosted by Death, whom none can escape. The highly moral subject matter of the Dance of Death was a favorite motif of the late Middle Ages, but few examples are preserved as well as this one.

La Ferté-Loupière, Saint-Germain, 12th century/15th century, Dance of Death fresco in the central aisle of the nave (detail), ca. 1500.

OPPOSITE:
Pontigny, former monastic church of Notre-Dame-de-l'Assomption, chevet, from 1186.

Appoigny, former collegiate church of Saint-Pierre-et-Saint-Paul, 1207 to 1220, central nave with the Renaissance choir screen.

Joigny, view across the Yonne to the historic city on the hill; in the center is Saint-Jean.

Joigny

Besides Auxerre itself, the other significant town in the Auxerre arrondissement is Joigny, a small, pretty city at the edge of the Othe Forest. The old city lies on a slope rising from the Yonne (illus. above). The elevation of Côte Saint-Jacques in the north of the city provides a lovely view over Joigny and the river valley.

Joigny has two churches, Saint-Jean and Saint-Thibault, both with similar construction histories. Saint-Jean, first mentioned in 1080, was later re-built numerous times. Records note that the unfinished church was consecrated in 1504. A fire in 1530 destroyed Saint-Jean, leaving only four 13th-century pillars standing in the eastern central aisle and a west tower with a portal dating from around 1500. Around these remains arose a new building with an unadorned exterior between 1548 and 1596. Its three-aisle nave is followed not by a transept, but by a kind of ambulatory opening into the central nave with three arches at the height of the arcades. The five-sided central apse is newer and was not part of the original plan. The elevation reveals three levels: a row of large, painted figural niches with consoles and baldachins separates the pointed arches of the columned arcade from the high clerestory. The clerestory windows in the east have Flamboyant tracery, while the western ones have Renaissance partitioning. Whereas the bays of the side aisles are covered with simpler stellar vaulting, the central aisle has a richly and imaginatively decorated coffered, shallow barrel vault with curved molding above the lunettes. This vaulting is a masterpiece by the architect Jean Chéreau. The forms of the coffering are probably based on the architectural treatise by Sebastiano Serlio (illus. opposite top).

In addition to 16th- and 17th-century panel paintings and an entombment group dating from before 1545 (illus. opposite bottom), the tomb of

Joigny, "Maison du Bois," half-timber house from the second quarter of the 16th century.

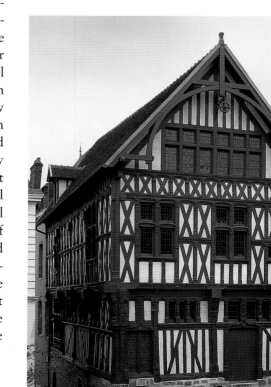

RIGHT: **Joigny**, Saint-Jean, 1548 to 1596, central aisle of the nave.

FAR RIGHT: **Joigny**, Saint-Jean, barrel vault of the central aisle of the nave by Jean Chéreau, late 16th century.

Joigny, Saint-Jean, floor plan.

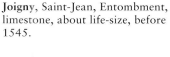

Joigny, Saint-Jean, Entombment, limestone, about life-size, before 1545.

Adélaïs de Joigny is also in Saint-Jean. The relief of the deceased on top is a supine figure clothed in contemporary fashion on a sarcophagus with four youthful figures under arcades on the front side and a scene from the once very popular novel *Barlaam and Josaphat* on the narrow end. The sarcophagus, dating from 1250/1260, came from the abbey of Dilo, which was destroyed in 1843.

In 1080 records mention a chapel in Joigny, that of the hermit Thibault, who had died a few decades earlier. In the course of city expansion in the 13th century, this chapel was rebuilt as the parish church of Saint-Thibault. In 1489–1529 a new building was again constructed, an irregular, rib-vaulted pillar basilica of four bays with a three-aisle nave choir with stellar vaulting, carved ceiling bosses, and a polygonal ambulatory. The chapel at the vertex of the sanctuary is an 1860 addition. The Flamboyant Gothic and the Renaissance come together in Saint-Thibault. Of the interior furnishings, all that remain are a kneeling figure of the donor, Etienne Porcher, from around 1380, two 14th-century virgins, and fragments of a Renaissance choir screen from 1544.

The work of Jean Chéreau, architect of Saint-Jean, is encountered once again in Château Gondi. Begun in 1569, it replaced a medieval castle. Since Jean Chéreau was well acquainted not only with Burgundian châteaux of the Renaissance, but also with Serlio's treatise on architecture, one might well expect a perfect Renaissance building. Instead, several changes in ownership led to long interruptions and numerous changes of plans. The result seen today makes a rather incomplete impression, though the somewhat newer two-story west façade is attractive. It has pilaster articulation in both stories and gabled niches between the windows of the ground floor. It is reminiscent of Ancy-le-Franc, but the ornamentation is more abundant, as though the *horror vacui* that befell late-15th and

early 16th-century château façades reappeared here in a classical form. The large dormers with triangular gables are firmly in the tradition of French château architecture.

Porte Saint-Jean, an entrance to the château square, is still part of the complex. In its axis is the Maison du Bois, once inhabited by the bailiff of the area (illus. p. 348). It is one of the many half-timber houses in Joigny, most of which were built after the fire of 1530. Many have intricately carved beams and late Gothic windows.

Saint-Florentin

At the confluence of the Armance and Armançon lies the small city of Saint-Florentin. Clearly visible from afar is the alluring church of Saint-Florentin (illus. below), rising above the surrounding town. After suffering great damage during the Hundred Years' War, a new building was begun at the start of the 16th century. Its choir and transept as well as two unfinished nave bays were consecrated in 1617. Saint-Florentin, too, is a stylistic mixture of Flamboyant Gothic and Renaissance. A five part,

non-projecting transept joins onto the three-aisle ambulatory around the choir, which has chapels only at the three straight bays. Chapels also accompany the two side aisles of the nave and enclose the transept. The vertical elevation of two stories with pointed-arch arcades, large tracery windows, and a walkway in front is pure Gothic. The floor plan, the stellar vaulting above the crossing and in the choir chapels, and the flying buttresses on the outside all belong firmly to this time period. Only the ends of the transept reveal the decorative canon of the Renaissance, with pilasters, gabled niches, fruit garlands, and engaged flat panels on the walls.

The interior is opulent and varied. The choir screen separating the choir and crossing was created in 1600. It is lovely, having three arches with Corinthian pilasters, a cornice, and a scrollwork frieze. Above the screen is a richly ornamented balustrade of pilasters and areas with decorative scrolling; at its center is a life-size pietà. Next to it, before the crossing piers, are the remains of an early 16th-century choir screen with profiled lateral pier buttresses, Gothic jamb figures, and playful, airy baldachins in the Flamboyant style (illus. right). The entrance portal dating from 1629 with angels playing music on the pediments gives the impression that the artist was familiar with Michelangelo's Medici tombs. The choir screen from 1539 forms a colonnade of the Corinthian order. In the baldachin niches on the columns of the chevet are St. Peter and St. Vincent. The altar wall from 1548 is articulated into three relief niches: from left to right are Christ in Misery, the Crucifixion, and the Resurrection. Above, there are large, completely sculpted figures of Christ (modern) and two saints, St. Martin and St. Florentine. The passion altar at the chevet of the ambulatory is from the same time as the main altar. The St. Nicholas chapel on the south side is also richly decorated and has a painted stone statue of St. Nicholas from the 16th century. There are many figures in the Sacré-Cœur chapel on the north side: a late 15th-century pietà, stone figures of the two Johns from the end of the 16th century, and a Visitation group. The remarkable unity of the series of glass windows is the work of the famous atelier in Troyes. The windows of the chapels and ambulatory around the choir were done largely between 1524 and 1529. In the chapel dedicated to Mary are lovely scenes from her life and the Tree of Jesse. The window at the chevet is dedicated to St. Martin of Tours; Genesis unfolds to the right. Left of the altar are the legends of St. Florentine and St. Nicholas, and in the Sacré-Cœur chapel, John the Baptist and a 1498 Apocalypse in the style of Dürer.

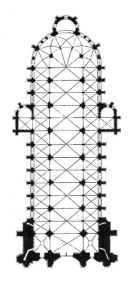

Sens, Saint-Etienne, floor plan.

Sens, Saint-Etienne Cathedral, from ca. 1140, central aisle of the nave.

Sens and the Sénonais

The arrondissement of Sens is the northernmost in Burgundy. In its countryside and geological composition, it resembles Champagne and Ile-de-France. It was not part of the late medieval duchy.

From about 500 BC, the Senones, one of the most powerful Gallic tribes, had their main seat here. After its Roman conquest, the city became capital of the Roman province by the name of Agedincum. In the second half of the third century, the martyr Sabinian proselytized here and supposedly erected the first church on the site of a heathen temple. From the 4th century on, Sens was a diocese; subsequebt bishops held the title Primas of Gaul and Germania from the 8th century on. The dioceses of Chartres, Auxerre, Meaux, Orléans, Paris, Nevers, and Troyes were under the jurisdiction of the Sens cathedral until Paris became an archdiocese.

In the early 7th century, records note the existence of a small family of three churches: a baptistery in the north and two basilicas, Saint-Jean and Notre-Dame. Like all the other dioceses and monasteries of Burgundy, Sens also suffered under attacks by the Hungarians, the Saracens, and the Normans. Archbishop Séguin consecrated a new church to St. Stephen in 982, shortly after a fire destroyed the older buildings. Beginning in about 1140, Archbishop Henri Sanglier (1122–1142) had this cathedral replaced by a basilica 377 feet (115 m) long. Two towers in the west frame an entrance bay onto which the nave and side aisles join with six six-part vaulted double bays. In the east, a semicircular ambulatory with a chapel (probably originally rectangular) at the vertex of the sanctuary leads around the choir. At the fifth double bay of the nave, where the transept would normally be, a chapel consisting of an antebay and a semicircular apse is joined to each of the side aisles. Pope Alexander III consecrated the high altar in 1164 and raised Sens to the temporary capital of all of Christendom.

The church, which once proceeded from nave to choir without the interruption of a transept, has a tripartite elevation (illus. left). The support for the arcades with pointed arches alternates between bulky piers with engaged semicircular or three-quarter pillars and pairs of columns. At the chevet of the choir, two pairs of columns meet. Above the vaulting of the side aisles are the galleries, slender double openings under blind arches—two underneath each high tracery window. After the southern tower collapsed in 1268/1269, these were restored; the original galleries were lower and had no tracery.

At the time that construction got under way in Sens, Cluny III had just been completed, the monastic church of Saint-Benoît-sur-Loire was at an advanced stage of construction, and the ambulatory choir with radiating chapels had become an established feature of large sacred buildings. Henri Sanglier did not, however, adhere to the Burgundian tradition. Instead, it seems he pursued a different vision for Sens: that of the monastic churches of Normandy. There, in Jumièges and Saint-Etienne in Caën, are the first appearances of a clear alternation in supports in combination with a three-fold vertical elevation of arcades, galleries, and clerestory. After 1120, a belated six-part rib vaulting was even successfully installed in Saint-Etienne in Caën. In Sens, vertical elevation

OPPOSITE:
Sens, Saint-Etienne Cathedral, southern end of the transept, early 16th century.

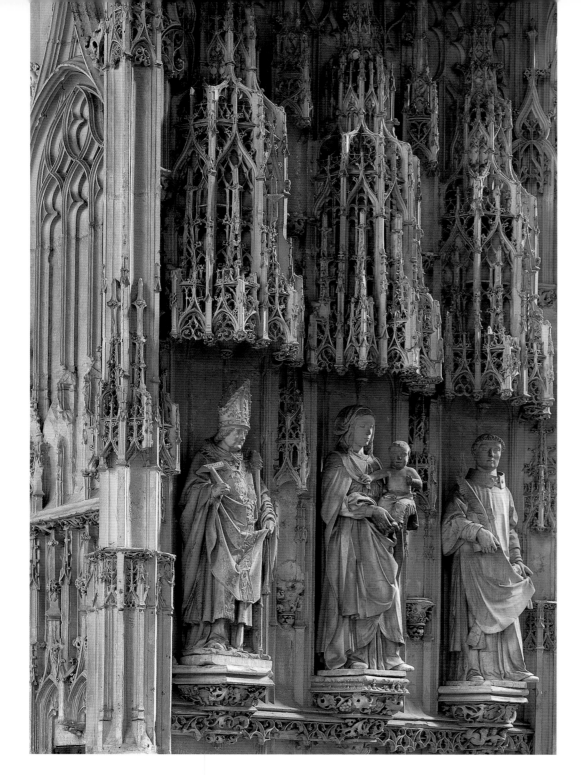

and vaulting were unified; it was only in the process of replacing the vaulting in 1268 that the height of the central nave was altered. In around 1300, chapels were joined to the central nave and side aisles, four on each side. In order to achieve a connection between them and the original chapel in the north, a transept was added. This was not completed until between 1500 and 1516 by the architect Pierre Chambiges and his son, who also worked on the southern transept after 1490. At the same time, the south tower, which had collapsed in 1267, was rebuilt.

Both transepts are elegant glazed structures in the Flamboyant style (see p. 353). Pier buttresses reminiscent of tabernacles frame the transept gable ends, which dissolve completely in the wind-

Sens, Saint-Etienne Cathedral, altar of Tristan of Salazar, Flamboyant figural sculpture under elaborately adorned baldachins.

Sens, Saint-Etienne Cathedral, St. Stephen, trumeau figure from the original central portal in the west, late 12th century.

ings of tracery in the upper story. Above the flat ogival arched portal are niches with baldachins and a recessed arch under a triangular gable, carrying Abraham in the north and (a restored) Moses in the south. The west has only kept its original articulation in the lower stories of the north tower; the middle section and the south tower were altered after the collapse. It has three portals, whose once impressive figural ornamentation was largely destroyed in the Revolution. All the jamb figures are missing, as well as many heads and hands. The oldest is the St. John portal, dating from about 1185. On the lintel, the tympanum, and in the archivolts, scenes from the life of St. John are depicted as in Auxerre. Avaritia and Largitas are on the base of the jamb. All that remains of the original late 12th-century central portal are the Wise and Foolish Virgins on the door jambs, the slender *trumeau* figure of St. Stephen (illus. below), and on the base, the liberal arts and depictions of the months. The first tympanum had also been dedicated to the preaching and stoning of St. Stephen, and the subject was repeated in the tympanum, created after 1268.

Angels, Virtues, and martyrs filled the archivolts. The right portal, dating from about 1300, is dedicated to Mary. The lintel and tympanum show the death, entombment, and ascension of the Virgin, while the base depicts the 24 Eldest.

The elaborate interior of the cathedral is well worth visiting. A stone relief depicting Thomas Becket, a 12th-century work, was first in the residence of the archbishop and is today in the square ambulatory chapel in the north (illus. below). The St. John's chapel has a very interesting wooden crucifixion group from the first half of the 13th century. In the chapel to the Virgin in the south is a Virgin with Child, donated by Canon Manuel de Jaulnes in 1334. In the central nave is the cenotaph for the parents of Archbishop Tristan of Salazar, which is from the same period as the transept arms. Next to it is the tomb of Cardinal du Perron and his brother, dating from the 17th century. The tomb created by Guillaume Coustou in 1777 for the dauphin Louis, son of Louis XV and father of Louis XVI, and for his wife Marie-Josephine of Saxony, was placed into the oval ambulatory chapel in the north in 1855. Last but

not least, the Sens Cathedral has numerous well-preserved stained-glass windows from the 12th to 17th centuries, including depictions of the legends of Saints Thomas Becket and Eustachius, as well as the Prodigal Son and Good Samaritan stories on the north side of the ambulatory.

The arch-episcopal and synodal palace (illus. above) bordering on the south side of the nave was built by Archbishop Gautier Cornut (1222–1241) around 1235/1240. The base or foundation is a two-aisle rib-vaulted structure, above which is a mezzanine floor with passageways and vaulted chambers that once served as a prison. Above is a light, spacious vaulted hall of six bays with a splendid façade of windows. The baldachin figures on the exterior of the building depict the builder, his king Louis IX, and local saints. The wings of the building were built around 1520 under Francis I and in 1557 under Henry II. Together with the Gothic bishop's palace, they form an expansive rectangular court in front of the south side of the cathedral. The entire building complex was thoroughly restored by Viollet-le-Duc. Today it houses the museums of Sens.

These museums are ordered chronologically, so begin your tour on the ground floor of the Aile François I with artifacts from prehistoric times and early history: ceramics, jewelry, skeletons from grave sites, and especially the so-called treasure of Villethierry. This comprises more than 800 pieces of Bronze-Age jewelry that were found in a vase. Next is the Gallo-Roman era, which is well docu-

Sens, synodal palace, 1235–1240, façade facing the street.

LEFT:
Sens, cathedral Saint-Etienne, Thomas Becket, stone relief, 12th century.

Sens, former palace of the archbishop, today museum, Aile
François I, reconstructed thermae
façade, 2nd century AD.

Villeneuve-sur-Yonne,
circular donjon of Philip II August,
1204 to 1211.

FAR RIGHT:
Villeneuve-sur-Yonne,
Porte de Joigny, city entrance from
the 13th century.

mented by numerous architectural fragments, floor
mosaics, ceramics, and sculptures from Agendi-
cum. The reconstructed façade of a second-century
thermae is very impressive indeed (illus. left).

The remains of a choir screen which stood in the
cathedral between 1762 and 1886 as well as a
model and various plaster casts of the Porte Dauphine, a monumental entrance gate at the south end
of the rue Dauphine (now rue de la République)
can be viewed on the first floor of the Aile Henry II.
It was erected in 1777 in honor of Dauphin Louis
and his wife, Marie-Josephine of Saxony, and torn
down again in 1883. On the second story are paintings from the 17th to 19th centuries. Comparatively little remains of the treasure the church
once called her own. There are, however, some
lovely, valuable liturgical garments on exhibit.

Villeneuve-sur-Yonne

Approximately a century before Louis IX founded
his famous planned city in the Camargue, Aigues-
Mortes, as the harbor city from which his crusade
should embark, Louis VII (1137-1180) had a city
with four gates built along the Yonne on the same
right-angled layout: Villefranche-le-Roy, today Villeneuve-sur-Yonne. The castle rose up in the northeast of the city. Phillip II August had a plain, massive, circular donjon erected in the moat in front of
the wall, a donjon that could only be reached by
way of a bridge (illus. below). The use of large
square ashlars was characteristic of building projects by this king, as can be seen here. A stairway
in the 13-foot- (4-m-) thick walls connected the rib-
vaulted round rooms with one another. This was
the model for the donjon of Aigues-Mortes. The
two city gates that remain, the Porte de Sens and
the Porte de Joigny (illus. below right), and probably also the towers of the city wall, all date from
the 13th century. Both gates were repaired and

expanded with corner towers after having been
damaged during the religious wars.

When Pope Alexander III stayed in Sens in
1163/1164, he laid the first stone for the parish
church of Notre-Dame in Villeneuve-sur-Yonne,
which wouldn't be completed for 300 years. By
about 1300, the choir and the three eastern nave
bays were finished. The other nave bays, the narthex, and the lower stories of the façade towers
were completed in the early 14th century. The
Hundred Years' War stopped all building activity
for a long time. Finally, in 1551, construction resumed, first on the façade, whose completion is
ascribed to Jean Chéreau of Joigny, and then on
the west bays, which were finished by 1597.

Just as construction of Notre-Dame was getting
underway, the cathedral of Sens was finished. It is
thus possible that the plan of this three-aisle basilica
with ambulatory choir and three radiating chapels,
but without a transept, was influenced by the other
church. At the first and third nave pier from the
east, a slight alternation of supports is noticeable.
Still, the vertical elevation is definitely Burgundian:
arcades, clerestory, walkway, and four-part rib vaulting above; there is stellar vaulting only in the first
bay after the narthex (illus. opposite). When construction resumed in the 16th century, lateral
chapels were added in the western nave bays. Their
decoration and interior fittings alternate between
themes and motifs of very late Gothic and those of
the fully developed Renaissance.

Looking at Notre-Dame from the east, you see
a thoroughly Gothic church, early Gothic at the
level of the chapels and High Gothic in the chevet.
The west façade is only Gothic in its architectural
conception: two towers and three portals between
low pier buttresses. No wavering is evident in the
decoration: it is purest Renaissance, laid over the
old concept like a new dress (illus. opposite top).

Villeneuve-sur-Yonne, Notre-Dame, 1163/1164 to 1597, central aisle and chevet.

ILLUS FAR RIGHT:
Villeneuve-sur-Yonne, Notre-Dame, main portal in the west façade, completed 1597.

Besides some original, in places only partially preserved stained glass windows, Notre-Dame has an entombment group by Jean Goujon (ca. 1510–1564/1569). The beginnings of classicism are evident in these quiet figures, whose clothes are reminiscent of contemporary costumes only in a few details. The robes and hairstyles of the four women, especially, are very much in a classical vein. Each one has her own space around her, and each one is exclusively attuned to the dead Christ.

Vallery

In the far north of the arrondissement, along the stream Orvanne, lies the château of Vallery (illus. below). In the first half of the 12th century there was already an extensive, irregular castle here, which was expanded around the mid-13th century. Jacques Androuet du Cerceau sketched a plan of the

entire complex in the 16th century that depicts a large, almost oval surrounding wall of about 500 by 325 feet (150 by 100 m) with moats, towers, and a gate flanked by towers.

In 1548 the estate became the property of Jacques d'Albon, marshal of France. He removed the courtines in the south and east, and had a new building begun. D'Albon planned a three-wing complex in the *brique et pierre* style typical at the time, with corner pavilions rising one story above the main building. All that was built in the end was the main wing with seven axes, the southeast pavilion, and the east wing. In the west, a wall with blind arcades and obelisks formed one side of the *cour d'honneur*; in the north, a simple wall that served to integrate the old double-towered gate into the new complex closed off the courtyard. In this manner, many an estate owner tried to feign a family tradition where in fact none existed. On the ground floor of the south wing is a gallery whose elegant, harmonious architecture prompted du Cerceau to compare it to the Louvre. Later this led to the assumption that Pierre Lescot was Vallery's architect.

Shortly before 1747 and again in the 19th century, numerous buildings were torn down here. Still standing are the pavilion and south wing, which is missing a part of the upper story. The cushion-like layers of ashlars frame the tall windows and articulate the corners of the building, giving the pavilion a strong, somewhat rustic plasticity. The gallery façade, in contrast, is completely clad with ashlars and marble. Double pilasters support the arcade arches, which were once open. Between them, flat marble panels have been fixed to the walls; triangular pediments emphasize the rhythm of the arcades. The low upper story was added in the 19th century.

Vallery, château, 12th/13th century and from 1548, view onto a corner pavilion and a partly preserved wing; in the foreground is a medieval gatehouse.

DÉPARTEMENT
NIÈVRE

The department of Nièvre is bordered to the west by the Loire River and its tributary, the Allier. In the north it abuts Puisaye, and in the east it includes the greatest part of the Morvan. Hills and plateaus follow one another in succession here, turning their softer slopes towards the Loire. West of Château-Chinon lies the Bazois, a fertile countryside with wetlands. Vegetables and grains are grown here, and the Charolais and Nivernais cattle that supply the markets in Paris are bred. In the north the land borders on Clamecy and Donzy. This is a forested area formed by the valleys of the Rivers Nièvre, Beuvron, Yonne, and Nohain. In Leuglay and Prémery, charcoal is produced in large factories. In the south, the Bourbonnais River leads to the neighboring Allier. The Bourbonnais region is enclosed by the Allier and the Loire, and has extensive wooded stretches. Prominent throughout the entire department are varied hedges of blackthorn, holly, oak, hazelnut, broom, fern, and many other plants that form natural boundaries for meadows, accompany streets, and divide the countryside into distinct spaces.

PREVIOUS TWO PAGES:
Morvan countryside near Château-Chinon.

LEFT:
View across **Lac des Settons**, made into a reservoir in 1861 through the construction of a 900-foot (277-m) dam, and covering an area of 359 hectares (898 acres).

Nevers

The capital of Nièvre is Nevers. Its geographically and topographically advantageous location at the confluence of the Loire and the Nièvre rivers was recognized by the Aedui, who established a settlement here about 2,000 years ago. After the Celtic tribe had formed an alliance with the Romans, the latter used the settlement as a base for military supplies. This was likely Noviodunum Aeduorum, a center mentioned by Caesar. In about 52 BC, the Aedui broke the alliance, attacked the city, and burned it to the ground. This event was one of the triggers of the rebellion of the Gallic tribes against their Roman conquerors. After the subjugation of the Gauls, the city was rebuilt and called Nervirnum, and it was enclosed by a wall for the first time in the 4th or 5th century. When the land was divided into administrative units called *pagi*, a count was appointed royal governor of Nevers.

The city has been a diocese since the 6th century, according to records. It seems that the cathedral, Saint-Cyr-et-Sainte-Julitte, has never moved from its original site. The oldest parts are the remains of an octagonal baptistery found underneath the cathedral dating from the founding of the bishopric. In the Carolingian era, a rotunda was erected above it. The building standing today is a conglomerate of 500 years. In the west, the three-aisle crypt and the three-apse west choir, which is several steps higher, are visible. Both belong to a cathedral building begun by Bishop Hugues de Champallement in 1031 and completed shortly after the middle of the century. This west choir with a broad, semicircular apse is barrel-vaulted, and its apse was painted in the 12th century. In front of it lies a projecting transept; the wings of the transept are separated from the former crossing by two rounded arches over each of its central supports, like a colonnade (illus. below left). The interior creates an unusual impression. Because there is no wall above the round arches, one has an open view from the nave into the Gothic vaulting of the transept. It is likely that a flat ceiling originally closed the room. The west transept and west apse were used primarily in Germany (Mittelzell/Reichenau, for example, and the cathedrals in Worms and Mainz). In France, the same features can be found in Saint-Bénigne in Dijon. Completed in 1018, it was likely the model for the cathedral in Nevers.

Nevers, cathedral of Saint-Cyr-et-Sainte-Julitte, west tower, 14th to 16th centuries, detail of the ornamentation.

RIGHT:
Nevers, Chapelle Sainte-Marie, 17th-century main façade.

Nevers, Palais des Ducs, ca. 1500 to the end of the 16th century, main façade with a spectacular stair tower. On its balustrade are panels with narrative reliefs.

Adjoining this west building is a broad High Gothic nave dating from the first half of the 13th century; its predecessor was destroyed in a fire at the beginning of that century. Its vertical elevation reveals an arcade with pointed arches on circular columns with engaged half or three-quarter columns, a triforium with three arcades in each bay, and a clerestory with simple Y-shaped tracery and a Burgundian walkway (illus. opposite, bottom right). Above lies the four-part rib vault. The small decorative figures on the triforium are beautiful. On the bases of the colonettes are additional figures, including monks, minstrels, and a bishop. In the spandrels we find angels above bands of clouds, and under the vaulting are richly profiled arches. This vertical structure carries over seamlessly into the eastern choir, as there is no eastern transept.

This choir was built during the first half of the 14th century. It is preceded by three antebays and is encircled by an ambulatory with radiating chapels. In accordance with the taste of the time, once rounded-off circular columns became compound piers and the triforium has been glassed in. Ornate tracery adorns the high windows. In the ambulatory one can see blind tracery décor in places on the walls and numerous very lovely piscinae. The lateral chapels, added during the 15th century, are decorated in Flamboyant style. The exterior of the building is dominated by the bell tower, rising 170 feet (52 m) in the west, constructed between the 14th and 16th centuries. A second tower on the north side was planned in order to complete the

cathedral façade, but here, as so often in France, the Hundred Years' War acted as a deterrent, particularly to the construction of sacred buildings.

Only a few steps separate the cathedral from the ducal palace, which was begun by Jean de Clamecy about 1500, that is, before the county became a duchy (illus. left). It was finally completed towards the end of the 16th century. Before this, the palace of the Count of Nivernais had been located here. This building was probably dismantled little by little, and Jean de Clamecy's first project was the renovation of one wing. Otherwise, by 1500 this would have been a three-wing complex with a courtyard. The ducal palace is flanked on the back by two circular towers and on the front by two slender, polygonal stairway turrets with simple, irregularly placed windows. A third stair tower, also polygonal, makes the château accessible from the center. Its windows and the decorative panels on the balustrade, which are amply adorned with scenic depictions, follow the course of the stairs. Three window axes open on both sides, culminating in dormers. This façade

Nevers, former priory church of Saint-Etienne, 1063 to 1097, choir with ambulatory and radiating chapels, transept, and crossing tower; the chevet has an exceptional dwarf gallery.

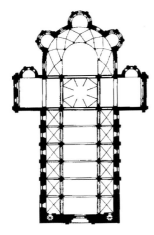

Nevers, Saint-Etienne, floor plan.

OPPOSITE:
Nevers, former priory church of Saint-Etienne, 1063 to 1097, view along the northern wall of the central nave with arcades, galleries, clerestory, and barrel vaulting into the choir with slender colonnaded arcades and a triforium instead of an emporium. Saint-Etienne is the first building in which the difficult engineering problem of constructing a barrel vault over a full clerestory was successfully mastered.

went through several periods of re-planning. The number of stories seems to have been changed: on both sides of the façade opens an axis with three windows, corresponding to the molding separating one story from another. One can also see differences in the decorations of the dormers.

In front of the main façade of the ducal palace lies the long Place de la République, which to the south adjoins the Montée des Princes, a park that slopes steeply down to the river and offers many lovely views of the surrounding countryside.

Heading north from the ducal palace, one soon reaches rue Saint-Martin with the 17th-century Sainte-Marie Chapel, which once belonged to the monastery of the Visitants. It has a beautiful façade (illus. p. 363). There, too, is the castle keep, a tower with an alarm bell that is a symbol of the pride of the 15th-century bourgeoisie. The city museum should not be missed. It has a comprehensive collection of the blue faiences that made Nevers both famous and wealthy in the 16th century. Lodovico di Gonzaga of Italy acquired the duchy in 1565 through marriage, and brought talented glass blowers and enamel artists from his hometown of Mantua, Italy to the Nivernais. They established an industry that was both highly respected and successful for many centuries.

Another substantially more monumental testament to the Christian faith is the former priory church of Saint-Etienne. It is among the most impressive and best-preserved Romanesque churches in France, and it is hardly possible to resist the

atmosphere of its festive, mysterious, and yet simple interior (illus. opposite). Saint-Etienne was one of the most important stops along the pilgrimage route to Santiago de Compostela in Spain, and the church dedicted to St. James in Santiago de Compostela had equal ranking with Rome and Jerusalem as a pilgrimage site. Four pilgrimage routes led through France to Spain. Count Guillaume I of Nevers endowed this priory and placed it under the authority of Cluny. It was constructed between 1063 and 1097, that is, exactly at the time that Abbot Hugh of Semur was planning the construction of Cluny III, which was begun in 1088. Saint-Etienne surely served as a kind of trial building, a dry run for Cluny III. The consistent design of the floor plan and the vertical elevation that intentionally desisted from decoration, concentrating entirely on the structure of the building, testify to the influence of Cluny and imbue the structure with great dignity and gravity. The three-story vertical elevation of arcades, galleries, and windows is typical of Romanesque churches. Innovative for the time is the barrel vaulting that spans it, replacing the flat ceiling that had been customary until then. Although previous attempts had been made to rest vaulting on walls without a clerestory or with small windows at the base of the barrel vaulting since about 1000 (as with Cluny II), Saint-Etienne represents the first successful vaulting over the full vertical elevation of a basilica.

The five-part transept is also spanned with a barrel vault. Like the cathedral, it has a strainer arch with an arcature above arcades which, to a certain extent, seem to optically dissolve the crossing. Squinches provide the transition to the octagonal crossing tower. Two lateral apses open out to the east. In the choir, the proportions and elevation are different. The arcades are as tall as the arcades in the nave, but significantly more slender. Above them runs a frieze of blind arcading surmounted by a row of windows, framed on either side by a small column. An ambulatory with three radiating chapels forms a hauntingly lit space behind the arcades of the chevet.

The exterior is also imposing (illus. left). Windows with round arches and sharp bevels have been cut into the smooth, carefully hewn ashlar masonry. The only adornment is lesenes in the chevet and ambulatory, an ornamental stone frieze that frames and connects the round arches of the windows in the ambulatory and the chevet, and the frieze of blind arcading that articulates the curving of the chevet bay. Although the upper stories of the crossing tower and the two west towers were dismantled in 1792, Saint-Etienne has lost hardly any of its former magnificence.

La Charité-sur-Loire

The former priory of Notre-Dame in La Charité-sur-Loire, only a few miles north of Nevers, was also a priory of Cluny. Founded by the Carolingians on a gentle slope above the Loire, the building was destroyed twice in the 8th century and then abandoned. In 1056, it was founded anew as one of the largest priories of Cluny. Soon thereafter, the new church was built and consecrated in 1107 by Pope Paschal II. This structure, too, was part of the chain of architectural experimentation that culminated in Cluny III. It had a five-aisle nave 400 feet (122 m) long (compared to Cluny III with 580 feet/177 m), a seven-part transept, and a deeply recessed choir faithful to the Cluny II model. The main apse was as wide as the central nave and spanned by a barrel vault, and was flanked on either side by three apses of equal width but decreasing in depth as one moves away from the nave. After Cluny III was completed, the choir of La Charité was also altered. The three central apses were abandoned in favor of an ambulatory with five deep radiating chapels (the center one was renovated in the form of a cross in the 14th century). The reconstruction work in the second half of the 12th century yielded a bright, transparent chevet of great elegance (illus. opposite). Slender, closely spaced supports that reveal the ambulatory and the deep chapels form a well-lit space behind them and support a blind triforium. The ogival arches of this blind walkway are reminiscent of Moorish style and occur as a recurrent motif on the exterior of the building. Above that is a row of narrowly spaced windows, above which the barrel vaulting begins. Also magnificent are details such as the capitals of the columns in the choir. The upper parts of the transept, which like the choir has three stories and barrel vaulting, were built at the time the choir was redesigned. The crossing is crowned by a richly articulated octagonal tower. Like many of the monumental churches of Cluny, the exterior of the choir, made of exquisite ashlar masonry, appears to be structured into four zones, since a tall, slender row of blind arcading adorns the vaulted area above the closely-spaced windows (illus. right). Below, the blind triforia in the interior are repeated in broad niches on the exterior of the transept.

Unfortunately, in 1204 the southern façade tower collapsed onto the nave after a fire. A bit later, the first seven bays of the northern lateral aisle were rebuilt as the parish church of Sainte-Croix. In the mid-16th century, the nave burned and was not immediately rebuilt. Then in 1695 four bays were built in the east in the style of the period. In 1789 the priory was disbanded, and Notre-Dame became the city's only parish church.

OPPOSITE:
La Charité-sur-Loire, former priory church of Notre-Dame, 1056 to 1107, view into the long choir. Influenced by Cluny III, it was rebuilt as a long choir with an ambulatory with radiating chapels after 1135/1140.

ABOVE:
La Charité-sur-Loire, former priory church of Notre-Dame, choir ambulatory, transept, and crossing tower seen from the northeast.

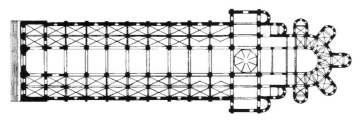

La Charité-sur-Loire, former priory church of Notre-Dame, floor plan.

Sainte-Croix, on the other hand, was sold. The still standing northern façade tower, the Tour Sainte-Croix, and both of the northern portals—once there were five—give only a pale impression of the church that was once so greatly admired by countless pilgrims. The outer northern portal is still in situ. On the lintel are scenes of the Virgin's life—the Annunciation, the Visitation, Birth of Jesus, Angels Appearing to the Shepherds—and in the tympanum is Christ in the mandorla. The inner north portal stands in the northern side aisle today. On the lintel is the Adoration of the Kings and the Presentation in the Temple. On the tympanum are a Christ standing in the mandorla, prophets, and apostles. The sculpture is not of poor quality, but bears no comparison to the sculpture in Vézelay or Autun of the same period.

Chevenon and Varennes-lès-Narcy

Two unusually picturesque and interesting examples of secular architecture are two donjons, one in Chevenon, south of Nevers near the Loire, and the other in Varennes-lès-Narcy, north of La Charité-sur-Loire. Almost identical, they were built about 1400. Chevenon was built for Guillaume de Chevenon, Varennes-lès-Narcy for Jean de Chevenon. The two brothers succeeded each other as commanders of the royal donjon of Vincennes and built donjons for themselves on their own estates (illus. right center). Both four-tower structures echo the donjon in Vincennes, albeit on a smaller scale and with simpler individual forms. Each is a rectangular, five-story building framed by massive circular corner towers. The portals are centered in the long side, framed by small turrets on angular pier buttresses. Battlements above a four-stepped *mâchicoulis* complete the façade vertically. Only the small, simple openings are original; the windows themselves date from the 16th century, as do the square towers, which partly replaced the circular ones.

Donzy

Following the small road leading out of Narcy to the north, you reach the little town of Donzy after a few miles. It lies at the confluence of the Nohain and Talvanne rivers. In its environs are a donjon from the 13th century, a Gothic church, and many lovely old houses from the 15th to the 17th centuries. These buildings reveal the former significance of Donzy as the center of a once influential barony. In a suburb, Donzy-le-Pré, parts of the Notre-Dame-du-Pré church have been preserved. It belonged to a priory that was given to Cluny in 1109. Shortly afterwards, construction of a new church must have begun. Essentially all that remains is the narthex, dating from the mid-

LEFT:
Donzy, former priory church of Notre-Dame-du-Pré, tympanum, mid-12th century. Depicted are the Virgin enthroned with the Child, the prophet Isaiah at her left and an angel with incense at her right.

BELOW:
Chevenon, four-tower donjon, from 1397, main façade with two massive circular towers and two slender towers flanking the entrance.

BOTTOM:
La Chapelle-Saint-André, Château de Corbelin, mid-15th century, view of the courtyard side of the logis with towers; at the left the two circular towers facing each other.

12th century with an important tympanum (illus. opposite above). The delicacy of the ornamentation, which seems to enmesh the archivolts, and the lovely sculptures with their richly pleated robes and flowing hems are reminiscent of the portal in Saint-Julien-de-Jonzy, created at about the same time. The subject of the tympanum, consisting of three stone panels, is the Virgin Mary. She is depicted in frontal position, presenting her Child. The Virgin is enthroned under a compact baldachin structure, symbolizing the Heavenly Jerusalem, above which the hand of God appears. At her right an angel is swinging incense, at her left, the prophet Isaiah is showing a scroll.

La Chapelle-Saint-André

Above Menou, which has a pretty château from the 1670s to 1680s, continue to the east to reach La Chapelle-Saint-André. Here, too, the Château de Corbelin has been preserved (illus. opposite). It was built around the mid-15th century, above the remains of a wooden fortification, as a square complex with round towers at the corners and a moat, a stone wing along one side of the courtyard, and a fortified gate with a drawbridge. Good fortune preserved Corbelin from greater changes, so that the complex standing today is considered one of the best preserved of this type and this era in Burgundy. Although the moats and the gatehouse have been lost, the walls, towers, and the two-story wing are largely intact. At both sides of a central entrance—the stair tower was taken down—an axis of lovely mullion windows with their typical late Gothic profiles opens up. They were likely once capped with dormers, but no longer are. Two charming turrets on conical corbels, a decorative form deriving from the four-tower donjon, adorned the corners of the logis. This was the environment in which the noblemen of Burgundy lived in the era of the great dukes.

Typical landscape of the Nivernais around Varzy.

ABOVE:
Clamecy, view showing the façades of houses facing the river.

TOP RIGHT:
Clamecy, former priory church of Saint-Martin, view of the central nave wall. Through the profiled arcades you look into the southern side aisle; above is the triforium with delicate colonettes and the clerestory with a Burgundian walkway. On the left, part of the choir screen by Eugène Viollet-le-Duc is visible.

Clamecy

Still farther to the east, in the hilly country where the Beuvron and Yonne valleys meet, lies Clamecy. For centuries, this was the center of logging trade in the Morvan, and until the first quarter of the 20th century, was one of the last places where logs were bound together into rafts and then steered by way of the Yonne and Seine rivers to Paris. In addition, the bishops of Bethlehem lived in exile in Clamecy from 1187—the year in which Muslim armies expelled the Christians from Jerusalem—until the French Revolution. In 1168, during the course of the crusades, Guillaume IV of Nevers had bequeathed the Hôpital de Pantenor in Clamecy to the bishop of Bethlehem in exchange for the privilege of being buried in Bethlehem after his death, something he dearly desired.

Saint-Martin, the former priory church, rises up in the midst of this charming, historical city. Its construction lasted from the 13th into the 16th century. Influenced by the cathedral of Auxerre, it was begun as a three-aisle basilica. The eastern end is formed by a rectangular choir ambulatory, which is a novelty. As in Auxerre, the walls of the three-zone vertical elevation of arcades, triforium, and clerestory have been minimized, creating an optical impression of lightness and transparency (illus. above). This impression is further enhanced by the two Burgundian walkways in front of the triforium and the clerestory. Apparently the minimization of walls was carried too far here, for in the 19th century, Eugène Viollet-le-Duc had to add a choir screen to support the piers. The old choir screen was destroyed in 1773.

Brinon-sur-Beuvron, Château de Brinon, 15th and 17th centuries, view of the complex and surrounding countryside.

Brinon-sur-Beuvron

A bit farther upstream on the Beuvron are two more 15th-century châteaux: Beuvron and Brinon-sur-Beuvron. In Beuvron the logis with two round towers on the exterior has been preserved. It still has original mullion windows and the polygonal stair tower that gave access to all rooms and connected them to one another. The service courtyard dates from the 18th century. Brinon-sur-Beuvron is a square complex with towers, owned by the Rabutin family. Its white limestone walls and beautiful nature park are reflected in the moat, which is fed by the Beuvron. In the 17th century, Pierre de Jaucourt had the buildings modernized and adapted to contemporary taste. Some of the windows date from this period, as do the dormers on the logis (illus. opposite).

Saint-Révérien

Continuing on the same road one arrives in Saint-Révérien, where another former Cluny priory has been preserved. The density of these priories attests to the import of the *Cluniacensis ecclesia*. A fire in 1723 destroyed the narthex and the nave (probably of the Cluny III type) of the church that had been built in the mid-12th century. Both were rebuilt in the 19th century. All that remains of the original building are the eastern sections, an ante-bay preceding the choir, the semicircular chevet, and the ambulatory with three radiating chapels. The chapel at the vertex of the sanctuary has vestiges of a 16th-century fresco. A Madonna with a sickle moon, accompanied by architectural elements, plants, and clouds, can be distinguished. Curving bands with Latin inscriptions inform us about what is depicted. The figural capitals of the chapels are worth seeing, as are the tomb slabs of Hugues de Lespinasse, Seigneur de Champallement (died 1374) and his wife, Marguerite de Thianges (died 1413), in the side aisle.

Saint-Saulge

The former priory church of Saint-Martin in Saint-Saulge is not a Cluny priory, but belonged to Saint-Lazare in Autun. It is famous for its 16th-century stained-glass windows (illus. above). The subjects include the Crucifixion with figures of donors, the Annunciation, a donor with John the Evangelist, the Virgin with Child and legends surrounding the relics of St. Cyriak, the Trinity, the Tree of Jesse, and saints' legends. The existence of a church here in the 10th century is recorded; it was probably renovated in the later 12th century. The eastern parts date from this period. In 1780, however, it was thoroughly restored together with the crypt. The nave had to be renovated again during the mid-16th century.

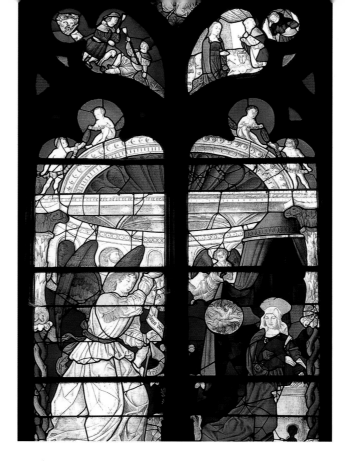

Saint-Saulge, former priory church of Saint-Martin, end of the 12th century, stained-glass window showing the Annunciation, 16th century.

Château-Chinon

At the edge of the famous Parc Naturel Régional du Morvan lies Château-Chinon. It has 2,700 inhabitants, making it the largest settlement in the Morvan! François Mitterand was the mayor of this small city for many years before becoming the president of France. The city itself is not terribly appealing. The medieval castle on the Calvaire, the 2000-foot (609-m) high "local mountain" of Château-Chinon, a castle that had replaced a Roman *castrum* and a Celtic settlement, is no longer standing, and a number of small industries have sprouted up here. For one, the city is the starting

Château-Chinon, fountain by Niki de Saint-Phalle.

Maux, Château de Champdioux, late 13th century, gatehouse with remains of a broad *bretèche*; in the background is the donjon.

Maux

Another plains castle is preserved as a picturesque ruin near Maux in a small hollow southwest of Château-Chinon: Champdioux. It represents the Burgundian castle architecture prevailing in the 13th century. Influenced by the castles of Philippe Auguste, primarily the Louvre, plains castles were regularized. The donjon was moved into a corner of the wall, while the other three corners were fitted with circular towers. Later, in the first decades of the 14th century, the donjon was left out completely and replaced by a fourth circular tower. The two entrances to the court, both protected by drawbridges, and the entrance to the donjon are very lovely in Champdioux. The large service courtyard on the far side of the moat (now filled in), the *basse-cour*, which itself was also fortified by towers and a gatehouse, is still used for agricultural purposes today. Like a *maison forte*, Champdioux illustrates what a feudal estate looked like and how it functioned in the late Middle Ages.

point for hiking tourism in the Morvan. With its multitude of brooks and rivers, reservoirs and moors, extensive woods and lonely high plateaus, the Morvan offers an ideal habitat for many rare plants and animals.

The name Morvan has been interpreted to mean *montagne noire* or "black mountain," a thoroughly fitting name for the dark granite rocks, the dense forests that often rise up out of banks of fog, black and heavy with rain, and the dark lakes. The climate of the Morvan is raw, with abundant precipitation—3.3 feet (1,000 mm) per year. In October 1970, much of the Morvan was declared the Parc Naturel Régional du Morvan, a measure which furthers not only the protection of nature and the countryside, but also tourism.

Bazoches

From Château-Chinon or Clamecy, it is a short trip to the castle of Bazoches. Records document the existence of a fortification on this site in the 12th century, which may have given the present complex its external form, an irregular rectangle. The donjon and moats are probably remnants of this early complex. In the 15th century the circular towers were added to the outer wall, along with the living quarters and encircling battlements on *mâchicoulis*, of which only a few are still intact. In 1675, the royal architect Sébastien Le Prestre de Vauban acquired Bazoches from Louis XIV in recognition of his services. Vauban had the residential buildings modernized and the rooms newly furnished. He also had the main entrance rebuilt and regularized the inner courtyard.

LEFT:
Countryside in the east of the Morvan near Mont Beuvray.

Countryside around Bazoches, about 6 miles (10 km) south of Vézelay.

Glossary

Abacus (Latin from Greek *abax*: tabletop) In architecture, the flat, often square slab of stone on top of a capital and directly underneath the entablature.

Alternating bands A layered technique of wall construction in which stone blocks or hewn stones and bricks of different colors are used in alternating layers, creating a decorative pattern. See also **ashlar**.

Apse A semicircular or polygonal projection of a building, usually vaulted or domed, especially at the east end of a church and housing the altar.

Arcade A series of arches resting on piers or columns.

Architrave A horizontal stone slab that rests on columns; in classical architecture it carries the frieze and cornice (i.e., the lowermost part of the entablature).

Archivolt A decorative molding around an arched wall opening, frequently in several successively receding rows over a church portal, forming a shallow porch (see **recessed portal**).

Ashlar A large stone masonry block, rough-hewn on the exposed surfaces. These have been used as a decorative element since the Italian Renaissance, especially in palace construction.

Avant-cour (French: preceding courtyard) In complexes with a double courtyard, the court preceding the *cour d'honneur* or interior courtyard (not the service courtyard).

Base A slab of masonry carrying the shaft of a pillar or column, also called a plinth.

Basse-cour (French: lower courtyard) In medieval or early Renaissance castles, a service courtyard usually in front of the entrance to the actual building complex.

Bay One segment of a structural system of a building. The term is used to describe the division of the vaulting of a building into regular spatial units. In multi-aisle systems, the exterior walls, transverse ribs and the columns of the arcades divide the building into vaulted bays.

Benedictine choir A choir extending outward with enlongated apses, often including the apses of the transept or double transepts.

Bifora A double-arched window in which the arches are separated by a small column.

Blind arcade An arcade engaged in a wall, thus decorative rather than supportive.

Bracket see **corbel**.

Bretèche (French) In medieval architecture, a small wooden gallery protruding from a fortified wall to provide a platform for defense.

Calotte A section of a sphere. In sacral architecture, usually a semidome over the apse.

Canonic According to a canon. In architecture, canon refers to the classical order of columns (including base, shaft, and capital) and its entablature (including architrave, frieze, and cornice). The five classical orders are the Doric, Ionic, Corinthian, Tuscan, and the composite order.

Canonize To declare a person to be a saint.

Capital The uppermost part of a column or pillar, often sculpted, forming the transition between the support and the load.

Cartouche A scroll- or shield-like architectural ornament bearing an inscription or heraldic device.

Caryatid A supporting column sculpted in the form of a draped female figure.

Castle (diminuative of Latin *castrum*: fort) A large building or group of buildings fortified for defense. In medieval times castle had fortification walls and corner towers.

Castrum (Latin: fort, town) In the Roman provinces, a town that evolved from a fort.

Cathedral (Latin *cathedra*: bishop's seat) The principal church of a diocese; (in English also a large, important church).

Chapter The members of a religious residence.

Chapter hall The representative meeting room of a cathedral or monastery chapter, usually in the east part of the cloister.

Château (French: castle, fortress, manor house) A large, often fortified residential complex of the nobility.

Choir ambulatory The passage or aisle that leads from the nave around the semicircular or polygonal apse without giving access to the restricted areas of the choir or altar. It provides access (often for pilgrims) to the chapels radiating around the apse.

Choir screen A partition of stone, wood, or wrought iron that separates the choir (reserved for clergy) from the areas accessible to the laity (nave, transept, and ambulatory). It is usually topped by a rood.

Clerestory The uppermost part of a nave wall. Rising above the arcade or triforium, it contains windows that provide light for the interior.

Cloister vault An arched masonry vault with diagonal or transverse raised ribs, also known as domical vault.

Collegiate church A church other than a cathedral that has a college, or chapter, of priests.

Colonnade A series of columns at regular intervals, usually supporting an architrave.

Colossal order An order of columns or pillars built on a large scale, stretching several stories high; also known as monumental order.

Column A supporting pillar consisting of a base, a cylindrical shaft, and a capital.

Compound pier A pier or column with multiple shafts, pilasters, or colonettes that are point-symmetrically arranged around an invisible core and form the transition to the supporting arches. (Typically found in Romanesque or Gothic architecture).

Confessio The most sacred grave in a church—usually that of a saint—located in the center of the crypt underneath the main altar.

Corbel A bracket of stone, wood, or brick projecting from the face of a wall; usually supporting a cornice or an arch.

Cornice The uppermost section of a classical entablature. More generally, any horizontal projecting element of a building surmounting a wall, dividing it horizontally for decorative purposes.

Cour d'honneur (French: literally, "court of honor") The interior courtyard formed by the wings of a building complex and preceding the logis.

Courtine The wall around the courtyard of a fortified complex.

Crocket A leaf-like, decorative element found in Gothic architecture, often on a capital, pinnacle, gable, or spire.

Crossing The area in a cruciform church where the transept crosses the nave. Because both sections are usually of identical width, a square central space is created, which is frequently accentuated with a dome or small tower.

Donjon In French châteaus, the keep, or fortified stronghold containing the residential and state rooms. It was frequently located in a corner of the complex and seldom freestanding.

Dormer A window gable that projects through a pitched roof surface.

Dormitorium Room where monks slept in a monastery.

Dwarf gallery A passage on the exterior of a wall screened in by a small-scale arcade; found in Romanesque architecture, especially in Italy and Germany.

Echauguette (French) A small, tower-like turret projecting from the upper story of a fortified wall or tower, often from a corner.

Entablature In classical architecture, the upper part of an architectural order (i.e., the roof structure between columns and roof), consisting of architrave, frieze, and cornice.

Epitaph An inscription in memory of a deceased person.

Exedra A semicircular bench inside the end of an apse.

Façade The front of a building, or any other side of it (i.e., courtyard façade), which has been architecturally embellished.

Fiale In Gothic architecture, a decorative ornament in the form of a slender pinnacle capped with a tall, pointed pyramid.

Finial A stylized ornament, often foliate, fixed to the peak of an arch or other vertical element.

Flamboyant (French: flaming) A style of tracery in late Gothic French architecture.

Fluting Ornamental vertical grooves in the shaft of a column or pillar.

Folie (French, in this case: extravagance) Used to describe posh leisure residences designed purely for the pleasure of their owners, often in eccentric forms with park-like gardens.

Frieze A continuous horizontal band of painted or relief-sculpted decoration along a wall.

Gallery A roofed passageway alongside a building, with an arcade forming the outer side. In French castles, beginning in the mid-14th century, they were located along the ground floor of the wings in combination with staircases; after the mid-15th century found as a free-standing two-story wing with open or glassed-in arcades.

Grande salle (French: great hall) In late Gothic castles of the dukes of Burgundy, the ceremonial hall for public occasions, generally a separate edifice combined with a donjon.

Grande vis (French: grand staircase) A large staircase leading to residential and/or representative rooms. It was the ceremonial entrance to the castles of King Charles V and his brothers, often the area where family portraits were displayed.

Groin The curved edge at the junction of two intersecting vaults.

Groin vault A cruciform vault created by the intersection of two barrel vaults of equal width. See also **crossing**.

Grisaille (French) A style of monochromatic painting in shades of gray; used to simulate the effect of relief sculpture.

Hall church A church in which the side aisles extend as far as the center nave, forming a unified and undivided sacred space; especially popular in the German Gothic style.

Hôtel (French) In a French city or town, a large, important building; generally an administrative office or a noble's residence.

Iconography In the visual arts, the study of the subject matter of a representation and its meaning.

Incarnat The representation of human skin in painting and polychrome sculpture.

Incrustation In architecture, decorative inlay of contrasting material in the wall paneling or in a floor surface, most often with colored marble. This technique has been known since antiquity.

Intrados The inner curve of an arch or vault.

Jamb The vertical elements framing an opening in a wall and supporting the lintel. They can be canted in windows; or profiled, stepped, or with colonettes or jamb figures in portals; and surmounted by archivolts.

Krater (Greek) A wide, two-handled bowl used in ancient Greece and Rome for mixing wine and water.

Lapidarium (from Latin lapis: stone) A collection of stone works.

Lesene A slightly protruding rectangular column without a base or capital set into a wall for reinforcement and decoration; also known as a pilaster strip. In Romanesque architecture often in conjunction with round arches or arched friezes.

Logis (French) Term for the main building of a complex, containing the residential and state rooms.

Lucarne An ornate dormer window.

Lunette (French: little moon) A semicircular or crescent-shaped decorative area over a door or window that may contain another window, a sculpture, or a mural.

Mâchicoulis (French) Projecting stepped corbels that support a battlemented parapet along the top of a castle wall or bretèche. See also **bretèche**.

Maiestas Domini (Latin maesta: majesty, dominus: lord) An enthroned Christ in an almond-shaped mandorla surrounded by the symbols of the evangelists, the apostles, or angels.

Maison forte (French: strong, substantial house) A fortified residence of the lower aristocracy. Often located along a trade route or on the border of a fief, it was a basic element of the feudal economic and judicial system of medieval France (see pp. 136f.).

Mandorla A halo or aureole appearing over the head of or around a holy figure to signify divinity.

Mannerist Term referring to a style of the late 16th century characterized by distortion of elements such as scale and perspective, as opposed to maintaining classical harmony.

Mansard roof (after French architect François Mansard) A roof having two different slopes on all sides, with the lower slope almost vertical and the upper one almost horizontal.

Memento mori (Latin: reminder of death) In art, the use of certain objects, such as a skull or an extinguished candle, which symbolize the transience of life and serve as reminders of one's inevitable death.

Metope (Greek: field in between) The rectangular field between the triglyphs in a Doric frieze, often decorated with elaborate narrative reliefs.

Mezzanine (Italian mezzano: intermediate) A story with a low ceiling between two main stories of a building.

Monopteros (Greek for single wing) A circular temple with a domed roof resting on a single row of columns.

Monolith (Greek for single, solid stone) A column, pilaster, or building made of a single block of stone.

Narthex An entrance hall or lobby leading into the nave of a church; originally separated from the nave by a railing or screen.

Nave The central part of a church's interior, especially the middle aisle.

Niches-à-banquettes (French: niches with benches) In medieval architecture, small benches placed perpendicularly into the deep intrados of windows.

Obelisk A tall, four-sided shaft of stone, usually tapered, monolithic, and pyramid-shaped at the top; erected by the ancient Egyptians as a commemorative monument.

Oculus (Latin: eye) A round window or opening in the summit of a dome, also known as an opaion.

Œil de bœuf (French: ox's eye) A circular lucarne window.

Octagonal Having eight sides and angles.

Ogival arch (from ogive: a diagonal rib of a Gothic vault) A pointed arch.

Oppidum (Latin) A fortified hilltop location in pre-Roman France and Italy.

Palais (French) An imposing town residence.

Parlatorium (Latin) A room in a monastery in which monks were permitted to have conversations and where they could receive lay visitors.

Pastoral (from Latin pastor: shepherd) In art, an idyllic shepherd scene.

Pedestal An architectural support for a statue, column, or pillar.

Piano nobile (Italian: noble story) The principal story in Renaissance buildings.

Pier A large architectural support, often square or rectangular in plan, without the entasis of antique columns; it may have a base and capital.

Pilaster A rectangular columnar element engaged in a wall for decoration and reinforcement. It has a base and capital.

Pilaster strip see **lesene**.

Piscina (Latin: pool) In late Gothic art, a small, often richly ornate fountain located in a side chapel near the altar.

Place Royale (French: royal plaza) An imposing monumental plaza with unified architecture, often with a statue of the ruler. This evolved into an important urban feature in 17th century France.

Pleurant (French: mourner) A weeping statue at a grave tomb, usually in the figure of a monk.

Plinth see **base**.

Polychrome (Greek) Many-colored.

Polygon (Greek) A closed figure consisting of three or more sides.

Profile The cross-section of an architectural element such as a rib, jamb, or cornice.

Quatrefoil (French) An ornamental tracery design made up of four lobes or foils.

Radiating chapels Apsidal chapels radiating around the choir ambulatory in the apse of a church.

Recessed portal A deeply stepped portal formed by staggered voussoirs forming the arch and staggered jambs. The stepped jams form a shallow porch, making the often relatively small entrance appear larger in relation to the thick wall.

Refectory (from Latin reficere: renew, restore) The monks' dining hall in a monastery, usually attached to the cloister wing opposite the church.

Retable An altarpiece or panel located above and behind the altar, usually bearing paintings, sculptures, carvings or other decorations.

Rhythmic travée or travers A section of a room that is rhythmically structured either by alternating open and closed areas or by the use of varying colossal orders. In the text: a decorative system with an alternating sequence of broad and narrow decorative axes framed by lesenes.

Rib A slender supportive and defining element of vaulting; the ribs form the framework of the vaulting.

Rib vault A vault having a framework of intersecting diagonal ribs.

Rocaille (French, from Italian: shell work) An 18th-century (Louis XV) style of ornamentation characterized by motifs of entwined vegetation and seashells.

Rococo The playful late Baroque phase of architectural style that derived its name from rocaille.

Rood A cross or crucifix mounted on the choir screen of medieval churches.

Rotunda A building with a circular plan (usually surmounted by a dome).

Sanctuary A sacred or holy place in a church, usually the choir and main altar.

Squinch A quarter-spherical segment of masonry vaulting or corbeling carried across an interior angle of a square wall system to support a circular or octagonal superstructure. This achieves the transition from dome to square.

Stele An upright stone or slab with an inscribed or sculpted surface; used as a monument or as a commemorative tablet in the face of a building.

Tambour (French: drum) Cylindrical or polygonal wall that supports a dome.

Tondo A circular painting or relief.

Tracery Ornamental stonework in a pattern of interlaced lines, used primarily in Gothic and late Gothic windows as support, but also as decoration on windows, screens, etc.

Translatio (from Latin translare: transfer) The transfer of a relic to a venerated place, usually to a confessio.

Transept The part of a cruciform church that is transverse, or perpendicular, to the nave.

Transverse arch A perpendicular supporting arch connecting two opposing walls of a building at right angles.

Trefoil An ornamental tracery design consisting of three rounded lobes adjacent to one another (clover leaf).

Triforium Originally a three-arched opening (compare to bifora) in the wall of the nave above the arcade and below the clerestory; or between the gallery and clerestory in four-story churches.

Triptych A work consisting of three painted or carved panels that are hinged together.

Trumeau (French: window column) The center post of a door or window supporting the lintel, in church doors often with a sculpture of the church's patron.

Turret A small tower or tower-shaped projection on a building.

Tympanum In antiquity, the recessed triangular pediment over the entrance of a temple, generally decorated with a relief sculpture. In medieval churches, the semicircular area between the arch and the lintel of the portal, frequently decorated with noteworthy, themed relief sculpture.

Vaulting shaft Rounded vertical profiles that run up a wall to the springing of a vault, anticipating the profiles of the arcades, ribs, or transverse arches.

Votive figure An image created and dedicated as a devotional offering.

Wall projection Projecting building section, frequently surmounted by a gable, often articulating the center part of a façade; also known as wing pavilion.

Westwork (from German Westwerk) In Carolingian, Ottonian, and German Romanesque architecture, the monumental west façade of a cathedral or monastery church, typically with towers that make it wider than the nave. Consists on the ground floor of the portal or narthex, and in the upper story of an imperial or royal gallery open to the nave in combination with a chapel dedicated to St. Michael.

Index of Names

Index of Places

Literature

Ambrose, Kirk. *The Nave Sculpture of Vézelay: The Art of Monastic Viewing.* Toronto: Pontifical Institute of Mediaeval Studies, 2006

Antoine, Elisabeth. *Art from the Court of Burgundy: 1364–1419.* Cleveland Museum of Art, 2005

Armi, C. Edson. *Design and Construction in Romanesque Architecture: First Romanesque Architecture and the Pointed Arch in Burgundy and Northern Italy.* Cambridge UK & New York: Cambridge University Press, 2004

Armi, C. Edson. *Masons and Sculptors in Romanesque Burgundy: The New Aesthetic of Cluny III.* University Park, PA and London: Pennsylvania State University Press, 1983

Bentley, James and Palmer, Hugh. *The Most Beautiful Villages in Burgundy.* New York: Thames & Hudson, 1998

Branner, Robert. *Burgundian Gothic Architecture.* London, 1960

British Museum. *Miniatures of the Virgin and Saints: from the Breviary of John the Fearless, Duke of Burgundy, Early Fifteenth Century.* London: British Museum.

Bromwich, James. *Roman Remains of Southern France.* New York: Routledge, 1996

Calkins, G. *Medieval Architecture in Western Europe: From A.D. 300 to 1500.* Oxford and New York: Oxford University Press, 1998

Conant, Kenneth John. *Carolingian and Romanesque Architecture 800–1200,* Pelican History of Art series. New Haven, CT: Yale University Press, 1992

Calmette, Joseph. *The Golden Age of Burgundy: The Magnificent Dukes and Their Courts.* London: Pheonix, 2001

Crumley, Carole L. and Marquardt, William H. *Regional Dynamics: Burgundian Landscapes in Historical Perspective.* San Diego: Academic Press, 1987

Dunlop, Ian. *Burgundy.* London: Hamilton and New York: Viking Press, 1990

Farr, James Richard. *Hands of Honor: Artisans and Their World in Dijon, 1550–1650.* Ithaca, NY: Cornell University Press, 1988

Forsyth, Ilene H. *Mary, the Throne of Wisdom: Dedication of a Sacred Image, Abbey and University Church of Saint John the Baptist, Collegeville, Minnesota, 24 October 1963.* Collegeville, MN: The Abbey, 1963

Grivot, Denis and Grivot, Zarnecki. *Gislebertus, Sculptor of Autun.* New York: Orion Press, 1961

Guillaume, Margurite. *La Peinture en Bourgogne au XVIe siécle.* Dijon: Musée des beaux-arts de Dijon, 1990

Hearn, M. F. *Romanesque Sculpture: The Revival of Monumental Stone Sculpture in the Eleventh and Twelfth Centuries.* Ithaca, NY: Cornell University Press, 1985

Hufgard, M. Kilian. *Bernard of Clairvaux's Broad Impact on Medieval Culture.* Lewiston, NY: E. Mellen Press, 2001

Hugonnet-Berger, Claudine. *Peintures murales en Bourgogne.* Dijon: Association pour la connaissance du patrimoine de Bourgogne, 1992

Huizinga, Johan. *The Waning of the Middle Ages: A Study of the Forms of Life, Thought, and Art in France and the Netherlands in the Fourteenth and Fifteenth Centuries.* Harmondsworth UK: Penguin, 1976

Lieftinck, Gerard Isaac. *Grisailles in the Book of Hours of Philip the Good in the Hague and the Master of Mary of Burgundy.* "Oud Holland" (Vol 85), 1970, 237–242

Loxton, Margaret. *Travels Through Burgundy.* Chicago: Trafalgar Square, 1991

McGuire, Brian Patrick. *Friendship and Faith: Cistercian Men, Women and Their Stories, 1100–1200* (Variorum Collected Studies Series 742). Burlington, VT: Ashgate Publishing, 2002

Miltoun, Francis. *Castles and Chateaux of Old Burgundy and the Border Provinces.* Boston: L.C. Page, 1909

Morand, Kathleen and Finn, David. *Claus Sluter: Artist at the Court of Burgundy.* University of Texas Press, 1991

Musée archéologique de Dijon. *D'ocre et d'azur: peintures murales en Bourgogne.* Dijon: Conseil régional de Bourgogne, Réunion des musées nationaux, 1992

Ousby, Ian. *Blue Guide Burgundy.* London & NY: W.W. Norton & Company, 1992

Raguin, Virginia Chieffo. *Stained Glass in Thirteenth-Century Burgundy.* Princeton NJ: Princeton University Press, 1982

Rouchon-Mouilleron, Véronique and Faure, Daniel. *Vézelay: The Great Romanesque Church.* New York: Harry N. Abrams, 1999

Stalley, Roger. *Early Medieval Architecture (Oxford History of Art).* Oxford and New York: Oxford University Press, 1999

Stoddard, Whitney S. *Art and Architecture in Medieval France: Medieval Architecture, Sculpture, Stained Glass, Manuscripts, the Art of the Church Treasuries.* New York: Harper & Row (Icon Editions), 1972

Stratford, Neil. *Studies in Burgundian Romanesque Sculpture.* London: Pindar Press, 1998

Taralon, Jean. *Les Vitraux de Bourgogne, Franche-Comté, et Rhône-Alpes.* Paris: Editions du Centre national de la recherche scientifique, 1986

Tobin, Stephen. *The Cistercians: Monks and Monasteries of Europe.* London: A & C Black Ltd, 1995

Toman, Rolf (ed). *Romanesque: Architecture, Sculpture, Painting.* Cologne: Könemann, 1998

Toman, Rolf (ed). *Gothic: Architecture, Sculpture, Painting.* Cologne: Könemann, 1999

Tovel, Ruth Massey. *Flemish Artists of the Valois Courts.* Toronto: University of Toronto Press, 1950

Vaughan, Richard. *Philip the Bold: The Formation of the Burgundian State (History of Valois Burgundy).* Woodbridge Suffolk and Rochester NY: Boydell Press, 2005

Vaughan, Richard. *John the Fearless: The Growth of Burgundian Power (History of Valois Burgundy).* Woodbridge Suffolk and Rochester NY: Boydell Press, 2005

Vaughan, Richard. *Philip the Good: The Apogee of Burgundy (History of Valois Burgundy).* Woodbridge Suffolk and Rochester NY: Boydell Press, 2004

Vaughan, Richard. *Charles the Bold: The Last Valois Duke of Burgundy (History of Valois Burgundy).* Woodbridge Suffolk and Rochester NY: Boydell Press, 2004

Photo Credits